SELF-DEFENSE IN INTERNATIONAL LAW

BY

D. W. BOWETT

M.A., LL.B.(Cantab.), Ph.D.(Manchester)
Of the Middle Temple, Barrister-at-law
Lecturer-in-law, University of Manchester

THE LAWBOOK EXCHANGE, LTD.
Clark, New Jersey

ISBN 978-1-58477-855-4

Lawbook Exchange edition 2009, 2014

The quality of this reprint is equivalent to the quality of the original work.

THE LAWBOOK EXCHANGE, LTD.
33 Terminal Avenue
Clark, New Jersey 07066-1321

Please see our website for a selection of our other publications and fine facsimile reprints of classic works of legal history:
www.lawbookexchange.com

Library of Congress Cataloging-in-Publication Data

Bowett, D. W.
Self-defence in international law / by D.W. Bowett.
p. cm.
Originally published: New York : Praeger, [1958].
Includes bibliographical references and index.
ISBN-13: 978-1-58477-855-4 (cloth : alk. paper)
ISBN-10: 1-58477-855-5 (cloth : alk. paper)
1. Self-defense (International law) I. Title.
KZ4043.B69 2009
345'.04--dc22

2008052811

Printed in the United States of America on acid-free paper

SELF-DEFENSE IN INTERNATIONAL LAW

BY

D. W. BOWETT

M.A., LL.B.(Cantab.), Ph.D.(Manchester)
Of the Middle Temple, Barrister-at-law
Lecturer-in-law, University of Manchester

FREDERICK A. PRAEGER
NEW YORK, N.Y.

BOOKS THAT MATTER

Published in the United States of America in 1958
by Frederick A. Praeger, Inc., Publishers
15, West 47th Street, New York 36, N.Y.

Library of Congress Catalog Card Number : 58–8188

PRINTED IN GREAT BRITAIN

PREFACE

This work was written in the belief that the right of self-defence was capable of legal analysis and that in the present state of international law such an analysis is essential. Where, as in the United Nations Charter, legal limitations are placed upon the individual state's right to resort to force, and the right of self-defence stands as the main, if not the only exception to the general prohibition of individual force, the scope and meaning of the exception become of paramount importance if the general prohibition is to have normative effect. State practice cannot be relied upon to give a consistent, logical explanation of the development of the right of self-defence. At the same time it has been thought preferable to deal with state practice, pointing out the anomalies and inconsistencies as they occur, rather than to expound a perfectly rational explanation of the right of self-defence based upon the premisses of fundamental rights but having all too vague a connection with international law as it has been developed in the practice of states.

Two occurrences of considerable impact upon the United Nations Organization, and upon this work, took place as the book was going to press; these were the Anglo-French intervention in Egypt in October, 1956, and the Soviet Union's intervention in Hungary in the same month. References to these had, of necessity, to be made; yet, in so doing, the writer is conscious of the contemporary nature of the sources upon which he relies, and also the lack of time for reflection upon the implications of these occurrences.

Acknowledgment must be made to the encouragement and advice of Professor B. A. Wortley of Manchester University, under whose guidance this work was prepared; to Dr. G. Schwarzenberger of University College, London, for valuable advice and criticism; to the Oxford University Press and the Royal Institute of International Affairs, who kindly permitted me to reproduce in Chapter X the gist of an article in the *British Year Book of International Law*, 1955–6; and to Miss R. Margeson, who has so patiently discharged the burden of copying the manuscript and the many alterations at successive stages.

Finally I should like to express my thanks for the co-operation of the Manchester University Press and for the generous contribution of Manchester University towards the cost of publication.

D. W. Bowett

Faculty of Law,
Manchester University

CONTENTS

TABLE OF CASES

TABLE OF TREATIES

ABBREVIATIONS

A.J. *American Journal of International Law.*
Annuaire. Annuaire de l'Institut de Droit International.
A.D. *Annual Digest of Public International Law Cases.*
A.C. *Appeal Cases* (Great Britain), 1891– .
Brit. and For. State Papers. British and Foreign State Papers, 1812– .
BYBIL. *British Yearbook of International Law.*
C.L.J. *Cambridge Law Journal.*
Co. Rep. Coke's Reports (Great Britain), 1572–1616.
Cmd. Command Papers, Cmd. 1– (1919–).
Cranch. United States, Supreme Court Reports, 1801–15.
De G.F. & J. De Gex, Fisher & Jones's Reports, Chancery, 4 vols., 1859–1862.
Documents. Royal Institute of International Affairs, Documents.
Dods. Dodson's Admiralty Reports (G.B.), 1811–22.
For. Rel. Foreign Relations of the United States, 1870– .
H.L.R. *Harvard Law Review.*
Hawk. P.C. Hawkin's Pleas of the Crown, 2 vols.
Int. Arb. J. B. Moore's *International Arbitrations*, 6 vols. (1906).
Int. & Comp. L.Q. *International and Comparative Law Quarterly.*
Int. Concil. *International Conciliation.*
I.C.J. International Court of Justice.
I.L.A. Reports. Reports of the Conferences of the International Law Association.
I.L.C. International Law Commission.
I.L.Q. *International Law Quarterly.*
L.Q.R. *Law Quarterly Review.*
L.R. Law Reports.
L.R.P.C. Law Reports, Privy Council, 6 vols., 1865–1875.
L. of N. League of Nations.
L.N.T.S. League of Nations Treaty Series.
Lofft. Lofft's Reports, King's Bench, 1 vol. 1772–1774.
Ld. Raym. Lord Raymond's Reports, Kings Bench & Common Pleas, 3 vols., 1694–1732.
Malloy. Malloy's Treaties.
Martens N.R.G. Martens, Nouveau Recueil Générale de Traités, 2nd Series.
Moore, *Dig.* *Digest of International Law*, etc., 6 vols. (1906).
Moore, *Int. Arb.* History and Digest of International Arbitrations to which the United States has been a party, etc., 6 vols. (1898).
Off. Journal. Official Journal of the League of Nations.
Off. Rec. Official Records.
Off. Rec. G.A. Official Records of the General Assembly.
Off. Rec. S.C. Official Records of the Security Council.
Parl. Debates (H.C.). Parliamentary Debates (Hansard), House of Commons Official Report.

Parl. Debates (H.L.). Parliamentary Debates (Hansard), House of Lords Official Report.

P.C.I.J. Permanent Court of International Justice.

Proceedings A.S. Proceedings of the American Society of International Law.

Q.B.D. Law Reports, Queen's Bench Division.

R.C. *Recueil des Cours de l'Academie de Droit International.*

Repertory. Repertory of Practice of the United Nations Organs, vols. 1–5, 1955.

R.G.D.I.P. *Revue Générale de Droit International.*

Rob.S. Robinson's Admiralty Reports (G.B.), 6 vols., 1798–1808.

R.I.I.A. Royal Institute of International Affairs.

Sc.L.T. *Scottish Law Times.*

S.G. Secretary-General of the United Nations.

S.C. Security Council.

Stat. United States Statutes at Large.

T.L.R. Times Law Reports.

Trans. Grotius Soc. Transactions of the Grotius Society.

Treaty Series. United Kingdom Treaty Series, 1892– .

T.A.M. Recueil des Décisions des Tribunaux Arbitraux Mixtes, 9 vols., 1922–1930.

U.N. United Nations.

UNCIO. *United Nations Conference on International Organization,* San Francisco, 1945.

UNRIAA. United Nations Reports of International Arbitral Awards, 6 vols., 1948–1956.

U.N.T.S. United Nations Treaty Series.

U.S. Treaty. United States Treaty Series.

Ven. Arb. Ralston & Doyle, Venezuelan Arbitrations of 1903, Washington, 1904.

Wheaton. Wheaton, United States Supreme Court Reports, 1816–27.

Yale L.J. *Yale Law Journal.*

INTRODUCTION

CHAPTER I

THE NATURE OF THE RIGHT OF SELF-DEFENCE

THE right of self-defence is common to all systems of law: *vim vi repellere omnia jura permittunt.*[1] As a legal concept its function and its scope may well vary with the degree of maturity attained by the system of law in which it finds a place. In any immature system of law, where there is absent any centralized machinery for the enforcement of the law and the protection of the rights of individuals, or where such machinery is inefficacious or dilatory in securing those ends, the need to allow to the individuals whose rights are endangered by a breach of the law the right to protect their rights by their own action is obvious. Yet, as the legal system gains in maturity, as its processes of enforcement and protection become more effective, the tendency is to allocate the duty of protection to a centralized authority and to restrict the right of unilateral action by individuals. For, if, in the interest of general peace and good order, society takes to itself the task of protecting the rights of individuals within society and prohibits the exercise of force by individuals, the right of self-defence assumes the character of an exceptional right, an exception to the general prohibition which must be carefully circumscribed. In some measure, however, the right must remain; for no matter how effective the means of protection afforded by the centralized machinery of society are, there will inevitably exist circumstances in which certain essential rights or interests of the individual can only be protected by conceding to the individual the right to take initial measures of protection until the centralized machinery comes into operation. It is difficult to envisage any legal system in which the prohibition of recourse to force has no exception in the form of an acknowledged right of self-defence.

In international society, characterized by a lack of centralized machinery and the immaturity of its legal system, the enforcement of the law and the protection of rights recognized by the law is, traditionally, a task delegated to or retained by the individual members, the sovereign states. Not unnaturally, the right of

[1] Decretals, Bk. V, Tit. XXXIX, cap. 3.

self-defence within such a society figures as the basic, fundamental right of every member. Yet, within the last fifty years, international society has moved towards a degree of centralization hitherto unknown; with that development the prohibition of individual use of force has come *pari passu.* The need to define the right of self-defence with some precision arises from this development, for, as the main exception to the general prohibition of force, the right of self-defence if left undefined and unregulated could virtually deny to the prohibition any real meaning.

To some extent the very universality of the right, its inevitable place in every system of law, afforded a basis for definition. Its universality indicated to the natural lawyers that its basis lay in natural law, that it existed as a fundamental precept of natural law, and that it could therefore be defined by reference to natural law. The attempts to define the right on this basis have, within this century and the last, been generally discredited. It is true, however, that certain characteristics of the right, as deduced from natural law, remain true today; it is worthwhile, therefore, to examine the formulation of the right of self-defence achieved by the natural lawyers.

SELF-DEFENCE UNDER NATURAL LAW

For the Natural lawyer the right of self-defence was not an independent problem but rather a part of the problem of defining the just war; it illustrated but one of the just causes of war, and a war *propulsare hostes* was recognized as a just war by the early theologians and schoolmen.[1] As adopted, and to some extent secularized, by later writers, it became an integral part of the concept of the *bellum justum*, but still essentially based upon natural law. Grotius stated:

> The right of self-defence, it should be observed, has its origin directly and chiefly in the fact that nature commits to each his own protection,[2]

---

[1] See generally Vanderpol, *La Doctrine Scolastique du Droit de Guerre* (1919). Also De la Brière, *Le Droit de Guerre Juste* (1938); De Solages, *La Théologie de la Guerre Juste* (1946).

[2] *De Jure Belli ac Pacis*, Bk. II, ch. I, s. iii, p. 172 of translation in Classics of International Law, ed. J. B. Scott, Publications of Carnegie Endowment. (All page references refer to this series.)

and Suarez refers to self-defence as 'the result of the innate tendency to preserve one's own life and one's own being, and both inclinations are common to men and to other animals'.[1]

Belli,[2] Gentili,[3] Victoria,[4] Ayala,[5] Wolff,[6] and Vattel[7] were equally of the opinion that natural law sanctioned the right of self-defence. Indeed, with some writers the right was not merely sanctioned but commanded[8]; self-defence was a duty imposed upon the state by natural law and owed to the subjects of the state by virtue of the social contract. Wolff states that:

> Each nation is bound to preserve itself . . . the whole is bound to the individuals to provide for them those things which are required as a competency for life, peace and security.[9]

There is, however, no unanimity as to the precise rights or interests of the state which may be protected by self-defence. In the extreme statement of Vattel it is available to protect the state against any injury, any violation of its rights.[10] For Ayala it is available for 'the defence of our own empire, of our persons, of our friends, of our allies, and of our property'.[11] More moderate formulations limit the scope of the right to the protection of the property of the state, and the lives and property of its subjects.[12] It is not, according to Grotius[13] and Victoria,[14] justified merely to extend state territory or to weaken a neighbour, nor for the sake of differences of religion or the glory of princes. The essential requirement, common to most writers, is that self-defence lies

[1] *Selections from Three Weeks*, Bk. II, ch. XVII, p. 329 trans.

[2] *De Re Militari et Bello*, Part II, ch. I, p. 61 trans.

[3] *De Jure Belli*, Bk. I, ch. XIII—'All laws and all codes allow the repelling of force by force. There is one rule which endures for ever, to maintain one's safety by any and every means', p. 59 trans.; see also ibid., Bk. III, ch. VI.

[4] *De Indis et de Jure Belli*, Appendix B, p. 55 trans.

[5] *De Jure et Officiis Bellici*, ch. II, p. 10 trans.

[6] *Jus Gentium*, p. 129 trans.

[7] *Le Droit des Gens*, Bk. I, ch. II, p. 13 trans.

[8] Vattel, *op. cit.*, pp. 13, 246 trans., Suarez, *De Bello*, Disputation XIII, p. 802 trans., but see *contra* Grotius, *De Jure Belli ac Pacis*, Bk. II, ch. I, p. 176 trans., who deems it praiseworthy to abstain.

[9] *Jus Gentium*, pp. 22–3 trans.

[10] *Le Droit des Gens*, Bk. II, ch. IV, p. 130 trans.

[11] *De Jure et Officiis Bellici*, ch. II, p. 10 trans.

[12] Grotius, *De Jure Belli ac Pacis*, Bk. II, ch. I, pp. 172–3 trans.; Wolff, *Jus Gentium*, ch. VII, s. 791, p. 409 trans.; Victoria, *De Indis*, Appendix B, pp. 52–3 trans.

[13] *De Jure Belli*, Bk. II, ch. I, p. 184 trans.

[14] *De Indis*, Appendix B, pp. 54–5 trans.

only for an injury received or threatened, and is to be used only against the state inflicting such injury.[1] De la Brière, writing of the second requirement of a just war, the just cause, according to the Thomistic doctrine defines it thus:

> Violation du droit, au sens strict du terme, violation de la justice: car la violation d'aucune autre obligation ne saurait légitimer la coercition par les armes, le recours à la force, comme dans une guerre.[2]

The insistence upon fault on the part of the state against which self-defence is directed, the '*propter aliquam culpam impugnationem mereantur*' of Aquinas,[3] is, perhaps, the most important contribution to the concept of self-defence made by these early writers; it is an essential condition of the lawful exercise of self-defence today. There was some measure of agreement that fault might exist where conduct merely threatens another state, for the right was conceded against an imminent or threatened injury, provided the danger was 'immediate and imminent in point of time'.[4] Yet in doubtful cases the state must abstain from anticipating injury, and must exercise care 'not to act upon vague and doubtful suspicions lest it should run the risk of becoming itself the aggressor'.[5]

One factor which limits the usefulness of these views in relation to the problem of definition under a maturer system of international law embodying a form of centralized machinery for enforcement of the law is that, since self-defence is only one aspect of the larger concept of *bellum justum*, little distinction is drawn between self-defence and the use of force for securing redress or inflicting punishment. Admittedly Grotius[6] distinguishes defence, recaption and punishment as different 'just' causes of war, as do also Ayala[7] and Wolff[8]; moreover Vanderpol,

[1] See Victoria's fourth proposition, relying on Augustine; 'There is a single and only just cause for commencing a war, namely, a wrong received'; *De Indis*, Appendix B, p. 54 trans.; Vattel, *Le Droit des Gens*, Bk. III, ch. III, p. 244 trans.

[2] *Op. cit.*, p. 64.

[3] De la Brière, *op. cit.*, p. 32.

[4] Grotius, *De Jure Belli*, Bk. II, ch. I, p. 173 trans.; Pufendorf, *De Jure Naturae*, Bk. II, ch. V, pp. 275–6 trans.; Vattel, *Le Droit des Gens*, Bk. II, ch. III, p. 244 trans.

[5] Vattel, *loc. cit.*, pp. 130, 244; Pufendorf, *loc. cit.*, p. 275.

[6] *Loc. cit.*, Bk. II, ch. I, p. 171 trans.

[7] *Loc. cit.*, Bk. I, ch. I, p. 11 trans.

[8] *Loc. cit.*, Bk. I, ch. II, p. 139 trans. The distinction had relevance in the context of civil law, for whereas self-defence was permissible to individuals,

summarizing the views of the Theologians, states that 'le droit de se défendre n'entraîne ni le droit de haïr l'agresseur, ni celui de se venger de lui'.[1] Yet for Vattel there is no real distinction, the concept of 'self-protection' is all-embracing, and for other writers this distinction is only relevant in characterizing a just war as 'defensive' or 'offensive'.[2] This distinction between self-defence and other forms of self-help may, in a more mature system of law, be vital; as we shall see, it is a distinction of the utmost importance in modern international law and results directly from the centralization of procedures for law enforcement.

Apart from this factor there are other serious limitations on the usefulness of relying upon the basis of the right of self-defence as propounded by the natural lawyers. For them the fundamental postulate was a right to exist, a right of self-preservation, and the limits of the right of self-defence are discernible by *a priori* argument from this postulate, reconciling the right of one state with the rights of others on the basis of equality and mutual recognition of rights. There is no real attempt at securing a correlation between the right of self-defence and the duties of other states, apart from the insistence that the state against which self-defence is used must be at fault. However, 'fault' had implications both of a juridical and a moral nature, and a failure to distinguish between legal and moral fault automatically reduced the concept of self-defence to a 'quasi-legal' concept.[3] Moreover, with the decline of the Universal Church,[4] the concept of 'morality' itself lost its universal character, its established criterion, and the tendency developed to consider self-defence as a right exercisable against inimical conduct; it ceased to be a right exercisable against breaches of established legal rules.

The final and most substantial argument against an acceptance of natural law as anything more than a guide as to the elements involved in the right of self-defence lies in the absence of an

the right of recaption and punishment was exercisable only by the state; see Victoria, *loc. cit.*, Appendix B, p. 52 trans. See also Vanderpol, *op. cit.*, p. 32 *et seq.*

[1] *Op. cit.*, p. 29.

[2] Suarez, *loc. cit.*, Disp. XIII, p. 804 trans.; Victoria, *loc. cit.*, Appendix B, p. 51 trans.; Pufendorf, *loc. cit.*, Bk. VIII, ch. VI, p. 1294 trans.

[3] The failure of Aquinas to distinguish legal and moral fault is discussed in De la Brière, *op. cit.*, pp. 33–4, 70–1.

[4] The phrase 'Universal Church' can, of course, at this stage mean only universal throughout Christendom.

objective determination of the justice of the resort to self-defence. The rightness of a state's action in resorting to self-defence could not be determined otherwise than by the state itself, relying on its conscience in the matter. As De la Brière points out:

> Dans la juste guerre, chacun se rend justice à soi-même, se procure justice à soi-même. Qui donc discerne qu'a été commise par autrui une violation grave, certaine et obstinée du droit? C'est l'Etat lésé lui-même . . . on est mauvais juge en sa propre cause.[1]

Under these circumstances it is believed that natural law concepts can, by themselves, afford no satisfactory answer to the question of the basis and character of self-defence. The preferable view, it is submitted, is one which involves an empirical examination of the rights for which international law has sanctioned the use of self-defence as a means of protection and the required proof of a necessary correlation between these rights and the duties imposed on other states by the law. Without that correlation the concept of self-defence loses its juridical character. For this reason Westlake rejected the basis of natural law, of natural, primary rights, relegating them to their proper place 'in that distributive justice which ought to govern in questions . . . *de lege ferenda*';[2] he said:

> We will therefore build nothing on a primary right of self-preservation, but inquire what are the limits which, for the better security of states all around, our international society has set to the inviolability of each.[3]

THE EMPIRICAL METHOD

The sounder approach is to be found in an analysis of the rights which, according to the practice of states, have been deemed capable of protection by the exercise of self-defence. For self-defence is in itself a 'privilege' or 'liberty' which justifies conduct otherwise illegal which is necessary for the protection of certain

[1] *Op. cit.*, p. 178. For criticism based on the same objection see Wehberg, 'L'Interdiction du Recours à la Force', *R.C.*, 1951 (1), p. 14 *et seq.*; Sturzo, *The International Community and the Right of War* (1929), Chapters VIII, XI; Hindmarsh, 'Self-help in time of Peace', *A.J.*, Vol. 26 (1932), p. 315, who regards the entire institution of self-help as based on the absence of state organization; Rodick, *The Doctrine of Necessity in International Law*, p. 6; Schwarzenberger, 'Jus Pacis Ac Belli', *A.J.*, Vol. 39 (1943), p. 464.

[2] *International Law* (1894), p. 113.

[3] Ibid., p. 114.

rights *stricto sensu.*[1] There are, therefore, two questions involved; firstly, in respect of which rights is this exceptional privilege permitted? In this connection, as we shall see, not all legal rights of states can be protected by self-defence, but only certain essential rights on which the security of the state depends. Moreover, it will be necessary to formulate these rights with reference to the correlative duties imposed by international law on other states, for without this correlation there can be no substantive right *stricto sensu*, and therefore no basis for the privilege of self-defence which presupposes delictual conduct violating those rights. Secondly there is the question of the conditions or limits imposed by the law upon the exercise of the right of self-defence itself for, even assuming a breach of one of the substantive rights to which self-defence applies, the actual use of self-defence is confined within limits imposed by general international law.

The essence of self-defence is a wrong done, a breach of a legal duty owed to the state acting in self-defence. This element is predominant in the writings of the early jurists and is clearly essential if self-defence is to be regarded as a legal concept. The breach of duty violates a substantive right, for example the right of territorial integrity, and gives rise to the right of self-defence. It is this precondition of delictual conduct which distinguishes self-defence from the 'right' of self-preservation and the 'right' of necessity.[2]

[1] See Hall, *Readings in Jurisprudence*, 1938, pp. 529–30, for a collection of definitions of the terms privilege and liberty. As to the distinction between right and liberty see Salmond, *Jurisprudence*, 3rd ed., 1910, p. 193. The notion is refined and termed a 'privilege' by Hohfeld, *Fundamental Legal Conceptions* (1913). Kocourek, reverting to the Austinian position, defines liberty as a 'non-jural' conception, being the negation of duty: see *An Introduction to the Science of Law* (1920), ch. IV; *Jural Relations*, 12th ed. (1928). But the classification of a privilege as a 'non-jural' conception is acceptable only on the premiss that there are factual situations outside the domain of law; it therefore follows that all legal relationships involve either a Claim-Duty or a Power-Liability situation. It is precisely this premiss which we reject. All factual situations come within the domain of law in the sense that there is a legal norm applicable. To assert otherwise is to argue a jurisprudentially impossible situation. See Lauterpacht, *The Function of Law* (1933), pp. 86–7.

[2] The distinction is drawn by Redslob, *Traité de Droit des Gens* (1950), pp. 243–52; Giraud, 'La Théorie de la Légitime Défense', *R.C.*, 1934 (111), p. 710; Kunz, 'Individual and Collective Self-Defence in Art. 51 of the Charter of the U.N.', *A.J.*, Vol. 41 (1947), p. 876; Cheng, *General Principles of Law* (1953), p. 69 *et seq.*; Schwarzenberger, 'The Fundamental Principles of International Law', R.C., 1955 (1), p. 343. The distinction is well-founded in English law, see R. v. *Dudley and Stephens* (1884), 14 Q.B.D., p. 273.

Self-preservation and the doctrine of necessity

It is doubtful whether self-preservation can have any meaning as a legal concept apart from a generic term for self-defence, self-help, and necessity; its appeal lies in the realm of ideology rather than of law.[1] In so far as self-preservation and necessity find a use as concepts justifying conduct which, though not lawful (and therefore distinct from self-defence) is yet excusable, their scope is necessarily limited. They cannot, in purporting to illustrate the maxim '*Salus populi suprema lex*', excuse all *prima facie* unlawful conduct against states which are not in breach of any duty under international law. That view, by which the whole of the duties of states are subordinated to the 'right' of self-preservation or the 'right' of necessity,[2] is destructive of the entire legal order. As Brierly has said:

> Such statements would destroy the imperative character of any system of law of which they were true, for they make all obligation to observe the law merely conditional; and there is hardly any act of international lawlessness which, taken literally, they would not excuse.[3]

The circumstances in which necessity may excuse the non-observance of the duties imposed by international law restricting the use of force are those in which, as an incidental to the exercise of the right of self-defence, the rights of an innocent state are infringed. The excusable character of this conduct towards an innocent state lies in the fact that, in order that a state may in self-defence protect its essential rights against a delinquent state, it may be necessary to disregard the rights of an innocent state which are thereby relatively little harmed in comparison to the harm which would have been suffered by the other state if denied the right to act out of necessity.[4]

If, then, by this pre-condition of delictual conduct on the part of the state against which action is taken, self-defence can be distinguished from self-preservation and necessity, it still remains to distinguish self-defence from both self-help and sanctions authorized by the collectivity of states through the medium of a competent organ.

[1] Schwarzenberger, *op. cit.*, p. 344.

[2] Hall, *International Law*, 8th ed., p. 322.

[3] Law of Nations, 5th ed., p. 317; for a restrictive view of the doctrine of necessity see *The Neptune*; Moore, *International Adjudications*, Modern Series, IV, p. 372, especially pp. 398, 433.

[4] For examples, see *post*, pp. 171–3.

Self-help

Self-help is, like self-defence, dependent on a prior illegal act by the state against which it is directed. Indeed it is often viewed as the larger concept of which self-defence forms a part. However, the two can and must now be distinguished. In essence the right of self-defence operates to protect essential rights from irreparable harm in circumstances in which alternative means of protection are unavailable; its function is to preserve or restore the legal *status quo*,[1] and not to take on a remedial or repressive character in order to enforce legal rights. This, the latter function, is the function of self-help, and, in a legal system which by its degree of centralization confines the task of law enforcement to collective organs, the positive, remedial role of self-help may well, at least to the extent that it involves the use of force, be taken from the individual states, leaving to them only the protective right of self-defence. This, it is believed, is the position which the United Nations Charter intended to achieve. The prohibition of the individual state's right to use or threaten force, coupled with the delegation to the Security Council of primary responsibility for the maintenance of international peace and security, and the agreement of individual members to accept the Council's decisions, brings about a situation in which self-help may be prohibited whilst self-defence remains under Art. 51.

The distinction between self-defence and self-help is important not solely because it is necessary to know precisely the scope of the right reserved to members under Art. 51, an express exception to the obligation not to resort to force or the threat of force, but also because the right of self-defence is only available against a use or threat of force which is delictual as being contrary to international law. It is therefore necessary to determine whether these other forms of self-help involving force or the threat of force are delictual. For if they are not delictual under the Charter, then they are not uses of force against which a state may resort to self-defence; self-defence against states can only be a reaction against a delict.

Under the Charter every use or threat of force may now, in general, be characterized under one of five heads:

1. Action authorized by a competent organ of the United Nations.

[1] Schwarzenberger, *op. cit.*, p. 343.

2. Action in the exercise of the right of individual or collective self-defence.
3. Delicts.
4. Action against 'enemy states' under Arts. 53(1) or 107.
5. Joint action by the five permanent members of the S.C. under Art. 106.

Apart from these last two heads, the last one avowedly of a transitional character, and the other presumably so in an organization of a permanent character, the Charter achieves the characterization of force or the threat of force into the trilogy of delict, sanction, and self-defence; these terms need definition and qualification[1] but are substantially accurate. This view would automatically involve the characterization of every form of self-help other than self-defence as delictual. Despite the attractive simplicity of this view, and the strong probability that this is what the framers of the Charter intended, the matter cannot be stated so categorically.

A difficulty arises from the ambiguity of Art. 2(4):

> All Members shall refrain in their international relations from the threat or use of force against the territorial integrity or political independence of any State, or in any other manner inconsistent with the Purposes of the United Nations.

Whether or not this article prohibits individual states from using force or the threat of force other than in self-defence or in pursuance of an authorization by a competent U.N. organ is uncertain. Some writers suggest that the prohibition is limited by its terms to action directed 'against the territorial integrity, etc . . .', and that action with aims other than those is permissible.[2] This is an argument particularly relevant to self-help, and the inter-

[1] See *post*, p. 19.

[2] See, for example, the views of Colbert, *Retaliation in International Law*, (1948), pp. 202–3; Goodhart, 'The North Atlantic Treaty of 1949', *R.C.*, 1951 (II), at p. 202; Stone, *Legal Controls of International Conflict*, pp. 234–6, also seems to adopt this argument in suggesting that the support of Members for S. Korea in 1950 would not be contrary to Art. 2(4) as not being directed against the 'territorial integrity or political independence of any State'. The contrary view is taken by Kelsen, *Principles of International Law* (1952), p. 45; Oppenheim, *International Law*, Vol. II, 7th ed., p. 154; Wehberg, 'L'Interdiction du Recours à la Force', *R.C.*, 1951 (I), p. 72; Verdross, 'Idées Directrices de l'ONU', *R.C.*, 1953 (II), p. 14; S.G.'s Report on the Question of Defining Aggression, October 3rd, 1952 (A/2211), p. 23.

pretation of Art. 2(4) is fully discussed later in Chapter VII. The existence of a certain ambiguity cannot, however, be denied and no firm answer can be given to the general question whether or not forms of self-help other than self-defence remain legal under the Charter. It may, therefore, be preferable to deal with the various forms of self-help in turn, indicating the distinction between these forms and self-defence, and expressing some view as to their continued legality under the Charter.

(*a*) *Reprisals* involving the use or threat of force are generally considered to be illegal.[1] As a form of self-help they have in common with self-defence the pre-requisite of an international wrong and the need for proportionality between the wrong done and the counter-measures taken.[2] In contrast to self-defence they are 'punitive' in character; their object is 'to compel the offending state to make reparation for the injury or to return to legality, by avoiding further offences'.[3] The right of self-defence does not extend 'en tirer réparation ou...infliger punition',[4] and the 'essentially preventive and non-retributive character of self-defence'[5] cannot be overstressed; the two forms of self-help are properly distinguished by reference to their aim. The view that reprisals are now illegal would appear to have been accepted by the Security Council. In dealing with the Syrian complaint concerning the attack on Syrian forces by Israeli forces of an avowedly retaliatory character near Lake Tiberias on December 11th, 1954, the Security Council unanimously condemned this attack as illegal.[6] The reasons advanced by the Security Council in the

[1] Waldock, 'The Use of Force by Individual States in International Law', *R.C.*, 1952 (II), p. 493; Schwarzenberger, *Manual of International Law*, 3rd ed., 1952, p. 62, and 'The Protection of British Property Abroad', *Current Legal Problems*, 1952, at p. 318; Stone, *op. cit.*, p. 287; Delbez, 'La notion juridique de guerre', *R.G.D.I.P.*, Vol. 24 (1953), at p. 196; Wehberg, *op. cit.*, R.C., 1951 (I), pp. 72–3. There is a contrary view in Colbert, *op. cit.*, at pp. 202–3.

[2] See the *Angola* Case (1928, 1930), Portugo-German Arbitral Tribunal, 2 UNRIAA, p. 1011 and the *Naulilaa* Case (1928), Portugo-German Arbitral Tribunal, 8 Recueil des Décisions des Tribunaux Arbitraux Mixtes, pp. 422–5.

[3] The *Angola* Case, 2 UNRIAA, p. 1011, at pp. 1025–6 trans.

[4] Théry, *Notion d'Agression* (1937), p. 235; see also Giraud, *op. cit.*, p. 709.

[5] Cheng, *op. cit.*, p. 94.

[6] S. C. Resol. of March 29th, 1955 (U.N. News, Release No. 16/55). Reports of the proceedings and of the Israeli and Syrian arguments are given in the *Manchester Guardian* of December 13th, 23rd, 1955. The Council stressed the complete lack of proportionality but refused to order compensation as Iran and the U.S.S.R. demanded.

terms of its resolution were that such an attack was inconsistent with Israel's obligations under the Armistice Agreement and the U.N. Charter, and a clear defiance of the Council's cease-fire resolution of 1948. Indeed, the Security Council had previously resolved that 'no party is permitted to violate the truce on the ground that it is undertaking reprisals or retaliation against the other party'.[1] It had been readily conceded that this prohibition did not deprive the parties of their right of self-defence. The Security Council's action on this occasion is, it is believed, based upon the belief that reprisals, as distinct from self-defence, are illegal under the Charter.

(*b*) *Intervention* by the use or threat of force is, apart from self-defence, probably also illegal under the Charter.[2] In the *Corfu Channel Case*[3] the United Kingdom sought to justify Operation Retail, the minesweeping operation in that part of Albanian territorial waters constituting the Corfu Strait subsequent to the actual mining of the destroyers *Volage* and *Saumarez*, as a justifiable intervention for the purpose of 'safeguarding evidence necessary for the purposes of justice', as intervention to abate an international 'nuisance' caused by the obstruction of the right of passage, and by the notion of 'self-protection or self-help'.[4] These arguments the Court rejected, stating that:

> The Court can only regard the alleged right of intervention as the manifestation of a policy of force, such as has in the past given rise to most serious abuses and such as cannot, whatever be the present defects in international organization, find a place in international law. Intervention is perhaps still less admissible in the particular form it would take here; for, from the nature of things, it would be reserved for the most powerful states, and might easily lead to perverting the administration of international justice itself.[5]

So far as the specific plea of self-protection or self-help was concerned, the Court said:

> The Court cannot accept this defence either. Between independent states, respect for territorial sovereignty is an essential foundation of international relations.[6]

---

[1] Off. Rec. S.C., 3rd Year, 354th Meeting, August 19th, 1948, p. 39 *et seq.*

[2] See *post*, p. 51 *et seq.*, for a fuller analysis of the 'right' of intervention.

[3] I.C.J. Reports, 1949, p. 5.

[4] *Oral Argument*, Vol. III, pp. 294–6, statement by Sir Eric Beckett; see also Pleadings, Vol. II, p. 282 *et seq.*

[5] I.C.J. Reports, 1949, p. 35.

[6] I.C.J. Reports, 1949, p. 35; and see the dissenting opinion of Judge Krylov, ibid., p. 77.

The judgment is not, however, free from ambiguity; it is possible to interpret these statements as a general condemnation of intervention and self-help, but on the other hand the Court may have regarded as illegal only such interventions as are 'the manifestation of a policy of force' and not, for example, interventions for the purpose of protecting the legal rights of the intervening state. The phrase 'intervention is perhaps less admissible in the particular form it would take here' also suggests a possibility of limiting the statement to the facts in issue.[1]

However, the view that intervention involving the threat or use of force otherwise than in self-defence is illegal finds some support in the condemnation by the General Assembly of the United Nations of the joint British and French intervention in Egypt in October, 1956,[2] and of the Soviet Union's intervention in Hungary in November, 1956.[3]

It is clear from statements made by members of the British government in both Houses of Parliament that justification for the intervention in Egypt was sought on the ground, *inter alia*, of self-defence.[4] However, in the absence of clear evidence that the hostilities arising out of the invasion of Egyptian-held territory by Israeli forces on October 29th, 1956 constituted an imminent danger to the Suez Canal, to shipping in the Canal, and to British lives and property, the plea of self-defence was unlikely to be accepted. Moreover, the action taken by the allied governments was directed not against the Israeli forces which, by their advance, threatened to bring hostilities to the Canal zone, but solely against Egypt. The fact that Israel had, and Egypt had not, agreed to the ultimatum issued by the allied governments on October 30th cannot be conclusive, for it raises the very question of the right of those governments to issue the ultimatum, involving, as it did, a threat of force. Therefore, treating the intervention as one not in self-defence, the condemnation by the General Assembly

[1] See Fitzmaurice, 'The Law and Procedure of the I.C.J.', *BYBIL*, Vol. 27 (1950), p. 5.

[2] Resolution of November 2nd, 1956, calling on all governments to halt the movements of military forces: *The Times*, November 3rd; and see the reiterations of this condemnation on November 8th and 24th; U.N. News, London Release, Nos. SCS/17, SCS/36.

[3] Resolution of November 6th, 12th, 1956; U.N. News Release, No. 54/56.

[4] Speech of the Lord Chancellor in the Lords, November 1st; text in *The Times*, November 2nd, 1956; Mr. Selwyn Lloyd in the Commons, October 31st; Parl. Debates (H.C.), Vol. 558, cols. 1569–71.

supports the view that, except in self-defence, intervention is legal.

The Soviet Union's justification for the intervention in Hungary rested not on self-defence but on the provisions of the Warsaw Pact of May 14th, 1955,[1] and the invitation of the Kardar government set up by the Soviet Union. The Warsaw Pact did not, however, envisage action against internal revolt within a member country[2] and it cannot be admitted that a state, having imposed a 'puppet' government by coercion of arms upon another state, can plead the consent of that government in justification of intervention within that state.[3] The General Assembly's resolution of December 12th, 1956, left no doubt of the views of fifty-five member states on the illegality of the Soviet Union's intervention, and again reinforces the view that intervention is generally illegal.

(*c*) A further form of self-help which must be distinguished from self-defence is that whereby a state resorts to force or the threat of force to compel a state either to agree to judicial settlement[4] of a dispute between the two states or, the dispute having been settled by a decision in its favour, seeks to compel the other state to execute the terms of the award. In the first case the use or threat of force clearly bears no relation to self-defence and is illegal. It may be possible for the Security Council to compel a state to resort to pacific settlement indirectly, by characterizing a refusal to comply with a recommendation to do so under Chapter VI of the Charter as a 'threat to the peace' under Art. 39 and then resorting to enforcement measures. It is not possible for the individual state to resort to the threat or use of force to achieve the same end, however serious the absence of compulsory jurisdiction may be. In the second case the position is more difficult.[5] Assuming an impartial determination as to the respec-

[1] See *post*, pp. 227–8; for convenient text see *A.J.*, Vol. 49 (1955), Supp., pp. 194–9.

[2] Art. 4, the operative article, envisages only an attack upon a member 'by any State or group of States'.

[3] *Post*, p. 53; see also the conclusions of the International Commission of Jurists in circular dated November 16th, 1956. And see the Report of the U.N. Committee on Hungary, *The Times*, June 21st, 1957.

[4] The term is here used to cover settlement on the basis of the legal rights of the parties whether by the I.C.J. or any arbitral tribunal.

[5] Those rejecting the legality of such action are Wehberg, *op. cit.*, pp. 22–3, Kelsen, *Law of U.N.*, p. 541; Verdross, *op. cit.*, p. 50. S. G.'s Report, *op. cit.*,

tive rights of the parties has been made, either by the International Court of Justice or by some arbitral tribunal, the individual state might argue that the use or threat of force in order to compel the recalcitrant state to carry out the decision is in no way 'inconsistent with the Purposes of the United Nations' or directed 'against the territorial integrity or political independence' of the recalcitrant state. It is in these circumstances that the question whether the prohibition of Art. 2(4) is absolute (except for the exceptions of self-defence, action authorized by the competent organs of the United Nations, action against 'enemy' states, and 'joint action' under Art. 106), or limited by the precise terms of the obligation becomes of vital importance. The weakness of this argument lies in the fact that, taken in the general context of the Charter, Art. 2(4) was intended to cover every use or threat of force save the exceptions mentioned.[1] Furthermore Art. 94(2) of the Charter provides a specific means by which the judgments of the I.C.J. may be enforced:

> If any party to a case fails to perform the obligations incumbent upon it under a judgment rendered by the Court, the other party may have recourse to the Security Council, which may, if it deems necessary, make recommendations or decide upon measures to be taken to give effect to the judgment.

The Security Council may possibly characterize the refusal of a state to comply with a judgment as a 'threat to the peace, breach of the peace, or act of aggression' under Art. 39, but this does not imply that the individual state has the right to resort to force against such a refusal. It may be that in exceptional cases the refusal to comply presents a real threat to the security of the state, and involves a violation of those legal rights for which protection may be sought in the exercise of the right of self-defence. This is perhaps what Rosenne had in mind when he wrote:

> Les conséquences de la non-observation devraient être d'une portée très grande avant qu'un Etat puisse chercher à justifier l'emploi de la

p. 23, by necessary implication rejects the legality of such action. Oppenheim, *op. cit.*, pp. 77–8, regards the cogency of arguments supporting individual action as doubtful. The legality of such action, in certain circumstances, has been accepted by Lissitzyn, *The International Court of Justice* (1951), pp. 76–7; Rosenne, 'L'Execution et la mise en vigeur des décisions de la Cour Internationale de Justice', *R.G.D.I.P.*, Vol. 24 (1953), p. 560; Vulcan, 'L'Execution des Décisions de la Cour Internationale de Justice d'après la Charte des Nations Unies', *R.G.D.I.P.*, Vol. 51 (1947), p. 187, at p. 195.

[1] This is apparently the view taken in the S.G.'s Report, *op. cit.*, p. 23.

force armée dans le dessein de constraindre le debiteur recalcitrant de la sentence à s'y conformer.[1]

However, in these circumstances the justification for the use of force would be self-defence, not self-help, and its reason a need to protect the legal rights of the state from violation, not to secure redress. Precisely what form of judgment would justify a state resorting to self-defence in order to compel compliance by another state is difficult to imagine. There may be substance in a distinction between judgments relating to title to territory and those merely awarding damages;[2] such a distinction might enable us to justify compulsion in the first category as self-defence . . . for refusal to comply would violate the state's right to territorial integrity, but never in the second category. It has been said:

> Art. 51 of the Charter could on occasion serve to justify the use of force to carry out a judgment of the Court. For example, the forcible occupation of a territory by the state entitled to possession under a judgment of the Court might be regarded as a lawful exercise of authority, armed resistance to which by another state would constitute an 'armed attack' within the meaning of Art. 51.[3]

Even here, since re-caption is not self-defence, it is possible that self-defence would only avail the state which has to some extent remained in possession of the territory, so that its action would take the form of expulsion by armed force rather than re-caption.

The position of this third form of self-help is clearly unsatisfactory under the Charter; so long as uncertainty remains as to its compatibility with Art. 2(4) of the Charter, the possibility of the lawful use or threat of force in self-help, other than self-defence, must promote an element of uncertainty in the concept of self-defence proper. This uncertainty arises precisely because it is not clear whether forceful self-help is illegal and, therefore, whether self-defence can be used against it. Moreover, even supposing that self-help other than self-defence is prohibited by the Charter, the position is scarcely satisfactory for, although this would clarify the concept of self-defence by determining the illegality of self-help, in a system of law which involves neither obligatory

[1] *Op. cit.*, p. 560.

[2] Ibid., pp. 554–6. For example, the distinction between the judgment on the *Legal Status of E. Greenland*, P.C.I.J., 1933, Series A/B, No. 53, pp. 22–147, and the *Corfu Channel Case* (Merits), I.C.J. Reports, 1949, p. 5.

[3] Lissitzyn, *op. cit.*, p. 76.

jurisdiction over disputes in the I.C.J. nor the assurance that decisions once given will be enforced, the prohibition of self-help is of doubtful value.[1]

This is not to say that the state is denied all forms of self-help, but only those forms involving the use or threat of force. Other forms may be available; the state may seize assets within its jurisdiction in settlement of an award, or it may undertake non-forceful measures of reprisals, or possibly persuade third states to hand over assets of the delinquent state refusing to pay the compensation awarded by a court.[2] There is, however, no assurance that these non-forceful measures of self-help will be always available or always efficacious. To this extent a serious injustice may remain unchecked by the remedies now available to the individual state under international law.

Sanctions

It is finally necessary to distinguish the right of self-defence from state action authorized by a competent organ of the international community. Such action will normally take the character of a sanction, a reaction against a delict, and throughout this work the term sanction will be used to describe action taken by a state or states on the authority of a competent organ of the international community. This is not always an accurate term in so far as action so authorized need not necessarily be a reaction to a delict—the enforcement action to be authorized by the Security Council is not inevitably a sanction in the strict sense[3]—but it

[1] For similar criticism see Kelsen, *Law of U.N.*, pp. 270, 544.

[2] In the Tripartite Agreement between the U.K., U.S.A. and France of April 25th, 1951, these governments agreed to hand over to the U.K. certain gold assets should an arbitration decide these assets belonged to Albania; these were to be in partial satisfaction of the Judgment in the *Corfu Channel Case*. Italy, as provided for in the statement accompanying the Agreement, applied to the I.C.J. and contended that (1) the Court had no jurisdiction in the matter since Albania had not accepted the Court's jurisdiction, (2) Italy had priority over the U.K. claim. The Court upheld this first contention and, therefore, could not decide the second. For a full account of these proceedings and the antecedent facts see *Case of the Monetary Gold Removed from Rome in* 1943, I.C.J. Reports, 1954, p. 21; see also D. H. N. Johnson, *Int. & Comp. L.Q.*, 1955, p. 93.

[3] This results from the fact that a 'threat to the peace, breach of the peace, or act of aggression' (Art. 39) is not elsewhere in the Charter characterized as delictual; the fundamental obligation not to resort to 'the threat or use of force' in Art. 2(4) is not phrased in terms corresponding to Art. 39. See Kelsen, *Law of the United Nations*, pp. 724–5; Oppenheim, *Int. Law*, 7th ed.,

will serve to indicate action distinct from either self-defence or delicts. As a general rule, however, both self-defence and sanctions (in this broad sense) have the common characteristic of being reactions to a delict. The distinction between the two lies firstly in the difference in purpose, and secondly in the fact that whereas self-defence is initially undertaken on the state's own authority and thereafter subject to the judgment of the international community, sanctions are taken only on the authority of the international community.

The purpose of self-defence is to protect certain essential legal rights; its aim is preventive and non-retributive, and, as we have seen,[1] it is this characteristic which distinguishes self-defence from reprisals and which certain of the early natural-law writers seized on to distinguish self-defence from other forms of the just war. The purpose of sanctions is not so limited; they may well secure the protection of the rights of the wronged state, but in so doing they may go beyond purely protective action and take a punitive form, for the ultimate aim of sanctions transcends the protection of an individual state's rights and envisages the protection of the general interest of the community in the preservation of the peace of the community. An example of this is seen in the definition of the purpose of enforcement action taken by the Security Council under Arts. 41 and 42 of the Charter; Art. 39 defines this purpose as being 'to maintain or restore international peace and security'. The second distinction between self-defence and sanctions is even more vital; it is inevitable that less freedom of action should be permitted to the individual state acting initially on its own authority than to the collectivity of states acting as the representatives of the international community as a whole. In the case of sanctions, authorized by a competent organ of the international community, the action is backed by a conviction of justice stemming from the international community; this cannot be presumed in the case of individual action by a state, acting in self-defence and without the prior authorization of a competent organ, and for this reason it is proper to deny to the individual state the right to

Vol. II, p. 160. The discrepancy between enforcement action and true sanctions is probably limited by the provision in Art. 1(1) of the Charter that the purpose of the U.N. is to 'take effective collective measures . . . for the suppression of acts of aggression or other breaches of the peace . . . in conformity with the principles of justice and international law . . .'

[1] *Ante*, pp. 13–14.

take action of a coercive character. De la Brière expresses the same distinction in referring to,

> . . . les coercitions internationales qui auraient le caractère d'une exécution collective par autorité de justice contre le transgresseur du droit. Ce serait, en effet, une solution essentiellement différente du recours à la guerre par la volonté de l'Etat offensé lui-même.[1]

If then, by these criteria, we can distinguish self-defence from other forms of self-help and from sanctions, the kind of action preserved to the individual state under its right of self-defence becomes clarified. There are, however, other distinctions which may have to be drawn between various forms of self-defence. In the first case it may be necessary to distinguish the 'external application' [2] of self-defence, what has been called 'active' [3] self-defence, from the 'internal application' [4] of self-defence, or 'passive self-defence'.[5] The distinction turns on the question whether the action in self-defence purports to take effect outside or inside the territorial jurisdiction of the state. In the first case, where the action takes effect within another state's jurisdiction, or upon the high seas, the necessity of the case will have to conform to extremely strict standards and it is submitted that the standard will be higher in the case of action within another state's jurisdiction than upon the high seas. It is as well to recall, in this connection, the statement of the I.C.J. in the *Corfu Channel Case* that 'between independent states, respect for territorial sovereignty is an essential foundation of international relations'.[6] The character of such action and the standard of necessity or immediacy will have to be determined in the light of the fact that here the state acting in self-defence acts in derogation of the sovereignty of another state. In the event of action upon the high seas, though not acting in derogation of another state's territorial sovereignty, the state exercising a right of self-defence does not do so on the basis of its own sovereign jurisdiction over its territory but in derogation of the principle of freedom upon the high seas. The

[1] *Op. cit.*, p. 65.

[2] The term is used by Cheng, *op. cit.*, ch. 2, p. 77, in relation to self-defence.

[3] Rodick, *The Doctrine of Necessity in Int. Law*, p. 36.

[4] Cheng, *op. cit.*, p. 32; the term is used in relation to self-preservation, not self-defence.

[5] Rodick, *op. cit.*, p. 36; a similar distinction is made by Wright, *The Enforcement of International Law through Municipal Law in the U.S.* (1915), p. 26.

[6] I.C.J. Reports, 1949, p. 35.

standard then required is strict but not so strict as in the former case.[1]

On the other hand, when the state invokes the right of self-defence as a justification for action within its own territorial jurisdiction, then it does so as sovereign and in the exercise of its sovereign rights. It is possible to contend that here the right of self-defence under international law is not relevant at all,[2] but, in circumstances in which a state acts against aliens or their property or the property of foreign states and possibly in breach of duties imposed by general international law or by treaty, it is difficult to assert that the state needs no justification other than its rights as territorial sovereign. Where such action is *prima facie* unlawful under international law it must find justification, if justification is to be found at all, in exceptional rights recognized by international law. It may be thought preferable to define such action as the state takes in self-protection within its territory as self-preservation, thus confining the term self-defence to action taken beyond the state's territorial limits. In our view this is not helpful or sanctioned by state practice; the essence of self-defence is that it is a reaction against a delict and, since this is not so with self-preservation, it is believed that the true distinction between the two terms should rest on this factor and not on the *situs* of the protective action. Of course the *situs* may be relevant to the burden of proof, but whether the action in self-defence is taken within or without the state's territorial limits, it is justified only in the form of a reaction to a delict violating its essential rights.

Secondly, it may be necessary to distinguish state action involving the use or threat of force from other action, and this distinction is relevant both to the action of the delinquent state and to that of the state acting in self-defence. *Prima facie* one would suggest that the right of self-defence finds its place in a legal system within the context of force, that it justifies the use of force against delictual conduct involving force or the threat of force. Certainly today the importance of the concept of self-defence lies in its character as an exception to the obligation not

[1] See *post*, ch. IV, and see Cheng, *op. cit.*, p. 95.

[2] Cheng, *op. cit.*, ch. 1, deals with the numerous instances of the territorial application of the principle of self-preservation (expulsion of aliens, measures to protect public safety or welfare, etc.) but does not deal with the legal concept of self-defence under this head, but only under the head of the 'external application' of the principle.

to resort to force or the threat of force, and Art. 51 of the Charter tends to suggest that self-defence is only a reaction to force by referring to the right of individual or collective self-defence 'if an armed attack occurs'. Kelsen has said of the right of self-defence, 'it is self-help against a specific violation of the law, against the illegal use of force, not against other violations of the law'.[1] There are, logically, four possible situations. Firstly, when the delinquent state uses force or the threat of force and the defending state's reaction in self-defence similarly involves force or the threat of force. Secondly, where the delinquent state uses force or the threat of force and the defending state's reaction involves measures less than force or the threat of force. Thirdly, where the delinquent state uses measures less than force or the threat of force and the defending state's reaction involves force or the threat of force. Fourthly, where the delinquent state uses measures less than force or the threat of force and the defending state's reaction similarly involves measures less than force or the threat of force.

The first situation is the classic one in which the defending state's reaction is properly described as the exercise of a right of self-defence, that is assuming the other requirements as to the reality of the threat to the state's essential rights, immediacy of the danger, lack of other means of protection, etc., are present. The second raises a certain difficulty for, if the right of self-defence only exists within the context of force, then the term 'self-defence' is not strictly appropriate to such action. Examples of such action would be the confiscation of assets, the enactment of discriminatory legislation directed against the delinquent state's interests or those of its nationals, or the expulsion of the nationals of the delinquent state; these measures are illustrations of the 'internal application' of the concept of self-defence and, taking effect within the jurisdiction of the state, they do not require the state to use force in its international relations (though they may demand a certain amount of force to carry them out within the state's own jurisdiction). It is not believed that by this fact alone such measures ought to be denied the term 'self-defence'; the criterion of force is an arbitrary one which does not find support in state practice. The reason why such measures will not normally be properly characterized as self-defence is rather that they are

[1] *A.J.*, Vol. 42 (1948), p. 784.

invariably retaliatory in character. They do not meet the delict in kind, nor are they apt to protect the actual rights threatened by the delictual use or threat of force; the whole purpose of the exercise of self-defence must be the protection of the very rights which are endangered. To take an example, where the delict of one state involves force in the transgression of the boundaries of another, the confiscation of the delictual state's shipping or other assets can scarcely be termed action appropriate to defend the right of territorial integrity (as the use of troops against the invaders would be). Such action is, therefore, as a general rule more in the character of reprisals than self-defence; but the fact that it does not involve force or the threat of force is not conclusive. It is possible that action designed to protect the very rights threatened by the delict, even though not involving force, can properly find justification on the basis of a right of self-defence.

In the third situation, when the delict does not involve force or the threat of force, it would similarly seem arbitrary to deny to the defending state the right to use force in the defence of its rights as a matter of fixed principle. As we shall see, there is something to be said for the view that economic or ideological aggression can be as detrimental to a state's security and, if illegal, as dangerous a violation of the state's essential rights as the use or threat of force. The relevance of any distinction between delicts involving force and those not so doing lies, in our submission, in the requirement of proportionality. The use of force as a reaction to a delict not involving force will scarcely ever be 'proportionate', but there is no rule of law to say it can never be so; indeed, it would be very questionable policy to introduce such a rule at this time and, even if introduced, the rule would be based on questions of policy rather than of juridical logic.[1]

In the fourth situation, if we reject the view that as a matter of principle the right of self-defence only exists within the context of force, the reaction of the defending state can also be properly characterized as self-defence assuming the other essentials of the right are present.

In the main, therefore, it is believed that the right of self-defence, though chiefly relevant as an exception to the prohibition of force and as a reaction to a delictual use of force, cannot be and has not been by state practice confined to this context. It has

[1] See *post* at pp. 47–50, 109–10 for circumstances relevant to this problem.

juridical significance when used to describe a state's reaction to a delict threatening its essential rights and to sanction action otherwise illegal which is undertaken by a state without the authority of any organ of the international community and which has as its object the protection of those essential rights by appropriate and proportionate measures. It is our purpose, in the following chapters, to analyse those substantive and essential rights which may be protected by the right of self-defence, and to examine the extent to which state practice bears out the nature of the right sketched out in this chapter.

PART ONE

THE SUBSTANTIVE RIGHTS FOR WHICH SELF-DEFENCE IS A PERMISSIBLE MEANS OF PROTECTION

CHAPTER II

THE RIGHT OF TERRITORIAL INTEGRITY

THE most obvious substantive right for which the right of self-defence serves as a means of protection is the right of territorial integrity, and it is in the defence of state territory that the right of self-defence is most clearly invoked. The analogy between natural persons and states, drawn by the natural lawyers of the Middle Ages, was used to identify the territory of the state with the body of the individual[1] and thus recognize an assault upon state territory as the clearest example of a situation affording to the territorial state a right of self-defence. Whilst the basis of analogy no longer serves to describe adequately the right to territorial integrity, it is certain that this right has been accepted as fundamental in international law and an essential foundation of the legal relations between states. As Komarnicki states:

> La violation des frontières d'un Etat est la violation de la compétence essentielle de cet Etat, c'est par conséquent la violation par excellence des limites posées par le droit.[2]

The general duty of non-intervention[3] was, in the Covenant of the League under Art. X, supplemented by the following specific duty:

> The Members of the League undertake to respect and preserve as against external aggression the territorial integrity and political independence of all Members of the League. . . .[4]

---

[1] Dickinson, 'The Analogy between natural persons and International Persons in the Law of Nations', *Yale L.J.*, Vol. 26 (1918), p. 565. On the view that this analogy had its origin in the mediaeval concept of mankind as an organic whole see Gierke, *Political Theories of the Middle Ages*, trans. Maitland (1900), p. 22.

[2] 'La Définition de l'Agresseur', *R.C.*, 1949 (II), p. 55; see also Baty, *Canons of International Law* (1930), p. 88; Stowell, *Intervention in International Law* (1921), p. 297; also the *Corfu Channel Case* (Merits), 1949, I.C.J. Reports at p. 35.

[3] See *post*, p. 44.

[4] On the difficulties of interpretation of this article see Komarnicki, *La Question de l'integrité territoriale dans le Pacte de la S.D.N.*, 1923; Fischer Williams, *Some Aspects of the Covenant*, 1934, pp.103–25; Williams, B., *State Security and the League of Nations*, 1927, ch. 3; Langer, *Seizure of Territory*, 1947, ch. 8.

In the Charter of the United Nations, whilst the guarantee is omitted, the right of territorial integrity is founded in the duty imposed on all members, and possibly non-members,[1] by Art. 2(4):

> All Members shall refrain in their international relations from the threat or use of force against the territorial integrity or political independence of any State, or in any other manner inconsistent with the Purposes of the United Nations.

It has, therefore, been regarded as axiomatic that the right of territorial integrity was the right *par excellence* which might be protected by the right of self-defence. In all the attempts to define aggression the invasion of or attack against the territory of a state has been made the starting-point of the definition.[2] It might even be said that a fixation with the 'territorial' concept of aggression has tended to obscure the need to recognize that there are other essential rights of the state, the violation of which ought equally well to be termed aggression, and the protection of which is equally well self-defence. In recent years increasing attention has been paid to the right of political independence and the need to protect it against subversive activities,[3] to something akin to a right of economic independence and the need to protect a state's economy against threats to its economic interests.[4] Yet, historically, the emphasis upon the right of territorial integrity is justified by the fact that aggressions which have placed states in the necessity of exercising their right of self-defence have, in the main, taken the form of a violation of the right to territorial integrity. The indictments against the Major War Criminals of the Axis Powers, heard at Nuremberg[5] and Tokyo,[6] show how predominantly the concept of a 'crime against the peace' was based upon the violation of the right of territorial integrity and, though this was not in issue and consequently never a direct finding, it is implicit in the judgments of the International Military Tribunal at Nuremberg and the International Military Tribunal for the Far East that the violation of this right afforded to the victim state a right of self-defence.[7] The subsequent formulation of the principles of the Nuremberg judgment by the International Law Com-

[1] This arises from Art. 2(6) of the Charter, theoretically at variance with the principle *pacta tertiis* but justified in the general interest of maintaining international peace and security; see *post*, p. 174 fn. 3.

[2] *Post*, ch. XI. [3] *Post*, pp. 47, 49. [4] *Post*, p. 106.

[5] *Post*, pp. 138–43. [6] *Post*, pp. 143–5. [7] *Post*, p. 139.

mission in 1950,[1] and the Draft Code of Offences against the Peace and Security of Mankind[2] reiterate this principle; the latter characterizes as criminal the following acts:

> Art. 2(4) . . . The incursion into the territory of a State from the territory of another State by armed bands acting for a political purpose.
>
> Art. 2(8) . . . Acts by the authorities of a State resulting in the annexation, contrary to international law, of territory belonging to another State or of territory under an international régime.

It cannot, therefore, be doubted that the right of territorial integrity is a right which may be protected against violation by the exercise of a right of self-defence. The matter cannot, however, be stated in such simple terms; it has been rightly said that 'territorial integrity is far from being an uncomplicated notion'.[3]

An initial difficulty arises over the question of interpretation of the term 'territorial integrity'; this is not identical with 'territorial inviolability' [4] and it can scarcely be supposed that a state has a right to have its frontiers inviolate in all circumstances. There might conceivably be circumstances in which one state is justified in action which, *prima facie*, constitutes a violation of the territory of another state, and this is particularly relevant to the situation in which a state acting in self-defence is forced to take action within the territory of another state. This illustrates the double aspect of the right of territorial integrity; on the one hand it is a right which may be protected by the exercise of self-defence, and on the other it may be subject to the right of self-defence of other states. It is a right which is never absolute in character but relative to the rights of other states; this principle of the 'relativity of rights' must necessarily impose a qualification on the statement, normally true, that the right of territorial integrity may be defended by the exercise of self-defence. Illustrations are not hard to find; the case of the *Caroline*, to which we shall refer in detail later,[5] illustrates

[1] See Report of the I.L.C. covering the Second Session, June 5th–July 29th, 1950, A/1316; Off. Rec. G.A., 5th Session, Supp. No. 12, Part III.

[2] Report of the I.L.C., Third Session, 1951, A/1858; Off. Rec. G.A., 6th Session, Supp. No. 9, ch. IV.

[3] Pompe, *Aggressive War an International Crime*, 1953, p. 104.

[4] *Contra* Oppenheim, *International Law*, 7th ed., Vol. II, p. 154.

[5] *Post*, p. 58.

the claim of one state to justify a *prima facie* violation of the territorial integrity of another by reference to its right of self-defence. Likewise the so-called right of Hot Pursuit[1] by which a state justifies the transgression of the boundaries of a neighbouring state in pursuit of marauders who have committed crimes within its territory is based upon the right of self-defence. Within recent years the Arab states and Israel have claimed to justify military operations outside the territory subject to their jurisdiction as measures of self-defence,[2] as have also Pakistan and India.[3] Britain and France similarly justified their intervention in Egyptian territory in October, 1956, on grounds of self-defence.[4]

In these circumstances the problem will invariably arise that states illegally transgressing the boundaries of another seek to justify their action on the ground of self-defence; it is a problem which is well-nigh inevitable once the relativity of the right of territorial integrity is admitted. For example, after China had invoked the attention of the Council of the League to the invasion of Manchuria by Japanese forces on September 21st, 1931,[5] the Japanese government made a statement to the Council justifying its action as 'justifiable measures of self-protection on the standard principle laid down in the *Caroline* case, that every act of self-defence must depend for its justification on the importance of the interests to be defended, on the imminence of the danger, and on the necessity of the act'.[6] Moreover, the Japanese government asserted that, since the right of self-defence was clearly reserved under the Kellogg Pact, its action was based upon this right and it was solely within the competence of that government to judge the legality of its action. This contention the League did not accept; the Lytton Commission, appointed on December 10th, 1931,[7] to study the situation on the spot and ascertain whether

[1] *Post*, p. 38.

[2] Off. Rec. S.C., 3rd Year, 301st and 302nd Meetings, May 22nd, 1948. For the Egyptian view see Doc. S/767; for the Israeli Doc. S/766; the Syrian Doc. S/753; Iraq Doc. S/769; Saudi Arabia Doc. S/772; Yemen Doc. S/774, Add. 1; Lebanon Doc. S/770.

[3] Off. Rec. S.C., 3rd Year, 227th–229th Meetings, January 6th to 17th.

[4] See *post*, pp. 104, 243.

[5] Off. Journal, 1931, p. 2453. For a brief summary of the facts leading up to this invasion see Langer, *op. cit.*, p. 56; Gathorne Hardy, *A short history of International Affairs*, 1920–38, p. 309 *et seq.*

[6] *Foreign Affairs*, October, 1932, p. 74.

[7] Off. Journal, 1931, pp. 2374–8.

Japan had acted in self-defence, rejected this plea as a pure question of fact in its report to the Council. 'The military operations of the Japanese troops during this night . . . cannot be regarded as measures of legitimate defence. In saying this the Commission does not exclude the hypothesis that the officers on the spot may have thought they were acting in self-defence.' [1]

Similarly in the Italo-Abyssinian affair, the League Council itself on October 7th, 1935, rejected the assumption of defensive necessity contained in the argument of the Italian delegate, Baron Aloisi.[2] The International Military Tribunal at Nuremberg rejected the plea that the invasion of Norway was an act of self-defence,[3] again, as a question of fact, whilst at the same time admitting that 'preventive action in foreign territory' could be justified under the conditions formulated in the *Caroline* case. Whether these conditions are satisfied, and whether, therefore, the transgression of the territory of another state is justified in self-defence must in final analysis be determined objectively by an impartial organ or tribunal representing the international community as a whole. So long as the distinction between illegal violations of a state's right to territorial integrity and *prima facie* violations justifiable in self-defence rests solely on the subjective judgment of the interested states, then the principle of relativity of rights can have only nominal application. Given the possibility of an objective determination of the legality of state action the principle is of real validity and it may then be stated that the right of territorial integrity is never absolute, but conditional on the absence of any real threat to the security of another state within the boundaries of the state claiming integrity.

It seems clear that by 'territorial integrity' it was never meant to acknowledge an absolute right to inviolability. Certainly President Wilson, the author of Art. X of the Covenant in the sense that he foresaw the guarantee contained therein as the 'very backbone of the whole Covenant', seems to have regarded the expression 'territorial integrity' as meaning 'immunity not from armed

[1] Off. Journal, 1931, Special Supp. No. 169, p. 148; and see the adoption of this report by the Assembly and the subsequent recommendations of the Assembly, Off. Journal, Special Supp. No. 112, pp. 22, 72, 75.

[2] Off. Journal, 1935, Records of Sixteenth Assembly, 15th Plen. Meeting, p. 104; and see Quincey Wright, 'The Test of Aggression in the Italo-Ethiopean War', *A.J.*, Vol. 30 (1936), p. 45.

[3] Judgment, p. 205 of text cited in *A.J.*, Vol. 41 (1947), Supp.

invasion but from forcible annexation'.[1] In the Corfu Incident of 1923[2] the whole question was raised by the bombardment of Corfu by Italy without any intention of annexation. It is not suggested that Italy's action could be characterized as self-defence,[3] but that action did raise the question whether the guarantee involved literal inviolability, as Greece contended, or only freedom from annexation or invasion with that intent. The enigmatic reply to this question, given by the Commission of Jurists, did not answer that question,[4] but it gave the implication that the right of territorial integrity was not absolute in character. Virtually the same question remains under Art. 2(4) of the Charter; we have previously suggested that forcible reprisals are no longer permissible, but it is, in our view, still maintainable that a right of absolute inviolability is not conferred by that provision and the right of territorial integrity remains, under the Charter, subject to the rights of other states to exercise self-defence within the conditions prescribed by general international law and the Charter.

A further problem arises from the complexity of the right of territorial integrity, and this relates to the position where the sovereignty over territory which a state claims to protect by the exercise of a right of self-defence is disputed. Once title to the territory is itself in dispute it can no longer afford a basis upon which to rest the right of self-defence, and again the situation may arise in which two states act under a claim of self-defence in respect of the same territory.

The dispute between Bolivia and Paraguay over ownership of the Chaco arose in precisely these circumstances. On June 15th, 1932, open hostilities began between these two states, the culmination of a series of 'frontier' incidents since 1928. The League of Nations Commission in its report of May 11th, 1934,[5] while

[1] Baker, 'The Meaning of the Covenant', in Munch, *Les Origines et l'Oevre de la S.D.N.*, II, 1924, p. 58; Fischer Williams, *op. cit.*, p. 118. It was, in fact, the last of his Fourteen Points.

[2] Off. Journal, 1923, pp. 1276 *et seq.*, 1412 *et seq.*; see Quincey Wright, 'The Concept of Aggression in International Law,' *A.J.*, Vol. 29 (1935), p. 384, and the extensive bibliography on the Corfu Affair cited in Briggs, *The Law of Nations*, 2nd ed., pp. 960–4.

[3] They were in fact characterized as reprisals by the Italian delegate, Salandra, on September 18th, 1923; Off. Journal, 1923, pp. 1313–14.

[4] Off. Journal, 1924, pp. 523–7; see *post*, pp. 124–5.

[5] For the full text of the report see *A.J.*, Supp., Vol. 28 (1934), p. 137 or C. 154.M.64, 1934, VII.

avoiding the question of responsibility for the war so long as attempts at pacific settlement were in progress, adverted to the difficulty resulting from disputed sovereignty in these words:

> In this dispute each party claims ownership of the Chaco, and therefore maintains it is waging a defensive war in its own territory. How is the aggressor to be determined in such a conflict? No international frontier has been crossed by foreign troops, since the Chaco question will only be settled by a determination of this disputed frontier.[1]

Similar difficulties exist in the Arab-Israeli dispute[2] and the dispute over Kashmir between India and Pakistan; it may be possible to provide a temporary solution by means of truce lines or 'neutral' zones, but it is clearly a situation in which a right of self-defence cannot be based on sovereignty over the disputed territory. The proper solution, it is submitted, lies in recognizing peaceful possession or *de facto* authority as a sufficient basis upon which to justify self-defence; the analogy of private law supports this view, for the English Common Law has long protected peaceful possession in fact, rather than actual title. It has been suggested that the effect of Art. X of the Covenant was to protect possession of territory, even against another state which might eventually prove to have a better title to the territory.[3] One of the five criteria applied by the Act relating to the Definition of the Aggressor prepared by the Committee on Security Questions of the Disarmament Conference in 1933[4] was the invasion of territory; in connection with this the Politis report stated: 'By territory is here meant territory over which a State actually exercises authority.'[5]

[1] *A.J.*, Supp., Vol. 28 (1934), p. 201. See generally Woolsey, 'The Settlement of the Chaco Dispute', *A.J.*, Vol. 33 (1939), pp. 126–9; Zimmern, *The League of Nations and the Rule of Law*, 1918–35; Hill, *Claims to Territory in International Law and Relations* (1945), pp. 206–7, 218–19, 425 *et seq.* For the text of the award in the dispute see *A.J.*, Vol. 33 (1939), pp. 126–9. In the previous dispute in 1933 between Columbia and Peru over the sovereignty of Leticia the Council was able to conclude that sovereignty lay in Columbia; but initially the problem was the same. See Report adopted by Council on March 18th, 1933; Off. Journal, 14th Year, No. 4, 71st Session of the Council, pp. 516–23.

[2] See discussion in Off. Rec. S.C., 3rd Year, 297th Meeting, May 20th, 1948.

[3] Fischer Williams, *Chapters on Current International Law and the League of Nations* (1929), pp. 468–9.

[4] League of Nations, Conference for the Reduction and Limitation of Armaments, Conference Documents, Vol. II, p. 679 (Doc. Conf. D/C.G. 108).

[5] Ibid., p. 681.

Further, in reply to Madriaga (Spain) who raised doubts as to the wisdom of this view, Politis replied that:

> The idea of that sentence was not to justify unlawful occupation, but solely to protect peaceful possession against any act of force, even when the legal titles on which possession was founded might accidentally be open to dispute.[1]

The same view appears to be implicit in the definition of aggression embodied in Art. 9 of the Inter-American Treaty of Reciprocal Assistance of 1947:

> Invasion, by the armed forces of a State, of the territory of an American State, through the trespassing of boundaries demarcated in accordance with a treaty, judicial decision, or arbitral award, or, in the absence of frontiers thus demarcated, invasion affecting a region which is under the effective jurisdiction of another state.[2]

In the acceptance of this view a solution is offered not only to those difficult cases where sovereignty over territory is disputed, but also to those cases in which territory is lawfully occupied by the forces of a state other than the territorial state, or to those cases where territory is under an international régime which does not transfer sovereignty in the territory from the territorial state. The situation of British troops in Egyptian territory under the Anglo-Egyptian Treaty of 1936[3] would illustrate the first case, and the joint occupation of Berlin[4] or the special international régime for Jerusalem[5] or for Trieste[6] the second. In all these cases it is suggested that the peaceful occupation of territory will afford a sufficient basis upon which to exercise the right of self-defence.

Where, of course, that occupation is lawfully terminated, as in the case where the consent of the territorial sovereign to the

[1] League of Nations, Records of the Conference for the Reduction and Limitation of Armaments, Series B (Minutes of the General Commission), Vol. II, p. 554.

[2] Signed at Rio de Janeiro, September 2nd, 1947; text cited *A.J.*, Vol. 43 (1949), Supp., p. 53.

[3] Treaty Series, No. 6 (1937), Cmd. 5360.

[4] Declaration of Governments of U.S.S.R., U.S.A., U.K. and France, June 5th, 1945, at Berlin; Germany No. 1 (1945), Cmd. 6648; see Kelsen, *A.J.*, Vol. 39 (1945), pp. 518–26.

[5] For text of General Assembly Resolution creating this régime see U.N. Yearbook, 1947–8, p. 254.

[6] Instrument for the Provisional Régime of the Free Territory of Trieste, approved by the Security Council, Off. Rec., 2nd Year, 91st Meeting, January 10th (S/224). For details see *U.N. Yearbook*, 1946–7, pp. 381–92.

presence of foreign troops within his territory is lawfully withdrawn, then the presence of those troops constitutes a violation of the right of territorial integrity which will justify the use of force in self-defence to bring about the expulsion of the foreign troops.[1]

The main defect in a system which permits the right of self-defence in the defence of territorial integrity without providing procedures for peaceful change is that in perpetuating the *status quo* it produces an incipient threat to the system itself.[2] It is not, in fact, permissible to assume that international society, or the distribution of territory amongst the members of that society, will be static; justice in the broad sense of appropriate distribution will be satisfied only when the prohibition of the use of force or the instrument of war as a means of change is accompanied by a procedure for peaceful change based upon equitable principles. In this respect the Charter of the United Nations provides even less solution to this problem than did Art. 19 of the Covenant of the League.[3] Moreover, in so far as the peaceful occupation of terri-

[1] The right of expulsion is dependent on the illegality of their presence; this may not always be clear. See the numerous complaints relating to the unlawful presence of troops on foreign soil which have been made. Complaint of U.S.S.R. by letter to President of S.C. dated January 21st, 1946 (Off. Rec. S.C., 1st Year, 6th Meeting) about presence of British troops on Greek territory; the Greek representative emphasized the consent of the Greek government to their presence. Complaint of U.S.S.R. against use of British troops in Indonesia, Off. Rec., 1st Year, 12th Meeting; Syrian complaint about presence of Soviet troops in Iran, letter to Secretary-General, January 19th, 1946 (Off. Rec. S.C., 1st Year, 3rd and 5th Meetings). Burmese complaint to General Assembly in Seventh and Eighth Session, 1953, on presence of Chinese troops, as to which see General Assembly Resolution 815 (IX), October 29th, 1954 (see *U.N. Yearbook*, 1954, p. 52 *et seq.*). Egyptian complaint about British troops in Egypt, letter to Secretary-General dated July 8th, 1947 (S/410); see discussion in Off. Rec. S.C., 2nd Year, 159th–201st Meetings.

[2] See the Canadian proposal in 1920 to delete Art. X of the Covenant because the guarantee of the existing territorial dispositions was not accompanied by a preliminary survey of the justice and adequacy of those dispositions and might, therefore, merely perpetuate injustice; Plenary Meetings, First Assembly, p. 279. An interpretative resolution submitted to the Fourth Assembly in 1924, affirming the principle of integrity against aggression rather than the perpetuation of the existing territorial and political organization was not adopted; Plenary Meetings, Fourth Assembly, p. 86.

[3] Art. 14 of the U.N. Charter, authorizing the General Assembly to 'recommend measures for the peaceful adjustment of any situation . . . etc.' is scarcely adequate, for the recommendations of the General Assembly would not be binding.

tory will afford a basis for the exercise of self-defence, this, too, has its defects in a system which contains no legal obligation to resort to judicial settlement in order to settle the question of title. The further elaboration of these defects is beyond the scope of the present work; suffice it to say that the principle that a state may use self-defence to defend its territorial integrity, whilst admitted as a principle of law, is one which needs complementary principles governing the peaceful settlement of disputes and peaceful change.

So far we have been concerned with self-defence of national territory on the assumption that the action in self-defence occurs within the national jurisdiction. Within these limits the right to defend territory in the lawful possession of a state clearly belongs to that state; it affords the least controversial example of the exercise of the right of self-defence. There are, however, more controversial cases in which the territorial state assumes the right to transgress the boundaries of a neighbouring state in pursuit of bodies of persons who have committed acts within its territory prejudicial to its safety and have then fled into the territory of a neighbouring state. This violation of territory has been justified as a continuation of action in self-defence taken within the national jurisdiction and bears some analogy to the right of Hot Pursuit on the High Seas.

THE SO-CALLED RIGHT OF HOT PURSUIT

The practice of the United States affords numerous illustrations of the exercise of this right of pursuit and, moreover, there is evidence that the right was claimed as justified on the basic principle of self-defence.[1]

In May, 1836, the forces of the U.S. under General Gaines invaded Mexican territory in order to pursue marauding Indians who had crossed into U.S. territory from the Mexican border and there committed acts of murder, arson and plunder before fleeing into Mexican territory. The U.S. justified its action as based on self-defence, whilst renouncing any intention of establishing anything in the nature of possession or of a claim to possession of

[1] Moore, *Dig.*, Vol. II, p. 418 *et seq.*; *International Arbitrations*, II, pp. 1212–14; III, p. 2430 *et seq.* Hyde, Vol. I, p. 240 *et seq.* Hackworth, *Dig.*, Vol. II, p. 282 *et seq.* Hershey, 'Incursions into Mexico and the Doctrine of Hot Pursuit', *A.J.*, Vol. 13 (1919), p. 568.

Mexican territory.[1] In a letter to Mr. Ellis, the U.S. Minister to Mexico, dated December 10th, 1836, Mr. Forsyth, the U.S. Secretary of State wrote:

> You will find no difficulty in showing to the Mexican government that it rests upon the principles of the law of nations, entirely distinct from those on which war is justified—upon the immutable principles of self-defence—upon the principles which justify decisive measures of precaution to prevent irreparable evil to our own or to a neighbouring people.[2]

This position, which the U.S. consistently maintained, was reiterated by the commission appointed on August 30th, 1912, by the U.S. Secretary for War to investigate the claims of U.S. citizens for damages arising out of hostilities in Mexico causing injuries to those citizens within U.S. territory.

> The ground upon which this position rests is simply that the right of self-defence rose superior in the particular circumstances to the right of territorial inviolability.[3]

These are cases of the pursuit of bodies acting without the authority or support of the state whose territory is invaded in hot pursuit, and they presuppose the inadequacy of the territorial state's own measures of prevention. The resultant derogation from the state's territorial sovereignty arises directly from that state's inability to secure to its neighbour respect for its territorial sovereignty. As Hyde puts it:

> Respect for the inviolability of the territory of a State rests on the theory that it possesses the power and the will to exercise control therein, and to a degree sufficient to ensure the administration of justice in a broad sense, throughout the national domain.[4]

From this point of view the infringement of the state's right to territorial integrity is justified on a reasoning analogous to the

[1] Moore, *Dig.*, Vol. II, p. 418. See also the invasions of W. Florida in 1814 and 1817 in derogation of Spanish sovereignty by U.S. forces for the pursuit and punishment of Indian Marauders, described by Adams, U.S. Secretary of State, as done 'not in the spirit of hostility to Spain, but as a necessary measure of self-defence'; Moore, ibid., p. 406. There are other illustrations drawn from the practice of Great Britain in the N.W. Frontier Provinces of India, involving the pursuit of tribesmen into Afghanistan territory as late as 1915. See *Cambridge Modern History*, Vol. XII, p. 489. *Cambridge History of India*, Vol. VI, p. 475.

[2] Cited in Moore, II, p. 418; Brit. & For. State Papers, Vol. XXVI, p. 1419.

[3] Cited in Hackworth, *Dig.*, Vol. II, p. 289.

[4] *International Law*, Vol. I, p. 646.

reasoning behind the principle of abuse of rights, of which Westlake has said 'no principle is more firmly established in the science of law than that which says to an owner *sic utere tuo ut alienum non laedas*'.[1] For it is the abuse of the rights of the territorial sovereign, in allowing his territory to harbour a danger to the security of a neighbouring state, that justifies the neighbouring state in resorting to measures *prima facie* unlawful.

In principle this reasoning would appear to be unobjectionable. In practice, however, the cases of incursions under the right of hot pursuit are drawn from a limited number of state relations, that is to say those cases where the invaded state found itself at a decided disadvantage in its power to resist the forces of the invading state. Although the U.S. readily conceded a similar right to Mexico on each occasion,[2] there seems to be no case in which the invaded state admitted the right of incursion apart from a treaty concession, or in any way regarded itself as being under a duty to submit to these incursions.[3] Moreover the analogy between the right of Hot Pursuit on land and the acknowledged right of Hot Pursuit on the High Seas is far from being exact; for the recognized limitation on the right on the high seas is that it must cease whenever the pursued vessel reaches the territorial waters of another state.[4] The right can never involve the violation of another state's territory; yet on land the right of hot pursuit involves precisely this.

A further reason for doubt as to whether the right of Hot Pursuit is properly involved in the right of self-defence is that in many cases the action of the pursuing state is distinctly punitive in character, and, therefore, since it goes beyond the necessities of protection, is more properly described as reprisals. This need not be so in all cases; it is conceivable that the only measures of protection against subsequent attacks or incursions by armed bands may lie in pursuing them to destruction across the frontiers of a

[1] *International Law*, Vol. II, p. 313. But see Schwarzenberger, 'The Fundamental Principles of International Law', *R.C.*, 1955 (1), pp. 341–2.

[2] Moore, *Dig.*, Vol. II, p. 421. Note of Mr. Marcy to Mr. Almonte, Mexican Min., February 4th, 1856.

[3] Westlake, *op. cit.*, Vol. I, p. 302, states that Mexico does not seem to have seriously objected; but see the reply of General Carranza, cited in Hackworth, *Dig.*, Vol. II, p. 288, and also Barrows, *William M. Evarts* (1941), p. 355, quoting the order to Mexican troops to 'repel force with force'.

[4] See *post*, p. 83.

neighbouring state. In these circumstances the essential purpose of the action would be the protection of the pursuing state's right of territorial integrity against future, imminent attack by the same bands. Yet even this would be permissible only within very stringent limits for, involving a transgression of another state's boundaries as it does, the onus of proving the necessity of the action and the reality of the imminent danger of subsequent attacks would be at its very highest. The right of hot pursuit, whatever its conditions in the past, must under present-day international law be subject to those same limitations and conditions which govern any exercise of the right of self-defence.

CHAPTER III

THE RIGHT OF POLITICAL INDEPENDENCE

It is significant that both Art. X of the Covenant and Art. 2(4) of the United Nations Charter link the right of territorial integrity with that of political independence; both together comprise the concrete existence of a state. In the main, delictual conduct of a state which violates the right of political independence will also violate the right of territorial integrity; the normal aggressive war endangers both rights, yet this is not necessarily so, for the political independence of a state is susceptible to impairment by conduct which need not involve an armed attack or the violation of its territorial limits. As Pompe has said:

> Through indirect action, via secret agents or internal groups supported by outside propaganda (the 'ideological' aggression), money, arms, and, at the critical moment of the disturbances, by direct intimidation and political pressure, a State can put an end to the independent existence of another as effectively as with the classical, external, military aggression.[1]

It is, therefore, in our submission, necessary to give separate treatment to the right of political independence and the exercise of a right of self-defence in protection of a state's political independence. The problem is not simplified by the vagueness inherent in any definition of this right, for, even as we have seen that the right of territorial integrity has its complexities, the formulation of a right of political independence presents even greater problems.

The right has been described as involving, *inter alia*, the right

[1] *Aggressive War*, 1953, p. 53; he instances the 'Anschlusz' of Austria in 1938, the Communist coup d'état in March, 1948, in Czechoslovakia, and the assistance given by Greece's northern neighbours to rebels within Greece from 1946 to 1949. See Secretary-General's Report on the Question of Defining Aggression, October 3rd, 1952 (A/2211), pp. 55–7, for a survey of the views of delegates to the United Nations and of the International Law Commission on the necessity for defining aggression so as to cover this 'indirect' aggression against a state's political independence. For an allegation that the U.S.S.R. had violated the political independence of Czechoslovakia see letter of March 12th, 1948, from Chile to Secretary-General, Off. Rec. S.C., 3rd Year, No. 73.

'to establish, maintain, and change its own constitution or form of government and select its own rulers . . . to negotiate and conclude treaties and alliances . . . and to maintain diplomatic intercourse with other members of the international community'.[1] It includes the right to maintain both the 'internal' and the 'external' sovereignty of the state, the latter term connoting the normal conduct of inter-state relations, and this external sovereignty of the state can obviously be impaired without a violation of the state's territorial integrity; this is yet another reason for affording separate treatment to the right of political independence. Recently, in the Draft Declaration on the Rights and Duties of States, a memorandum submitted by the Secretary-General of the United Nations in accordance with the General Assembly's resolution of November 21st, 1947, the right was defined in these terms:

> Every state has the right to its own independence in the sense that it is free to provide for its own well-being and to develop materially and spiritually without being subjected to the domination of other states provided always, that in so doing it shall not impair or violate the legitimate rights of other states.[2]

The memorandum also cites various precedents defining the right and all illustrating the connection between the right of independence and the principle of self-determination of peoples,[3] a principle to which the United Nations is pledged in the purposes of its Charter. This connection, however true, serves to indicate the lack of precision which surrounds the right of political independence. For this reason it is proposed to concentrate on the existence of duties imposed by international law which find their correlation in the right of political independence; only to the extent that such duties exist can there be said to be a right of

[1] Hershey, *Essentials of Public International Law*, 1912, p. 147. See the view in Oppenheim, *International Law*, 3rd ed., Vol. I, at p. 207, denying that it is ever a right in the strict sense but rather a quality; this contrasts curiously with the postulate of a duty to refrain from acts injurious to a state's independence (ibid., p. 208).

[2] U.N. Publications, A/CN.4/2, December 15th, 1948, Art. 4, p. 58.

[3] This principle has defied definition, and international law has never truly recognized any such legal right or known standards by which any group may be said to be entitled to self-determination. See Eagleton, 'Excesses of Self-Determination', *Foreign Affairs*, July 1953, p. 593; Cobbah, *National Self-Determination*, 1945, p. 46, adverts to these difficulties in defining the right as not absolute, but relative to the circumstances.

political independence *stricto sensu*, for 'the rights of states under general international law are always the reflection of the duties imposed by general international law'.[1] To a great extent the duties embodied in Art. X of the Covenant, and now Art. 2(4) of the Charter, cover the use or threat of force against the political independence of any state; it is also necessary to consider the more comprehensive duty of non-intervention which covers conduct not within the scope of the prohibition of Art. 2(4).

THE DUTY OF NON-INTERVENTION

Under General International Law. In 1758 Vattel formulated the duty of non-intervention as a re-statement of the right of independence from the negative side.[2] The conviction that intervention against a state without just cause constituted an infringement of the state's legal rights gradually developed, so that when the French Constitution of 1792 enunciated the following principle:

> La Convention nationale déclare qu'elle accordera secours à tous les peuples qui voudront recouvrir leur liberté, et elle charge le pouvoir exécutif de donner des ordres aux généraux des armées françaises pour secourir les citoyens qui auraient été ou qui seraient vexés pour la cause de la liberté,

the protest was so general as to cause its repeal on April 13th, 1793.[3] Despite this the practice of states in the eighteenth and nineteenth centuries showed scant respect for the principle of non-intervention. A revival of the system of the Balance of Power after the Congress of Vienna in 1815 brought the Holy Alliance into a unity of aim—that aim being the suppression and prevention of revolution in Europe and in the European colonies of Latin-America. Indeed the Monroe doctrine, proclaimed in 1823, was largely a reaction to this policy,[4] and that doctrine did much to strengthen the idea of a duty of non-intervention. By the nine-

[1] Kelsen, 'The Rights and Duties of States', *A.J.*, Vol. 44 (1950), p. 264.

[2] *Le Droit des Gens* (1758), Bk. II, para. 54. See also Winfield, 'History of Intervention in International Law', *BYBIL*, Vol. 2 (1922), p. 131.

[3] Phillimore, 'Droits et Devoirs Fondamentaux des Etats', *R.C.*, 1923 (1), p. 41; and see Laprade, *England and the French Revolution*, 1909, p. 106.

[4] Hershey, *op. cit.*, p. 152. See the British reaction in the circular of Castlereagh, January 19th, 1821, to the circular from Metternich at Troppau on December 8th, 1820, proclaiming the policy of the Holy Alliance; British State Papers, 1820–1, Vol. 8, pp. 1160–2.

teenth century to some extent the general duty was admitted, but subject to those cases where intervention was 'justifiable' . . . and the degree of uncertainty as to what amounted to justifiable intervention, to lawful exceptions to the duty of non-intervention, emphasized the lack of definite legal content in the 'right' of political independence. The enthusiasm for a recognition of the right was most marked in the Americas; the Sixth International Conference of American States resolved in 1928 that 'No state has the right to intervene in the affairs of another,' [1] and this conviction was repeated in a protocol at Buenos Aires in 1936,[2] and in the Declaration of American Principles at Lima in 1938.[3] It now finds a place in Art. 5 of the Draft Declaration on the Rights and Duties of States which states that 'No state has the right to interfere in the internal or external affairs of another state'.[4]

If intervention is construed strictly, as 'dictatorial interference in the sense of action amounting to a denial of the independence of the state',[5] then the duty of non-intervention is also comprised in the obligation contained in Art. 2(4) of the Charter to refrain from force or the threat of force against the political independence of any state. This follows necessarily once intervention is envisaged, as traditionally it has been, as involving coercion or the threat of coercion. On the other hand political independence is today susceptible to impairment by means not involving force or the threat of force; the development of techniques of ideological warfare, of subversive activities, has led to an increased concern with the duties imposed on states which are apt to meet these newer and more subtle methods of destroying a state's political independence. It is necessary, therefore, to summarize briefly what these duties are.

Firstly it is clear that the state must not organize hostile expeditions within its territory and directed against another state; nor must it encourage the formation of such expeditions by

[1] Cited Hyde, *International Law*, Vol. I, p. 251. The U.S. delegation put forward certain reservations where circumstances called for 'interposition of a temporary character . . . for the purpose of protecting the lives and property of its nationals', ibid., p. 252. See also the Convention of Montevideo in 1933, Art. 8; cited Hackworth, *Dig.*, Vol. I, p. 98.

[2] Cited Hackworth, *Dig.*, Vol. V, p. 463; 'Intervention by one state in the internal or external affairs of another state is condemned.'

[3] Ibid., p. 464.

[4] U.N. Publications, Doc. A/CN.4/2, December 15th, 1948.

[5] Lauterpacht, *International Law and Human Rights* (1950), p. 167.

non-state agencies or private persons.[1] Stowell rightly treats the latter as a 'constructive attack' by the state within whose territory the preparations take place,[2] and both forms of injurious conduct would be in breach of Art. 2(4). Where, however, the state conducts subversive activities which do not involve force or the threat of force, then those activities are delictual not by reference to Art. 2(4) but only by reference to a somewhat extended duty of non-intervention. The Draft Code of Offences Against the Peace and Security of Mankind[3] provides that the following are offences:

> Art. 2(5). The undertaking or encouragement by the authorities of a State of activities calculated to foment civil strife in another State, or the toleration by the authorities of a State of organized activities calculated to foment civil strife in another State.
>
> Art. 2(6). The undertaking or encouragement by the authorities of a State of terrorist activities in another State, or the toleration by the authorities of a State of organized activities calculated to carry out terrorist acts in another State.

These, however, are statements *de lege ferenda*; they certainly go beyond any precedent Nuremberg set[4] and, in so far as they suggest the prohibition of conduct not involving the use or threat of force, they may well go beyond what can be accurately stated as the present law. The borderline between encouragement and toleration, the question as to what constitutes 'toleration' and above all the question of how far existing law prohibits indirect state support are matters of some uncertainty. The policy of the U.S.A. as revealed in the Mutual Security Act of 1951[5] is on this

[1] Oppenheim, Vol. I, 8th ed., pp. 292–3; Hackworth, *Dig.*, Vol. VII, p. 396 *et seq.*; Curtis, *A.J.*, Vol. 8 (1914), pp. 1–37, 224–55, for the practice of the United States. See General Assembly Resolution 707 (VII) determining assistance to hostile forces in Burma to be contrary to the Charter and a violation of the territory and sovereignty of Burma (Repertory, Vol. I, p. 32).

[2] *Intervention in International Law*, p. 373; and see Phillimore, *International Law*, Vol. I, p. 230.

[3] Adopted by the International Law Commission in its Third Session, May 16th–July 27th, 1951; see Report on Third Session, ch. IV, pp. 10–14. Resolution 290 (IV) of the General Assembly on the Essentials of Peace (Repertory, Vol. I, p. 25), calls upon every nation 'to refrain from any threats or acts, direct or indirect, aimed at impairing the freedom, independence or integrity of any State, or at fomenting civil strife and subverting the will of the people in any State'.

[4] Pompe, *op. cit.*, pp. 340, 353.

[5] 65 Stat. 373, text in *A.J.*, Vol. 46 (1952), Supp., p. 14. The U.S.S.R. has proposed that this be characterized as aggression, November 22nd, 1951

ground of a questionable character; s. 101 of the Act envisages financial support 'for any selected persons who are residing in or escapees from the Soviet Union, Poland, Czechoslovakia, . . . either to form such persons into elements of the military forces supporting the North Atlantic Treaty Organization or for other purposes . . .' in order to contribute to the security of the United States.

A particularly difficult problem arises from the use of propaganda calculated to impair the political independence of a state. When propaganda is conducted by the state itself then, although it has been said that 'a State is bound under international law to refrain from spreading propaganda in a friendly country hostile to the latter's government',[1] this has been doubted by Stone[2] on the ground that the required *opinio necessitatis* to support such a customary duty is lacking. The propaganda broadcasts of the 'Voice of America', a state broadcasting agency, which have been transmitted to the U.S.S.R. since February, 1947, have recently been justified by Whitton as a form of retorsion or reprisals for a breach by the U.S.S.R. not only of this customary duty, but also of the specific obligation contained in the exchange of notes comprising the Roosevelt–Litvinoff agreement of 1933.[3] The same

(A/1968/Rev. 1), as has also Czechoslovakia, October 15th, 1952 (A/2224/Rev. 1): see also discussions in First Committee of General Assembly at 582–584 Meetings, March 23rd to 26th, 1952. The basis of the Act may well be that of reprisals for subversive activities organized by the Communist states.

[1] Van Dyke, 'The Responsibility of States for International Propaganda', *A.J.*, Vol. 34 (1940), p. 58 at p. 73; see also Stowell, *op. cit.*, p. 378; Whitton, 'Efforts to Curb Dangerous Propaganda', *A.J.*, Vol. 41 (1947), p. 900; Preuss, 'International Responsibility for Hostile Propaganda', *A.J.*, Vol. 28 (1934), p. 649 *et seq.*; Lauterpacht, 'Revolutionary Propaganda by Governments', *Trans. Grotius Soc.*, Vol. 13 (1927), p. 143 at pp. 145–6; Fenwick, 'Intervention by way of Propaganda', *A.J.*, Vol. 35 (1941), p. 626. And see the protest by U.S. Secretary of State Colby on August 10th, 1920, to the U.S.S.R., particularly on the use of the diplomatic corps as a medium of revolutionary propaganda, cited Stowell, *op. cit.*, p. 580. See, for a recent example, the view of the British government in protesting to Greece on the transmission of broadcasts from Athens Radio likely to inspire sedition and rebellion in Cyprus through the organization EOKA; *Manchester Guardian*, January 31st, 1956.

[2] *Legal Controls of International Conflict*, p. 319.

[3] J. B. Whitton, 'Cold War Propaganda', *A.J.*, Vol. 45 (1951), p. 152; for the text of the agreement, see *A.J.*, Vol. 28 (1934), Supp., p. 3. The agreement is mainly declaratory of existing law, although s. 3 of the note of Mr. Litvinoff would seem to go beyond the duties normally required.

writer explains that 'the action of the American government i solidly grounded on considerations of self-defence as fundamenta as those invoked by Marshall in the early case of *Church* v *Hubbart*'.[1] The whole problem is beset with uncertainty, in par due to its novelty, in part due to the lack of any clear notion o what is meant by propaganda. Can the truth ever be propaganda It may well be that even true statements, broadcast to the peopl of a friendly state with the primary object of promoting civi unrest rather than disseminating impartial information, migh constitute propaganda.[2]

Equally controversial is the extent of the state's responsibilit in failing to suppress activities of private persons or agencie within its territory which are designed or tend to impair th political independence of a friendly state. Where those activitie take the form of hostile, armed expeditions the position is toler ably clear; it is correctly stated by Lauterpacht thus:

> International law imposes upon the state the duty of restrainin persons resident within its territory from engaging in such revolu tionary activities against friendly states as amount to organized acts o force in the form of hostile expeditions against the territory of thos states.[3]

This is well supported by the municipal law of the United State and Great Britain. The U.S. Criminal Code of 1909, s. 13, make it a criminal offence to prepare a military expedition against foreign, friendly state within the territory or jurisdiction of th United States.[4] The British Foreign Enlistment Act of 1870, s. 2 is to the like effect,[5] and the same view was taken by the Institut

[1] J. B. Whitton, 'Cold War Propaganda', p. 153. See *post*, p. 68, wit reference to the case of *Church* v. *Hubbart*.

[2] But see General Assembly Resolution 127 (II) inviting Governments o Member States to consider measures of combating 'the diffusion of *false* *distorted* reports likely to injure the friendly relations between States'; Repe tory, Vol. I, p. 23. See also Resolution 277 (III), ibid., p. 24, on Freedom o Information.

[3] 'Revolutionary Activities by Private Persons against Foreign States *A.J.*, Vol. 22 (1928), p. 126 *et passim*, for review of authorities; for the Unite States practice see Curtis, *op. cit.*, p. 1 *et passim*; Hackworth, *Dig.*, Vol. VI p. 396 *et seq.*

[4] 35 Stat. 1088, 1090; convenient text in Hackworth, *op. cit.*, p. 397 and se decisions there cited. See also *U.S.* v. *Arjona* (1887), 120 U.S. 479. See als the U.S. Neutrality Act of 1917; convenient text in *A.J.*, Vol. 11 (1917 Supp., p. 186.

[5] 33 and 34 Vict. c. 90. On the interpretation of s. 2 see R. v. *Sandova* 3 T.L.R. 411, and 436 (a re-trial), and R. v. *Jameson*, 12 T.L.R. 551.

of International Law in their Resolution on the 'Rights and Duties of Foreign Powers as regards the Established and Recognized Governments in cases of Insurrection', adopted in 1900.[1] Yet, even here, it is the failure to exercise due diligence to suppress the preparation which founds the responsibility of the territorial state;[2] the duty is not absolute, but only strict, and the state has committed no breach where due diligence has been exercised but has still failed to suppress the hostile expedition.

The real difficulty lies in the duty of the territorial state to suppress activities by private persons which do not involve hostility by the use of arms. The Anglo-American view would tend to deny any such duty where the activities do not involve armed hostility, or terrorist activities, or attempts to commit common crimes against life or property.[3] In other words, no duty of suppression would exist in relation to subversive activities and private propaganda; the view in Oppenheim is that 'there is no duty to suppress revolutionary propaganda on the part of private persons directed against a foreign government'.[4] Again, Van Dyke states:

> It may therefore be said that the principle that states must use due diligence to prevent the use of their territory as a base for the spreading of propaganda hostile to foreign governments has never, in general practice, been accepted as law.[5]

On the other hand continental jurists have tended to widen the duty of restraint to include all cases where there exists a threat to

[1] Annuaire, 18 (1900), p. 227, Art. II, s. 3.

[2] See the case between Nicaragua and Honduras on the one hand, and Guatamala and Salvador on the other, before the Central American Court of Justice, December, 1908. Judgment quoted in *A.J.*, Vol. 3 (1909), pp. 434–6. For the U.S. practice see Hackworth, *Dig.*, Vol. II, p. 334 *et seq.*

[3] Oppenheim, Vol. I, 8th ed., pp. 292–3; Hackworth, *Dig.*, Vol. II, pp. 334–5. The special problem of terrorist activities was studied by a Committee of Experts of the League, and they recommended the conclusion of a Convention to deal with the problem; see League of Nations, Doc. A.7.1936 V. For the eventual Convention on Terrorism, signed at Geneva on November 16th, 1937, but never adopted, see *BYBIL*, Vol. 19 (1938), pp. 214–17. See the Resolution of the Council of the League, December 10th, 1934 . . . 'that it is the duty of every state neither to encourage or tolerate on its territory any terrorist activity with a political purpose; that every state must do all in its power to prevent and repress acts of this nature and must for this purpose lend its assistance to Governments which request it'; Off. Journal, July–December, 1934, p. 1759.

[4] *Op. cit.*, Vol. I, p. 260.

[5] *Op. cit.*, p. 68.

the security of a foreign power, that is all cases where, if the acts were committed by nationals against the state, they would render the actors liable to an indictment for treason.[1] As we have seen, the formulation of Art. 2(5) of the Draft Code of Offences Against the Peace and Security of Mankind is much nearer the continental view, including, as it does, a duty to suppress all organized activities 'calculated to foment civil strife in another State'.

The degree of uncertainty as to the extent of a state's duties in relation to conducting, encouraging, or failing to suppress activities detrimental to another state's political independence must necessarily be reflected in the claim of a right of self-defence against such activities by the injured state. For, since a breach of duty is the essential pre-requisite of the injured state's right to exercise self-defence against another state, so long as those duties remain ill-defined the position of self-defence against subversive activities or 'indirect' intervention must remain uncertain.

Under Treaty. There is, of course, no bar to a state undertaking by treaty to enlarge the scope of its duties towards other states. This may be done vis-à-vis one particular state, as with the Roosevelt–Litvinoff agreement of 1933,[2] or vis-à-vis several states parties to a general or multilateral convention. The International Convention concerning the Use of Broadcasting in the Cause of Peace,[3] signed at Geneva on September 23rd, 1936, ratified by more than twenty states and coming into force on April 2nd, 1938, obliged the parties *inter se* to refrain from broadcasting within their respective territories matter of 'such a character as to incite the population of any territory to acts incompatible with the internal order or the security of a territory of a High Contracting Party' (Art. 1); and to ensure that transmissions 'shall not constitute an incitement either to war against another High Contracting Party or to acts likely to lead thereto' (Art. 2).

[1] Calvo, *Le Droit International*, 5th ed. (1896), III, para. 1298; Rivier, *Principes du Droit des Gens* (1896), I, p. 226; Pradier-Fodéré, *Traité du Droit International*, Vol. I, paras. 238, 260; Fauchille, *Traité* (1922), Vol. I, Part I, No. 255; Redslob, *Histoire des Grands Principes du Droit des Gens* (1923), p. 511.

[2] *Ante*, p. 47.

[3] For text see *A.J.*, Vol. 32 (1938), Supp., p. 113. This convention was ratified by G.B., France, the Dominions, but not by either the U.S.S.R. or the U.S.A.

THE EXERCISE OF THE RIGHT OF SELF-DEFENCE AGAINST STATES IN PROTECTION OF THE RIGHT OF POLITICAL INDEPENDENCE

The exercise of a right of self-defence against another state in the defence of a right of political independence is, as we have already stated, dependent on a prior breach of the duty of non-intervention by that state.[1] Yet neither the duty of non-intervention, nor the right of political independence are absolute in character; the relativity of the right is apparent when it is shown that there are 'justifiable' grounds for intervention. The formulation of the right of independence in the Draft Declaration on the Rights and Duties of States is subject to the proviso that, in providing for its own well-being, a state 'shall not impair or violate the legitimate rights of other states'.[2] The comment of the United Kingdom on Art. 4 of the Draft indicated that there might be exceptions to the right, and 'instances of a state acting with the utmost barbarity and inhumanity to its own nationals, or making preparations which appear to foreshadow a policy of aggression, or again of pursuing a course which leads to the economic strangulation of another state occur to the mind in this connection'.[3] The idea is not novel; it bears analogy with the doctrine of abuse of rights and, as Stowell has said:

> . . . there is no absolute or perfect right, but all rights are to be asserted with due regard to the preservation of the independence, security, and property of neighbouring states.[4]

Perhaps the most important limitation on the right of political independence today is the right of intervention assumed by the Security Council in the general interest of the international community as a whole. Whereas the right of political independence is normally assured to states by Art. 2(7) of the Charter:

> Nothing contained in the present Charter shall authorize the United Nations to intervene in matters which are essentially within the

---

[1] The same idea is expressed by Hyde, *International Law*, Vol. I, p. 247, when he states that 'the absence of internationally illegal conduct removes the possibility of lawful intervention'; see also Kelsen, *Principles of International Law*, p. 64, 'dictatorial interference . . . is permitted only as a reaction against a violation . . . of rights'.

[2] *Ante*, p. 43.

[3] A/CN.4/2, at p. 59.

[4] *Intervention in International Law*, p. 455; see also Brierly, 'Règles du Droit de la Paix', *R.C.*, 1936 (IV), p. 126, criticizing the notion of absolute, inherent rights advocated by Pillet, *Droits Fondamentaux des Etats*, p. 3, and Hall, *International Law*, 8th ed., p. 65.

domestic jurisdiction of any state or shall require the Members to submit such matters to settlement under the present Charter; . . .

this is immediately followed by the proviso

. . . but this principle shall not prejudice the application of enforcement measures under Chapter VII.

This means, therefore, that the right of political independence is conditional upon its not constituting a 'threat to the peace, breach of the peace, or act of aggression' within the terms of Art. 39. It has already been determined that the conduct of a state's external relations with another state constituted a breach of the peace when the North Korean authorities invaded the Republic of South Korea in June, 1950.[1] It has also been mooted whether the internal aspect of independence can come within the terms of Art. 39. A sub-committee of the Security Council on April 29th, 1946, rejected a Polish proposal to apply Art. 41 to Spain on the ground that the internal régime in Franco Spain did not come within those terms;[2] at the same time they acknowledged that the internal régime of a state might constitute a threat to international peace. What is clear is that, should the United Nations intervene, having properly characterized the political independence of a state as involving a 'threat to the peace, breach of the peace, or act of aggression', the intervention must be deemed to be lawful and the state concerned cannot claim the right of self-defence against such intervention.

The other cardinal limitation on a state's right of political independence is the right of self-defence vested in other states. Traditionally acknowledged as but one of the heads of 'justifiable' intervention, today it stands as an acknowledged and undoubted

[1] S.C. Off. Rec., 5th Year, No. 15, at p. 18; Resolution of June 25th adopted 473rd Meeting. See *post*, p. 194.

[2] Off. Rec. S.C., 1st Year, Special Supp. (Doc. S/75); see also Off. Rec., 1st Year, No. 31, p. 602 *et seq*. For the actual appointment and terms of reference of the sub-committee see First Series, No. 2, 38th Meeting, p. 239; and for the resolution of the General Assembly leading up to the appointment, see Off. Rec. G.A., 1st Year, 59th Meeting (Doc. A/64), p. 39. A similar proposal that the situation in Indonesia constituted a threat to the peace was made by Australia, letter of July 30th, 1947 (Doc. S/449), to the Secretary-General. It is not clear that the Security Council acted under Art. 39, see Resolution of August 26th, 1947 (Doc. S/521), and in any event the Security Council ruled out the Netherlands contention that this was a matter within her own domestic jurisdiction. Off. Rec. S.C., 2nd Year, No. 67, p. 1622 *et seq*.

head whilst its companions rest in a condition of uncertainty.[1] It is distinct from the broader concept of self-preservation;[2] it is also distinct from the so-called Doctrine of Contagion,[3] a doctrine permitting intervention where the internal situation of a neighbouring state promotes the fear in another state that the unrest will spread to its own people. The limitation of self-defence is, in so far as the exercise of the right is directed against the state claiming political independence, subject to the same conditions which govern every exercise of the right of self-defence; the danger must be immediate, no alternative means of protection available, and the measures taken proportionate to the danger which results from the delinquent state's breach of duty. Against the lawful exercise of a right of self-defence there can be no right of self-defence in the state claiming political independence.

Assuming, however, that the infringement of a state's political independence is unlawful, that is to say does not fall within any of the heads of 'justifiable' intervention and is in breach of an established duty, then the state clearly has the right of self-defence in the protection of its independence. The measures of self-defence which may be permissible are, of course, subject to the conditions governing the right of self-defence generally, and of particular relevance here is the condition of proportionality; there must be a proportionate relationship between the delict and the action in self-defence. This would mean, therefore, that where

[1] For the traditional heads of 'justifiable' intervention see Winfield, *op. cit.*, p. 149; Hall, *International Law*, 8th ed., p. 339; Fauchille, *Droit International Public*, Vol. I, Part I, Nos. 300 *et seq.*; Stowell, *op. cit.*, ch. II. The traditional heads must now be read subject to the Charter and the strictures of the I.C.J. in the *Corfu Channel Case* (Merits), 1949, I.C.J. Reports, p. 35. Apart from self-defence and possibly humanitarian intervention, state intervention would still be justified where in pursuance of a treaty right; e.g. Art. 1, Treaty between U.S.A. and Japan, September 8th, 1951 (text *A.J.*, Vol. 46 (1952), Supp., p. 91). Also where consent of lawful government is given *ad hoc*, as with the Greek government's consent to the intervention of British troops in Greece in 1946 (see *ante*, p. 37 fn.). The difficulty here is that the intervening state may recognize as the lawful government an authority which it may itself have put in power by force: see the Soviet Union's recognition of the Kardar government and the deposition of Nagy's government during the intervention in Hungary in October–November, 1956.

[2] *Ante*, p. 10.

[3] This doctrine was rejected by Hall, *op. cit.*, pp. 299–300; Stowell, *op. cit.*, p. 385; and Westlake, *International Law*, Part I, Peace, pp. 318–19, who regards the circular from Troppau as an assertion of a 'right of self-preservation against the contagion of revolution' but supports Canning's plea for proof of actual danger.

the delict involves the use or threat of force against a state's political independence, the use or threat of a proportionate amount of force will be permissible in self-defence. Naturally the presumption of legality is stronger when the defending state confines its use of force or threat of force to its own territory, but even beyond its own territory and within the territory of another state this may well be permissible if no other means of protection against an imminent danger are available. It cannot be supposed that the inviolability of territory is so sacrosanct as to mean that a state may harbour within its territory the most blatant preparation for an assault upon another state's independence with impunity; the inviolability of territory is subject to the use of that territory in a manner which does not involve a threat to the rights of other states.

Where, on the other hand, the delinquent state's conduct does not involve the use or threat of force it will be rarely that the requirement of proportionality permits the use or threat of force in self-defence. The defending state will have to have recourse to other means of protection. For example, where the delict involves the broadcasting of propaganda the state may have recourse to 'jamming', which may be illegal *prima facie* but justifiable as self-defence. Thus the decision of the British government to 'jam' the broadcasts from Athens Radio in January, 1956,[1] was justifiable as a measure of self-defence against delictual conduct by Greece, and this would be so whether or not jamming is *per se* illegal.[2] Similarly, where the state is using its embassies as centres for espionage in the receiving state's territory, or using them as centres for the organization of subversive activities, the receiving state would be justified in closing those embassies. Again, where the state conducts subversive activities in another state through the medium of its nationals within the latter state's territory, self-defence would justify the large-scale deportation of those nationals. Fitzmaurice, the U.K. delegate to the Sixth Committee

[1] See *Manchester Guardian*, January 31st, 1956.

[2] It is doubtful whether it is illegal; the Convention of 1936 (*ante*, p. 50) made no reference to this practice, and the condemnations of the practice by the U.N. Sub-Commission on Freedom of Information, Montevideo, May, 1950 (Dept. State Bull., Vol. XXII, No. 571, p. 954), by the Economic and Social Council (U.N. Doc. E/1827, pp. 1–2), and by the General Assembly Resolution, December 14th, 1950 (U.N. Doc. A/1746) have no normative effect.

of the General Assembly criticized the U.S.S.R. proposal defining aggression for its failure to take account of 'indirect aggression involved in an attempt to attack the political integrity of a country by subversive action against its government' [1] and, on another occasion, stated:

> If a State were to send several million unarmed men into a small neighbouring State, it would give the small State a reason for exercising its right of self-defence, for several millions of even unarmed men were capable of taking over the nerve centres of a State and thus weakening it.[2]

It seems that here Fitzmaurice had in mind the use of force in self-defence. Without excluding that possibility we would contend that, on the same principle, a state could consider far lesser numbers of aliens a threat to its political independence once evidence of their subversive intention was obtained, and therefore resort to mass deportation. It was said by the Umpire in the *Maal Case*:

> There is no question in the mind of the Umpire that the Government of Venezuela in a proper and lawful manner may exclude, or if need be, expel persons dangerous to the welfare of the country . . . since it exercises [the right of expulsion] rightfully only in a proper defence of the country from some danger anticipated or actual;[3]

and again, this would be so even if such action were *prima facie* contrary to a treaty between the two countries providing for freedom to travel in or reside in the territory of each for their nationals. There seems no logical reason why such action of an executive character, not involving the threat or use of force in the accepted sense, should not be characterized as self-defence and thus afford a legal justification for action which would otherwise be illegal.

THE EXERCISE OF THE RIGHT OF SELF-DEFENCE AGAINST INDIVIDUALS

The situation may arise in which the threat to a state's political independence originates in the conduct of individuals or groups

[1] Off. Rec. G.A., Sixth Session, Sixth Committee, 281st Meeting, para. 9.

[2] Ibid., 292nd Meeting, para. 40.

[3] Neth.-Ven. M.C.C. (1903), Ven. Arb., 1903, p. 914; see also the *Paquet Case*, Ven. Arb., 1903, p. 265 at p. 267; the *Ben Tillet Case* (1898), G.B./Belgium, Brit. & For. State Papers, Vol. 92, p. 78 at p. 105. These cases are all cited by Cheng, *General Principles of Law*, pp. 32–3.

of individuals for which no state bears international responsibility. The most obvious example is the case in which a state uses due diligence, and therefore fulfils the duty imposed on it by international law, but is still unable to prevent individuals from organizing a hostile expedition or conducting other activities involving an immediate danger to another state's political independence. In these circumstances the state on whose territory these preparations or activities occur is not in breach of any duty and, therefore, no action in self-defence can be directed against it by the state threatened by these preparations or activities. This is not to say that the threatened state is powerless to do anything to protect itself; it may take action in self-defence but such action must be directed solely at the individuals or groups responsible for the threat to or violation of its rights.

> The action which it is necessary to take against an expedition still within the jurisdiction of the state of its origin must not be considered as directed against the state so invaded.[1]

It is apparent here that such action as is necessarily taken against the state so invaded is taken by virtue of a right of necessity, and not of self-defence, for there is here no breach of a duty by the state invaded to justify action against it in self-defence. As against the individuals the action may be self-defence in so far as the individuals are in breach of the defending state's own law, but necessity in so far as they are not, for, in the main, those individuals will not, under the dualist doctrine, be regarded as subject to duties imposed by international law. This is a position which ignores the very real potentialities for endangering a state's security which individuals possess, and it will only be rationalized when international law imposes on individuals duties relating to the protection of a state's essential rights of the same kind as those imposed on states.

The current trend is towards a recognition of the need to impose responsibility on individuals for the same acts which, if undertaken by a state, involve state responsibility. To a limited extent the Nuremberg Judgment[2] illustrates this trend, but that precedent is not really applicable to the present problem for there the individuals on whom responsibility was imposed were acting

[1] Curtis, 'The Law of Hostile Military Expeditions as Applied by the United States', *A.J.*, Vol. 8 (1914), p. 236.

[2] October 1st, 1946; text in *A.J.*, Vol. 41 (1947), p. 172.

as authorities of the state; the problem with which we are now concerned is that of the international responsibility of individuals who do not act as state officials and whose acts are not authorized by the state. The more recent Draft Code of Offences Against the Peace and Security of Mankind[1] goes further and envisages, in limited circumstances, the possibility of individual responsibility under international law even where the individuals are not acting for or upon the authorization of a state. For example, Art. 2(1) makes 'any act of aggression' a crime under international law 'for which the responsible individuals shall be punishable' (Art. 1). Art. 2(4) provides that

> The incursion into the territory of a State from the territory of another State by armed bands acting for a political purpose

is also a crime.[2] Moreover individual responsibility can arise under Art. 2(12) which makes conspiracy in, or incitement to commit, or complicity in any of the offences under Art. 2 criminal under international law. However, apart from Art. 2(4), it is doubtful whether individual responsibility will be imposed even under the Draft Code except where there is a crime for which a state is also responsible. The phrase 'any act of aggression' in Art. 2(1) is not defined, but will presumably be limited by the concept of aggression used at Nuremberg, and will cover only armed, military aggression undertaken by a state.[3] It cannot be over-emphasized that the Draft Code at the moment represents only the views of the International Law Commission upon the desirable and future development of the law; it goes far beyond the precedent of Nuremberg and at the present time the position is that which obtains under traditional international law.[4] Under

[1] Adopted Third Session of the International Law Commission, May 16th to July 27th, 1951; see Report on Third Session, A/1858. See generally Fenwick, 'Draft Code of Offences Against the Peace and Security of Mankind', *A.J.*, Vol. 46 (1952), pp. 98–100; Potter, ibid., p. 98.

[2] Pompe, *op. cit.*, p. 349, suggests that this crime 'can only become dangerous for the offended State, and for peace and security, when the activity of these bands is supported or tolerated, notwithstanding protests, by the authorities of a State'; this can scarcely be true in all cases.

[3] Pompe, *op. cit.*, p. 347, criticizes the lack of definition in saying, 'But to suggest that acts of aggression can be committed without any element of armed force is to allow any tribunal applying this Code to punish persons for all sorts of unfriendly acts which are qualified as economic or ideological aggression.'

[4] Pompe, ibid., p. 343; Stone, *Legal Controls of International Conflict*, p. 23, describes it as part of a 'programmschriften for an unborn world'.

that law, as we have suggested, there is no responsibility on individuals as such for these activities calculated to overthrow the political independence of a state, whether those activities take the form of armed, hostile expeditions or of subversive action and propaganda. In that case there is no right of self-defence against the individuals but only a right of necessity in which other states must acquiesce. This acquiescence will preclude them from extending diplomatic protection to the individuals concerned.[1]

The *locus classicus* of the right of self-defence, the *Caroline* case,[2] affords an excellent example of the position under traditional international law which arises when a hostile expedition is organized on the territory of a state against which no breach of duty is alleged. In 1837 certain factions aiming at insurrection against the British rule in Canada had been established both inside Canadian territory and within U.S. territory adjacent to the Canadian border. The U.S. Secretary of State wrote to the governors of those states adjoining Canadian territory requesting their 'prompt interference to arrest the parties concerned, if any preparations are made of a hostile nature against a foreign power in amity with the U.S.'[3] Preparations of precisely this nature had become evident at Buffalo, in U.S. territory, on December 13th, 1837, involving the looting of the state arsenal. The U.S. Marshal, arriving at Buffalo on December 28th, found that a force which had within a matter of days grown from 200 to 1,000 men, well-armed, was encamped on Navy Island in Upper Canada. This force had been supplied with reinforcements of men and materials by the steamer *Caroline*. On December 29th a British force from Canada entered U.S. territory, seized the steamer *Caroline* then at Schlosser in the State of New York, set her on fire and sent her to destruction down the Niagara Falls. During the skirmish two U.S. citizens were killed. In a letter from Mr. Fox, the British Minister at Washington, dated February 6th, 1838, the basis of the British position was stated in these terms:

> The piratical character of the steam boat Caroline and the necessity of self-defence and self-preservation, under which Her Majesty's sub-

[1] Schwarzenberger, 'The Fundamental Principles of International Law', *R.C.*, 1955 (1), p. 332.

[2] See Moore, *Dig.*, Vol. VII, p. 919 *et seq.*; Vol. 2, p. 409. R. Y. Jennings, 'The Caroline and McLeod Cases', *A.J.*, Vol. 32 (1938), p. 82; Cheng, *op. cit.*, pp. 84–7.

[3] Moore, *Dig.*, Vol. II, p. 409.

jects acted in destroying that vessel, would seem to be sufficiently established.[1]

However, the controversy was only really taken up after the arrest by the United States authorities of one Alexander McLeod in 1840 on a charge of murder and arson in connection with the events of December 29th, 1837. Indeed this very fact indicates that in 1837 the U.S. was not prepared to contest the strength of the British position. McLeod was a British subject who had been a member of the expedition which crossed into United States territory to effect the destruction of the *Caroline*. The British protest to this arrest rested on the justification of the act of state in which McLeod had participated and, since the issue of piracy was dropped, that of self-defence became vital. Mr. Webster, the U.S. Secretary of State, in a note to Lord Ashburton on July 27th, 1842, stated what in the opinion of the United States were the essential requirements of action in self-defence. In what is now regarded as the *locus classicus* of self-defence, he called upon Great Britain to show a

necessity of self-defence, instant, overwhelming, leaving no choice of means, and no moment for deliberation

and went on to state that:

It will be for it to show, also, that the local authorities of Canada, even supposing the necessity of the moment authorized them to enter the territory of the U.S. at all, did nothing unreasonable or excessive, since the act, justified by the necessity of self-defence, must be limited by that necessity and kept clearly within it.[2]

Lord Ashburton replied, justifying the action in these terms and adding an apology: this was accepted and there the matter ended.[3]

Whatever the merits of the controversy it is clear that at no stage did Great Britain rest her case on the allegation of a prior breach of duty by the United States.[4] Strictly speaking, therefore, vis-à-vis the United States the action taken by Great Britain was

[1] H. EX. Docs. 302 and 73, 25th Congr., Second Session.

[2] Parl. Papers (1843), Vol. LXI; Brit. and For. State Papers, Vol. XXX, p. 193.

[3] Lord Ashburton to Mr. Webster, July 28th, 1842; Parl. Papers (1843), Vol. LXI.

[4] Curtis, *A.J.*, Vol. 8 (1914), p. 242, suggests that it was in part the failure of the U.S. authorities which justified the invasion by British forces; whether this was so or not, and possibly a case for this could be made out, the official British position did not rest on this assumption.

taken by virtue of its right of necessity, though the principles governing the actual exercise of the right, as stated by Webster, were applicable both to necessity and self-defence. Certainly these principles were approved by the International Military Tribunal at Nuremberg when it stated:

> It must be remembered that preventive action in foreign territory is justified only in case of an 'instant and overwhelming necessity for self-defence, leaving no choice of means and no moment for deliberation' (The Caroline Case).[1]

The lawfulness of action which is kept within the limits defined in the statement of Mr. Webster means that the territorial state which suffers an incidental transgression of its frontiers must acquiesce in such action. We have previously stated that the right of territorial integrity is never absolute, and in this particular instance its relativity is illustrated by the fact that it gives precedence to the rights of the state which acts in self-defence. The duty of acquiescence is, therefore, not unreasonably imposed,[2] for the condition on which one state may claim respect for its own integrity is that it should not itself contain a threat to the security of another state. As Lauterpacht has said,

> It is equally clear that a state is entitled to expect that the exclusiveness of other states' jurisdictions over their territory will not result, even indirectly, in a serious menace to its existence and safety. For it is only and alone the respect for the sovereignty of the neighbouring state that induces the menaced state to refrain from invading the territory of its neighbour in order to put an end to an impending danger.[3]

It is as a result of the failure of international law to contain duties relating to the conduct of individuals which threatens the security and political independence of states that states impose penalties under their own municipal law as a protection against such conduct and thereby assume a somewhat extensive juris-

[1] *A.J.*, Vol. 41 (1947), p. 205.

[2] Curtis, *op. cit.*, p. 6; Hyde, *International Law*, Vol. I, p. 248; Stowell, *op. cit.*, p. 50; Vattel, Bk. III, ch. 2, paras. 35, 36. In fact this attitude, that the action is pacific vis-à-vis the invaded state has often been taken. See the attitude which the United States assumed in relation to her invasions of Florida in 1814 and 1817; as Secretary of State Adams explained to Mr. Ewing, U.S. Minister to Spain, the invasions were 'not in a spirit of hostility to Spain, but as a necessary measure of self-defence'. Letter of November 28th, 1818, cited in Moore, *Dig.*, Vol. II, p. 406.

[3] 'Revolutionary Activities by Private Persons against Foreign States', *A.J.*, Vol. 22 (1928), p. 106.

diction which can be justified by reference to the right of self-defence. Where the state acts in self-defence against a threat to its security or independence, which is caused neither by another state nor in circumstances which constitute a breach of an international obligation by that other state, the state so acting must fall back on the provisions of its own law or constitution to authorize whatever measures of protection it deems necessary. The position has been put by Lauterpacht in these terms:

> . . . as against individuals, the right to protection cannot be deduced from the rights inherent in the international personality of states, but only from the principle, if there be such a one, that the legal system embodied in the constitution of a particular state is part of the international legal order, and, accordingly, an interest which states are under a duty actively to defend against all attacks.[1]

The legal order of a particular state cannot, of itself, justify measures of protection except in so far as these are sanctioned by the international legal order, for the question of jurisdiction is one which by its very nature falls within the province of international law. That apart, the individuals against whom the state acts must, then, be considered to be in breach of a duty imposed on them by the law of the particular state whose existence is threatened by their action. They cannot be held liable for a breach of international law;[2] the function of international law is merely to sanction those claims to jurisdiction which are consistent with the general practice of states.

Whenever the state purports to qualify the acts of its nationals within or without its territory, or of aliens within its territory, the general principles of personal and territorial jurisdiction will afford sufficient justification. The difficulty really arises where the

[1] Ibid., p. 106.

[2] A possible view is to regard these acts as 'offences against the law of nations', defined by one writer as 'acts committed with intent to violate a fundamental interest protected by international law, or with knowledge that the act will probably violate such an interest, and which may not be adequately punished by the exercise of its normal jurisdiction by any state'—Quincy Wright, 'Proposals for an International Criminal Court', *A.J.*, Vol. 46 (1952), p. 71. Yet, as this writer admits, the basis for this must be that international law recognizes a duty on states to include those acts in their national criminal codes. It is precisely the existence of such a duty which we deny, and, indeed, it is because the state's duty does not extend to acts falling short of armed expeditions by individuals or groups of individuals, that the endangered state must assume its own measures of protection.

acts qualified are those of foreigners, committed outside the territorial jurisdiction.

In practice, where these acts are prejudicial to the security and independence of the state, this jurisdiction over foreigners for crimes committed abroad is generally assumed. Its basis is, of course, neither territorial nor personal, but rather the nature of the interests threatened or injured by the acts of the foreigner and the necessity of self-defence of those interests. The departure from the normal principles of personal or territorial jurisdiction can also be justified by the principle of 'real protection' which antedates the foundation of the national state and the formulation of the modern territorial theory of penal competence.[1] A further justification for this jurisdiction may be found in looking to the *lex situs* of the effect rather than of the cause, a view which would meet the normal principle of territorial jurisdiction;[2] but in all those cases where the conduct of individuals threatens the security and political independence of the state there is good reason for recognizing the right of self-defence as sufficient justification. Moreover, as the Permanent Court of Justice has itself stated:

> the territoriality of criminal law is . . . not an absolute principle of international law and by no means coincides with territorial sovereignty.[3]

There are many examples of this type of protective jurisdiction.[4] The French Code of Criminal Procedure of 1808, Art. 7, provides:

> Tout étranger qui, hors du territoire de la France, se sera rendu coupable, soit comme auteur, soit comme complice, d'un crime attentatoire à la surêté de l'Etat, ou de contrafaçon du sceau de l'Etat . . . pourra être poursuivi et jugé d'après les dispositions des lois françaises, s'il est arrêté en France ou si le gouvernement obtient son extradition.[5]

---

[1] Pella, 'Towards an International Criminal Court', *A.J.*, Vol. 44 (1950), p. 46.

[2] See Lauterpacht, *C.L.J.*, Vol. 9 (1947), p. 344, and Beckett, *BYBIL*, Vol. 6 (1925), pp. 44–60.

[3] *Lotus Case*, 1927, P.C.I.J., Series A, No. 10, p. 20.

[4] For a collection of examples see the Harvard Draft Convention on Jurisdiction with respect to Crime, *A.J.*, Supp. (29), 1935, p. 546 *et seq.* Also, a more recent collection, the U.N. Legislative Series, 1951, Laws and Regulations, Vol. II.

[5] Receuil Sirey, 1955, Code d'Instruction Criminelle, Art. 7.

The Chinese Criminal Code of 1935, Art. 5, which speaks of 'offences against the internal or external security of the State' is typical of a number of general formulations.[1] Indeed the need for this extended jurisdiction was acknowledged by the Institute of International Law in 1883 in cases 'd'une necessité toute à fait urgente', thereby indicating the essential connection which this question of jurisdiction has with the right of self-defence.[2] In the *Bayot Case*, on February 22nd, 1923, the Cour de Cassation said:

> Attendu que, si le droit de punir qui émane du droit de souveraineté, ne s'étend pas, en principe, au délà des limites du territoire, il n'est autrement au cas prévu par l'art. 7.C. instr. crim. dont la disposition, fondée sur le droit de légitime défense, attribue compétence à la jurisdiction française pour connaître des crimes attentatoires à la surêté de l'Etat commis hors du territoire de la France par un étranger dont l'arrestation a en lieu en France.[3]

The Harvard Draft Convention on Jurisdiction provides in Art. 7:

> A state has jurisdiction with respect to any crime committed outside its territory by an alien against the security, territorial integrity, or political independence of that state, provided that the act or omission which constitutes the crime was not committed in exercise of a liberty guaranteed the alien by the law of the place where it was committed.[4]

The statement purports to be one which reflects the actual practice of States in the question of jurisdiction. The proviso seems necessary to exclude from the jurisdiction those offences which are the result of an abnormally sensitive political régime and which are not found in the penal laws of the majority of states. For example, the recent Act for the Protection of Peace, passed on December 25th, 1950, in Bulgaria, is typical of a number of recent Peace Defence Laws passed within the Soviet satellite states and claiming an extensive jurisdiction quite beyond that normally accorded to states under general international law.[5] The effect of the proviso is to deny a state jurisdiction over acts which are legally permissible under the *lex loci commissi*.

[1] U.N. Legislative Series, Vol. I, p. 24.

[2] Annuaire, 1883–5, pp. 132 and 140.

[3] Sirey, 1923, I, 330.

[4] *A.J.*, Supp., Vol. 29 (1935), p. 543.

[5] See Nicoloff, *A.J.*, Vol. 45 (1951), p. 353; also 'Soviet Bloc Peace Defense Laws', *A.J.*, Vol. 46 (1952), p. 537. The texts of the legislation on this subject by the U.S.S.R., Czechoslovakia, and Yugoslavia are given in *A.J.*, Supp., Vol. 46 (1952).

Our conclusion, therefore, is that this extended jurisdiction over aliens committing abroad acts detrimental to a state's independence and security is not only reflected in the actual practice of States, but also based on the principle of self-defence. Much of the opposition to this jurisdiction is based on the view that adequate protection is afforded by the penalties imposed by the *lex loci commissi*; yet, as we have seen, the protection afforded by the majority of legal systems really extends only to the prohibition of the preparation or organization of armed military expeditions. This is clearly inadequate to deal with the very real threat to the security of a State presented by subversive activities of individuals or groups of individuals which are equally prejudicial to the security of the State. Moreover, much of the protection which the municipal systems do afford to foreign states in this connection is conditioned not by a desire to protect that foreign state but by the fear of a reaction against the municipal state. For example, the French Penal Code contains under Art. 79 prohibitions against 'des actes hostiles non approuvés par le gouvernement, exposés la France à une déclaration de guerre . . . (or) . . . exposés des Francais à subir de réprésailles'.[1] Quite clearly the provision has in mind the protection of France and its citizens from undesirable repercussions rather than the protection of the independence of a foreign friendly state from interference.

Admitting, then, the generality of this protective jurisdiction in state practice, it must also be admitted that the U.S.A. and the U.K. still base their own penal competence almost exclusively on the personal or territorial principles.[2] It may remain for political necessity to convert this practice to that more generally adopted by states.

Finally, it will be obvious that these claims to jurisdiction are

[1] Receuil Sirey, 1955, Bk. III, ch. I, p. 9.

[2] See Beckett, 'The exercise of Criminal Jurisdiction over Foreigners', *BYBIL*, Vol. 6 (1925), p. 44, who does not regard as established a rule of international law which goes beyond allowing states the exercise of jurisdiction based upon the territorial and personal principles. This would seem, at least today, to be inconsistent with the practice of states. See U.N. Legislative Series, *op. cit.*, Vol. II. Bourquin criticizes Beckett's view as outmoded and inconsistent with practice and the general consensus of state opinion which Beckett admits is necessary to found a new rule of jurisdiction; 'Crimes et Délits contre la surêté des Etats Etrangers', *R.C.*, 1927 (I), p. 117, at p. 174. And see Lauterpacht, 'Allegiance, Diplomatic Protection and Criminal Jurisdiction over Aliens', *C.L.J.*, Vol. 9 (1947), pp. 330–42.

in the main illusory in those cases where the state claiming jurisdiction has not the presence of the offender within its territory or cannot secure that presence. For this reason Art. 7 of the French Criminal Code contains the proviso 'if he is arrested in France or the Government secures his extradition'.[1] One might assume that the logical corollary of a duty of non-intervention would be a duty to surrender to a State whose independence had been threatened by the acts of individuals those of the individuals who were found within the territory of another friendly state. In fact no such duty exists under general international law, although it was conceded in part between certain signatories of the Terrorist Convention of 1937.[2] On the contrary, it is precisely the 'political offender' who is excluded from the obligation to surrender contained in the normal extradition treaty. The anomaly would seem to be that whereas a state may be under a duty to acquiesce in such reasonable violations of its territory or in extended claims to jurisdiction made by a state acting in self-defence, the duty of non-intervention is passive merely, and does not involve any active assistance in surrendering to a state individuals who commit acts endangering the security of that state. In the light of all these considerations it is submitted that the jurisdiction which a state claims over aliens abroad who have committed acts prejudicial to its security and independence is not unreasonably asserted and is soundly based upon the right of self-defence.

[1] See *ante*, p. 62.

[2] For the Final Draft of this Convention for the International Prevention and Suppression of Terrorism see Hudson, *International Legislation*, VII, p. 862, and see the earlier resolution of the Council of the League following the assassination of the King of Yugoslavia in Marseilles in 1934 maintaining that 'it is the duty of every State neither to encourage nor tolerate on its territory activity with a political purpose; that every State must do all within its power to prevent and repress acts of this nature and must for this purpose lend its assistance to Governments which request it': Off. Journal, July–December, 1934, p. 1759.

CHAPTER IV

DEFENCE OF THE STATE'S SECURITY ON THE HIGH SEAS

In certain circumstances the state cannot await the arrival of a danger to its security within its own territorial jurisdiction, but must take measures to prevent that danger from materializing while still outside its territorial jurisdiction. In this case the state may claim a measure of 'protective jurisdiction' and use force in the exercise of that jurisdiction beyond the limits of state territory.

It is accordingly generally recognized that a state may exercise its authority on the high seas in exceptional circumstances where this is necessary to forestall a real threat to its territorial integrity and general security;[1] there is, however, no agreement on the precise nature of the circumstances which enable this protective jurisdiction to be exercised or on the forms of prevention to which the state may have recourse in the exercise of its right of self-defence. The principle of the freedom of the high seas cannot be of any greater sanctity than that of territorial integrity which, as we have seen, is subject to qualification in the interests of security of a neighbouring state; it cannot, therefore, be contended that the freedom of the high seas is any the less subject to qualification. As Jessup states:

> 'It must be remembered that the great principle of the inviolability of national territory is qualified by the right of self-defence. Why should it be denied that the freedom of the high seas may also be subject to qualification?' [2]

The right to assume this protective jurisdiction and to enforce it by force if necessary, is bound up with the somewhat broader theory of the 'Contiguous Zone' which, as Gidel points out,[3] has

[1] See Oppenheim, *International Law*, Vol. I, 8th ed., p. 497. Stuyt, *General Principles of Law*, p. 136 *et seq.* Brierly, *Law of Nations*, 5th ed., 1955, p. 241; and see the Dissenting Opinion of Judge Moore in *The Lotus Case*, 1927, P.C.I.J., A.10, p. 69: 'No state is authorized to interfere with the navigation of other states on the high seas in time of peace except . . . in extraordinary cases of self-defence.'

[2] *The Law of Territorial Waters and Maritime Jurisdiction* (1927), p. 76.

[3] 'La Mer Territoriale et le Zone Contigue', *R.C.*, 1934 (II), p. 241 *et seq.*

long existed side by side with the cannon-shot rule limiting the extent of territorial waters and of the normal jurisdiction of states to three miles from the shore. The essential difference between these contiguous zones and territorial waters is that, whilst only limited jurisdictional rights are claimed in the former, within territorial waters a state may exercise all the normal jurisdictional rights of full sovereignty. It is generally assumed that these exceptional claims to jurisdiction within the contiguous zone are, within the recognized limits, exercisable as of right, as being based upon a general custom accepted by states.[1] The other view, that they are not in the nature of rights but simply claims to jurisdiction based upon the acquiescence of affected states, was put forward by Dr. Twiss as arbitrator in the case of the *Cagliari*[2] in which he was concerned with the claim to exercise a right of visit and search for revenue purposes beyond the marine league. Masterson,[3] however, points out that this view overlooks the extent to which the practice has found acceptance by states, and that there is ample evidence for regarding these jurisdictional claims as exercisable as of right. A survey of the recent United Nations publication on the Laws and Regulations on the Régime of the High Seas will indicate the strength of Masterson's contentions at the present time.[4]

Our present task is to examine how far these claims to jurisdiction beyond the limits of territorial waters are based upon the concept of self-defence. For this purpose, and for the sake of convenience, we propose to examine these claims under the following heads.

CUSTOMS AND REVENUE ENFORCEMENT

States have tended to claim a certain power of control over the high seas adjacent to territorial waters for the protection of their fiscal and revenue laws and, moreover, have based this claim on the grounds of self-protection and self-defence.[5]

The British Hovering Acts[6] which extended this jurisdiction to

[1] Ibid., p. 244. [2] Moore, *Dig.*, I, pp. 729, 730.

[3] *Jurisdiction in Marginal Seas* (1929), pp. 128, 379. Also Jessup, *op. cit.*, ch. II; and Hackworth, *Dig.*, Vol. II, p. 709.

[4] U.N. Legislative Series, Vol. I (1951), *passim*.

[5] See Jessup's conclusions, *op. cit.*, p. 105.

[6] For a detailed survey of the Acts see Masterson, *op. cit.*, chs. III–IV.

a distance of eight leagues were, according to Lord Stowell in the case of *Le Louis*,[1] based in part upon purposes 'immediately affecting their (the State's)[2] safety and welfare'.[3] Piggott, in summarizing these extensions of jurisdiction, states that 'this form of legislation rests, as has already been hinted, not on the rule of jurisdiction but on the principle of self-defence'.[4] Moore treats the Hovering Act of 1763 and the earlier security zones of James I and Charles II under the general heading of 'Questions of Defensive Power',[5] and Westlake[6] also bases these claims to jurisdiction on grounds of self-defence, finding them difficult to distinguish in principle from the case of the *Virginius*.[7]

The practice of the United States affords similar illustrations of these extended claims to jurisdiction. After an Act of March 2nd, 1799, had authorized the visit and search of vessels bound for the United States within four leagues of the coast, Marshall, C.J., in *Church* v. *Hubbart* said: 'Its (the State's) power to assure itself from injury may certainly be exercised beyond the limits of its territory.'[8] Again, in *Rose* v. *Himmely*, Johnson, J., in his dissenting judgment nevertheless maintained that:

> 'Whatever the great principle of self-defence in its reasonable and necessary exercise will sanction in an individual in a state of nature, nations may lawfully perform upon the ocean.'[9]

The Anti-Smuggling Act of 1935[10] gave the President power to declare a 'customs enforcement' area up to a possible distance of 100 miles from the coast, and Dr. Yntema has referred to this as 'implicitly involving some sort of residual right of self-defence against flagrant violation of revenue laws'.[11]

Whatever the historical justification for treating these cases of extended jurisdiction as pertaining to the general theory of pro-

[1] (1817) 2 Dods. 210. [2] Brackets mine. [3] Ibid., p. 245.

[4] *Nationality*, Part II, p. 45. [5] *Dig.*, Vol. I, p. 722.

[6] *International Law*, 2nd ed. (1910), Vol. I, p. 175. He would, however, admit the justification of seizure only in those cases when the vessel was actually engaged in illicit trade. See now 8th ed., Vol. I, p. 496.

[7] See *post*, p. 72. [8] (1804) 2, Cranch, 187, pp. 234–5.

[9] (1807) 4, Cranch, 241, at p. 287.

[10] For the text of this Act see 'Laws and Regulations on the Régime of the High Seas', U.N. Legislative Series, Vol. I, p. 107; and see Jessup, *A.J.*, Vol. 31 (1937), pp. 101–6.

[11] Hyde, *International Law*, Vol. I, p. 789 fn. Colombos, *op. cit.*, p. 108, doubts the consistency of this power with international law.

tection and the more specific right of self-defence, the present position would appear to indicate that this is an assumed jurisdiction, admittedly going beyond the normal limits of personal and territorial jurisdiction, but in reality based upon customary international law; its basis is found in the general practice of states rather than in the exceptional right of self-defence. Oppenheim refers to 'a customary rule of law . . . which allows littoral states in the interest of their revenue and sanitary laws . . .' [1] to establish this extended jurisdiction. Jessup likewise asserts the normality of the jurisdiction provided it satisfies the criterion of reasonableness.[2] Masterson would base it on a theory of interests and admit the legitimacy of the jurisdiction to protect the state's special interests,[3] and Gidel, whilst accepting the theory of interests which he deems inadvisable to define with any precision, stresses the normality of the jurisdiction in these words:

> Les lois de protection douanière et fiscale aux termes desquelles un Etat s'attribue unilatéralement le droit d'exercer à l'égard des pavillons étrangers certaines mesures d'autorité au-delà de la limite de son territoire maritime doivent être considérées comme jouissant en principe d'une valeur internationale. . . .[4]

This view would seem to be borne out by the Provisional Articles concerning the Régime of the High Seas; Art. 4, dealing with Contiguous Zones, adopted by the International Law Commission in its fifth session states:

> On the high seas adjacent to its territorial sea, the coastal state may exercise the control necessary to prevent and punish the infringement, within its territory or territorial sea, of its customs, immigration, fiscal or sanitary regulations. Such control may not be exercised at a distance beyond twelve miles from the base line from which the width of the territorial sea is measured.[5]

The general acceptance which this view finds today would tend to exclude any necessity for regarding this jurisdiction as being based on the right of self-defence; the legality and normality of the jurisdiction make an appeal to this exceptional right unnecessary in this age.

[1] *Op. cit.*, Vol. I, p. 450.
[2] *Op. cit.*, p. 92.
[3] *Op. cit.*, p. 381.
[4] 'La Mer Territoriale et la Zone Contigue', *R.C.*, 1934 (II), p. 244.
[5] See Off. Rec. General Assembly, Eighth Session, Supp. No. 9, A/2456, ch. III; cited in *A.J.*, Vol. 48 (1954), Supp., pp. 43–4. See especially the comment of the U.K. on this Article, *A.J.*, Vol. 50 (1956), p. 278.

SECURITY

The state's interests in its security as distinct from its interests in the protection of its customs and revenue laws are far more readily brought within the concept of self-defence as we have attempted to define it. Even under this head there appears to be no real agreement on the classification of those interests. For example, Gidel adopts a classification unfamiliar in English and American literature of 'sécurité sanitaire',[1] 'sécurité de navigation', and 'sécurité générale'. At least the first two species are, as we have seen, now protected by jurisdiction assumed as a customary right, without any pretence at the immediacy characteristic of the right of self-defence. The issue of a general security zone in which jurisdiction is exercised in virtue of the right of self-defence is more controversial.

In 1930 at the Hague Codification Conference on Territorial Waters, Great Britain[2] refused to accept the view that a state was justified in establishing a general security zone, contiguous to its territorial waters, but recognized that a state may in exceptional circumstances invoke the right of self-defence in taking measures of protection on the high seas. That this narrower and exceptional right does exist, independently of the question of whether a general security zone is permissible, can scarcely be doubted. Art. 20 of the Harvard Draft Code on Territorial Waters states:

> On the high seas adjacent to the marginal sea, however, a State may take such measures as may be necessary for the enforcement within its territory or territorial waters of its customs, navigation, sanitary, or police laws or regulations, or for its immediate protection.[3]

It is submitted that while this last necessity for 'immediate protection' is properly one of self-defence, the others are, given the element of reasonableness, clearly covered by the customary law of nations as evidenced in state practice. It is, therefore, with the exercise of jurisdiction for the state's immediate protection that

[1] Great Britain established a two league quarantine zone as early as 1835 (6 Geo. IV, c. 78, ss. 8 & 9).

[2] See the British response of December 6th, 1928, to the Questionnaire of the Preparatory Committee for the Codification Conference. Territorial Waters, C.74.M.39, 1929, V, p. 162: quoted in Hyde, *op. cit.*, Vol. I, p. 466. See now the U.K. Comment on Art. 4 of the Provisional Articles on the Régime of the High Seas, cited *A.J.*, Vol. 50 (1956), p. 278.

[3] *A.J.*, Vol. 23 (1929), Supp., p. 245.

we are primarily concerned. It is to be noted that in the Provisional Articles concerning the Régime of the High Seas, the International Law Commission makes no provision for a contiguous zone for security purposes; indeed the Memorandum prepared by the Secretariat,[1] whilst recognizing that the basis for exercising jurisdiction in a contiguous zone is self-protection, suggested that the principle of the *Virginius*[2] was no longer admissible, and called in aid the decision of the International Court of Justice in the *Corfu Channel Case*[3] to support this view. This view has been rightly criticized by Waldock;[4] not only does the *Corfu Channel Case* judgment not warrant such a view, but also the distinction between a state's interests in its customs, immigration and fiscal laws on the one hand, and its interests in its general security on the other is extremely artificial. It can scarcely be contemplated that a state must remain passive whilst a serious menace to its security mounts on the high seas beyond its territorial sea. It is accordingly maintained that it is still permissible for a state to assume a protective jurisdiction, within the limits circumscribing every exercise of the right of self-defence, upon the high seas in order to protect its ships, its aircraft,[5] and its rights of territorial integrity and political independence from an imminent danger or actual attack.

The assertion of jurisdiction may take two forms. It may take the form of the use of force to repel an imminent danger to the state's security and, to a lesser degree, the exercise of a right of visit and search backed by force. Or it may take the form of an assertion of jurisdiction by legislation, purporting to qualify the nature of acts done on the high seas and affecting the security of the state. It will be convenient to treat the two forms separately.

The use of force and the right of visit and search

The case here envisaged is that the littoral state uses force or otherwise asserts a 'protective jurisdiction' in virtue of its right of

[1] U.N. Doc. A/CN.4/32 (1950). [2] *Post*, p. 72.

[3] I.C.J. Reports, 1949, p. 5; and see *ante*, p. 14.

[4] 'The Regulation of the Use of Force by Individual States in International Law', *R.C.*, 1952 (II), at p. 464 *et seq.*

[5] See Art. 6 of the North Atlantic Treaty which treats an attack upon the ships or aircraft of any of the parties as an attack within the meaning of Art. 5; this treaty is expressly based upon the right of self-defence reserved in Art. 51 of this Charter. See *post*, p. 224.

self-defence under international law, the question whether these claims have authorization in the state's municipal law being irrelevant.

The right to use force on the high seas against non-national vessels, or indeed the right to exercise visit and search over those vessels, are normally belligerent rights exercisable only in time of war. Nevertheless, there are exceptional cases, quite apart from treaty concessions,[1] when these rights may be invoked in self-defence by a state at peace.

> The notion that the right of self-defence is a purely belligerent right and cannot be exerted in time of peace is unfounded. It proceeds upon the manifestly erroneous assumption that the rights of a nation upon the high seas cannot be attacked or endangered except in time of war.[2]

It is clear, as the case of the *Marianna Flora*[3] shows, that the right may be exercised against acts of piratical aggression if the circumstances are such as to reasonably warrant the apprehension of real danger by the state. The fact that the ship subsequently proves innocent of piratical character would seem to be irrelevant if the initial suspicion is well-founded.

In the *Virginius*,[4] the classical example of this position, an American vessel owned by and in the service of Cuban insurgents was captured on the high seas off the coast of Cuba by a Spanish warship. She was at that time carrying a large quantity of arms and ammunition, and a large number of passengers who were justifiably believed to be intending to join the insurgent forces in Cuba. After a trial for piracy, part of the crew, including British and American citizens, were executed. Great Britain recognized the validity of the original capture as an exercise of self-defence, contesting only the subsequent detention and execution of her nationals without prosecution on a definite charge and according to the due legal forms.

[1] For example, the Anglo-U.S. Liquor Treaty of 1924; Treaty Series No. 22 (1924), Cmd. 2199. See also Rodick, *The Doctrine of Necessity in International Law*, 1928, p. 38.

[2] Speech of J. C. Carter, U.S. Counsel, Behring Sea Fur Seal Arbitration, 1893; 12, Proceedings, p. 255.

[3] 1826 11 Wheaton, 1, involving the interception of a Portuguese ship on suspicion of piracy by a U.S. vessel.

[4] 1873; Parl. Papers (1874), Vol. LXXXI; Moore, *Dig.*, Vol. II, pp. 895–903. See also the *Mary Lowell* (1879), Moore, *Int. Arb.*, Vol. 3, p. 2772, where, on similar facts, the vessel was held to have 'forfeited the right to the protection of the American flag' and her seizure was justified by self-defence.

Much may be excused in acts done under the expectation of instant damage in self-defence by a Nation as well as an individual. But after the capture of the Virginius and the detention of the crew was effected, no pretence of imminent necessity of self-defence could be alleged.[1]

Arising out of the same case Mr. Cass, the U.S. Secretary of State, in a note to the Peruvian Minister, declared that:

. . . there is no case in which such entry (visit and search upon the high seas in time of peace[2]) is a lawful act. It may be an excusable one under peculiar circumstances of entrance and conduct, which might well induce the aggrieved party to renounce all claims for reparation, as, for instance, if a piratical vessel was known to be cruising in certain latitudes, and a national ship should fall in with a vessel sailing in those regions, and answering the description of the pirate, the visitation of a peaceable merchantman in such a case, with a view to ascertaining the true character, would give no reasonable cause of offence to the nation to which she might belong and whose flag she carried.[3]

The view that there is no right of visit and search based upon a general concept of security, at least in times of peace, has had other adherents;[4] it has naturally followed from the International Law Commission's rejection of a contiguous zone for security purposes that Art. 21 of the Provisional Articles limits the right of visit and search in such a way as to exclude the more general right which we are now discussing.

A further question is that of the extent of the assumed jurisdiction. Does it extend to the punishment of the vessel, or does it end with the prevention of the danger? Rodick concludes that, since the jurisdiction is 'merely protective and not punitive',[5] a vessel arrested as a result of visit and search should be placed at the disposal of the flag state for punishment according to its own municipal law.[6] Yet it seems clear that if the vessel is of a piratical character the capturing state could exercise a punitive jurisdiction under general international law. Moreover, assuming the circumstances were such as to justify a reasonable apprehension of a

[1] Ibid., p. 85. [2] Brackets mine.

[3] Quoted in Rodick, *op. cit.*, p. 37; Moore, *Dig.*, Vol. II, p. 892.

[4] See Fauchille, *Traité de Droit International*, p. 66, who, whilst recognizing a right of police protection, declares the right of visit and search to be non-existent in times of peace with the exception of piracy.

[5] *Op. cit.*, p. 40.

[6] See *The Salvador*, L.R., 3 P.C., 218; and see Art. 4 Provisional Articles (*supra*) which, so far as 'customs, immigration, fiscal or sanitary regulations' are concerned, recognizes the right to 'prevent and *punish*' any breach.

threat to the security of the state, there seems no reason to regard the state as acting at its peril so that if the vessel proves innocent the state should be bound to offer an apology and indemnity.

Any punishment which the capturing state might choose to inflict would be based upon its own municipal law, apart from the exceptional cases of pirates, who, as *hostes humani generis*, come under a universal jurisdiction and are punishable under customary international law. It is noticeable that in the case of the *Virginius*[1] what was denied was not the right to punish, but merely that, since the necessities of self-defence were no longer present, there was no right to punish summarily and without the normal and due processes of the law. It may well be that, if the right of self-defence does involve the right to administer sanctions, the act of prevention and the act of punishment must not be too far separated in time, for otherwise the 'immediacy' of the occasion would be lacking.[2]

Another example of a situation in which a state may invoke this jurisdiction in self-defence is where the imminent or actual action of belligerent vessels constitutes a danger to the security of a peaceful state. The *Kearsage* and *Alabama* incident in 1864[3] affords the classical example of this. During the American Civil War the *Kearsage* lay off the port of Cherbourg, just outside territorial waters, waiting to commence action with the cruiser *Alabama* which was sheltering in that port. The U.S. Government acknowledged the protest of the French Government and ordered the *Kearsage* to refrain from action at a distance close enough to the French shore, albeit on the high seas, to prejudice the safety of the littoral state. Writing of this incident, Moore states:[4]

> We claim also that the sovereign of the shore has the right, on the principle of self-defence, to punish and pursue marauders on the sea to

[1] *Ante*, p. 72.

[2] James C. Carter, Counsel for U.S. in Behring Sea Fur Seal Arbitration, 1893, speaking of the breach of a blockade or conservation zone established by a state, considered that legislation providing for the trial and punishment of offenders, involving the seizure of vessels, 'would transcend the necessities of self-defence and assume the character of legislation' if aimed at *past* offences.

[3] Moore, *Dig.*, Vol. I, p. 723; Jessup, *op. cit.*, p. 96.

[4] Ibid., p. 721. The statement seems to be that of Secretary Bayard to Secretary Manning of May 28th, 1886. See *A.J.*, Spec. Supp., Vol. 23 (1929), p. 336.

the very extent to which their guns would carry their shot, and that such sovereign has jurisdiction over crimes committed by them through such shot, although at the time of shooting they were beyond three miles from the shore.

The rationale of this claim is not difficult to justify, since it aims at the prevention of acts which take effect on the territory of the state by causing damage there, even though the actors are outside the territory; this principle of 'constructive presence'[1] is a recognized basis of jurisdiction.

It is in the same interest of security that many states declare 'Defence Zones', areas of the high seas extending far beyond their territorial waters, in which the states prohibit acts of belligerency in a war to which they are not parties.[2]

Legislation

The cases we now envisage are those in which the authorities of the state act in pursuance of powers granted to them under the laws of that state. The necessity for such legislation arises from the fact that where the security of the state is threatened by conduct of individuals who are normally, except when engaging in piracy, not subject to duties imposed by international law, the state must impose such duties under its own municipal law. The difference between these cases and those under the preceding head is, however, purely formal, since the validity of those powers, or of the legislation by which they are given is, so far as other states are concerned, again dependent on the extent to which the jurisdiction is recognized by general international law.

[1] See *The Araunah*, Moore, *Int. Arb.*, I, pp. 824–5, in which Lord Salisbury invoked this doctrine to justify seizure of vessels lying outside the three-mile limit but using small boats to take seals within that limit. In the *Tenyu Maru* (1910) 4 Alaska 129, a U.S. court adopted the same view, quoted in Jessup, *op. cit.*, p. 112.

[2] See Comment to Art. 20, Harvard Draft Code on Territorial Waters, *A.J.*, Vol. 23 (1929), Supp., p. 245, for instances of this. The Declaration of Panama, 1939, by which the governments of the various American Republics claimed such a zone to 300 miles from their coasts was such a 'measure of continental protection . . . as of inherent right'. Final Act of Meeting of the Foreign Ministers of the American Republics, Dept. of State Bull., October 7th, 1939, pp. 321–2; cited in Colombos, *op. cit.*, p. 536; Hyde, Vol. III, p. 2350, doubts the legality of so wide an extension, though he admits the principle. Great Britain contested this declaration after the *Graf Spee* incident.

As Hyde states:[1]

> It should be observed that, as an incident in the defence of itself from the commission of acts which it may assert the right to thwart on the High Seas, a state may not unreasonably seek to impose penalties by judicial process upon the actors as a means of preventing the recurrence of illegal activities—to exercise the judicial power as a subsidiary means of vindicating its rights.

There would seem to be no objection in principle to a state qualifying by its own legislation the nature of an act committed on the high seas and prejudicial to its own security. In the *Lotus Case* in 1927 the Permanent Court of International Justice stated:

> Though it is true that in all systems of law the principle of the territorial character of criminal law is fundamental, it is equally true that all or nearly all these systems of law extend their action to offences committed outside the territory of the state . . . The territoriality of criminal law, therefore, is not an absolute principle of international law and by no means coincides with territorial sovereignty.[2]

Reference to the 'Hovering Laws' and similar enactments both in this country and the U.S.A. has already been made; whilst these aimed at the protection of customs and revenue interests, there is no reason why the interests of national security should not be similarly protected.

However, it is believed that neither the U.S.A. nor Great Britain has enacted legislation dealing with national security: reference has already been made to the opposition by Great Britain to the idea of a general security zone.[3] Numerous other countries have, however, enacted legislation by which they purport to qualify acts committed abroad by non-nationals which are inimical to the security of the state. For example, Art. 7 of the French Code of Criminal Procedure, November 17th, 1808, as revised, gives jurisdiction over aliens committing outside the territory of the state, either as principal or accessory, a crime against the security of the state.[4] The Hungarian Penal Code of 1950, s. 4, assumes a similar jurisdiction where the acts are 'detrimental to the basic interests of the democratic functioning

[1] *International Law*, I, p. 763.

[2] Series A, No. 10, p. 20. But see Art. 10 of the Provisional Articles concerning the Régime of the High Seas.

[3] See *ante*, p. 70.

[4] Laws and Regulations on the Régime of the High Seas, Vol. 2, U.N. Legislative Series, 1952, p. 43.

of the economic order'.[1] In similar vein the Costa Rican Penal Code of 1941, s. 4, speaks of acts 'detrimental to the political or economic interests of the nation'.[2] There are numerous other examples of this jurisdiction given in the second volume of the U.N. Legislative Series of 1952.

This derogation, in the interests of security, from the normal principles of territorial and personal jurisdiction is accepted when within reasonable limits. As Oppenheim states, referring to the view that jurisdiction is either personal or territorial, 'it is not a view which consistently with the practice of states and with common sense can be rigidly adopted in all cases . . . (nor) can it cover . . . serious crimes against (their) own safety'.[3]

There is no reason why the judicial power may not be regarded as a proper means of safeguarding the state, and an act of jurisdiction of this sort regarded as an act of self-defence. Even though this power must, in the nature of things, be exercised after the event and therefore after the particular danger has been met, if any particular exercise of the power is regarded as a means of preventing the recurrence of activities which provide a constant threat to the state's security, it may still be correct to regard the exercise of the judicial power as incidental to the right of self-defence. Perhaps the stronger objection to this inclusion of judicial acts within the principle of self-defence is that this jurisdiction is commonly accepted in state practice and exercised as of customary right. This being so, it lacks the essential features of self-defence as an exceptional right.

FISHERIES

Many of the claims to an extended jurisdiction are based upon an alleged special interest in the preservation or even exclusive

[1] Ibid., p. 61. [2] Ibid., p. 28.

[3] *International Law*, Vol. I, 8th ed., p. 332. For a recent case in British practice, see *The Naim Molvan* (1948), A.C. (P.C.), 851, involving the seizure of the vessel *Asya* flying a Turkish flag on the high seas off the Palestinian coast and confiscation under the Immigration Ordinances 1941 s. 12(3) for 'abetting unlawful immigration'. It was held that, the inference that the vessel had intended to land passengers illegally being a proper one, the seizure was not contrary to any established principle of international law. There can be little doubt that by 1946 these illegal landings of immigrants were indeed prejudicial to the security of Palestine.

right of exploitation of fisheries on the high seas. It is conceivable that an economic interest of this nature may be far more vital and essential for a state's existence than its interest in the inviolability of a portion of its territory. The question arises whether, under the right of self-defence, a claim to jurisdiction and control over fisheries on the High Seas can be maintained.

Clearly the first distinction between the 'economic' and the 'territorial' interest in the hypothetical situation envisaged above is that the territory of the state is subject to its sovereign control; this is not so *prima facie* with fisheries on the high seas. As Fauchille states:[1]

> Le droit de pêche appartient à tous les peuples. Nulle puissance ne saurait se réserver d'une manière absolue et vis-à-vis de tous les Etats le monopole de la pêche dans aucune partie de la haute mer,

and consequently

> aucun Etat ne peut édicter des règlements de pêche applicables aux sujets d'autres États.[2]

Yet not least of the reasons advanced for this principle is that 'les produits de la pleine mer sont inépuisables et suffisent à tous'.[3]

However, if this basic reason should no longer hold good, if in fact there is extreme likelihood of exhaustion, may any one state immediately and drastically affected by this state of exhaustion assume some measure of jurisdiction in self-defence? Fauchille admits that the users cannot abuse their common rights to the extent of exhausting these fisheries. Oppenheim, summarizing the attitude of states in this position, states:

> States have relied either on the right of self-protection against activities threatening the existence of an industry vital to the economic life of the nation or on the narrower ground of an alleged right of property in animals attached in some way to the territory . . . of the state concerned.[4]

This, in fact, was the position assumed by the U.S. Government in the Behring Sea Arbitration of 1893.[5] It may be useful to summarize the events leading up to this arbitration.

[1] *Traité de Droit International* (1922), Vol. I (2), p. 49. [2] Ibid., p. 50.

[3] Pradier-Fodéré, *Traité de droit international public*, p. 573.

[4] *Op. cit.*, p. 499.

[5] For a general outline of the facts see Moore, *Dig.*, Vol. I, p. 893; Jessup, *op. cit.*, p. 54. The U.S. argument is put by James C. Carter, Behring Sea Arbitration, Proceedings, XII.

By a ukase of the Emperor Alexander of Russia, dated September 7th, 1821, sanction was given to regulations limiting the rights of sealing and fishing in the Behring Sea to Russian subjects. Both the U.S. and Great Britain contested this claim, and Mr. Adams for the U.S. maintained that:

> The citizens of this Union will remain unmolested in the prosecution of their lawful commerce, and no effect will be given to an interdiction manifestly incompatible with their rights.[1]

By treaties of 1824 and 1825 Russia renounced her claims against the U.S. and Great Britain respectively. In 1867 Russia ceded 'all the territory and dominions . . . on the Continent of America and in the adjacent islands' of which she was possessed to the U.S.A.

By legislation of 1868, 1873 and 1889 the U.S.A. purported to protect the seal fisheries off the coast of Alaska from depredation by unlicensed vessels, and from 1886 onwards a number of seizures of British sealing schooners took place for violations of these laws. In a report on the negotiations which took place between the U.S.A. and Great Britain after the latter had repeatedly protested, Mr. Phelps, U.S. Minister in London, stated:

> And it is suggested that we are prevented from defending ourselves against such depredation because the sea at a certain distance from the coast is free . . . there are many things that cannot be allowed to be done on the open sea with impunity, and against which every sea is *mare clausum*. And the right of self-defence as to person and property prevails there as fully as elsewhere.[2]

At a later stage Mr. Blaine of the U.S. Government spoke of 'the necessity of defending the traditional and long-established rights of the U.S.': it is interesting to note that Russia had previously maintained her restrictions under the ukase of 1824 were a 'measure of legitimate self-defence'.[3]

By a treaty of arbitration, signed at Washington in 1892, the dispute was submitted to arbitration, the U.S. resting her case on succession to rights originally claimed by Russia and not affected by the treaty of 1825 with Great Britain, on a right to protect a 'property' in the seals, and on the more general ground of self-defence against abuses by the fishing vessels of Great Britain.[4]

[1] Cited in Moore, *Dig.*, Vol. I, p. 891.

[2] Ibid., p. 898. [3] Moore, *Dig.*, Vol. I, p. 909.

[4] See the oral argument of James C. Carter, 12 Proceedings, p. 255. 'The government of the U.S., therefore, bases its claims to defend its

The arbitrators rejected these claims and asserted the primacy of the principle of the freedom of the high seas over any alleged right of self-defence.[1]

Probably, so far as the claim to a right of self-defence is concerned, the decision indicates only that the interests of the U.S. were not of a sufficiently vital nature to support a plea of self-defence, and must, therefore, be subordinated to the interests of all nations in the freedom of the high seas. It is interesting to note that the policy of the British government followed the principle of this award in the later case of *Mortensen* v. *Peters*.[2] In that case the captain of a Norwegian fishing vessel was convicted of illegal trawling in an area of the Moray Firth outside the limits of territorial waters under the Herring Fishing (Scotland) Act, 1889. Although the High Court of Justiciary upheld the conviction on the ground that, however contrary to international law, the courts must apply an Act of Parliament, the British government remitted Mortensen's fine and pardoned him. By the Trawling in Prohibited Areas Prevention Act of 1909[3] this excessive jurisdiction was relinquished.

Within recent years numerous states have adopted a policy of conservation, by which they claim jurisdiction over areas of the high seas for the purpose of preserving and protecting fisheries there essential to the economic need of the nation. The Presidential Proclamation No. 2668, of September 28th, 1945,[4] is typical of many of these claims; it sets out the policy of the U.S. Government by establishing 'conservation zones' which, in so far as they 'have been or shall hereafter be developed and maintained by nationals alone' shall be regulated by the U.S. In so far as they have been 'legitimately developed and maintained jointly by the nationals of the U.S. and nationals of other states' these zones are to be established by agreement between the U.S.A. and such other

property interest in the seal herd and its industry upon the following grounds:

(i) the reason and necessity of the thing, there being no other means adequate to the defence of such rights.

(ii) the practice and usage of nations which always employ this means of defence.'

[1] For the text of the award see Moore, *Dig.*, Vol. I, p. 911.

[2] (1906) 14 Sc. L.T. 227.

[3] 9 Edward VII, c. 8.

[4] For full text see Laws and Regulations, U.N. Legislative Series, 1951, p. 112. Department of State Bull., Vol. 13 (1945), p. 486.

states. The proclamation makes no mention of any right of self-defence, although it does recite the need for protection of these resources in which the U.S. has special rights and equities. Gidel, earlier, points out[1] that the problem posed by these proclamations is twofold; firstly, can the state extend areas reserved to its own nationals (the territorial waters are clearly so reserved), and secondly, can the state assume a protective jurisdiction common to aliens and subjects alike? His own conclusion[2] is that international law does not recognize the unilateral declaration as a basis for establishing fishery conservation zones. It is noticeable, however, that to those claims which are clearly defined and rest content with a protective jurisdiction rather than a claim to sovereignty, no protest has been made; in the absence of protest, there is a basis at least for the development of customary rights.[3]

This, in effect, appears to be the basis upon which the International Law Commission felt that draft articles relating to Fisheries could be included in the Provisional Articles concerning the Régime of the High Seas. The basic assumption behind the old statements on the freedom of the high seas was, as we have seen, that the resources were inexhaustible and, therefore, free to all. The validity of this assumption is now seriously challenged. The summary of the Commission's Report on the Fourth Session states that:

> The resulting position constitutes, in the first instance, a danger to the food supply of the world. Also, in so far as it renders the coastal state or the states directly interested helpless against wasteful and predatory exploitation of fisheries by foreign nationals, it is productive of friction and constitutes an inducement to states to take unilateral action, which at present is probably illegal, of self-protection.[4]

The present trend, therefore, is to place the regulation of fisheries under a régime acceptable on a basis of state practice; the details of this régime are set out in Chapter II of the Provisional Articles. It should no longer be necessary to resort to the right of self-defence to justify measures of protection or conservation of fishery resources beyond territorial waters.

[1] 'La Mer Territoriale et le Zone Contigue', *R.C.*, 1934 (II), p. 266.

[2] Ibid., p. 268.

[3] For other claims see Vol. I, Laws and Regulations, U.N. Legislative Series, 1951.

[4] *A.J.*, Vol. 48 (1954), Supp., p. 40.

It is also evident that, whatever the principles involved in relation to fisheries, the interest which a state may claim to protect cannot be limited to fisheries. An analogous position could well exist in relation to oil and other mineral deposits on or under the sea-bed beyond the limits of territorial waters but contiguous to the shore of the claimant state. The Presidential Proclamation of September 28th, 1945[1] establishes similar conservation zones for petroleum and other minerals and, whilst basing this claim to jurisdiction mainly upon grounds of reason and justice, recites that 'self-preservation compels the coastal nation to keep close watch over activities off its shores'. Again, this is typical of a number of claims by various states.[2]

Jessup's conclusion in 1927 was that:

> . . . there is a tendency on the part of many states to claim in the interests of self-protection, a certain power of control over the high seas adjacent to territorial waters. It is obvious that this tendency is not universal and no general principle of international law may be deduced therefrom. It is merely possible to say that 'reasonable claims' advanced on the ground of self-defence, particularly in time of war, are logically sound and legally defensible.[3]

This may still be the case, although the growth of state practice in this respect in recent years is tending more and more to establish the basis of a customary right. However this may be, the cases where such claims can be justified in self-defence are not yet apparent. Moreover the acceptance as law of the Draft Articles on the Continental Shelf, adopted by the International Law Commission at its 234th Meeting in its Fifth Session[4] will tend to oust self-defence as a basis for a claim to jurisdiction over the resources of the sea-bed and sub-soil in the submarine areas contiguous to the state's coast up to a depth of two hundred metres and substitute the firmer basis of an acknowledged rule of law.

The right of hot pursuit

The right of hot pursuit developed as an ancillary right, a logical consequence of the assertion of jurisdiction over terri-

[1] No. 2667 U.S. Statutes at Large, Vol. 59 (1945), p. 884; U.N. Legislative Series, p. 38.

[2] For other similar proclamations see Vol. I, U.N. Legislative Series, Laws and Regulations on the Régime of the High Seas.

[3] *Op. cit.*, p. 105.

[4] Text in *A.J.*, Vol. 48 (1954), Supp., p. 28.

torial waters. The Harvard Draft states this right in these terms:

> A state may continue on the high seas the pursuit of a vessel of another state and may effect its arrest for a violation of international law, if such pursuit was begun while the vessel was in the territorial waters of that state.[1]

As the Comment on the Draft states,[2] the right of pursuit ends when once interrupted by the fugitive vessel reaching the territorial waters of another state. In the *Itata*,[3] a vessel which had been seized and charged with breach of the American neutrality laws at San Diego, California, escaped and reached Iquique, a Chilean port, without being intercepted. She was pursued there by U.S. naval vessels and surrendered to them by the Chilean authorities. The U.S. and Chilean Claims Commission, established under the Convention of August 7th, 1892, acknowledged that this act of entry into foreign territorial waters for the purpose of seizing a fugitive vessel was a 'clear violation of the laws of nations'. [4]

To this rule there is possibly one exception, suggested by Hackworth,[5] in that the pursuit of pirate vessels can be continued within the territorial waters of another state if that state is not in a position to take up the pursuit itself; even then it is suggested that the right of trial devolves on the territorial state within whose waters capture is effected.

It was generally assumed that the right does not exist unless the pursued vessel has actually committed an offence within the territorial waters of the pursuing state; in other words, the right of hot pursuit did not extend, apart from treaty,[6] to the so-called 'contiguous zone'.

[1] *A.J.*, Vol. 23 (1929), Spec. Supp., Art. 21. See generally Bluntschli, *Le Droit international codifié*, 3rd ed., Art. 342; Rivier, *Principes*, I, p. 151; Jessup, *op. cit.*, pp. 106–10; Hall, *op. cit.*, 7th ed., p. 266; Piggott, *Nationality*, Vol. II, pp. 35–40; Glanville Williams, 'The Juridical Basis of the Right of Hot Pursuit', *BYBIL*, Vol. 20 (1939), pp. 83–98.

[2] Ibid., p. 358.

[3] Moore, *Dig.*, Vol. VII, pp. 905–65; Jessup, *op. cit.*, p. 106. See also Hershey, *A.J.*, Vol. 13 (1919), p. 568, who doubts whether the *Itata* was ever pursued into Chilean waters and regards the surrender as a voluntary act rather than one impressed upon the Chilean authorities by a display of force.

[4] The Commission here adopted the statement of Storey J. in the *Apillon* (1824), 9. Wheaton, 361, 371.

[5] *Dig.*, Vol. II, p. 683.

[6] As in Art. 9 of Convention for Suppression of Contraband Traffic in Alcoholic Liquors, 1925, L.N.T.S., XLII, 73.

In the case of the *I'm Alone*,[1] arising out of the sinking of a Canadian vessel by U.S. Coastguard vessels after a pursuit beginning not within territorial waters but within the one hour zone permitted to the U.S. authorities for the purpose of visit and search of British vessels under the Anglo-U.S. Liquor Treaty of 1924,[2] the Commissioners found it unnecessary to decide whether the right of hot pursuit was involved in the grant by treaty of this extended jurisdiction. However, in *The Vinces*[3] a seizure of a British vessel in hot pursuit 13 miles from the shore in pursuance of an offence committed 7½ miles from the shore and within the one-hour sailing distance was held lawful. On appeal to the Circuit Court of Appeals the court, having accepted evidence of the intended destination of the vessel being the United States and of her intention to land cargo contrary to the Tariff Act, 1922,[4] held that seizure beyond the 12 mile limit authorized by that Act for the purpose of visit and search was justified as an exercise of the right of hot pursuit. The effect of the 1924 Treaty was not considered relevant, since that Treaty was intended to cover ships hovering outside territorial waters but within the one-hour zone; in this case there was an obvious intention to enter U.S. territorial waters. The whole question whether the right of hot pursuit extends to these wider 'security' or 'contiguous' zones remains unsettled. It will become settled if the Provisional Articles drafted by the International Law Commission are accepted and become law; Art. 22 on the right of pursuit provides that 'if the foreign vessel is within a zone contiguous to the territorial sea, the pursuit may only be undertaken if there has been trespass against the rights for the protection of which the said zone was established'.

Of immediate importance for present purposes is the basis of this right. Not unnaturally, since many authorities have based these claims to an extended jurisdiction beyond the limits of territorial waters on a right of self-defence, there is a tendency to

[1] See *A.D.*, 1933–4, Case No. 86. Hackworth, *Dig.*, Vol. II, p. 703; Garner, *BYBIL*, Vol. 16 (1935), p. 173; Fitzmaurice, ibid., Vol. 17 (1936), p. 88; Dennis, *A.J.*, Vol. 23 (1929), p. 359; Hyde, *A.J.*, Vol. 29 (1935), p. 299.

[2] *A.J.*, Vol. 18 (1924), Supp., p. 127. There were sixteen of these Treaties with various states.

[3] (1927) 20 Fed. (2d) 164. U.S. District Court of S. Carolina. On appeal under the title of *Gillam* v. *U.S.* (1928), 27 Fed. (2d) 296. See Hudson, *Cases*, p. 681.

[4] Relevant section quoted in Briggs, *Law of Nations*, 2nd ed., p. 374.

base this ancillary right on a similar ground. In the case of *The North*[1] before the Canadian Supreme Court, Idington, J., said:

> The right of pursuit . . . springs from the necessity of the case. It rests upon what in the last analysis is the basis of so much international law in many analogous cases, the necessities of self-defence and protection.[2]

Hyde,[3] whilst not excluding the possibility of an exercise of the right being based on self-defence, considers that 'conditions justifying immediate pursuit and capture on the high seas on grounds of self-defence are rarely present'.

However, one may again question whether the doctrine of hot pursuit may be properly classified as pertaining to the concept of self-defence, since the extent of its acceptance into the general practice of states as a normal exercise of jurisdiction suffices to place it within the domain of customary rights. At the Hague Conference of 1930, when dealing with the proposed codification of the law of territorial waters, the Preparatory Committee, after submitting a questionnaire to governments on the question of hot pursuit, made the following observation:

> With one exception, all the replies on this point recognize that a state is entitled to continue on the high seas a pursuit begun within its territorial waters.[4]

There seems little basis, therefore, for regarding this as an exceptional right, or for denying to it the character of a right *stricto sensu*. Sir Charles Russell in the course of his argument in the Behring Sea Arbitration had described it as 'not a right in the strict sense by international law, but something which nations will stand by and see done'.[5] Yet later he admits that it is based on 'acquiescence' and the 'general consent on the part of nations'.

A more practical explanation of this right, tending away from the exceptional classification of self-defence, is that of Westlake,

[1] 37 Canada Supreme Court Reports, 385 (1906). Hudson, *Cases*, p. 678, and see discussion of this case in Jessup, *op. cit.*, pp. 107–8.

[2] 37, Canadian Supreme Court Reports, pp. 400–1.

[3] Vol. I, p. 794. See also Hershey, *A.J.*, Vol. 13 (1919), p. 13, basing hot pursuit on 'the right of self-protection and self-defence'.

[4] League of Nations Publications C.74, M.39, V, p. 93. Earlier contrary views had been expressed by M. Asser, arbitrator between U.S.A. and Russia in the cases of the *James Hamilton Lewis* and the *C. H. White*; Moore, *Dig.*, Vol. I, pp. 927–9.

[5] 13, Proceedings, p. 300.

who describes it simply as 'necessary for the effective administration of justice',[1] and of Hall, who describes it as 'a continuation of an act of jurisdiction which has begun or which but for the accident of the immediate escape would have begun within the territory itself and that it is necessary to pursue it in order to enable the territorial jurisdiction to be effectively exercised'.[2] Gidel expresses the same rational need for giving effect to state jurisdiction by the grant of this right:

> La force public doit, sur mer comme sur terre, proportionner la vigueur de ses moyens à l'obtention de résultats qu'elle se propose : il s'agit d'empêcher un navire de se soustraire par la fuit à la répression d'infractions qu'il a commises.[3]

The specific provision for the right of pursuit in Art. 22 of the Provisional Articles endorses the view that, whatever place the right of self-defence may have had in the origin of the right of pursuit, it is now no longer necessary to look further than the normal, customary practice of states.

Our conclusion is, therefore, that though in the defence of its security a state may exercise the right of self-defence upon the high seas adjacent to its territory, the tendency is for the law to recognize the need for protection of certain essential interests of the state by developing customary rights of a jurisdictional character. Where such customary rights exist the legality of state action needs no further justification, and self-defence remains appropriate only to action of an exceptional character, not sanctioned by customary right, which has as its purpose the protection of the state's essential rights against a danger, actual or imminent, resulting from the delictual conduct of another state, or from the conduct of individuals, upon the high seas.

[1] *International Law*, Vol. I, p. 173; approved in Hyde, Vol. I, p. 794.
[2] *International Law*, 4th ed., p. 267. Cited by Davies, J., in *The Ship North* v. *King*, (1906), 37 Supreme Court of Canada Reports, p. 394.
[3] R.C., 1934 (II), p. 239.

CHAPTER V

THE RIGHT OF PROTECTION OF NATIONALS

It cannot be doubted that the state may defend its nationals or any person within its territorial jurisdiction from hostile attack. In so far as such hostile attack emanates from groups within its own territory the state may rely on the procedures of its own administrative and legal system to justify the necessary defensive measures. Where, however, the attack emanates from a foreign state, or from groups outside the defending state's own territorial jurisdiction, the necessary defensive measures can be taken in the exercise of a right of self-defence recognized in international law. It is significant that in Art. 9 of the Inter-American Treaty of Reciprocal Assistance of 1947,[1] an armed attack against the 'people' of the signatory state within the area defined by the treaty is treated as a *casus foederis*, the occurrence of which will bring into operation the right of collective self-defence.

The more difficult problem arises when the state purports to intervene within the territory of another state to protect its nationals. It is our present purpose to examine how far the protection of nationals abroad can be said to fall within the concept of self-defence.

THE PROTECTION OF NATIONALS ABROAD

The right of the state to intervene by the use or threat of force for the protection of its nationals suffering injuries within the territory of another state is generally admitted, both in the writings of jurists and in the practice of states.

In the arbitration between Great Britain and Spain in 1925, one of the series known as the *Spanish Moroccan Claims*, Judge Huber, as rapporteur of the commission, stated:

> However, it cannot be denied that at a certain point the interest of a State in exercising protection over its nationals and their property can take precedence over territorial sovereignty, despite the absence of any

---

[1] *A.J.*, Vol. 43 (1949), Supp., p. 53, and see *post*, pp. 228–31.

conventional provisions. This right of intervention has been claimed by all states; only its limits are disputed.[1]

Oppenheim states in similar terms:

> The right of protection over citizens abroad, which a state holds, may cause an intervention by right to which the other party is legally bound to submit. And it matters not whether protection of the life, security, honor or property of a citizen abroad is concerned.[2]

In certain cases, where diplomatic protection in the sense of diplomatic interposition or of the presentation of a claim on behalf of a national by his state has either failed or is inadequate to prevent an immediate danger to life or property which would otherwise be irremedial, states have resorted to the threat or use of force as a means of protection. It is with this form of protection that we are here concerned. We now envisage action by the protecting state which involves a *prima facie* violation of the independence and territorial inviolability of the territorial state. In so far as this action takes effect in derogation of the sovereignty of the territorial state it must necessarily be exceptional in character and limited to those cases in which no other means of protection are available. It presupposes the inadequacy of any other means of protection against some injury, actual or imminent, to the persons or property[3] of nationals and, moreover, an injury which results either from the acts of the territorial state and its authorities or from the acts of individuals or groups of individuals which the territorial state is unable, or unwilling, to prevent.

> Ces violences motivant l'intervention militaire consistaient en des excès commis par le population (émeutes, massacres, pillages) ou en des illégalités graves commises par des fonctionnaires (arrestations arbitraires, par exemple).[4]

No exhaustive enumeration of the cases affording the right to have recourse to this extreme form of protection is possible; we

[1] Anglo-Spanish Arbitrations, *Beni-Madan, Rzini Claim* (1925), UNRIAA, Vol. II, p. 616.

[2] *International Law*, Vol. I, 8th ed., p. 309. See generally Borchard, *Diplomatic Protection of Citizens Abroad* (1916); Dunn, *Protection of Nationals* (1932); Gaston Leval, *De la Protection Diplomatique des Nationaux à l'Etranger* (1907); E. Pittard, *Protection des Nationaux* (1896). Moore, *American Diplomacy* (1905), p. 131, is even more categorical: 'The right of the government to intervene for the protection of its citizens in foreign lands was never doubted.'

[3] But see *post*, p. 100.

[4] Giraud, 'Théorie de Légitime Défense', *R.C.*, 1934 (III), p. 735.

can enumerate the conditions that govern it, but not all the occasions which justify it. Moreover, the problem is not simply one of state responsibility. In most cases the right of the protecting state to intervene in this way is occasioned by a breach of a duty imposed on the territorial state under general international law to use 'due diligence'[1] in safeguarding the lives and property of aliens within its territory from unlawful infringement. To this extent the notions of state responsibility and protection are supplementary; both depend on the failure of the territorial state to conform to minimum standards based upon general international law, to a 'standard of justice, very simple, very fundamental, and of such general acceptance by all civilized nations as to form part of the international law of the world'.[2] It is equally clear that not all cases of state responsibility will involve another state's right of protection by means of armed intervention, for many and indeed most forms of breach do not carry any immediate threat of irreparable injury to the life or property of aliens.

Nevertheless, it is conceivable that, even where 'due diligence' has been exercised by the territorial state, there may be a threat to the lives and property of these aliens originating from groups of individuals for which the territorial state can bear no responsibility. This is not to suggest that there cannot be responsibility for 'mob violence',[3] but only that it is feasible for this to occur in circumstances where the territorial state has nevertheless acted with due diligence. In such a case the right of the protecting state

[1] The *Alabama Award*, 1872, was founded upon the failure of Great Britain to exercise 'due diligence': Moore, *Int. Arb.*, Vol. 1, p. 656. See Art. 10 and 12 of the Harvard Draft Convention on State Responsibility, *A.J.*, Vol. 23 (1929), Supp. On the fundamental question of the basis of state responsibility see Eagleton, *Responsibility of States* (1928); Leval, *op. cit.*, p. 169. Dunn, *op. cit.*, p. 175, rejects the notion of *culpa* as the basis of responsibility as unworkable and chooses instead to look upon 'the institution of diplomatic protection as a device for allocating the risks of injuries and losses that are necessarily associated with the normal conduct of international trade and intercourse'. For our purposes if state responsibility does exist then it does so as the result of extremely abnormal conduct on the part of the territorial state.

[2] Elihu Root, 'The Basis of Protection to Citizens Residing Abroad', Presidential Address to the 10th Meeting of the A.S. of International Law; cited in Stowell, *Intervention in International Law*, p. 159. See also Borchard, *op. cit.*, p. 28.

[3] See J. B. Moore, *Responsibility of Governments for Mob Violence*, Collected Papers, I, p. 217. Eagleton, *Responsibility of States in International Law*, 1928, ch. VI.

arises from the exigencies of the situation, not from the breach of any obligation, and is, for this reason, more properly classed as an exercise of the 'right', or more strictly the qualified privilege, of necessity[1] rather than the right of self-defence. This is yet another example of the anomaly which arises from the fact that, although groups of individuals are rarely under duties imposed by general international law, they are capable of injuring the interests of states. The action taken by a state in defending these interests only assumes the character of a legal right when the injurious action of the individuals or groups of individuals can be characterized as delictual under international law. It is of interest to note the developments envisaged by the Draft Code of Offences against the Peace and Security of Mankind,[2] Art. 2(9) of which provides that the following will be criminal acts under international law:

> Acts by the authorities of a State or by private individuals, committed with intent to destroy, in whole or in part, a national, ethical, racial or religious group as such, including
> (i) Killing members of the group;
> (ii) Causing serious bodily or mental harm to members of the group;
> (iii) Deliberately inflicting on the group conditions of life calculated to bring about its physical destruction in whole or in part;
> (iv) Imposing measures intended to prevent births within the group;
> (v) Forcibly transferring children of the group to another group.

In these circumstances, where the protective action is not based upon a breach of an obligation by the territorial state, such action as the protecting state may take must in no way be directed against the territorial state.[3] The territorial state is 'legally bound to submit' [4] to such action as is reasonably taken, and the prin-

[1] *Ante*, pp. 9–10.

[2] Drafted by the I.L.C. on the directions of the General Assembly (Resolution 177 (ii) of November 21st, 1947). Text of Draft Code in *A.J.*, Vol. 45 (1951), Supp., p. 126.

[3] See Art. 7 Harvard Draft Convention, *op. cit.*, which draws a clear distinction between cases where the alien suffers injury inflicted by an individual or group of individuals for which the state is not responsible, and where the injury results from an act of an authority of the state.

[4] Oppenheim, *op. cit.*, p. 309. On similar reasoning Stowell, *op. cit.*, p. 50, refers to a 'corresponding obligation on the part of all nations not to interfere with the recognized and orderly procedure for the enforcement of the law', and refutes any right of resistance to such reasonable force as may be necessary. This tends to suggest the action of the protecting state partakes of the nature of a sanction; in the absence of an international delict, as in the case we suppose, this is clearly not so.

ciple of relativity of rights prevents the territorial state from asserting its right of territorial integrity to the extent of obstructing the action of the protecting state. This is so even though the measures of protection are not due to the territorial state's fault, but are due to circumstances in which the protecting state must insist on the precedence of its right of protection over the rights of the territorial state.

Now whether this protective action is seen as a form of 'justifiable' intervention, 'intervention by right' as Oppenheim has it,[1] and therefore an exception to the general principle of non-intervention, or as a form of action in self-defence has not in the past affected the question of the legality of the action. It may well be, however, that now Art. 2(4) of the Charter contains a prohibition of 'the use or threat of force against the territorial integrity or political independence of any State', thereby precluding intervention,[2] and Art. 51 preserves the 'inherent right of individual and collective self-defence', the question of classification has become more than one of mere form. For the moment our purpose is to examine how far the threat or use of force in the protection of nationals abroad can come within the concept of self-defence.

THE DEFENCE OF NATIONALS AS THE DEFENCE OF THE STATE

Political theories of the social contract gave rise to the view that protection, as the duty of the state, afforded the consideration of the *pactum subjectionis*, and that protection of the nationals of the state was, in effect, protection of the state itself. Within the definition of the state the requirement of a community is essential, and without nationals, without the community, the state ceases to exist.

> Le citoyen est l'essence de l'Etat; c'est aussi sa raison d'être... les citoyens forment un élément constitutif de l'Etat.[3]

[1] *Op. cit.*, p. 276; also Borchard, *op. cit.*, p. 448, classes this action 'not as a case of intervention, but as non-belligerent interposition'. He bases the right of protection on the necessity of sanctioning 'the right of international intercourse between states and individuals according to the standards of conduct and treatment recognized as proper and lawful by international law and practice'. Ibid., pp. 353–4. Leval, *op. cit.*, p. 7, distinguishes from intervention, but admits 'la limite est souvent difficile à fixer'.

[2] See *ante*, chs. II, III.

[3] Pittard, *op. cit.*, p. 1. This view is dependent on a particular theory of the state, that the state exists for the protection and promotion of the rights of the citizens, the individuals who comprise it. See Duguit, *Etudes de Droit Public*, 1901, p. 288. Bluntschli, *Theory of the State*, 1898, p. 305.

It has been contended that an injury to the nationals of a state constitutes an injury to the state itself,[1] and that the protection of nationals is an essential function of the state.[2] On this reasoning it is feasible to argue that the defence of nationals, whether within or without the territorial jurisdiction of the state, is in effect the defence of the state itself.

Le droit d'exercer une action en vue de protéger des nationaux à l'étranger est étroitement apparenté au droit d'intervention, dont il fait même, peut-être, partie intégrante... il sembleraient s'étendre à tous les droits dont peuvent jouir l'état et ses nationaux sur le territoire d'un autre Etat, comme à chacun des nationaux. C'est à ce point de vue que cette action coïnciderait avec le droit de légitime défense...[3]

Indeed, it may reasonably be argued that the defence of members of the community of a state, of its nationals, is as much a part of the defence of the state as the defence of any portion of its territory or of its political independence. Redslob has stated that:

... où le citoyen subit une agression, soit de la part des autorités territoriale, soit de la part de personnes individuelles. C'est alors la légitime défense qui entre en jeu... et cela pour deux raisons... il considéra son citoyen comme partie de lui-même ou se prévaudre de la faculté générale de s'associer à la légitime défense d'autrui.[4]

Writers have, in fact, deduced the right of protection from the fundamental right of self-preservation[5] or, achieving the same result, defined an attack upon the state as including 'all violations of the legal rights of itself or its subjects'.[6]

This identification of the interests of the state and the interests

[1] Vattel, Bk. II, ch. VI, s. 71. But obviously not every injury; see Borchard, *op. cit.*, p. 351.

[2] Borchard, *op. cit.*, p. 31.

[3] Potter, 'L'Intervention en droit international moderne', *R.C.*, 1930 (II), p. 647. See the dictum of the umpire of the Commission in the *Great Venezuelan Railroad Case*, holding official acts null and void in so far as they conflict with the 'highest law of any nation, the safety of its people'. Ven. Arb., 1903, p. 632.

[4] *Traité de Droit des Gens*, 1950, pp. 255–7. *Contra* Théry, *Notion d'Agression*, 1937, pp. 191–2.

[5] Hall, *International Law*, 8th ed. Pearce-Higgins, Sec. 87. Pittard, *op. cit.*, p. 77: 'L'Etat possède le droit de protéger ses sujets en vertu de ses droits d'existence, de conservation . . .'

[6] Westlake, *International Law*, Vol. I, pp. 312–13. He would, however, omit from such a definition violations of a trivial nature, on the principle '*de minimis non curat lex*'. An interesting judicial attempt to identify the rights of the state and its nationals occurred in the case of *The Commonwealth* v. *William P. Blodgett* (1846) 12 Metcalf, p. 56, at p. 84. Soldiers of the State of Rhode Island entered the State of Massachusetts without permission and there

of its nationals, however attractive theoretically, tends to obscure the real basis of the right of self-defence. A too ready acceptance of this view leads to a ready acceptance of the proposition that the defence of the interests of nationals is, *ipso facto*, the defence of the interests of the state. In practice it cannot be said that a threat to the safety of nationals abroad constitutes a threat to the security of the state. Obviously, to imperil the safety of a single national abroad is not to imperil the security of the state; and yet there may be occasions when the threat of danger is great enough, or wide enough in its application to a sizable community abroad, for it to be legitimately construed as an attack on the state itself. It is submitted that, in deciding at what stage a threat to nationals involves a threat to the state, no process of 'counting heads' will serve any useful purpose. The proper course is to have recourse to the principle of relativity of rights which demands a weighing of the one state's right of territorial integrity against the other state's right of protection. This is also demanded by the requirement of proportionality which is common both to reprisals[1] and to self-defence. The measures of self-defence, of protection, must be proportionate to the danger, actual or imminent, to the nationals in need of protection. It follows, therefore, that action in self-defence must be conditioned by respect for the equal rights of other states and that it must not be, in the words of Mr. Webster, 'unreasonable or excessive . . . (but) justified by the necessity of self-defence, . . . limited by that necessity and kept

arrested several rebels. On being tried before a Massachusetts court the direction to the jury contained this identification of the defence of the state with the defence of the lives and property of nationals. 'If there existed a necessity for the defence or protection of the lives and property of the citizens of Rhode Island, or for the defence of the State of Rhode Island, that the defendants should do the acts complained of . . . they were to acquit them.' Cited in Cheng, *General Principles of Law*, p. 84. See also Rutgers, *R.C.*, 1931 (IV), p. 1, who at p. 69 accepts as a defensive war any war waged for the protection of nationals and their property abroad or on the high seas.

[1] See the Arbitration between Germany and Portugal over the *Naulilaa Incident*; Decision of July 31st, 1928, 8 Receuil des Décisions des Tribunaux Arbitraux Mixtes, 409, pp. 422–5: 'Reprisals are an act of appropriate justice . . . a certain proportion between offences and reprisal is a necessary condition of the legitimacy of the latter.' Colbert, *Retaliation in International Law*, 1948, pp. 76–9, maintains the proportion may be not only to damage done but also to the prospect of future injuries, as a deterrent, citing the *Barrier Forts Incident*. (Offutt, *op. cit.*, p. 39), also Commodore Hollins after the Greytown Incident . . . 'as a guarantee for future protection'. Brit. and For. State Papers, Vol. 46, p. 880.

clearly within it'.[1] The principle of relativity of rights and the notion of proportionality involve a strict adherence to the measure of proportionality which the occasion demands, so that a state may not lightly violate the independence and integrity of another state in defence of its own right to the treatment of its nationals according to established standards.

This would mean in practice that a large-scale naval demonstration or military landing could never be justified as action in the defence of a single national; to undertake such action would be to totally disregard the rights of the territorial state by the disproportionate enforcement of the rights of the protecting state. On the other hand the use or threat of force by the protecting state would be justified where the magnitude of the danger to its nationals satisfied the requirement of proportionality, for the relativity of rights would have been properly assessed.[2]

We would submit, therefore, that any argument for the inclusion of the protection of nationals within the concept of self-defence is better founded on an examination of the conditions which state practice has imposed on the threat or use of force as a means of protection, rather than on the controversial premiss of fundamental rights. As we shall see, these conditions correspond in essentials with the conditions which general international law imposes upon the use of the right of self-defence. It is to a consideration of these conditions that we now turn.

THE CONDITIONS OF PROTECTION

The nationality of the person

The normal condition precedent to the protection by the state is the allegiance of the person protected to that state,[3] and, in-

[1] Parl. Papers (1843), Vol. LXI; Brit. and For. State Papers, Vol. 30, p. 193.

[2] Rodick, *Doctrine of Necessity*, p. 49, speaking of intervention for the protection of the lives and property of nationals, says 'an intervention in the form of landing troops will be the subject of legal excuse only in case that refraining from such action would result in a more vital breach in the sovereign rights of the state affected. Intervention would perhaps be the subject of legal excuse if the lives of a large number of aliens were in imminent danger'. At p. 50 he doubts whether excusable in the protection of property alone and is unable to recall a single instance when justified solely in the protection of property rights.

[3] Borchard, *op. cit.*, p. 462. Hackworth, *Dig.*, Vol. III, p. 285. J. Bassett Moore, *Collected Papers*, II, p. 329. Hurst, 'Nationality of Claims', *BYBIL*, Vol. VII (1926), pp. 163–82.

deed, the correlation of protection and allegiance has been close enough for the state to refuse protection where that allegiance has been broken by the existence of allegiance to another state,[1] the non-fulfilment of the duties of citizenship,[2] acts inconsistent with that allegiance, such as piracy,[3] or slave-trading.[4] For this purpose corporations organized in or incorporated in the territory of the state are assimilated to natural persons owing allegiance to the state.[5] In the absence of this condition it is difficult to see how the act of protection can be brought within the concept of self-defence, for the nexus of nationality, essential if this assimilation between state and community is to be well-founded, is absent. That is not to deny that a state may afford protection to persons other than its own nationals,[6] for such right may be given under treaty or under request from the state whose nationals those persons are,[7] or even under the principle of humanitarian intervention. What is denied is that, in the absence of the nexus of nationality, the use or threat of force in the protection of persons is part of the concept of self-defence.

Given the nationality of the subject, it is commonly supposed that the state has not only a right but a duty to extend its protection to that subject. This notion has its support in the writings of the earlier jurists[8] and has been put in the following terms by the Supreme Court of the U.S.A. in the case of *Luria* v. *U.S.*[9]

> Citizenship is membership of a political society and implies a duty of allegiance on the part of the members and a duty of protection on the part of the society.

---

[1] Hackworth, *Dig.*, Vol. III, p. 360; V, p. 710.
[2] Ibid., Vol. III, p. 285, 315. [3] Ibid., Vol. II, p. 681.
[4] Borchard, *op. cit.*, p. 738. [5] Hackworth, II, p. 500; III, p. 423.
[6] See *ante*, p. 94 fn. 3. Also Lauterpacht, *C.L.J.*, Vol. IX (1947), p. 336. Beckett, *Trans. Grotius Soc.*, Vol. 17, p. 178; great weight of opinion against protection on grounds other than nationality.
[7] Hackworth, *Dig.*, Vol. II, p. 329. Borchard, *op. cit.*, pp. 471–5, for a number of illustrations. In particular see letter of Mr. Innes, British Chargé d'Affairs in Washington to Secretary Knox, dated June 13th, 1912, requesting U.S. protection for British lives and property, Hackworth, p. 329.
[8] Wolff, *Jus Gentium*, ed. J. B. Scott, trans., pp. 22–3; Vattel, *Droit des Gens*, Bk. I, ch. II, ss. 13–16; Fiore, *Diritto Internazionale Codificato*, Title XVI, 5th ed., 1918, trans., Borchard, p. 259; Grotius, *De Jure Belli ac Pacis*, Bk. II, ch. XXV, ss. 1 & 2.
[9] (1913) 231, U.S. 9, pp. 22–3. See also Blutschli, Code, s. 380. Leval, *op. cit.*, p. 14; Pittard, *op. cit.*, p. 85.

Again, more recently, we find in the decision in *Joyce* v. *D.P.P.*[1] in the House of Lords, the Lord Chancellor relying on the principle established in *Calvin's Case*,[2] that '*protectio trahit subjectionem et subjectio protectionem*', and saying:

> The principle which runs through feudal law and what I may perhaps call constitutional law requires on the one hand protection and on the other fidelity: a duty of the sovereign lord to protect, a duty of the liege or subject to be faithful.

On the other hand it has been denied that the subject has any absolute right to protection,[3] or, what amounts to the same thing, that if there is a right it is limited by 'la prudence politique et les circonstances'.[4] Whatever the position may be in constitutional law, and clearly in the law of both England[5] and the U.S.[6] the 'right' is conditional on the fulfilment of the duties of allegiance, this seems to represent more accurately the position in international law. For there can be no doubt that the state, in exercising its right to protect, is asserting its own right, a right recognized by international law and, we submit, a right which emanates from the more general right of self-defence.[7] Moreover, the exercise of that right is conditioned by the same requirements which international law imposes upon any exercise by the state of its right of self-defence.

The imminence of danger to life or property

The occasions on which states have asserted their right to protection are not susceptible to conclusive analysis on the basis of legal rights, for, though it has been alleged that these occasions

[1] [1946] A.C. 347 at p. 368.

[2] (1608) 7 Co. Rep. la at 5a, 'because they are bound to obey and serve him he is called their liege lord, because he *should* maintain and defend them'.

[3] Opp., Vol. I, 8th ed., p. 686; Borchard, *op. cit.*, pp. 29, 356 says at best an imperfect right. *Contra*, Moore, *op. cit.*, p. 131.

[4] Leval, *op. cit.*, p. 16.

[5] See Lauterpacht, 'Allegiance, Diplomatic Protection and Criminal Jurisdiction over Aliens', *C.L.J.*, Vol. IX (1947), p. 330, an article reviewing the general problem in the light of the Joyce Case. Also Glanville Williams, *C.L.J.*, Vol. X (1948), p. 54.

[6] See *ante*, p. 95.

[7] The right of diplomatic protection is certainly the right of the state: see Borchard, *op. cit.*, ss. 371–8; Freeman, *The International Responsibility for Denial of Justice* (1938), pp. 456–96; Lipstein, *BYBIL*, Vol. XXII (1945), pp. 130–45; Moore, *Dig.*, Vol. VI, p. 294; see also the *Mavrommatis Concession Case*, P.C.I.J., Series A, No. 2, p. 11.

were almost always free from interference in the internal political affairs or administration of the country,[1] considerations of national honour, political prestige and economic advancement have confused the issue. Clearly, in so far as the state taking measures of protection is motivated by factors other than the need for protection they cease to be within the concept of self-defence. For acts which have as their real object the infringement of the territorial integrity or political independence of the state cannot be termed acts of self-defence against that state.

The practice of the U.S. affords the greatest source of instances of action in protection of the lives and property of citizens. In a Memorandum published in 1912 by Mr. Clarke, Solicitor for the Department of State, we find the statement that:

> . . . no nation, it would seem, has with more frequency than this government used its military forces for the purpose of occupying temporarily parts of foreign countries in order to secure adequate safety and protection for its citizens and property.[2]

In fact, from 1813 to 1899, U.S. military forces were employed on at least 46 occasions to protect American citizens abroad,[3] and between 1900 and 1927 on at least 24 occasions.[4] On many of these occasions the acknowledged basis of the U.S. action was the necessity to protect life and property, a duty which the territorial state either denied or found impossible to fulfil.

After the intervention of the U.S. in Cuba, during the revolution of 1895–8, President McKinley in his special message of April 11th, 1898, justified the intervention on the ground that, *inter alia*,

> We owe it to our citizens in Cuba to afford them that protection and indemnity for life and property which no government there can or will afford, and to that end to terminate the conditions that deprive them of legal protection.[5]

---

[1] Borchard, *op. cit.*, p. 448.

[2] Right to Protect Citizens in foreign countries by landing forces, 1912 (revised ed., 1929), p. 33; for a list of interventions in chronological order see p. 34.1(*a*) and in co-operation with the forces of other powers, p. 37(7). This Memorandum is a partial justification of the use of armed force by the U.S. Executive without the sanction of Congress needed for a declaration of war under Art. 1, s. 8, para. 11, of the Constitution.

[3] Milton Offutt, *Protection of Citizens Abroad by the Armed Forces of the U.S.* (1928), chs. II, III.

[4] Ibid., ch. IV. For an account of the Greytown incident in 1854 see Moore, *Dig.*, Vol. II, pp. 414–18; Hindmarsh, *op. cit.*, p. 78; Stowell, *op. cit.*, pp. 39–43.

[5] Hyde, Vol. I, p. 259.

Again in Haiti, in 1915, although in this case a prominent American author has found it 'extremely difficult to reach an unbiased conclusion concerning the propriety of acts committed on behalf of the U.S. in Haiti in 1915',[1] one ground of intervention was the imminent danger to American lives and property.[2] Moreover, Secretary Lansing on that occasion specifically stated that in so acting the U.S. 'has no design upon the political or territorial integrity of Haiti'.[3]

It is interesting to note that on only one occasion has the U.S. government refused its approval of the decision of a local commander to use armed force to protect U.S. citizens abroad.[4] The Regulations for the Government of the Navy of the U.S., under which action has been taken on many occasions, are of interest in so far as they set out the basis upon which intervention is justified in these terms:

> The right of self-preservation, however, is a right that belongs to states as well as to individuals, and it includes the protection of the state, its honour, and its possessions, and the lives and property of its citizens against arbitrary violence, actual or impending, whereby the state or its citizens may suffer irreparable injury. . . . It (the use of force in time of peace[5]) must be used only as a last resort, and then only to the extent which is absolutely necessary to accomplish the end required. It can never be exercised with a view to inflicting punishment for acts already committed.[6]

It is believed that this accurately states the conditions upon which the right of self-defence may be exercised in the protection of nationals and their property, the question of the protection of the 'honour' of the state apart. For in these terms protection is seen as an exceptional measure, available as a last resort to prevent irreparable injury, and never as an act of reprisal for acts already committed.

It is on this basis that we must disagree with the examination by Borchard of the purposes for which troops may be landed, at least in so far as we attempt to bring these purposes within the

[1] Hyde, Vol. I, p. 261. [2] Ibid., p. 261.

[3] Report of Senate Investigating Committee, Senate Docs. No. 794, p. 315.

[4] Offutt, *op. cit.*, pp. 8, 14. The occasion was that of Commodore Porter's landing in Porto Rico in 1824.

[5] Brackets mine.

[6] 1913, para. 1647. Cited in Hindmarsh, *op. cit.*, p. 76.

concept of self-defence.[1] Of these five purposes only the first, and possibly the third, meet the conditions set out in the U.S. Naval Regulation quoted above. Again, for the same reasons, we must exclude from the concept of self-defence the many acts of reprisals which states have taken in the past. The action of Italy in bombarding Corfu in 1923,[2] of France in bombarding Damascus in 1925,[3] and the joint occupation of Vera Cruz by the naval forces of Great Britain, France, and Spain in 1861 are illustrations of reprisals of this sort. All these measures had the character, at least in intention, of sanctions for an injury already suffered; the essence of action in self-defence is that it should be a measure of protection, not punishment, against an injury which is actual or imminent. By these tests it is possible to distinguish self-defence in the protection of nationals from measures of reprisals and also from intervention in the accepted sense, both of which may, as we have seen, be no longer legal under the Charter. The present tendency is to distinguish self-defence from intervention. Certainly such action as we have been considering in this chapter was specifically reserved from the prohibition of intervention by the Havana Conference of 1928, when Mr. Hughes, U.S. delegate, said:

> What are we to do when government breaks down and American citizens are in danger of their lives? . . . Now it is a principle of international law that in such a case a government is fully justified in taking

---

[1] *Op. cit.*, p. 449. These purposes are:

(*a*) for the simple protection of American citizens in disturbed localities,
(*b*) for the punishment of natives for the murder or injury of American citizens in semi-civilized or backward countries,
(*c*) for the suppression of local riots and the restoration and preservation of order,
(*d*) for the collection of indemnities, either with or without the delivery of a previous ultimatum,
(*e*) for the seizure of customs-houses, as security for the payment of claims.

It should be admitted, in fairness to Borchard, that these are stated as purposes for which force *has* been used, relying on the Solicitor's Memorandum cited above.

[2] See Colbert, *Retaliation in International Law*, pp. 81–7, Off. Journal of League, 1923, see pp. 1276 *et seq.*, 1412 *et seq.*, Toynbee, *Survey of International Affairs*, 1920–3, 1925, p. 349, for a brief statement of the facts; Hindmarsh, *op. cit.*, pp. 79–81.

[3] See Quincy Wright, 'The Bombardment of Damascus', *A.J.*, Vol. 20 (1926), pp. 264–74.

action—I would call it interposition of a temporary character for the purpose of protecting the lives and property of nationals. I could say that that is not intervention. One can read in text books that that is not intervention.[1]

There are, of course, instances of the use of force in the protection of the lives and property of nationals to be found in the practice of other states.[2] The Don Pacifico Incident in 1850, in which Great Britain laid an embargo on all Greek merchant vessels in Greek ports to secure the protection of the rights of a British subject (the right in this case being one to compensation for damage done by rioters) is an extremely controversial instance.[3] It is doubtful whether Great Britain would be prepared legally to maintain the same position today. Recent examples of the use of force in the protection of the lives and property of nationals are found in the claims of both the Arab states and Israel to justify military operations outside the territory subject to their jurisdiction. In reply to a questionnaire drafted by the Security Council in 1948, the Arab states gave this as one reason, *inter alia*, justifying such action; Israel similarly stated that its own action was 'in order to protect the Jewish population, traffic and economic life, including the protection of those Jewish settlements where . . . that life and property are in imminent danger'.[4] There was, so far as can be ascertained, no categorical ruling by the Security Council that these claims were inconsistent with the right of self-defence recognized by the Charter.

A substantial problem is whether the protection of the property of nationals, as opposed to their lives, can ever be said to be self-defence. The problem is really two-fold; firstly does the right of

[1] Report of the Delegates of the U.S. to the Sixth International Conference of American States, Washington, 1928, pp. 14–15. Cited in Hyde, Vol. I, p. 252.

[2] See Memorandum of Mr. Clarke, Right to Protect Citizens in Foreign Countries by Landing Forces, 1912, p. 37(7) for list of cases involving co-operation between U.S. and other powers. See also Sicilian Sulphur Monopolies, 1836; cancellation resulting in loss to British subjects and subsequent threat of naval blockade by H.M. government; State Papers, Vol. 28 (1839–40), pp. 1163–42; Vol. 29 (1840–1), pp. 175–204; Vol. 30, pp. 111–20.

[3] See Colbert, *Retaliation in International Law* (1948), p. 70; also Hansard, Parl. Debates, 3rd Series, Vol. 112, p. 382, for an admission by Palmerston of a denial of justice as a condition precedent to this form of coercion.

[4] Questionnaire adopted by S.C. at 295th Meeting, 1948 (S/753). For the replies see the Arab statements at 301st Meeting, May 22nd, 1948; Off. Rec. S.C., 3rd Year, p. 7, and the Israeli statement, ibid., p. 10.

self-defence cover the defence of property of nationals at all, and secondly if it does, then in what circumstances and in respect of what sorts of property? As to the first, it will readily be appreciated from previous illustrations in this chapter that the right of self-defence has in the past been invoked to comprise the defence of property. In fact a number of states undertook certain limitations on the use of force for the recovery of contract debts in the Hague Convention of 1907.[1] This apart, states have always asserted their right to protect their nationals' property, and for this reason the Drago doctrine[2] has never been admitted as part of general international law. However, the term property is currently used in international law as co-extensive with any type of right or interest in property—it has become in practice largely synonymous with foreign investments.[3] It is submitted that protection in the sense of the use of military force or the threat of such use can rarely, if at all, be extended to the property rights of nationals abroad. This is not to imply that other forms of protection by way of diplomatic protest or the taking up of the national's claim before an international tribunal are prohibited. What is suggested is that an actual or threatened injury to property can seldom meet the requirement that it may injure the security of the state. Perhaps this is somewhat more realistic than making a complete distinction between persons and property. In the Definition of Aggression drafted by the Security Committee (Litvinoff Committee) of the Political Commission of the Disarmament Conference of May 24th, 1933,[4] the Annex stated that no act of aggression could

[1] See Scott, J., *The Hague Conventions and Declarations of* 1899 *and* 1907 (1915), p. 89.

[2] First advanced in a Note of December 29th, 1902, to the Argentine Minister at Washington on the occasion of the joint intervention of G.B., Italy and Germany against Venezuela. In brief, his position was that 'the public debt cannot occasion armed intervention, nor even the actual occupation of the territory of American nations by a European power'. See For. Rel., 1903, pp. 1–5 for full text. The appeal to the Monroe Doctrine and thereby the support of the U.S. is obvious. For authorities in support see fn. 34 of Hershey's article in *A.J.*, Vol. I (1907), p. 37.

[3] Schwarzenberger, 'The Protection of British Property Abroad', *Current Legal Problems*, 1952, p. 296. See also Art. 78 (9a) of the Italian Peace Treaty for a similarly wide definition; Cmd. 7481, 1948. See Friedmann, *Expropriation in International Law* (1953), p. 145.

[4] League of Nations Conference for the Reduction and Limitation of Armaments, Docs. Vol. II, p. 679, at pp. 683–4. The relevant texts are given in U.N. Doc. A/2211, October 3rd, 1952.

be justified by any of a number of circumstances, including 'the violation or the danger of violation of the moral or material rights or interests of a foreign state or its nationals'. This would appear to suggest that the protection of the moral or material rights of nationals, as opposed to their lives, would not fall within the limits of self-defence as permitted by the proposed Act relating to the Definition of the Aggressor. It is a wider view of the limits of self-defence than that advocated in the proposals of the U.S.S.R. delegation that justification for attack cannot be found in 'possible danger to life or property of foreign residents' in that it concedes the right to protect the lives of nationals. On the other hand it may be narrower in that the U.S.S.R. delegation's proposals reject 'possible danger' as a sufficient cause but do not eliminate *actual* danger. The real criticism of the Committee's view lies, in our submission, in the making of an arbitrary distinction between lives and property. Moreover, in so far as it implies that the protection of the lives of nationals can never be part of the right of self-defence, it is clearly not accepted by all states. Fitzmaurice, the United Kingdom delegate to the Sixth Committee of the General Assembly in 1952 stated, *à propos* the recent Soviet proposal defining aggression in similar terms to the 1933 definition and similarly excluding mistreatment of foreigners as a justification for action otherwise defined as aggression, that:

> . . . by mistreating foreigners on its own territory, a State committed an act of aggression against the country of which the foreigners were nationals: and in defending itself, the State concerned was exercising its right of self-defence.[1]

The second problem, then, is one which must be posed if we reject the distinction between the lives and the property of nationals as artificial. It is submitted that the principle is correctly stated in this way: the right of protection extends to those cases where the interests of the nationals endangered, whether they be interests in personal safety or in property, are essential in the sense that their destruction involves an irremedial and serious injury directly to the nationals involved, and indirectly to the state affording them protection. In many cases the injury to property rights is capable of being satisfactorily met by compensation from the territorial state; breaches of contracts or concessions, whether

[1] Off. Rec. G.A., Sixth Committee, Sixth Session, 292nd Meeting.

by private persons or by public authorities, are normally of this nature. Only in the most limited category of property rights, normally where the property is of a physical nature, corporeal in the true sense, and of an especial value due to intrinsic worth or uniqueness, would the injury be irremedial in this sense. The conclusion is, therefore, that the protection of property within the concept of self-defence will only be justified when the property is really endangered and the destruction of the property cannot be met by *restitutio in integrum* or adequate compensation.

Recently the problem was posed by the Iranian Nationalization Laws of 1951[1] directed at the expropriation of the property of the Anglo-Iranian Oil Company, a British company, in breach of concessionary rights. The question which arose, and which was posed to the Foreign Secretary of the United Kingdom, Mr. Morrison, in the House of Commons, was whether the U.K. was in a position to protect the lives of British subjects in Iran, and also to protect the oil installations belonging to the A.I.O.C. from seizure or sabotage. Mr. Morrison replied that 'the Government certainly take the view that we have every right, and indeed the duty, to protect British lives'.[2] In fact a cruiser was despatched to Abadan, later supported by seven other vessels,[3] and the debates show exactly how narrowly the decision to avoid the use of force was avoided. The omission by Mr. Morrison to reply to the question in identical terms, that is to say to include the right to protect property, may well be significant. It may, however, possibly be explained on the assumption not that the U.K. had no right to protect British property by the use of force, but that the injury to the property of the A.I.O.C. was neither irremedial nor irrevocable.

[1] Law of March 15th, 1951, supplemented by a law of May 1st, 1951. See Friedmann, *op. cit.*, pp. 154–5. Schwarzenberger, *op. cit.*, p. 308. Cheng, *The Anglo-Iranian Dispute*, 1951, Vol. V, *World Affairs*, p. 387. Frankel, 'The Anglo-Iranian Dispute', 1952, *Year Book of World Affairs*, Vol. VI, p. 56. Ford, *The Anglo-Iranian Oil Dispute* 1951–2 (1954). And see Waldock, 'The Regulation of the Use of Force by Individual States in International Law', *R.C.*, 1952 (11), at p. 503, who rightly rejects the artificial distinction between persons and property and suggests self-defence would have justified the landing of troops had British lives been in danger without, however, excluding the right to similarly protect certain types of property.

[2] Hansard, Parl. Debates (H.C.), Vol. 488, p. 43. See also Vol. 491, p. 995, for the statement by Churchill that 'if violence is offered to them we must not hesitate to intervene if necessary by force'.

[3] Ibid., Vol. 489, col. 491, p. 1010.

An even more recent example from British state practice of the view that the use of force in the protection of the lives and property of nationals is to be justified in self-defence is to be found in the statements made in Parliament by government spokesmen on the intervention in Egypt in October, 1956.[1] The Lord Chancellor stated on November 1st:

> . . . we have three good grounds for intervention: the danger to our nationals, for example, those at Ismalia; the danger to shipping in the canal . . .; and the danger to the enormously valuable installations in the canal itself . . .[2]

Mr. Butler, the Leader of the House, stated on the same day that 'there is no doubt that our action is in accordance with customary international law and Art. 51 of the Charter'.[3] The defect of this argument lay not in the principle it assumed, but in the application of the principle to the facts.[4] There was, prior to the intervention of United Kingdom and French forces, no evidence that the Egyptian government had failed to protect foreign nationals from acts of violence. Moreover, the action taken involved the use of force not against the Israeli forces which, by their advance, threatened to bring hostilities to the Canal Zone, but solely against Egypt.

In conclusion, therefore, it is submitted that, in the absence of international guarantees of the protection of the lives and property of aliens, the state may exercise its right of self-defence to protect the lives, and in exceptional cases the property, of its subjects. For,

> . . . the price of inviolability of any territory is the maintenance of justice therein. Accordingly, when that price is not paid in relation to foreign life and property, the landing of forces for their protection is to be anticipated.[5]

It is inevitable that this exercise of the right of self-defence, being initially based on a subjective evaluation of the interests to

[1] *Ante*, pp. 15–16.

[2] Speech in House of Lords, *Manchester Guardian*, November 2nd, 1956.

[3] Speech in House of Commons, ibid.; see also speech of the Foreign Secretary in the House on October 31st, *Manchester Guardian*, November 1st.

[4] Thus Lord McNair, former President of the I.C.J., whilst admitting the principle in a speech in the House of Lords (Parl. Debates (H.L.), September 12th, col. 661), condemned the action taken as illegal: letter to *The Times*, November 6th, 1956.

[5] Hyde, Vol. I, p. 649. See also Potter, *op. cit.*, R.C., 1930 (II), p. 648.

be protected, should be subject to the abuses so often involved in an individual measure for the protection of rights. The likelihood of such a measure becoming a mere cloak for intervention needs no stress; such is the inherent danger of 'diplomacy of the quarter-deck'.[1] The fear which lies behind a refusal to recognize the defence of nationals abroad as within the concept of self-defence is that this recognition would permit large-scale intervention totally unrelated to the danger to which the nationals are exposed. This cannot be so if the requirement of proportionality is complied with, and this requirement is essentially part of the lawful exercise of a right of self-defence. Moreover, since the exercise of the right depends upon the international legal system it must be capable of evaluation in the light of the standards imposed by that system. This is particularly so where the right to resort to these extreme forms of protection is dependent upon a prior breach of the standards of state responsibility imposed by that same system. If the question of breach is capable of being objectively determined, then the reaction to that breach must equally be so. Any state invoking the right of self-defence must be prepared to justify the measures it takes in pursuance of that right before an impartial international tribunal.

[1] Chester, 'Diplomacy of the Quarter Deck', *A.J.*, Vol. 8 (1914), p. 443.

CHAPTER VI

THE DEFENCE OF ECONOMIC INTERESTS

We have indicated previously that in practice the interest which a state may have in the safe preservation of the national economy, of its essential economic interests, may be equally as great as its interest in safeguarding its territory, its political independence, or its people. Indeed, states have become increasingly aware of their vulnerability to 'economic aggression', a term used as early as 1916 by the British delegation at the Paris Conference in drafting a resolution calling for joint action after the war by the Allies to protect their economic interests against German 'economic aggression' by 'necessary measures in self-defence'.[1] Since the Charter an increasing concern has been evident about the question of economic aggression and the very real possibility of a political independence becoming valueless if unaccompanied by some kind of economic independence. The original Brazilian proposal at San Francisco to extend the terms of Art. 2(4) to include 'economic' force was rejected,[2] but there are cases in which states have complained to the Security Council of various forms of economic aggression.[3] More recently the problem has achieved prominence in relation to the task of defining aggression; the view has been taken that a definition should comprehend forms of indirect aggression, including economic aggression. The Bolivian draft definition submitted to the Sixth Committee of the General Assembly on January 11th, 1952,[4] stated:

[1] Parl. Debates (H.C.), August 2nd, 1916, Vol. 85, col. 341.

[2] *UNCIO*, Docs. VI, pp. 339–40.

[3] See complaint of Hyderabad in cable to the Secretary-General, August 21st, 1948 (S/986), containing a charge against India that it had exposed Hyderabad to (*inter alia*) a crippling economic blockade 'intended to coerce it into a renunciation of its independence'. Also the Jewish Agency's justification for operations by its armed forces outside the territory subject to its control as necessary to protect Jewish 'traffic and economic life' from Arab aggression; S.C. Off. Rec., 3rd Year, 301st Meeting, p. 10, May 22nd, 1948.

[4] A/C.6/L.211, cited in Report by the Secretary-General on the Question of Defining Aggression, A/2211, October 3rd, 1952, at p. 58. See also the views of representatives of China, Indonesia, Netherlands, Pakistan and Yugoslavia during the 278th–295th Meetings, January 5th and 22nd, 1952, in the Sixth Committee.

> Also to be considered as an act of aggression shall be . . . unilateral action to deprive a state of the economic resources derived from the fair practice of international trade, or to endanger its basic economy, thus jeopardizing the security of that state or rendering it incapable of acting in its own defence and co-operating in the collective defence of peace.

This view reflects the principle found in Art. 15 of the Bogota Charter of 1948[1] which phrases the duty of non-intervention widely enough to include intervention directed against the internal economy of a state.

> No state . . . has the right to intervene . . . the foregoing principle prohibits not only armed force but also any other form of interference or attempted threat against the personality of the state or against its political, economic, and cultural elements.

The question arises, relevant to the concept of self-defence, as to whether or not there exists as a counterpart to this 'economic aggression' a right of self-defence in respect of a state's economic interests. In our submission there is logically no reason why such a right should not be admitted; the fact that it is not generally recognized as part of the concept of self-defence is attributable to two factors. Firstly there is no duty of non-intervention which, as a parallel to the duty of non-intervention relating to political independence or territorial integrity, generally prohibits action by states detrimental to the economy of another state. Therefore, in the absence of conduct of a delictual character, there can be no violation of a state's legal rights which calls for the exercise of self-defence. This position does not arise logically, from the nature of things, but from the fact that international law has as yet little economic 'content'; the sphere of international economic law is exceedingly restricted,[2] although there is no inherent reason why it should not contain rules as comprehensive as those governing state conduct in the political field. Admittedly there are certain duties based upon treaty, and it could be argued that to the extent that such duties exist the delictual character of state conduct in breach of those treaties can be established, and therefore

[1] Pan-American Union, Law and Treaty Series, No. 23 (Washington, 1948), p. 27. And see also Art. 4, Draft Declaration on the Rights and Duties of States, A/CN.4/2, December 15th, 1948, which includes the right to 'develop materially'.

[2] See Schwarzenberger, 'The Province and Standards of International Economic Law', *I.L.Q.*, Vol. 2 (1948), p. 402; Alexandrowicz, *International Economic Organizations*, (1952), ch. XIV.

self-defence is available as a reaction to that breach. On this argument one can formulate something akin to a duty to protect another state's monetary system,[1] a duty which has found expression in the International Convention for the Suppression of Counterfeiting of Currency,[2] in the provisions of the General Agreement on Tariffs and Trade,[3] the Articles of Agreement of the International Monetary Fund,[4] the Convention for European Economic Co-operation,[5] and bilateral agreements of a similar pattern which restrict the freedom to manipulate exchange values and which check depreciation by one state to the detriment of another.[6] One can also formulate a limited duty of non-discrimination, the corollary of what might be called a 'right to trade'.[7] It has been suggested that the principle of non-discrimination 'belongs to positive international law (and) may be considered to be the fountain-head of obligations in the same way as the general principles of international law create obligations between states'.[8] The preferable, and more accurate, view is expressed by Wilson thus:

> Traditionally, whilst agreeing upon freedom of the seas to commerce carriers in time of peace, states have claimed the right, without

---

[1] Mann, *The Legal Aspect of Money*, 2nd ed., p. 435, regards this duty as based solely on treaty and not on customary law. But see Nussbaum, *Money in the Law* (1939), p. 33, referring to the many penal codes making counterfeiting of foreign currency illegal. In *U.S.* v. *Arjona*, 120 U.S. 479 (1887), the view was taken that a duty existed to enact such provisions; see also *Emperor of Austria* v. *Day* (1861), 3 De G.F. & J., 217. But see the *Serbian and Brazilian Loans Case*, P.C.I.J., Ser. A, Nos. 20–1, at p. 44, for the view that, treaty obligations apart, the manipulation of a state's currency is entirely a matter within its domestic jurisdiction.

[2] Hudson, *International Legislation*, Vol. IV, p. 2692.

[3] U.N. Treaty Series, Vol. 55, p. 187.

[4] U.N. Treaty Series, Vol. 20, p. 41, especially Arts. 4 and 8; the latter provides 'No member of the I.M.F. shall engage in or permit its fiscal agencies to engage in any discriminatory currency arrangements or multiple currency practices except as authorized by the Agreement or approved by the Fund' (s. 3).

[5] Text in *A.J.*, Supp., Vol. 43 (1949), p. 94, especially Art. 7.

[6] For a list of such agreements to which the U.K. is a party see Mann, *op. cit.*, pp. 429, 352, fn. 2.

[7] Such a right is maintained, as an 'imperfect' right, by many classical writers. Victoria, *De Indis Novis Inventis*, Sec. III, titles 1–7; Grotius, *Mare Liberum*, ch. VIII; Gentili, *De Jure Belli*, Libri Tres, Bk. I, ch. XIX; Vattel, *Le Droit des Gens*, Bk. II, ch. II, paras. 23–5.

[8] Van Essen, *Nederlands Tijdschrift Voor Int. Recht*, Vol. 1 (1953–4), p. 417.

infringing international law, to withhold commercial advantages to foreign nationals, vessels and goods. The granting of trading privileges and advantages has, in general, come through treaties, principally bilateral ones.[1]

Many such bilateral treaties do exist, incorporating the Most Favoured Nation Clause, and now the duty of non-discrimination has become the crux of the multilateral General Agreement on Tariffs and Trade.[2] It might also be possible, within the limits of treaties like the General Agreement on Tariffs and Trade, or the treaty constituting the International Union for the Protection of Industrial Property of 1883,[3] to formulate a duty not to compete unfairly. Trading practices such as dumping, subsidization and the granting of export bounties can destroy the competitive economy of a foreign state[4] and the need for the international regulation of such practices has been in part met by the General Agreement. Yet even the duties imposed under the General Agreement are modified by escape clauses which tend to destroy the normative character of these provisions and suggest a guide to policy rather than definite legal prohibitions.[5] In the main unfair competition can only be met with retorsion, with a reaction of the same legal character; it can rarely be described as delictual in the proper sense.

The second factor which tends to preclude a recognition of a right of self-defence in relation to the state's economic interests is that, as we have seen, that right is primarily important as an exception to the prohibition of the use of force. The context in which the right of self-defence has the most significance is that of

[1] Wilson, *The International Law Standard in Treaties of the U.S.* (1953), p. 87.

[2] Art. 1. See also Art. 5 providing for freedom of transit for goods and vessels, and Arts. 11–15 limiting the extent to which members may impose quantitative restrictions. Somewhat similar provisions are found in the Treaty constituting the European Coal and Steel Community, signed at Paris on April 18th, 1951; *A.J.*, Supp., Vol. 46 (1952), p. 107.

[3] Martens, N.R.G., 2nd Series, XXX, pp. 449–77. This treaty contained an obligation to assure all members of 'effective protection against unfair competition'; apparently construed as 'dishonest' competition, see Parl. Papers, Cmd. 5842 (1911), pp. 95–6.

[4] For views as to the effect of these practices on a state's economy see Viner, *Dumping, A Problem in International Trade* (1923), p. 3 *et seq.*, also p. 140; Gregory, *Tariffs, A Study in Method* (1921), p. 177 *et seq.*; Towle, *International Trade and Commercial Policy* (1947), especially ch. 21; Haberler, *Theory of International Trade*, ch. 18; Strausz-Hupé and Possony, *International Relations*, 2nd ed. (1954), ch. 21.

[5] For example, Arts. VI(5), XII(2)(*a*)(i), XIX, XX, of GATT.

force, and that context is not normally relevant to the defence of economic interests. This is so because the injurious conduct of a state against which measures necessary to protect the national economy must be taken will rarely involve the use or threat of force; when it does, then it would invariably violate one or other of the substantive rights previously examined, the right to political independence or territorial integrity for example, and self-defence would be invoked in the defence of those rights rather than in the defence of economic rights. Moreover, not only will the delict not involve force or the threat of force, but the requirement that self-defence shall be proportionate will generally mean that the reaction to the delict, the measures in self-defence, cannot lawfully involve force. This need not be so inevitably; we may recall the United Kingdom comment on Art. 4 of the Draft Declaration on the Rights and Duties of States[1] to the effect that there may be exceptions to the duty of non-intervention where a state is 'pursuing a course which leads to the economic strangulation of another state'. However, the cases in which self-defence would justify the use of force against a delict not involving force would be extremely rare; the defending state would be put to the most stringent proof as to the necessity of the case, the proportionate nature of the reaction, and the lack of alternative means of protection.[2] Delictual conduct *per se* does not warrant the exercise of self-defence, nor can every illegality be deemed to be aggression against which a state may use force to defend its rights. As Fitzmaurice, the United Kingdom delegate in the Sixth Committee of the General Assembly, stated in 1952:

> If all aggression was in fact illegal, every illegality was not aggression. It was not desirable to brand certain minor illegalities as acts of aggression. Such definitions might even mention as 'aggression' some acts which were not illegal. There was a danger of that kind in the Bolivian draft resolution which dealt with economic aggression in vague terms.[3]

---

[1] A/CN.4/2, December 15th, 1948.

[2] See the refusal of the Assembly of the League to recognize the military action by Japan against China in 1931 as legitimate self-defence against the Chinese boycott of Japanese commerce. Report adopted by the Assembly February 24th, 1932: cited in Théry, *Notion d'Agression*, pp. 211–12. See also Lauterpacht, 'Boycott in International Relations', *BYBIL*, Vol. 14 (1933), p. 125.

[3] Off. Rec. G.A. Sixth Session, Sixth Committee, 292nd Meeting, paras. 47 & 48.

The field in which the right of self-defence can apply to those measures of protection which a state takes to protect its economy is, therefore, necessarily limited. It can only apply where the injurious conduct is delictual in character, and will rarely, if ever, justify measures involving the use of force. This does not, however, exclude its application to the defence of economic rights entirely, for, assuming the existence of a threat to those rights which is delictual, there may still be room for the application of the right of self-defence in those circumstances in which a state claims to justify action not involving force but *prima facie* illegal.

For example, a state may on grounds of self-defence justify discrimination against the products of another state despite a duty of non-discrimination assumed towards that state under treaty. In the *Oscar Chinn Case*[1] Belgium adduced an argument closely allied to this. Belgium was bound to treat Great Britain and her nationals on a basis of 'commercial equality' by Art. 1 of the Convention of Saint-Germain of 1919. Although the Belgian contention which succeeded before the Court was that their protective measures were in fact not inconsistent with this obligation, the alternative argument, brought lest a breach was proved, was that:

> The measures which it adopted became necessary in order to safeguard the interests of the community as a consequence of the position of colonial products in the markets of the world.[2]

The resemblance of this plea to one of self-defence is close. Again the problem may arise in the claim of a state to maintain anti-dumping measures, or anti-bounty measures, despite an obligation of non-discrimination contained in the Most Favoured Nation clause of a treaty,[3] or even in a claim to suspend or terminate a treaty obligation owed to a state whose delictual conduct imperils the state's economy. Here the argument begins to resemble that behind the *clausula rebus sic stantibus* doctrine which allows termination in circumstances which 'threaten or cause the sacrifice of a state's development, or its vital requirements for

[1] P.C.I.J. Series A/B., No. 63, Judgment, December 12th, 1934.

[2] Hudson's World Court Reports, Vol. 3, p. 439.

[3] See Schwarzenberger, 'The M.F.N. Standard in British State Practice', *BYBIL*, Vol. 22 (1945), p. 96, at p. 114 *et seq.*, where he argues that the basis of the claim to derogate is estoppel. Viner, *op. cit.*, pp. 316–17, prefers the basis of *volenti non fit injuria*. See also Hornbeck, 'The M.F.N. clause in Commercial Treaties', Bulletin of the University of Wisconsin, VI (1910), p. 73, cited Viner, *op. cit.*, p. 318.

political or economic existence, or . . . are inconsistent with the right of self-preservation'.[1] It is, however, a distinct argument, for, whereas the right of self-defence would only be applicable where the termination or suspension was a reaction against a delict, the fundamental change of conditions essential to the doctrine of *rebus sic stantibus* does not necessarily presuppose a delict in the other contractual party. It is also an argument distinct from that behind retorsions, for there the conduct is not delictual. It is, furthermore, distinct from reprisals, for the measures taken in self-defence would have to be appropriate for the protection of the very interests threatened, and directed specifically to that end; they could not, as with reprisals, take on a punitive or retaliatory character.

A noticeable feature of recent economic treaties is the manner in which they specifically recognize and regulate the right to take measures *prima facie* inconsistent with the main obligations assumed under the treaty, when necessary to protect a state's economy. In a sense these provisions are analogous to Art. 51 of the U.N. Charter and, indeed, the recognition of something akin to a right of 'economic self-defence' seems inevitable in a system which aims at the regulation of the world economy but which can only achieve regulation gradually. As Alexandrowicz has said:

> It is, however, extremely unlikely that we could achieve its (the world economy's)[2] balance and its growth without permitting member states by the application of measures of economic self-defence first to restore individual equilibrium.[3]

Hence numerous qualifications, giving to members the right to take defensive measures to protect infant industries,[4] to counteract dumping,[5] to forestall a decline in monetary reserves,[6] to conserve natural resources,[7] or generally to protect their security,[8]

[1] Woolsey, 'The Unilateral Termination of Treaties', *A.J.*, Vol. 20 (1926), pp. 349–50. See also the Reports of the Law Officers of the Crown cited McNair, *Law of Treaties* (1938), pp. 236–41, particularly the Report dated March 18th, 1867. Also Tobin, *The Termination of Multilateral Treaties* (1933); Harvard Draft Law of Treaties, *A.J.*, Supp., Vol. 29 (1935), comment on Art. 28. The question of termination in wartime is rather different; as to this see *Techt* v. *Hughes* (1920), 229 N.Y. 222, at pp. 241–7.

[2] Brackets mine. [3] International Economic Organizations, 1952, p. 162.

[4] Arts. VI(5), XIX, G.A.T.T. [5] Art. VI(5), G.A.T.T.

[6] Art. XII(2) (*a*) (i) G.A.T.T.; a reservation to the general obligation to abolish quantitative restrictions.

[7] Art. XX, G.A.T.T. [8] Art. XXI, G.A.T.T.

appear in these treaties. The analogy between these provisions regulating state action in the economic field, and Art. 51 regulating state action involving the use or threat of force is not an exact one; the right to take these measures of 'economic self-defence' is not necessarily dependent on a prior breach of duty by the state against which the reserved right is exercised. It is, therefore, all the more desirable that this kind of right, more accurately described as economic 'self-preservation', should be carefully defined by the treaties and, where possible, its exercise made subject to the prior approval of an international organ.

Our conclusion is, therefore, that the right of self-defence has, due to these factors and for the reasons given, little relevance to the problem of safeguarding the state's economic rights. Admittedly the lack of a comprehensive system of duties relating to the conduct of economic policies may not be a permanent feature of international law; but even when injurious conduct can really be characterized as delictual, the rôle of self-defence will not, except in the most exceptional circumstances, be to sanction the use of force. It may, within a very limited field, find some application as a justification for other conduct which is *prima facie* illegal but which is designed solely to protect a state's economic rights against unlawful injury.[1]

This is not to imply that the term 'economic aggression' has no value; our contention is that it has little relevance in international law as a term descriptive of conduct justifying the victim state in resorting to self-defence. There is, however, no necessary reason why, for the purposes of an international executive organ like the Security Council, entrusted with responsibility for the maintenance of international peace and security, the term should not be applied to economic policies which in fact endanger international peace and security.[2] The League of Nations was not prepared to exonerate China completely from responsibility for the

[1] For illustrations of legislative measures designed to this end see Milhaud, 'L'Organisation économique de la Paix', *R.C.*, 1926 (V), p. 281, at p. 323 *et seq.*; also Patterson, 'Les Bases économique de la Paix', *R.C.*, 1931 (III), p. 419 *et seq.* See also Alexandrowicz, *op. cit.*, p. 162, justifying measures 'of economic self-defence . . . to restore individual equilibrium'.

[2] See the view of the Egyptian delegate, Mr. Moussa, in the Sixth Committee; referring to a breach of the obligation of economic co-operation he said, 'If the breach became very serious and developed into a threat to the peace, any State could always complain to the Security Council', 291st Meeting, para. 9.

conflict between herself and Japan which Japan justified as measures of self-defence against the Chinese boycott of Japanese goods,[1] and the position may arise in the future in which economic policies will constitute a 'threat to the peace' within the terms of Art. 39 of the United Nations Charter. It does not appear that at present states are prepared to concede so extensive an interpretation of the concept of aggression, but the possibility of this becoming desirable in the future cannot be excluded. Moreover, there is not, with an international executive organ, the same need for confining the right to take enforcement action to cases where the delictual conduct of a state involves the use or threat of force as there is for confining the right of the individual state to use force in self-defence to those cases. Whether, as a matter of policy, it is advisable to define aggression for the purposes of an international executive organ widely enough to include economic aggression is a question beyond the scope of the present work.

[1] See *ante*, p. 32.

PART TWO

THE ANTITHESIS OF THE RIGHT OF SELF-DEFENCE AND THE 'RIGHT' OF WAR

CHAPTER VII

SELF-DEFENCE AND WAR

THE preceding chapters have been concerned with an analysis of those substantive rights which the state may protect by the use or threat of force in self-defence: the privilege of self-defence operates as a justification for action which would otherwise be illegal. Confining the analysis to the law of peace, this provided a coherent explanation of a privilege invoked for the protection of certain rights which were established as rights *stricto sensu* by the correlative duties imposed on states, such as the duty of non-intervention. State practice, particularly in the nineteenth century, abounded with illustrations of the use of force in self-defence which remained susceptible to analysis within the law of peace,[1] for the reason that the state against which the force was directed chose to regard the action in self-defence as 'pacific' in character. Certainly this had advantages,[2] for the normal system of inter-state relations was not ruptured by a condition of war *de jure*, and the attitude of third states, to whom the status of neutrals might prove inconvenient, often determined the 'pacific' character of the action by bringing pressure to bear on the participants.

However, though the factual conditions which such a 'pacific' exercise of the right of self-defence brought about might well be indistinguishable from those in which war *de jure* existed,[3] the legal character of self-defence on the one hand and war *de jure* on the other were, under the positivist doctrine of the nineteenth century, entirely dissimilar.

Self-defence existed only as a privilege justifying action otherwise illegal, and the purpose of the privilege was the protection of certain rights *stricto sensu*. The condition precedent to the lawful exercise of the privilege was the breach of those established duties correlative to those rights, and there were legally recognized

[1] Hindmarsh, *Force in Peace* (1933), p. 38. And see *ante*, ch. II, p. 39.

[2] See Colbert, *Retaliation in International Law* (1948), p. 98, who puts forward the mutual advantages of this relationship. Also Hogan, *Pacific Blockade*, pp. 12–13; Borchard, *Diplomatic Protection*, p. 450.

[3] Wilson, *A.J.*, Vol. 26 (1932), p. 327, Editorial Comment; and see Fenwick, 'Intervention: Individual and Collective', *A.J.*, Vol. 39 (1945), p. 647.

limitations on the privilege: for example, the limitation that the force used should be proportionate, and that it should not go beyond what was necessary to secure the protection of those rights. In contrast war, or rather the state's freedom to go to war, was not dependent on any prior breach of a duty by the victim state. Once undertaken, the aim of complete subjugation of the victim was apparently permissible, and the reaction of the victim was legally indistinguishable from the attack of the 'aggressor'. Once war *de jure* existed the two states engaged in action of a like kind. In war the duty of non-intervention disappeared, the substantive rights upon which self-defence depended were non-existent, and the 'right' of self-defence became meaningless. Indeed, it became somewhat pointless to invoke a right of self-defence, curtailed by legal rules, when it was permissible to resort to war and use the same or a greater degree of force without any kind of legal restriction.

The paradox of the positivist doctrine was that any state, by its own election to treat a 'pacific' use of force in self-defence as an act of war bringing about war *de jure*, could transform the legal privilege of self-defence into conduct legally indistinguishable from its own. This arose directly from a system in which war could begin

> . . . upon the commission of an act of force under the authority of a state, which is done *animo belligerendi*, or which, being done *sine animo belligerendi* but by way of reprisals or intervention, the other state elects to regard as creating a state of war either by repelling force by force, or in some other way. . . .[1]

The same equivocal position was enjoyed by the right of intervention,[2] of which, according to some writers,[3] self-defence forms a 'justifiable' part. Hall, writing from the positivist standpoint, admitted this in saying that 'regarded from the point of view of the state intruded upon it must always remain an act which, if not consented to, is an act of war', whilst from the point of view of the intruding state it may well be 'a measure . . . for the express

[1] McNair, 'The Legal Meaning of War', *Trans. Grotius Soc.*, Vol. XI (1926), p. 36. See ibid., pp. 31–4, for a collection of views and definitions.

[2] See Winfield, 'The History of Intervention in International Law', *BYBIL*, Vol. II (1922–3), p. 131, who reached the conclusion that 'there appears to be no distinction between forcible intervention and war'.

[3] See *ante*, p. 53.

purpose of avoiding war'.[1] The 'right' of a state to go to war, a 'right' only so-called by a travesty of legal terminology, made nonsense of the legal privilege of self-defence: the essence of such a privilege is the absence of any right to resist the exercise of the privilege.

The positivist rejection of the concept of *bellum justum* expounded by the scholastics, and developed by Grotius on the basis of natural law,[2] meant that the positivists were forced into recognizing war as 'a circumstance beyond the power of the law to control'.[3] It became a fact, a state of affairs, recognized by international law and producing certain legal consequences, but in itself not subject to legal criteria. War possessed the dual and irreconcilable function of asserting rights under the law, the *ultima ratio legis*, and of challenging those rights without reference to the law, the *ultima ratio regis*.[4] The incompatability of a right of self-defence and the unfettered freedom to resort to war could, therefore, only be resolved by embodying within positive international law a prohibition of the freedom to resort to war and, since this could be avoided by the delinquent state refusing to declare war, to the use or threat of force. The right of self-defence could only achieve a full, juridical connotation in a legal system which could characterize every use or threat of force, whether within the technical definition of war or not, as either a delict, or self-defence, or a sanction. The only lawful use of force, other than self-defence, would be that in the nature of a sanction authorized by the community of states: and against either

[1] *International Law*, 8th ed., Pearce-Higgins, p. 337.

[2] For a general survey of the scholastic doctrine and its development see Vanderpol, *La doctrine scholastique du droit de guerre* (1919); Rolin, *Le droit moderne de la guerre*, I, p. 144 *et seq.*; De la Brière, *L'Organisation Int. de la Papauté Souveraine*; Sturgo, *The Int. Community and the Right of War* (1929), ch. X; Von Elbe, 'The Evolution of the Concept of the Just War in International Law', *A.J.*, Vol. 33 (1939), p. 665; Wright, 'Changes in the Conception of War', *A.J.*, Vol. 18 (1924), p. 765; 'Eagleton, Attempt to define Aggression', *Int. Concil*, 1930, pp. 581–3. The concept of *bellum justum*, although variously defined, achieved its most famous definition in the Grotian trilogy of wars of defence, recaption, and punishment. *De Jure*, Bk. II, 1, II, 2: '*Plerique bellorum tres statuunt causas justas, defensionem, recuperationem rerum, et punitionem.*'

[3] Eagleton, *op. cit.*, p. 583.

[4] Fenwick, *International Law* (1924), p. 428; Oppenheim, Vol. II, 7th ed., pp. 177–8; Wright, *op. cit.*, p. 761; Westlake, *International Law*, Vol. II, p. 3; Hershey, *Essentials*, p. 545.

self-defence or a sanction the use of force would be delictual. It is to the gradual prohibition of war and the use or threat of force, and, therefore, the establishment of a coherent and juridical concept of self-defence, that we now turn.

POSITIVISM PRIOR TO THE PACT OF PARIS

The movement towards an elimination of the state's unlimited freedom to wage war by its express prohibition in positive international law signified a rejection of the concept of the *bellum justum* as a satisfactory basis for the regulation of international relations.[1] Yet this movement accepted the notion, implicit in the concept of the *bellum justum*, that no prohibition should include wars of self-defence. The Third and Seventh World Peace Congresses at Rome and Budapest in 1891 and 1896, while condemning offensive wars, recognized the right of states to defend themselves.[2] Yet this distinction between offensive and defensive wars, regarded as fundamental by the scholastics, found no echo in the typically positivist approach adopted at the Hague Conferences of 1899, 1907.[3] For, with one exception, the Conventions produced by those Conferences aimed at the provision of machinery for pacific settlement and, in the event of its failure, the imposition of certain restrictions on the manner of waging war. In accordance with state practice over the preceding two centuries, no reference was made to the legality of the war as such. Even the Third Convention of 1907, Regarding the Outbreak of Hostilities, provided only for the observance of certain formalities accompanying a declaration of war; of the right of declaring war nothing was said, the restriction being purely 'formal' in character. As Scott has said:

It must be admitted that the convention is very modest, for it leaves

---

[1] For an exhaustive collection of the treaties, both general and particular, embodying a restriction of the right to resort to war or armed force see Harvard Draft Convention on Rights and Duties in Case of Aggression, *A.J.*, Supp., Vol. 33 (1939), p. 823.

[2] Troisième Congrès Int. de la Paix, Rome, 1892, pp. 142–3; Bulletin Officiel du VII Congrès Universelle de la Paix, Berne, 1856, pp. 46–55.

[3] See generally, The Proceedings of the Hague Peace Conference, Vols. I–III (1921); Choate, *The Two Hague Conferences* (1913); Scott, *The Hague Peace Conferences of 1899 and 1907*, Vols. I and II (1909).

the Powers free to declare war at their pleasure, provided only that the pretext be capable of formulation.[1]

The one exception, apart from this purely formal limitation, was the Second Hague Convention of 1907 respecting the Limitation of the Employment of Force for the Recovery of Contract Debts, which in Art. I provided:

> The Contracting Powers agree not to have recourse to armed force for the recovery of contract debts claimed from the Government of one country by the Government of another country as being due to its nationals.[2]

Subject to certain exceptions, such as the refusal to arbitrate or, having accepted arbitration, to give effect to the award, this Convention forbade the recourse to force as a legal remedy for the enforcement of the obligations of a state in respect of contract debts. Within these admittedly narrow limits, and confined to the signatory states, we have a duty the breach of which would constitute a delict and afford to the state against which force is wrongly used the right of self-defence. It is arguable that the prohibition extends only to the recourse to force and not to the mere threat of force or, at the other extreme, war *de jure*; on this reasoning the state could avoid the qualification of its actions as delictual by the simple expedient of declaring war in accordance with the formalities of Hague Convention III of 1907. The better opinion would seem to be that the duty embraces all recourse to force, irrespective of its character as measures falling short of war or as war *de jure*.

[1] Scott, *op. cit.*, Vol. I, p. 522. The only restriction he describes as a pious hope 'that the difficulty of a perfect justification may exercise a restraining influence upon prospective belligerents': ibid., p. 519. This Convention can only refer to 'hostilities' with belligerent intent; the continuing legality of force short of war is implicit in the specific limitations of the 2nd Convention of 1907 prohibiting recourse to armed force for the recovery of contract debts. See Hindmarsh, *op. cit.*, p. 95; Théry, *Notion d'Agression* (1937), p. 22 *et seq.*

[2] Scott, *op. cit.*, Vol. II, p. 357. Text is given in *A.J.*, Vol. 2 (1908), Supp., p. 81, and see general discussion of the limitations of the provision in Hyde, *Int. Law*, Vol. II, pp. 1007–9. The especial value of this Convention can be seen in the light of the decision of the Hague Tribunal on February 22nd, 1904, which acceded to the argument that the allies, by their coercive blockade of Venezuela in 1902, were entitled to preferential treatment in respect of their claims. For the award see J. B. Scott, *Hague Court Reports*, p. 56.

The Bryan Treaties of 1914[1] later introduced an obligation on contracting states not to resort to war prior to the report of a conciliation commission, thus imposing a 'moratorium', a prohibition procedural rather than substantive in character but, in so far as war prior to a report by the commission would be delictual, affording a right of self-defence to the attacked state. The use of the term war, introducing as it did all the pitfalls of a technical definition, appears distinctly retrogressive in view of the Hague Convention II; in affording a state the opportunity of escaping the prohibition by having recourse to force without a declaration of war it introduced an error which was later to be perpetuated in the League Covenant. It might be argued that the customary interdiction of intervention sufficed to characterize as illegal most of the acts of force lacking the character of war. Whilst within limits this was true, the advantages of including within the prohibition acts of force short of war were obvious. There was an initial tendency, in this positivist era, to argue that a particular prohibition gave complete freedom outside its terms—on the dubious principle '*expressio unius est exclusio alterius*'. Furthermore in addition to the differences held as to the cases of justifiable intervention, outside the customary prohibition, these cases were by no means capable of classification under the headings of 'sanctions' or 'self-defence'. Yet, as we shall consistently maintain, the right of self-defence achieves full recognition only when all other acts of force can legally be characterized as delicts or sanctions. Against any given delict a reaction involving the use of force would be, ideally, either action backed by the authority of the international community, or else action in self-defence, taken within the narrow limits set by the law of that community and in protection of legally recognized interests.

Prior to 1915, apart from these minor prohibitions, the general freedom of the state to resort to unlimited war remained; it was impossible, as yet, to characterize force or war as being a delict, or self-defence, or a sanction.

As the Report of the Peace Conference Commission on Responsibilities of 1919 admitted, 'even a war of aggression may not be considered as an act directly contrary to positive

[1] For example see Treaty with Great Britain of September 15th, 1914, Treaty Series (1914), No. 16, Cmd. 7714. On the general pattern of these treaties see Editorial Comment in *A.J.*, Vol. 8 (1914), p. 565.

law',[1] and this despite the controversial Art. 231 of the Treaty of Versailles implying the illegality of aggressive war.[2]

The inadequacy of this position posed a problem which the League Covenant failed to solve. Art. 10[3] introduced material criteria for distinguishing between legal and illegal wars:

> The Members of the League undertake to respect and preserve as against external aggression the territorial integrity and existing political independence of all Members of the League.

This imposed upon the Council in the case of any such aggression, or threat of aggression, the duty of advising 'upon the means by which this obligation shall be fulfilled', but the elimination of the freedom of using force against the territorial integrity and political independence, contained in Arts. 12 to 15, was by no means complete. The criteria of illegality adopted in those Articles were purely formal, with the result that the Covenant introduced a distinction between permissible and prohibited wars, this dichotomy being based entirely on the question whether or not the procedures for pacific settlement laid down in the Covenant had been followed. The connection with the idea of a 'moratorium' embodied in the earlier Bryan Treaties is undeniable, and as Miller states:

> Here there is first a covenant for delay, that is, a covenant against war during arbitration or inquiry and for three months thereafter. . . . Then follows an absolute covenant against war where there is compliance with an arbitral award, and an absolute covenant against war where there is compliance with a Council recommendation.[4]

---

[1] Cited in Wright, 'The Outlawry of War', *A.J.*, Vol. 19 (1925), p. 76, at p. 84.

[2] For a rejection of this principle as part of general international law see Eagleton, *op. cit.*, p. 587. Also Wright, *op. cit.*, pp. 83–4.

[3] On the construction of this Article see Komarnicki, *La question de l'Integrité Territoriale dans le Pacte de S.D.N.* (1923); Williams, *State Security* (1927), ch. III. And on the meaning of aggression in relation to Art. X, Ray, *Commentaire*, p. 364. See also the Report of the Commission of Jurists on Article X, League Documents A 24(1), 1921, V(A.C. 26(*a*)). The Committee on Amendments recognized that 'changes may be effected . . . by various means . . .'; to which the Sub-Committee added, 'and even by war, provided that the peaceful measures laid down in the Covenant have been exhausted', cited Williams, *op. cit.*, p. 99.

[4] *The Drafting of the Covenant*, I, p. 326.

The question of illegality under the Covenant had no necessary relation to the intrinsic merits of the case, and, as Eagleton pointed out, 'under the Covenant it is even possible for a war in self-defence to be illicit'.[1] War remained possible in a number of cases which could by no means be classified as sanctions or self-defence.[2] No specific reservation of the right of self-defence appears in the Covenant, possibly because this was deemed to be superfluous; however, the opinion that 'pursuant to the Covenant, defensive war is never prohibited . . . the military defence of a country is not only a right but even a duty for a member state of the League',[3] seems to have been generally admitted, with possible reservations to the use of the term 'duty'. The right of self-defence could, however, only be stated in terms which corresponded to the specific obligations not to resort to war contained in the Covenant; in so far as the Covenant contained no general prohibition, apart from self-defence and sanctions, there could be no general right of self-defence.

Not least of the failures of the Covenant as a legal instrument was its restrictive use of the word 'war'; the restriction appears curious in view of the earlier Hague Convention II of 1907 which, as we have seen, possibly erred on the other side in confining its prohibition to 'recourse to force'. The explanation which appears most likely is that the whole approach to the Covenant was conditioned by the earlier Bryan Treaties; the similarity, not only in the use of the restrictive term 'war', but in the general principle of a 'moratorium', is striking. The problems which this particular restriction posed were clearly illustrated in the bombardment and occupation of Corfu by Italy in 1923 as a measure of reprisals, without a declaration of war; a Commission of Jurists appointed by the Council to determine whether coercive measures, lacking the character of war, were inconsistent with the Covenant produced the enigmatic reply that 'coercive measures which are not

[1] *Op. cit.*, p. 591.

[2] For an analysis of the cases in which war remained legal see Whitton, 'La Neutralité et la S.D.N.', *R.C.*, 1927 (II), pp. 478–92, and of those in which war was illegal, Eagleton, *op. cit.*, p. 586 *et seq.* Also Wehberg, *The Outlawry of War* (1931), p. 9 *et seq.*

[3] Wehberg, *op. cit.*, p. 10. To regard self-defence as a duty seems erroneous, as does the further statement that war in self-defence could only be waged 'on the demand of the League' (ibid., p. 101). A draft of the Deustche Gesellschaft für Völkerrecht contained in Art. 20 a specific reservation of the right of self-defence. See Wehberg, p. 101 fn.

intended to constitute acts of war may or may not be consistent with the provisions of Art. 12 to 15 of the Covenant, . . .'[1]

Dissatisfaction with this partial solution became evident within and without the League. Outside the League, and particularly in the United States, a movement developed for the complete prohibition of war.[2] Within the League itself the attitude towards a complete prohibition of war was unenthusiastic, probably gauging more accurately the range of possibilities in view of the current temper of states. The abortive Draft Treaty of Mutual Assistance of 1923[3] contained no specific reference to a right of self-defence. Another approach, which had been suggested in the debates on the Draft Treaty,[4] lay in an increased emphasis on Art. 12 of the Covenant, containing an obligation to arbitrate or submit to the Council any disputes likely to lead to a rupture and in no case to resort to war until three months after the award or report by the Council. The Geneva Protocol of 1924[5] represented an attempt, again ultimately abortive, to link the prohibition of war with a

[1] Off. Journal, 1924, pp. 523–7. The same problem was later posed by the Japanese invasion of Manchuria in 1931, although on that occasion the Report of the Assembly leaves no doubt that this action was inconsistent with the Covenant; even then, however, the Report chose to regard the case as not being one in which a country declared war without previously exhausting the procedures of the Covenant. See *ante*, p. 33. A positive finding of illegality and breach of Art. 12 was returned by the Council of the League in the Italian invasion, without a declaration of war, of Abyssinia in 1935. See *A.J.*, Vol. 30 (1936), Supp., pp. 1–57.

[2] See the Levinson proposals of March 9th, 1918: text in Shotwell, *War as an Instrument of National Policy* (1929), p. 103. Some difference existed on whether self-defence should be specifically excepted. Moore, 'The Draft Treaty and the Outlawry of War', *The New Republic*, August 27th, 1924, argued it should not: the Shotwell Plan (printed in Int. Concil., 1924, p. 201) of 1924 accepted the distinction between offensive and defensive wars.

[3] See text in Williams, *op. cit.*, Annex V, p. 277; ch. V contains a full discussion of the text, and the reactions of various governments to it are given as appendices. The objections to the draft were aimed, in the main, at Part III allowing complementary defensive agreements, and at the method of determining aggression; this was, under Art. 4, to be left undefined except for the provisions of Art. 1, and in the entire discretion of the Council, who would reach a decision within five days: Eagleton, *op. cit.*, pp. 592–4; Wehberg, *op. cit.*, pp. 14–15. For the discussions see Off. Rec. Fourth Assembly, Minutes of the Third Committee (Off. Journal, Spec. Supp., No. 16).

[4] See M. Lange before the Third Committee in 1923; Plenary Meetings, Fourth Assembly, pp. 23–7.

[5] Off. Journal, Spec. Supp., No. 21 (October, 1924), p. 21. And see generally Baker, *The Geneva Protocol* (1925); Wehberg, 'Le Protocol de Genève', *R.C.*, 1925 (II), p. 5; Miller, *The Geneva Protocol* (1925).

more comprehensive system of pacific settlement than the Covenant itself afforded. The Preamble contained an assertion 'that a war of aggression constitutes a violation of this solidarity and an international crime'; in Art. II:

> The signatory states agree in no case to resort to war either with one another or against a state which, if the occasion arises, accepts all the obligations hereinafter set out, except in the case of resistance to acts of aggression or when acting in agreement with the Council or the Assembly of the League of Nations in accordance with the provisions of the Covenant and of the present Protocol.

This provision approximated closely to the position which, we submit, must ideally exist if the right of self-defence is to be a juridical concept; that is to say, the trilogy of delict, sanction, and self-defence was roughly established. The necessity of excluding self-defence from the prohibition was stated in the preliminary Report of M. Politis and M. Benes:

> Le prohibition n'atteint que la guerre d'agression. Il va de soi qu'elle ne s'étend pas à la guerre défensive. Le droit de légitime défense demeure respecté comme il doit l'être. L'état attaqué conserve entière la liberté de résister de toute ses forces aux actes d'agression dont il serait victime... il peut et doit commencer pour se défendre par ses propres moyens.[1]

In the exercise of the right of self-defence the victim state was, under Art. II, assured of the assistance of the other signatory states in accordance with Art. 16(3) of the Covenant, the obligation being both joint and several.[2] Moreover, the exercise of the right of self-defence, and the subsequent support of other states by means of sanctions under Art. 16(3), was in no way dependent on the prior approval of the Council; the definition of the aggressor was established by means of the presumptions in Art. X and could be rebutted only by the unanimous vote of the Council.

The most significant defect, from the point of view of establishing a right of self-defence, was the use of the term 'war'; the lesson of the Corfu Incident[3] had by this time, presumably, been learnt,

[1] Cited Wehberg, *op. cit.*, *R.C.*, 1925 (II), p. 42.

[2] The formula of the Protocol afforded a greater elasticity than that in the Covenant, providing that a Member was to render aid 'in the degree which its geographical position and its particular situation as regards armaments allows' (Art. II).

[3] See *ante*, p. 34.

yet the proposal of M. Limburg (Holland) to extend the prohibition to cover 'recourse to force' was rejected.[1] Of lesser importance was the introduction of the notion that self-defence became a duty on the attacked state, owed, apparently, to other signatories. Wehberg argued forcibly against this, maintaining that the better course was for the attacked state to demonstrate its faith in the Council by appealing to it in the first instance.

> Quand un Etat renonce, pour l'instant, à se défendre par les armes, il rend un service immense à la cause de la paix universelle.[2]

Implicit in this view was not only a faith in the Council, but an assumption that the Council would act unanimously and quickly; this proved subsequently to be yet another faith that was misplaced. The refusal of Great Britain to accept the basic idea of general guarantees of security ultimately sealed the fate of the Protocol and the labours of the Fifth Assembly.[3] This in itself indicated that the more likely solution lay in the conclusion of particular treaties of guarantee, and the Pact of Locarno of 1925 adopted this course.[4]

The Locarno Pact[5] applied two basic principles—a guarantee of territorial integrity, and a guaranteed process of arbitration; to this end, in Art. 2, Germany, France and Belgium undertook 'that they will in no case attack or invade each other, or resort to war against each other'. The escape from the technical term 'war' was a notable advance, although it is debatable whether the use of terms like 'attack' and 'invade' offer any improvement on the simpler and more comprehensive form 'recourse to force'. [6] The exceptions to this prohibition were stated in Art. 2:

[1] Records of the Fifth Assembly, First Commission, pp. 35–7.

[2] Wehberg, *op. cit.*, *R.C.*, 1925 (II), p. 44. Limburg, too, opposed this innovation, and there followed a lively discussion in the First Committee (Records of Fifth Assembly, pp. 36, 71, 121).

[3] The reasons advanced by Mr. Chamberlain, and set out in the British Memorandum, are cited in Williams, *op. cit.*, pp. 208–9. Amongst them is the reason that the prohibition of warlike preparations (Arts. 7 and 8) might jeopardize the state's right of self-defence.

[4] Wehberg, *The Outlawry of War*, p. 33, traces the political history of Locarno back to Versailles and the French desire to obtain security against Germany by defensive treaties with Great Britain. See also Williams, *op. cit.*, ch. VI; Eagleton, *op. cit.*, pp. 600–2.

[5] Treaty of Mutual Guarantee, Locarno, October 16th, 1925. Text in *A.J.*, Supp. (1926), p. 22.

[6] As it appeared in the earlier Hague Convention (II), 1907.

This stipulation shall not, however, apply in the case of:

(1) The exercise of the right of legitimate defence, that is to say, resistance to a violation of the undertaking contained in the previous paragraph or to a flagrant breach of Article 42 or 43 of the said Treaty of Versailles, if such breach constitutes an unprovoked act of aggression and by reason of the assembly of armed forces in the demilitarized zone immediate action is necessary.

(2) Action in pursuance of Article 16 of the Covenant of the League of Nations.

(3) Action as a result of a decision taken by the Assembly or by the Council of the League of Nations or in pursuance of Article 15(7) of the Covenant of the League of Nations, provided that in this last event the action is directed against a state which was the first to attack.

The effect of Art. 2 was to achieve a rough approximation to the classification of acts of force into delicts, sanctions, and self-defence, although it was in effect confined to the three states of Germany, France and Belgium.[1] However, the right of self-defence was qualified: no mention was made of any duty of self-defence, as in the Protocol, but the paramount duty in case of a violation of Art. 2 was to 'bring the question at once before the League of Nations' (Art. 4(1)). In the main, therefore, the signatory states were deprived of the right to react instantly in self-defence; their action was dependent on the prior approval of the Council and, this given, partook more of the character of a sanction than of action in self-defence. The right of self-defence was unqualified, in the sense that it enabled immediate action, only in cases of a 'flagrant violation' of Art. 2 or the demilitarization provisions of the Treaty of Versailles (Arts. 42 and 43), provided this constituted an 'unprovoked' act of aggression and 'by reason of the assembly of armed forces in the demilitarized zone immediate action is necessary'. Similarly, the guarantee of assistance by other signatory powers was, under Art. 4(2), operative as a general rule only when the Council had reached its finding; it was operative immediately only in cases of 'flagrant' violation within the terms of Art. 2. However, between the three signatory states of the Western Pact, and within these limits, the prohibitions of Art. 2 contained a duty correlative to a right of self-defence.[2]

[1] Great Britain and Italy were also signatories, but only the three states named above are named in the treaty as bearing the obligations of Art. 2.

[2] The point may well be made that the introduction of terms like 'flagrant violation' and 'unprovoked' acts of aggression heightens the risk of unilateral interpretation of these terms so as to deprive the limitation on the right of self-defence of most of its force. See *post*, p. 230.

So far, then, only the League Covenant and the Locarno Pact contained prohibitions of war or, in the latter case, of attack or invasion; the Covenant was general, though not universal, in its application; the Locarno Pact bound only France, Germany and Belgium.[1] To this extent positive international law enabled war, or attack or invasion, to be characterized as delictual and, consequently, the reaction by force of another state to be characterized as the exercise of the right of self-defence.

We have already seen how the Geneva Protocol postulated a 'duty' of self-defence and how Wehberg had opposed this approach as detrimental to the very basis of the League, faith in the efficacy of the Council.[2] A related problem was that of the connection between the Council and the state directly attacked; was the state, in the exercise of the right of self-defence, to act, initially, independently of the Council, or should such action be consequent on a decision of the Council? Prior to the Locarno Pact the first alternative was assumed to be the correct view; the Locarno Pact, however, introduced a compromise between these two alternatives by allowing independent action against 'flagrant' violations of the obligations set out in Art. 2 but in all other cases obliging restraint until the Council had reached its decision. Within the League opinion veered towards the restriction of the state's right to resort to immediate self-defence in favour of an increased reliance on the Council; this is clearly shown in the Council's handling of the Graeco–Bulgarian Conflict which broke out on October 19th, 1925.[3]

Briefly, the conflict developed out of an exchange of fire between Greek and Bulgarian frontier guards, and the commander of the Greek troops, believing the Greek frontier to be menaced, ordered an advance into Bulgarian territory. In the event Bulgaria chose not to reply with counter-measures but referred the matter to the Council under Arts. 10 and 11 of the Covenant. The Greek justification of her action was contained in a telegram to the Secretary-General on October 24th; it stated, *inter alia*:

It is therefore clear that all the measures which the military command

---

[1] We are here speaking specifically of the obligation under Art. 2 of the 'Western' Pact.

[2] See *ante*, p. 127.

[3] See Off. Journal, November, 1925, Part II. A brief account is given in Wehberg, *op. cit.*, pp. 46–8.

has been compelled to take are nothing but measures of legitimate defence.[1]

The reactions of both the British representative, Mr. Chamberlain,[2] and of the French, M. Briand as President of the Council, are clear in their deprecation of impulsive action in self-defence rather than resort to the machinery of the League. M. Briand, noting the Greek argument that the measures taken were necessary for the legitimate defence and protection of the country, stated:

> It was essential that such ideas should not take root in the minds of nations which were Members of the League, and become a kind of jurisprudence, for it would be extremely dangerous. Under the pretext of legitimate defence, disputes might arise which, though limited in extent, were extremely unfortunate owing to the damage they entailed. These disputes, once they had broken out, might assume such proportions that the Government, which started them under a feeling of legitimate defence, would be no longer able to control them.[3]

It cannot be supposed that the Council intended to interdict defensive warfare or deny the right of self-defence; nor can it be supposed that, as a matter of law, the Council determined the right of self-defence to be operative only after recourse to the League and after obtaining the sanction of the Council. What the Council did was to emphasize that, as a matter of practice, states would do well to resort to the Council rather than to self-defence.[4]

The argument for prior resort to the Council rested on the assumption that the Council would protect a state's 'menaced and violated rights and interests' and, moreover, do this speedily before the results of an aggression were irreparable. To this end the Draft Treaty of 1923, Art. 4,[5] provided that the Council should reach a decision as to which of the parties were the victims of aggression and therefore entitled to assistance under the treaty within four days. However, Art. 4 did not suggest the

[1] Off. Journal, November, 1925, Part II, p. 1697. This view was rejected by the Commission of Inquiry and the Council adopted the Commission's Report on December 14th, 1925; Off. Journal, 7th Year, No. 2, 37th Session of Council, pp. 172–7.

[2] Ibid., p. 1699 and also p. 1709.

[3] Ibid., p. 1709.

[4] This is borne out by the Council's attitude in the Chaco Dispute where it clearly admitted the right to take 'military measures of a defensive character': Off. Journal, 1929, pp. 72–3. For a contrary interpretation of the Council's view in the Graeco-Bulgarian Dispute see Borel and Politis in Annuaire (Lausanne, 1927), II, p. 698.

[5] See *ante*, p. 125.

attacked state's own right of defence lay in abeyance for these four days. In a resolution of December 14th, 1925,[1] the Council instituted a study of the special facilities for transmission and transit which would be available to the Council in case of danger of war. The Memorandum of De Brouckère,[2] rapporteur to the Commission appointed by the Council, whilst admitting the right of defensive warfare, adverted to the difficulty of making a finding of aggression within the minimum of time; he suggested that the emphasis be placed on Arts. 11 and 15, rather than 16, in other words that the Council should proceed with preventive action immediately,[3] leaving the more difficult question of determining the aggressor until the irreparable effects of aggression had been prevented. This solution, more realistic than a categorical denial of the right of self-defence prior to the sanction of the Council, was the one which met most squarely the practical difficulties involved and has, as we shall see, been adopted by the U.N. Charter.[4]

The counter-argument, as it was put forward by Wehberg,[5] seems quite unrealistic. However desirable it may be that centralization of the use of force should be achieved, and consequently the exercise of the right of self-defence proscribed except when sanctioned by a central agency, such as the Council, the practical problems were firstly that the Council might not reach a decision,[6] and secondly that if it did it might be too late to prevent irreparable damage to the attacked state, hamstrung by the prohibition against undertaking its own defence. In the light of modern conditions of warfare even the four days of the Draft Treaty seem far too long a period in which to allow the aggressor freedom of action; entire cities may be destroyed, and a continent entirely occupied.

[1] Off. Journal, February, 1926, p. 175.

[2] League of Nations Docs., Series III, 1927, pp. 100–1; C. 740. M.279, 1926, IX.

[3] Pacific blockade is cited as an example; Documents, Series III, p. 68.

[4] *Post*, ch. XI.

[5] *Ante*, p. 127.

[6] In this connection the operation of the unanimity rule within the Council caused concern, for the rule that interested parties must refrain from voting, rejected by De Brouckère (Documents, Series III, p. 68) and Lord Cecil (ibid., pp. 68–70), was supported by M. Paul Boncour. This problem has not really been solved by the U.N. Charter; see *post*, p. 179. The presumptions established by Art. 10 of the Geneva Protocol were, of course, an attempt to solve this problem as well as the second problem of delay in reaching a decision.

THE PACT OF PARIS

In the United States the movement for a prohibition of war, started by Levinson in 1918[1] and followed by the Shotwell drafts in 1924 and 1927,[2] began to find a more general sympathy. The projects of the American Institute of International Law,[3] the resolutions of Senator Borah before the Senate in December, 1927,[4] and the resolutions of the Sixth Pan-American Conference in the spring of 1928 condemning wars of aggression[5] created an atmosphere entirely favourable to the message of M. Briand, the French Minister for Foreign Affairs, addressed to the American people through the Associated Press on April 6th, 1927.[6] The message called for a joint effort by the two countries to outlaw war and in particular a treaty between them by which they would renounce war as an instrument of national policy vis-à-vis the other party.

The subsequent negotiations between the two governments[7] revealed a disagreement which went beyond the mere question of terminology. In brief, the United States advocated a simple and unqualified renunciation of war as an instrument of national policy; otherwise, in the words of Secretary Kellogg, 'the effect would be very greatly weakened and its positive value as a guarantee of peace virtually destroyed. The ideal . . . is arresting and appealing just because of its purity and simplicity'.[8] To the French this simplicity carried its own danger, and Briand favoured a renunciation only of wars of aggression, the object of this being the reservation of action in self-defence, and also action taken in consequence of obligations under the Covenant or the Locarno Pact, from the terms of the prohibition.[9]

[1] *Ante*, p. 125. See generally Myers, *The Origin and Conclusion of the Paris Pact* (1929).

[2] Shotwell, *War as an Instrument of National Policy* (1929), p. 53.

[3] See the summary of these projects in Wehberg, *Outlawry of War*, pp. 68–9.

[4] Congress Record, Vol. 69, Pt. I, p. 477: text in Shotwell, *op. cit.*, p. 103.

[5] Text in *A.J.*, Vol. 22 (1928), p. 356 *et seq.*

[6] For the full text see Shotwell, *op. cit.*, p. 39 *et seq.* The initial reception was actually insignificant until Dr. Murray Butler published the offer in a letter to the *New York Times* on April 25th, 1927: see Miller, *The Peace Pact of Paris* (1928), pp. 8–9.

[7] These negotiations are reviewed in Shotwell, *op. cit.*, Pt. II; Miller, *op. cit.*, chs. IV—XII.

[8] Note of February 27th, Miller, *op. cit.*, Doc. 7.

[9] See Miller, *op. cit.*, p. 38. The French terms are contained in the Draft Treaty of April 20th, 1928; see Miller, ch. XII.

So far as the right of self-defence was concerned, Kellogg readily conceded this in these terms:

> There is nothing in the American draft of an anti-war treaty which restricts or impairs in any way the right of self-defence. That right is inherent in every sovereign state and is implicit in every treaty. Every nation is free at all times and regardless of treaty provisions to defend its territory from attack or invasion and it alone is competent to decide whether circumstances require recourse to war in self-defence.[1]

He did not deem it necessary to make any express reservation, and the comments of Germany, Great Britain[2] and Japan revealed their agreement with this view.[3]

The reservation of action taken in consequence of obligations under the Covenant or the Locarno Pact occasioned more difficulty. Again, the United States, supported by Germany, Great Britain and Japan, took the view that the American formula in the Draft of April 13th, 1928[4] was in no way inconsistent with the Covenant or Locarno, whereas the French Draft of April 20th, 1928,[5] contained, in Art. 4, provisions safeguarding rights and obligations under prior international agreements. Despite the majority opinion, as Miller points out, there was substance in the French objection:

> . . . no one would say that action of any nature by a third state under the obligations of the Covenant or of the Treaties of Locarno was 'aggression'; and yet some might say that it did not come within the term 'self-defence'. In other words, while such action could not be argued to be within the French formula of a 'war of aggression', it might be argued to be within the American formula, 'war as an instrument of national policy'.[6]

In fact the real contradiction lay not between the American formula and a state's 'obligations' under the Covenant or Locarno, but between the cases of licit war, possible because of the purely procedural limitations imposed by the Covenant, and the renunciation of war as an instrument of 'national policy'. The argument that a war of sanction under Art. 16 of the Covenant is a war of 'international' rather than of 'national' policy is readily accepted;

[1] Note of June 23rd, 1928. Shotwell, *op. cit.*, App. VI; Miller, *op. cit.*, Doc. 23. Shotwell, *op. cit.*, p. 139, makes the point that this admission was tantamount to recognizing the French formula of 'aggressive' war.

[2] Sir Austen Chamberlain's Note of May 19th (Miller, Doc. 14). He later maintained this view before the House of Commons on July 31st, 1928.

[3] See generally Miller, *op. cit.*, ch. XIII.

[4] Miller, Doc. 10.

[5] Ibid., Doc. 11.

[6] Miller, *op. cit.*, p. 40.

the same cannot be said of a war waged pursuant to the liberty of Art. 15(7), or 15(8) for example. Subsequently these contradictions became an endless source of discussion within the League itself, an unhappy testimony to the wisdom of the French objections.[1]

In the outcome the Pact as signed on August 27th, 1928 marked the rejection of the French arguments; it stated in Art. 1:

> The High Contracting Parties solemnly declare in the names of their respective peoples that they condemn recourse to war for the solution of international controversies, and renounce it as an instrument of national policy in their relations with one another.[2]

With the general criticisms of the Pact we are not here concerned,[3] except in so far as they are relevant to the problem we are now considering, that is to say the prohibition of war and the development of a right of self-defence. The initial advantage conferred by the Pact was the generality of the prohibition: as Wehberg states, 'for the first time it established the principle of the outlawry of all aggressive war in an international convention'.[4] However, no attempt was made to define aggressive war, or, to correct Wehberg, 'war as an instrument of national policy'. The French Draft of April 20th, 1928, had defined it thus:

> ... c'est à dire comme instrument d'une action personelle, spontanée et indépendante dont elles prendraient l'initiative et non d'une action dans laquelle elles se trouveraient entraînées par l'obligation d'un traité tel

[1] See in particular the carefully formulated proposals for modification presented by Sir Cecil Hurst before the First Commission in the Fifth Session on September 17th, 1929; text given in Wehberg, *op. cit.*, p. 89. Also Colombos, 'The Paris Pact', *Trans. Grotius Society*, Vol. XIV (1928), p. 87, at p. 96. Manning, 'The Proposed Amendments to the Covenant of the League of Nations', *BYBIL*, Vol. XI (1930), p. 158. Rauchberg, 'Les Obligations juridiques des Membres de la Société des Nations pour le Maintien de la Paix', *R.C.*, 1931 (III), p. 146 *et seq.*, and especially sec. 11. Rutgers, 'La Mise en harmonie du Pact de la S.D.N. avec le Pacte de Paris', *R.C.*, 1931 (IV), p. 80. For the minutes of the Committee appointed by the Council in 1930 to consider the proposed amendments see League Docs. C.160 M.69, 1930, V.

[2] *The General Pact for the Renunciation of War*, Washington Printing Office, 1928.

[3] See Shotwell, *op. cit.*, Part III; Wehberg, *op. cit.*, p. 80 *et seq.*; Rauchberg, *op. cit.*, p. 151 *et seq.*; Rutgers, *op. cit.*, p. 74 *et seq.*

[4] *Outlawry of War*, p. 81. Contrast with this view that of Hindmarsh, *op. cit.*, p. 123, to the effect that the Pact of Paris cannot be regarded as a significant part of the post-war peace structure; Nuremberg would seem to support Wehberg's view, see *post*, p. 138.

que le pacte de la Société des Nations ou tout autre traité enregistré à la Société des Nations. Elles s'engagent dans ces termes à ne se livrer l'une contre l'autre à aucune attaque ou invasion.[1]

This definition, as part of a rejected draft, cannot be accepted as an aid in construction, and the only real source of interpretation was the partial definition of self-defence, for most purposes the opposite of the prohibited wars of national policy, in Kellogg's note of June 23rd. He there stated:

. . . every nation is free at all times and regardless of treaty provisions to defend its territory from attack or invasion, and it alone is competent to decide whether circumstances require recourse to war in self-defence.[2]

The absence of a satisfactory definition of either 'war as an instrument of national policy' or self-defence becomes even more of a defect in view of the possible interpretation of this last clause in the note to mean that a state remained the sole judge of the legality of its recourse to war in self-defence. As we have seen,[3] it was precisely this interpretation which Japan adopted as part of a specious argument to justify her action in Manchuria in September, 1931, as self-defence. So interpreted the obligation of Art. 1 of the Pact becomes entirely illusory.

A further criticism of the Pact is that, assuming the only sanction provided by the Pact is that 'any signatory Power which shall hereafter seek to promote its national interests by resort to war should be denied the benefits furnished by this Treaty', in other words, the other signatory states assume a freedom of action in relation to the delinquent state, this sanction is entirely de-centralized.[4] It may be argued that American participation in concerted sanctions was unattainable in 1928; whilst this may be true, the fact remains that, in the absence of centralized sanctions, the sphere of self-defence must necessarily be larger and ill-defined.

The final criticism lies against the reliance on the term 'war', despite the general knowledge of the dangers which factual situations lacking the techincal requisites for prohibition as 'war'

[1] Miller, Doc. 11, p. 188.

[2] Miller, *op. cit.*, Doc. 23, p. 213. France concurred in this unilateral competence, note of July 14th.

[3] *Ante*, p. 32. This trend is, of course, quite contrary to the Locarno idea of making self-defence, in the main, dependent on the prior approval of a central organ.

[4] See generally Oppenheim, Vol. II, 7th ed., p. 190. The words are contained in the preamble to the Pact.

could bring about in international relations. It has been argued[1] that the Pact does prohibit force short of war by virtue of Art. 2 which provided that the settlement or solution of disputes 'shall never be sought except by pacific means'. It is submitted that this argument is invalid for, under the accepted terminology of international law (and without defending that terminology), measures involving the use of force but falling short of war are characterized as 'pacific'; in this case Art. 2 cannot be invoked as a reason for departing from the plain meaning of the terms of Art. 1. The importance of the problem can be gauged by the fact that within four years of the conclusion of the Pact there were three instances of the use of force, plainly contrary to the spirit of the Pact, but because of this defect not easily characterized as contraventions of Art. 1. These were the outbreak of hostilities without a declaration to war between Russia and China in 1929 over the Chinese Eastern Railway,[2] the Japanese occupation of Manchuria in 1931,[3] and Peru's invasion of the Columbian province of Leticia in 1932.[4]

In September, 1934, the Conference of the International Law Association adopted the celebrated 'Budapest Articles of Interpretation' of which Art. 2 purported to extend or interpret Art. 1 of the Paris Pact to cover armed force in general; these articles cannot, it is submitted, affect the legal limitations of Art. 1, and only serve to demonstrate its inadequacy.[5] That

[1] Wright, *A.J.*, Vol. 27 (1933), pp. 51–4. Miller, *op. cit.*, pp. 125–6. A similar argument is that Art. 2 limits the right of self-defence to cases where the state so defending has attempted pacific means of settlement. See Woolsey, *A.J.*, Vol. 23 (1929), p. 382.

[2] See Toynbee, *Survey of Int. Affairs*, 1929, pp. 344–89; Documents, 1929, pp. 274–84. In the note of December 4th, 1929, to the U.S. (Docs., p. 279), Russia also relied on the right of self-defence, presumably admitting her action otherwise fell within the prohibition.

[3] *Ante*, p. 32.

[4] *Ante*, p. 35 fn.

[5] The text of these Articles is given in *Trans. Grotius Soc.*, Vol. XX (1934), p. 205. Lauterpacht, 'The Pact of Paris and the Budapest Articles of Interpretation', ibid., pp. 197–201, doubts the legality of this interpretation, since the signatory powers were clearly aware of the limitations involved in the term 'war'. See also Viscount Sankey, L.C., in debate in House of Lords, February 20th, 1935, describing the I.L.A. as a 'purely private and unofficial conference' and denying to its views any legal effect. Parl. Debates, H.L., 5th Series, Vol. 95, cols. 1007, 1043. There is a strong reliance on the Articles by Mr. Stimson, U.S. Sec. of War before the House Committee on Foreign Affairs, January 16th, 1941; cited Hackworth, *Dig.*, Vol. VII, pp. 680–1.

inadequacy was only in small part met by subsequent bilateral treaties for the renunciation of both war and force short of war[1] and the restrictions imposed on the executives of certain states under the terms of their constitutions;[2] in substance it remained until the Charter of the United Nations abandoned the restrictive term 'war'. However, the subsequent failure of the Pact to mitigate the injustices and the illogicalities which the liberty of waging war brought about, came not so much from the defective terminology of the Pact as from the patent unwillingness of states generally to fulfil their obligations under both the Covenant of the League and the Pact of Paris.

In 1931 on the occasion of the Japanese invasion of Manchuria, in 1935 in connection with the Italian invasion of Abyssinia,[3] in 1937 when Japan invaded China,[4] and in 1939 when Russia attacked Finland[5] there were authoritative pronouncements on the illegality of the action by virtue of the provisions of the Covenant and the Pact. Yet, in the main, the signatory Powers failed to pursue the course which these findings logically indicated as necessary if their own international obligations were to be fulfilled.[6] In 1937 and 1938 the German aggression against Austria and Czechoslovakia, and Italy's aggression against Albania in 1939, failed to promote even the reaction of an authoritative pronouncement by the League. It remained for the International Military Tribunal at Nuremberg in 1945 to draw the necessary conclusions from German aggression against Poland in 1939 and subsequent aggression throughout Europe. Only at this tardy

[1] For a list of these treaties see Oppenheim, Vol. II, 6th ed., pp. 152–3 fn.

[2] The French Constitution of 1790, and especially the decree of May 22nd, 1790, limited even the power of the executive to wage a defensive war. See generally Wehberg, *op. cit.*, pp. 108–16. Also Morrison, *The Outlawry of War* (1927), p. 43.

[3] Report of the Committee of Six, adopted by the Council of the League, October 7th, 1935. Off. Journal, 1935, pp. 1223–6.

[4] Off. Journal, Spec. Supp., No. 177, p. 42. See also Langer, *Seizure of Territory*, 1947, for a summary of these various incidents between 1931 and 1939, especially Part III, Diplomatic Practice.

[5] Off. Journal, 1939, p. 540.

[6] There were, of course, reactions against the delinquent state; the Stimson Doctrine of Non-Recognition, economic sanctions, and radical departures from the normal practice of neutral impartiality were constant gestures of this era. The opinion is nevertheless held that these did not, in view of the circumstances, amount to a fulfilment in good faith of the obligations assumed under the Covenant. See generally Oppenheim, Vol. II, 6th ed., p. 131 *et seq.*; Déak and Jessup, *A Collection of Neutrality Laws*, 2 Vols. (1939).

stage was the contrast between the international delict of waging war in contravention of these express prohibitions and the right of self-defence made, and the legal character of the Pact of Paris vindicated.

THE INTERPRETATION OF THE PACT OF PARIS AND THE RIGHT OF SELF-DEFENCE BY THE INTERNATIONAL MILITARY TRIBUNAL

So far we have indicated that the positive prohibition of war as an instrument of national policy contained in the Kellogg-Briand Pact of 1928 made possible amongst signatories the characterization of belligerent action as either a delict, a sanction, or self-defence. The possibilities of such a characterization, and its consequences, were not realized immediately after the Pact, at least in so far as the practice of states generally can be taken to evidence such a realization. However, at the conclusion of the Second World War in 1945 this characterization was made in respect of the German and Japanese belligerencies and it is to the proceedings of the International Military Tribunals that we now turn.

Nuremberg

At Nuremberg the International Military Tribunal gave judgment on the major German war criminals and the indictments were framed on the basis of Art. 6 of the London Charter[1] which set out the crimes over which the Tribunal was to assume jurisdiction. 'Crimes against the Peace' were there defined as the 'planning, preparation, initiation, or waging of a war of aggression, or a war in violation of international treaties, agreements, or assurances . . .' From this definition it will be seen that no attempt was made to indicate the rights of the victims of aggression which had been violated or to define aggression; the Charter relied upon the general, and necessarily vague, concept of aggression and the fact of contravention of treaties, agreements, and assurances. However, in the earlier discussions at the London

[1] Charter of the Int. Military Tribunal, in Report of Robert H. Jackson, U.S. Representative to the Int. Conference on Military Trials, London, 1945 (Dept. of State Publication 3080, released February, 1949), p. 423. For a history and analysis of the Charter and Judgment, see the Memorandum of the Secretary-General, 1949, A/CN.4/5, March 3rd. Also Pompe, *Aggressive War an International Crime*, 1953.

Conference on Military Trials the original drafts submitted by the United States and Great Britain to some extent defined the concept of aggression and also specifically indicated that the Axis belligerency was aggressive because of its attack against or invasion of the territories of other states;[1] that is to say they indicated that the victims were in self-defence of a specific right, namely a right to the integrity of their territory. A later United States' definition of aggression on July 19th, 1945,[2] closely followed the Litvinoff definition of 1933[3] but the difficulties inherent in this task of definition were such that, in the absence of agreement, the final agreed formulation was undefined. In the result, therefore, the actual Charter affords no indication of the substantive rights involved in the right of self-defence.

It must, however, be supposed that since the Allied belligerency was in resistance to aggression, and taken either by the actual victims of the aggression or by states coming to their aid, that belligerency was in self-defence or collective self-defence. This is nowhere stated in the Judgment but, since it can scarcely be argued that the Allies were taking sanctions in the sense in which we have defined the term,[4] the conclusion is irresistible. The absence of such an express finding is explicable since the legality of the allied belligerency was not in question before the Tribunal.

What was, of course, directly in issue before the Tribunal was the question whether the Axis belligerency was waged in self-defence. This argument was inevitable and had been anticipated; in the U.S. Draft Definition of Aggression of July 19th, 1945,[5] the United States representative had tried to introduce certain limitations on the scope of self-defence as a defence before the

[1] U.S. Dept. of State Pub. 3080. American Draft of Definitive Proposal, Executive Agreement, p. 24. British Memorandum of May 28th, 1945, p. 40. It is of interest to note the British substitution of 'war' for the American phrase 'force or threat of force', in order to bring the Article into line with the Paris Pact. Though this was no doubt correct it involved a limitation on the concept of aggression; see S.G.'s Memo., *op. cit.*, p. 49. For example, the invasions of Austria and Czechoslovakia were not charged as aggressive wars, but as aggressive acts, a distinction necessitated apparently by the technical definition of war. For comment on this see Finch, 'The Nuremberg Trial and International Law', *A.J.*, Vol. 41 (1947), pp. 26–7.

[2] Ibid., p. 294.

[3] See League of Nations, Records of the Conference for the Reduction and Limitation of Armaments, Series D, Vol. 5, p. 237.

[4] *Ante*, p. 19.

[5] International Conference on Military Trials, *op. cit.*, p. 294.

Tribunal, whilst admitting that, where used in its proper sense, the defence must be valid. The Draft Definition provided that:

> No political, military, economic or other considerations shall serve as an excuse or justification for such actions; but exercise of the right of legitimate self-defence, that is to say, resistance to an act of aggression, or action to assist a state which has been subjected to aggression, shall not constitute a war of aggression.

In the outcome neither the definition of aggression nor the express reservation of the defence of self-defence found a place in the Charter, but the existence of the defence was never doubted, and it was in fact relied upon by defence counsel at Nuremberg, as the following statement by Professor Jahrreiss indicates:

> War in self-defence is permitted as an inalienable right to all states; without that right, sovereignty does not exist; and every state is sole judge of whether in a given case it is waging a war of self-defence.[1]

This statement contains in fact an assertion of two distinct principles; firstly that a right of self-defence exists, and secondly that each state is alone competent to judge the question whether it is acting in self-defence. To the first of these principles no objection was, and could be, taken; we have already shown how the reservation of the right of self-defence from the prohibitions of the Paris Pact was an incontestable fact. To the second principle the Prosecutor for the United Kingdom replied in these terms:

> Neither the Pact of Paris nor any other treaty was intended to—or could—take away the right of self-defence. Nor did it deprive its signatories of the right to determine in the first instance, whether there was any danger in delay and whether immediate action to defend themselves was imperative; and that only is the meaning of the express proviso that each state judges whether action in self-defence is necessary. But that does not mean that the state thus acting is the ultimate judge of the propriety and of the legality of its conduct. It acts at its peril. Just as the individual is answerable for the exercise of his common law right of defence, so the state is answerable if it abuses its discretion, if it transforms 'self-defence' into an instrument of conquest and lawlessness, if it twists the natural right of self-defence into a weapon of predatory aggrandisement and lust. The ultimate decision as to the lawfulness of the action claimed to be taken in self-defence does not lie with the state concerned, and for that reason the right of

---

[1] Trial of Major War Criminals, Nuremberg, 1948, Vol. XVII, p. 469; reliance was placed on the statement of Secretary of State Kellogg in connection with the position of self-defence under the Paris Pact, see *ante*, p. 133.

self-defence, whether expressly reserved or implied, does not impair the capacity of a treaty to create legal obligations against war.[1]

The prosecution invited the Tribunal to assume the right to judge for itself, as a question of fact, whether the Axis belligerency was waged in self-defence. As the United States Prosecutor stated:

> I do not doubt that if a nation arrived at a judgment that it must resort to war in self-defence, because of conditions affording reasonable grounds for such an honest judgment, any tribunal would accord it great and perhaps conclusive weight, even if later events proved that judgment mistaken. But the facts in this case call for no such deference to honest judgment because no such judgment was even pretended, much less honestly made.[2]

The Tribunal treated the question of aggression as one entirely of fact[3] and concluded in every case where, as a question of fact, the aggression was proved that it was therefore illegal and also criminal. We are not here concerned with examining the validity of the premisses from which that conclusion was drawn; it is perhaps true that the Tribunal was on surer ground in starting from the alternative basis of 'violation of international treaties, agreements, or assurances . . .', and relying on the positive prohibition contained in the Paris Pact rather than on the undefined concept of aggression.[4] However, in either case the defence of self-defence would have been equally valid. Of the Pact itself the opinion of the Tribunal was that 'this Pact was violated by Germany in all cases of aggressive war charged in this Indictment'.[5] The Tribunal went on to say that:

[1] Shawcross, Vol. XIX, pp. 461–2. There then follow certain arguments based upon the position of self-defence under Art. 51 of the U.N. Charter which, with respect, could not but be irrelevant to these indictments.

[2] Mr. Justice Robert H. Jackson, Vol. XIX, p. 421.

[3] Judgment, October 1st, 1946, *A.J.*, Vol. 41 (1947), p. 203. Telford Taylor, *op. cit.*, p. 340.

[4] It has been doubted whether aggression can be determined by reference to a general notion of international law, as opposed to the breach of specific obligations. See Harvard Research Draft Convention, Definition of Aggression, Art. 1(c): *A.J.*, Vol. 33 (1939), Supp., p. 847.

[5] Judgment, *op. cit.*, p. 216. The omission of the war against France and Great Britain from the Indictment is explained by the fact that these two countries first declared war on Germany—see Pompe, *op. cit.*, p. 23. This affords a clear illustration of the limitations on the Charter inherent in the technical definition of war. The declaration of war is, in itself, irrelevant to whether the war is one in self-defence; see the view taken by the Tokyo Tribunal in relation to the Netherlands declaration against Japan, *post*, p. 144. For a critical account of the Paris Pact as a basis of the Indictments see Pompe, *op. cit.*, p. 248.

. . . the solemn renunciation of war as an instrument of national policy necessarily involves the proposition that such war is illegal in international law, and that those who plan and wage such a war, with its inevitable and terrible consequences, are committing a crime in so doing. War for the solution of international controversies undertaken as an instrument of national policy certainly includes a war of aggression, and such a war is therefore outlawed by the Pact.[1]

As we have shown, the plea of self-defence was equally relevant to this aspect of the Indictment; Professor Jahrreiss relied specifically on the 'reservation' of the right of self-defence from the Pact by U.S. Secretary of State Kellogg.[2] However, the only occasion[3] on which the Tribunal deemed it necessary to consider this plea as having any possible validity was in connection with its judgment on Raeder. On his behalf it had been argued that the invasion of Norway was a necessary act of self-defence to forestall an imminent Allied landing;[4] in the words of the judgment:

The defence that has been made here is that Germany was compelled to attack Norway to forestall an Allied invasion, and her action was therefore preventive.

It must be remembered that preventive action in foreign territory is justified only in case of 'an instant and overwhelming necessity for self-defence, leaving no choice of means and no moment for deliberation' (The Caroline Case).[5]

On the facts the Tribunal rejected the immediacy of the occasion and stated:

It is clear that when the plans for an attack on Norway were being made they were not made for the purpose of forestalling an imminent Allied landing but, at the most, that they might prevent an Allied occupation at some future date,[6]

---

[1] *A.J.*, Vol. 41 (1947), p. 218. Quincey Wright, 'The Law of the Nuremberg Trial', ibid., p. 38, at p. 42, fn. 14, gives an exhaustive list of authors supporting this conclusion as to the criminality of aggressive war. For a contrary view see G. A. Finch, 'The Nuremberg Trial and International Law', ibid., p. 20, at p. 33.

[2] *Ante*, p. 133.

[3] Excluding the frivolous plea that the aggressions against Greece and Yugoslavia were defensive in view of the British landings in Greece, with the consent of the Greek Government. See as to this Judgment, *op. cit.*, p. 211.

[4] There seems to be no question of the possibility of this; see Churchill, *The Second World War*, Vol. I, pp. 421–39. Hankey, *Politics, Trials & Errors*, 1950, pp. 78–9, points out that the Norwegian Leads had been mined by Great Britain on April 8th, 1940, prior to the German invasion; and see Neilson, *The Tragedy of Europe*, 1940, Vol. I, p. 436.

[5] *A.J.*, Vol. 41 (1947), p. 205.

[6] Ibid., p. 206.

thereby indicating that the classical formulation of self-defence in the *Caroline* case must be supplemented by the requisite of 'purpose', or, in other words, an intention formed in good faith and honesty of conviction to protect one's own safety, that safety being immediately threatened. Clearly, whatever the threat of an allied landing, the primary purpose was to secure operational bases in Norway.[1] The Tribunal also met the argument that the right of self-defence necessarily involved the right to self-judge the necessity of the occasion by stating:

> But whether action taken under the claim of self-defence was in fact aggressive or defensive must ultimately be subject to investigation and adjudication if international law is ever to be enforced.[2]

Tokyo

The International Military Tribunal for the Far East[3] exercised jurisdiction on the basis of its own Charter, a Charter adopted from the London precedent but varying slightly in that the words 'declared or undeclared' appeared before 'war of aggression'.[4] As in the case of the Nuremberg Tribunal, the plea of self-defence was made, its validity as such accepted, but rejected on its application to the facts.[5] Speaking of the Japanese invasions (with one exception in the case of Thailand where the evidence pointed to a considerable degree of consent by Thailand) the Tribunal stated:

> They were unprovoked attacks, prompted by the desire to seize the possessions of those nations. Whatever may be the difficulty of stating

---

[1] Ibid., p. 307. The Tribunal noted the circulation of a questionnaire dated October 3rd, 1939, by Raeder which sought comments on the desirability of securing bases in Norway.

[2] Ibid., p. 207.

[3] Set up by a proclamation issued by the Supreme Commander for the Allied Powers in the Pacific on January 19th, 1946, with the Charter annexed to the Proclamation.

[4] For the reasons for and a criticism of this phraseology, see Pompe, *op. cit.*, p. 25. See generally *History of the United Nations War Crimes Commission and the Development of the Laws of War*, London, H.M.S.O. (1948), p. 257. Horwitz, 'The Tokyo Trial', *Int. Concil.*, 1950, p. 465. Comyns Carr, 'The Judgment of the International Military Tribunal for the Far East', *Trans. Grotius Society*, Vol. 34 (1948), pp. 141–51. Schwelb, 'Crimes against Humanity', *BYBIL*, Vol. 23 (1946), pp. 214–16.

[5] Its validity as a defence was in fact recognized in respect both of the charges of Crimes against the Peace and of Murder; Comyns Carr, *op. cit.*, pp. 142–3.

a comprehensive definition of a 'war of aggression', attacks made with the above motive cannot but be characterized as wars of aggression.[1]

This affords a clear statement of the 'territorial' concept of aggression; as in the case of Nuremberg there is no general statement to the effect that the attacked states acted in self-defence of their territorial integrity, but this again is accounted for by similar reasons. The only specific recognition of the victims' right of self-defence which was made was in respect of the Netherlands' action in declaring war on December 8th, 1941, prior to any actual attack on Netherlands territories. The evidence had shown that an attack was clearly planned, indeed an order of the Japanese Imperial General Headquarters on November 10th had fixed December 8th for the commencement of the attack. In view of this the Tribunal rightly recognized the right of the Netherlands to anticipate the attack in self-defence and stated:

> The fact that the Netherlands, being fully apprised of the imminence of the attack, in self-defence declared war against Japan on the 8th December and thus officially recognized the existence of a state of war which had been begun by Japan cannot change that war from a war of aggression on the part of Japan into something other than that.[2]

In conclusion it may be stated that the trials at Nuremberg and Tokyo revealed little about the content of the right of self-defence which was not known before. As we have seen, the Tribunal was able to rely on the classical definition formulated by U.S. Secretary of State Webster in the *Caroline* case; the aggressions in question were of the most blatant character, including direct attacks on the territories of other states, so that there was little need to embark on detailed discussions of the precise nature and limits of the right of self-defence. The essential contribution which these judgments make lies in the clear characterization of war as an instrument of national policy, of aggressive war, as illegal and criminal; for only by so doing does it become possible to speak of a right of self-defence *stricto sensu*. It is the solemn enunciation of that principle which elevates the right of self-

[1] Judgment, November 4th–12th, Part B, ch. VII, p. 994; cited Horwitz, *op. cit.*, p. 549.

[2] Judgment, *op. cit.*, pp. 994–5; Horwitz, *op. cit.*, p. 560. It is perhaps fair to state that the judgment of the International Military Tribunal for the Far East was not unanimous; see the impressive dissenting judgment of Justice Pal, published by Sweet & Maxwell, 1953.

defence into a position within the framework of legal rules which is logically defensible and permits its coherent exposition in the whole field of international law, without differentiating between the law of peace and of war.

This principle, together with the other principles of international law recognized by the Charter of the International Military Tribunal and the judgment of the Tribunal, have been affirmed without dissent by the General Assembly,[1] an indorsement which, although lacking normative character, signifies the generality of the recognition of those principles. The subsequent formulation of those principles by the International Law Commission, presented to the General Assembly in 1950, adds little to this recognition, but the Draft Code of Offences against the Peace and Security of Mankind illustrates the deductions which those jurists on the Commission see fit to draw from Nuremberg. Art. 2(i) of that Code defines as an offence against the peace and security of mankind:

> Any act of aggression, including the employment by the authorities of a State of armed force against another State for any purpose other than national or collective self-defence or in pursuance of a decision or recommendation by a competent organ of the United Nations.[2]

This definition is based upon the principle which Nuremberg foreshadowed, the principle which we have maintained must be recognized before a legal right of self-defence exists, namely that every employment of armed force by the authorities of one state against another can be characterized into the trilogy of delict, sanction, or self-defence.

THE UNITED NATIONS CHARTER

It remains for us to examine exactly how far this trilogy of delict, sanction, and self-defence has been achieved under the

[1] Resolution I (95), December 11th, 1946. Pompe, *op. cit.*, pp. 316–18, regards the resolution as the mere recognition of the existence of an international criminal law, not the creation of such law.

[2] See Report of the I.L.C. Third Session, 1951, U.N. Doc. A/1858: *A.J.*, Supp., Vol. 45 (1951), p. 103. Also cited in Pompe, *op. cit.*, p. 340. See comments by Fenwick, *A.J.*, Vol. 46 (1952), pp. 98–100; Pitman B. Potter, ibid., p. 101; also Observations of Governments on the Draft Code and on the Question of the Definition of Aggression (1952) A/2162 and Add. 1. Also Parry, 'Some Considerations upon the Content of a Draft Code', *I.L.Q.*, Vol. 3 (1950), p. 208. D. H. Johnson, 'Code of Offences against Peace and Security', *Int. and Comp. L.Q.*, Vol. 4 (1955), p. 445.

Charter and, in consequence, a right of self-defence *stricto sensu* established. The defects inherent in a system which confines its prohibition of unilateral action to the technical definition of 'war' have already been indicated. It was, therefore, as a marked departure from the prohibitions of the Covenant and the Pact of Paris that the Dumbarton Parks Proposals formulated, as one of the Principles of the proposed organization, the following obligation:

> All members of the Organization shall refrain in their international relations from the threat or use of force, in any manner inconsistent with the purposes of the Organization.[1]

This formula, in its rejection of the term war far more comprehensive than its predecessors, introduces an objective criterion for the ascertainment of whether the obligation has been broken. The existence of a 'threat or use of force' is a question of fact,[2] and there is now no possibility of the parties to a conflict determining for themselves its juridical nature, namely whether or not war existed, and thereby evading the binding prohibition of war. It is a matter for some regret that at San Francisco, in response to the demand of certain smaller states that specific guarantees of their territorial integrity and political independence be included,[3] this formula was qualified to become, in the wording of Art. 2(4) of the Charter:

> All Members shall refrain in their international relations from the threat or use of force against the territorial integrity or political independence of any State, or in any other manner inconsistent with the Purposes of the United Nations.

The meaning of this prohibition is not free from all ambiguity, and as yet the practice of the organs of the United Nations is extremely limited in so far as it affects directly this question of interpretation. The General Assembly on November 27th, 1948,[4] endorsed the finding of the majority of the United Nations Special Committee on the Balkans that the material and moral assistance to armed bands invading Greek territory, provided by Albania, Bulgaria and Yugoslavia, constituted a threat to the political independence and territorial integrity of Greece. The Assembly

[1] Commentary on the Charter of the U.N., H.M.S.O., Cmd. 6666, p. 25.
[2] Pompe, *Aggressive War*, p. 97.
[3] *UNCIO*, Docs., Vol. VI, pp. 69, 346.
[4] Resolution 193 (iii) at 167th Plenary Meeting.

also, in 1952, passed a resolution[1] which considered that the 'presence, hostile activities and depredations of foreign forces in the territory of Burma . . . constitute a violation of the territory and sovereignty of the Union of Burma'. In the *Corfu Channel Case* the Albanian government alleged that the minesweeping operations of the British fleet on November 12th–13th, 1946, to collect evidence following the mining of the two British destroyers,

> ... a violé d'une manière flagrante le souveraineté de l'Etat albanais et toutes les règles du droit international.[2]

The Albanian contention rested on general principles and on Art. 5 of the Hague Convention VIII of 1907 rather than on Art. 2(4). However, the Albanian rejoinder to the British reply did cite Art. 2(4), but more for the basis of a proposition that since the Charter the right of intervention had completely disappeared.[3] Unhappily the judgment of the Court was framed in general terms and found that 'the action of the British Navy constituted a violation of Albanian sovereignty'.[4]

This paucity of authority on the interpretation of Art. 2(4) is due largely to the fact that complaints by states which might have been framed in terms of a breach of Art. 2(4) have almost invariably been framed in terms of Art. 39. The inquiry has been whether a 'threat to the peace, breach of the peace, or act of aggression' has occurred, and not whether Art. 2(4) has been violated. As we shall see,[5] the terms of these two articles are not co-extensive, and a determination under Art. 39 might be made regardless of whether Art. 2(4) had been broken or, *vice versa*, a breach of Art. 2(4) need not necessarily assume the character of a 'threat to the peace, breach of the peace, or act of aggression'. There have been numerous cases in which Art. 2(4) could have been directly in issue. Where there has been an armed invasion of territory, as in the Indonesian,[6] Palestine[7] and Korean[8] affairs;

[1] Resolution 707 (vii).

[2] Albanian Counter-Memorial, *Corfu Channel Case*, Pleadings, Vol. II, p. 138, para. 141.

[3] Albanian Rejoinder, ibid., p. 370, paras. 151 and 154.

[4] I.C.J. Reports, 1949. *Corfu Channel Case* (Merits), p. 35. [5] *Post*, p. 176.

[6] See Australian draft resolution of July 31st, 1947. Off. Rec. S.C., 2nd Year, No. 67, p. 1626.

[7] See the communication from the Jewish Agency; Off. Rec. S.C., 3rd Year, No. 66, 292nd Meeting, p. 2, S/744.

[8] See the S.C. Resolution of June 25th, 1950, S/1501. Off. Rec. S.C., 5th Year, 473rd Meeting, pp. 13 and 14.

or where a complaint is made that troops are maintained in territory contrary to the wishes of the territorial sovereign, as in the Soviet complaint against the U.K. in 1946,[1] the Egyptian complaint against the U.K. in 1947,[2] and the Burmese complaint against the Nationalist government of China in 1953[3]; or where the allegation is that support is being given to armed invading bands as in the Greek question in 1947,[4] or the Guatemalan complaint of 1954[5]—in all these cases Art. 2(4) appears relevant, and these illustrations are not exhaustive. In certain cases complaints framed almost in the terms of Art. 2(4) have been made, as, for example, in the Soviet complaint against the U.S.A. regarding the alleged invasion of Taiwan,[6] but no firm finding of a breach of Art. 2(4), soundly based on the construction of that article, is known to exist.

In the absence of authoritative decisions on the meaning of the article it becomes necessary to discuss its interpretation in the light of accepted rules of construction. Taking the words in their plain, common-sense meaning, it is clear that, since the prohibition is of the 'use or threat of force', they will not apply to economic or political pressure but only to physical, armed force.[7] This does not imply that the independence of a state may not be imperilled by means other than the use or threat of force. In so far as this may be the case, the threatened state may still have the right of self-defence, but the preceding breach of an obligation will be not the breach of Art. 2(4), but of some other duty im-

[1] Statement of U.S.S.R. representative, Off. Rec. S.C., 1st Year, 6th Meeting, p. 73. [2] Off. Rec. S.C., 2nd Year, No. 59, p. 1343.

[3] Burmese proposal on March 25th, 1953 (A/2375), adopted on the agenda of the General Assembly on March 31st: see subsequent resolution of G.A. (707 (vii)), April 23rd.

[4] Statement of Greek representative to U.N., addressed to President of S.C. U.N. Docs. S/389.

[5] For discussion in the S.C., see Off. Rec. S.C., 9th Year, 675th Meeting, June 20th, 1954. The complaint is made in a cablegram from Min. for Foreign Affairs of Guatemala to President of S.C. U.N. Doc. S/3232.

[6] Soviet draft resolution submitted September 2nd, 1950. U.N. Doc. S/1757. See also joint resolution submitted by Central People's Govt. of China at 527th Meeting on November 29th, 1950. U.N. Doc. S/1921; neither were adopted. See also the Chilean complaint that the threat of force by the U.S.S.R. had violated the political independence of Czechoslovakia, made on March 12th, 1948; U.N. Doc. S/694.

[7] See Waldock, *op. cit.*, ch. III. A Brazilian proposal to extend the prohibition of Art. 2(4) to include economic force was rejected; *UNCIO* Docs., VI, pp. 339–40.

posed by international law—in all probability the duty of non-intervention. Against such a breach of duty, given the requirements of the right of self-defence, that right may still be exercised; but the requirement of proportionality, coupled with the obligations of Art. 2(4) and Art. 2(3), would suggest that the defending state should, as a general rule, exercise force only against threats which are delictual under Art. 2(4). Against other delicts, not involving the use or threat of force, the measures of self-defence will take the form of, possibly, a denial of trading rights, a refusal of the right of diplomatic representation within its territory,[1] or some other non-hostile action which the emergency demands.

A second qualification of the prohibition contained in Art. 2(4) results from the phrase 'in their international relations'. *Prima facie*, the prohibition does not extend to force used within the state's own metropolitan area, in its colonies and protectorates.[2] This qualification harmonizes with the general limitation on the scope of the authority of the organization contained in Art. 2(7), which preserves to the members matters 'essentially within the domestic jurisdiction'. It is, of course, possible for force used within a state's own territory to be characterized as a 'threat to the peace, breach of the peace', but it can scarcely be said to be contrary to Art. 2(4) and this anomaly arises solely from the difference in wording of Arts. 2(4) and 39. Under normal circumstances, however, the qualification introduced by the phrase 'in their international relations' will cause no difficulty, for, since the state's relations with these territories are not 'international', not governed by international law, no problem arises. There may be, however, exceptional circumstances in which a group or community within these territories claims international personality, or statehood; this is a claim that any threat or use of force against the group or community would be 'international' and therefore subject to Art. 2(4). It implies also that the group or community is endowed with international personality and can not only plead a breach of Art. 2(4) but against that breach exercise the right of

[1] This might be an appropriate form of self-defence where an embassy has been used as a base for activities aimed at overthrowing the political independence of the receiving state.

[2] For the same view see Goodrich & Hambro, *Charter of the U.N.*, 2nd ed., p. 103; Wehberg, 'L'Interdiction du Recours à la Force', *R.C.*, 1951 (I), p. 73; Pompe, *op. cit.*, p. 106; Waldock, 'The Regulation of the Use of Force by Individual States in International Law', *R.C.*, 1952 (II), ch. III.

self-defence. It is not difficult to envisage a situation in which the established state claiming sovereignty over the territory occupied by the group or community resists this claim and contends its action is not subject to the prohibition of Art. 2(4).

The situation in Indonesia in 1947 may be taken as an illustration of how the problem can arise. Following a letter dated July 30th from the Australian representative on the Security Council,[1] the Security Council became seised of the question whether the hostilities undertaken by the Netherlands against Indonesian forces on July 20th, 1947, constituted a breach of the peace under Art. 39. The Netherlands contended that the matter was essentially within its own domestic jurisdiction,[2] so that the issue was on the application of Arts. 39 and 2(7). It could, however, have been framed as a contention that the action of the Netherlands was not a use of force in its international relations, had the question of a breach of Art. 2(4) arisen. In the outcome, though the precise basis of the Security Council ruling is not clear, the Council apparently proceeded to assume jurisdiction on the view that by the Linggadjati Agreement the Netherlands had accorded *de facto* recognition to the Indonesian Republic.[3]

This problem arises more from the de-centralized system of determining whether 'international relations' exist between communities, that is to say whether recognition of statehood should be accorded, than from any ambiguity in the phrasing of Art. 2(4). The recognition of new states in international law remains largely a matter for the individual appreciation of states, whereas the breach of Art. 2(4) is a question which purports to be objective. Until such time as recognition of new states is made a collective function this difficulty will persist, and in the meanwhile it is possible for a community to allege a breach of Art. 2(4) and claim to exercise the right of self-defence at the same time as its opponent denies statehood to the community and the application of Art. 2(4).

The phrase 'against the territorial integrity or political independence of any state' may, on one construction, mean that the element of intent is introduced into the prohibition; namely, that the use or threat of force contravenes this obligation only where

[1] U.N. Doc. S/449.

[2] Off. Rec. S.C., 2nd Year, No. 67, 171st Meeting, pp. 1619–20, 1045–6.

[3] For a summary of the action taken by the Security Council see *International Organization*, Vol. II (1948), pp. 80–5, 297–9, 500–2. Also *U.N. Rep. of Practice*, Vol. I, p. 115 *et seq.*

intended to jeopardize the political independence or territorial integrity of another state. Or, if specific intent is not required, it may mean that at least the use or threat of force must have this effect before being in contravention of Art. 2(4). This, in effect, was the construction which the U.K. agent, Sir Eric Beckett, sought to place on the article in contending before the International Court of Justice in the *Corfu Channel Case* that 'Operation Retail', the subsequent minesweeping operation, was not contrary to Art. 2(4). He said:

> But our action on the 12th/13th November threatened neither the territorial integrity nor the political independence of Albania. Albania suffered thereby neither territorial loss nor any part of its political independence.[1]

As previously indicated, the finding of the Court, against the United Kingdom on this point, made no specific reference either to this argument or indeed to Art. 2(4).

Against this view there are strong reasons which would deprive this phrase of any qualifying effect on the prohibition. Firstly there is the fact that its origin is found in the desire of the smaller powers to secure some express guarantee of their territorial integrity and political independence;[2] the introduction of this phrase at San Francisco had not, as its purpose, the qualifying of the obligation. Secondly, to introduce the subjective element of 'intent' seems anomalous once 'war' had been replaced by the more objective phrase 'threat or use of force'. Moreover, in the initial stages at least, it may be extremely difficult to ascertain the intention of a state, and even the most obvious aggression may be accompanied by statements to show a lack of any such specific intent. As Pompe says . . . 'intention can hardly be ascertained by the international security organ. For the maintenance of international peace and security it is the effect of the act that counts'.[3] This is supported by the view of Wehberg, who states: 'La menace et l'emploi de la force sont proscrits en eux-mêmes et quels que puissent être leurs motifs'.[4]

[1] I.C.J. Pleadings, *Corfu Channel Case*, Vol. III, pp. 295–6. See also the argument by Stone, *Legal Controls of International Conflict*, pp. 234–6, that the U.N. action in Korea could not violate Art. 2(4), since it was not directed against the territorial integrity or political independence of any state.

[2] *Ante*, p. 146.

[3] *Op. cit.*, p. 166.

[4] *Op. cit.*, p. 64.

Similarly, Lauterpacht states:

> Neither is the obligation not to resort to force or threats of force limited by the words 'against the territorial integrity or political independence of any state'. Territorial integrity especially where coupled with 'political independence', is synonomous with territorial inviolability. . . . Thus a state would be acting in breach of its obligations under the Charter if it were to invade or commit an act of force within the territory of another state, in anticipation of an alleged impending attack or in order to obtain redress, without the intention of interfering permanently with the territorial integrity of that state.[1]

Despite these reasons it is submitted that, the phrase having been included, it must be given its plain meaning. Moreover, to give it its plain meaning coincides with the limitations on the obligation of non-intervention which traditional international law recognizes. The rights of territorial integrity and political independence have never been absolute, but always relative to similar rights in other states, so that 'integrity' has always been a more accurate term than 'inviolability'. The right to territorial integrity or political independence is never absolute but is conditional on the non-existence of any threat to the security of another state within its borders. In our view, therefore, invasion of territory necessitated by the imminence of an attack from that territory, and justified by the conditions governing the exercise of the right of self-defence under general international law, would not be prohibited by Art. 2(4). It is precisely because self-defence cannot be, by definition, 'against the territorial integrity or political independence of any state', that the opinion could be held at San Francisco that the right of self-defence was left unimpaired by Art. 2(4). Similarly, when circumstances justify the landing of troops to protect the lives and property of nationals, this use of force, if confined to the requirements of self-defence, will never be aimed at impairing the territorial integrity or the political independence of the territorial state; once it has that aim it ceases to be self-defence and transgresses Art. 2(4).

The reference to 'any State' at once signifies that the benefit of the obligation of Art. 2(4) is extended even to non-signatory states, in the interest of international peace and security. Bearing in mind the provision of Art. 2(6), it may now be said that, on principles of reciprocity and by regarding the general interest in

[1] Oppenheim, *International Law*, 7th ed., Vol. II, p. 154.

the maintenance of international peace and security as paramount, the obligation of Art. 2(4) is also incumbent on 'any State'. Whatever are the theoretical objections to this, based on the maxim '*pacta tertiis nec nocent nec prosunt*', the imposition of this basic obligation on non-signatory states is soundly based on the essential inter-dependence of all members of the international community. Action by any state against any other state, regardless of membership of the United Nations, which is contrary to the terms of Art. 2(4), cannot but jeopardize the security of the entire international community as a whole. It is worth noting, in passing, that neither the Republic of South Korea, nor the 'authorities of North Korea' (the latter unrecognized as a state by the United Nations) were members of the United Nations, yet, though Art. 2(4) was not specifically in issue, the latter was determined to be responsible for, and the former the victim of what was certainly action contrary to its terms.

Two other difficulties present themselves in this reference to 'any State'; one lies in the possibility that the attacking state may not recognize the 'statehood' of its victims and therefore deny the application of Art. 2(4). A situation of this nature arose when in 1948 the Arab States sent forces into Palestine but elected to regard the 'State' of Israel as a rebellious minority in an independent nation which had requested the assistance of the Arab states in restoring law and order.[1] Here again the argument turned more on the terms of Art. 39 than of Art. 2(4), and the real question became one as to whether 'international' peace had been threatened or broken; in essence the argument is not dissimilar. In the outcome the majority of members of the Council disregarded the question of statehood and concentrated on the fact of invasion by states of territory not their own.[2] This attitude, and also that taken in relation to Indonesia,[3] suggests that the U.N. organ will not interpret statehood too literally and limit the obligation of Art. 2(4) to cases of attack against a recognized state; more particularly, they will not allow the attacker, by

[1] Off. Rec. S.C., 3rd Year, 292nd Meeting, statement of Mr. Nakleh (Arab Higher Committee), pp. 7–9.

[2] Off. Rec. S.C., 3rd Year, 293rd–299th Meeting. At the 302nd Meeting on May 22nd, 1948, the Security Council rejected a determination under Art. 39, and adopted a resolution calling upon 'all governments and authorities' to abstain from hostile military action. U.N. Doc. S/773.

[3] *Ante*, p. 150.

withholding recognition from its victim, to evade the prohibition. The other difficulty arises where the territory invaded is territory in respect of which sovereignty is disputed. It has already been suggested that here the test of *de facto* occupation ought to be applied, so that the threat or use of force against territory in *de facto* occupation of another state should be characterized as delictual under Art. 2(4). This is not to suggest that a *de facto* but illegal occupation of territory will be perpetuated; there remains the obligation of Art. 2(3) which would suggest that *de facto* occupation must be reinforced with willingness to have the question of title adjudicated pacifically. Moreover, without such willingness, continued illegal occupation of territory would probably assume the character of a threat to international peace and warrant the Security Council taking coercive measures under Chapter VII. It is also clear that the illegality of a use of force or threat of force is not determined solely by the criterion of use 'against the territorial integrity or political independence of any State', for there is added to this criterion that of use 'in any other manner inconsistent with the Purposes of the United Nations'. Of those purposes, stated in Art. 1, that which is paramount is the purpose 'to maintain international peace and security'; to that end the Members are

(1) to take effective *collective* measures for the prevention and removal of threats to the peace and for the suppression of acts of aggression or other breaches of the peace,
(2) to bring about by peaceful means, and in conformity with the principles of justice and international law, adjustment or settlement of international disputes or situations which might lead to a breach of the peace.

Both these obligations restrict the capacity of members to take measures involving the use or threat of force, except as a 'collective measure' (which here means a measure authorized by the collectivity of states represented in a competent organ of the United Nations), or as action in self-defence. We have previously seen[1] that the legality of individual self-help, other than self-defence, is doubtful under the Charter; certainly Art. 2(4) provides criteria of legality which, though not free from ambiguity, must be complied with.

Apart from these doubts as to the continued legality of forms

[1] *Ante*, pp. 11–19.

of self-help, and apart from the somewhat anomalous exceptions of action against 'enemy states' (Arts. 53, 107), and 'joint action' under Art. 106,[1] it is now possible to characterize the use or threat of force as either a delict, or a sanction, or self-defence. This possibility is, for our purposes, the greatest advance secured by the Charter. This threefold classification of the use or threat of force not only avoids the pitfalls of a prohibition of 'war',[2] but brings about a restriction on the freedom of individual action which makes self-defence legally meaningful. It involves the delictual character of the use or threat of force, other than in self-defence or authorized by a competent United Nations organ, and thereby provides the basis upon which the concept of self-defence achieves a juridical connotation.

[1] *Ante*, pp. 11–12. [2] *Ante*, pp. 124–5.

CHAPTER VIII

NEUTRALITY AND SELF-DEFENCE

THE development of neutrality as an institution of international law demanding impartiality towards belligerents was inevitably linked with the rejection of the concept of *bellum justum*, for strict impartiality had found no place in a system which differentiated between the just and the unjust war,[1] and in which states had been entitled to discriminate against the belligerent whose cause was unjust. As stated by Jessup and Déak:

> The problem of neutrality came to be considered from the point of view of whether a war was 'just' or 'unjust' and neutral duties towards a nation waging a 'just' war were thus measured differently from those which existed toward a nation embarking on an 'unjust' war.[2]

The ascendancy of positivism brought not only a rejection of the *bellum justum* but, as a corollary, a new concept of neutrality as a condition of absolute impartiality towards opposing belligerents. It was this element of impartiality which characterized the positivist definitions of neutrality,[3] and when Oppenheim described the principle of impartiality as 'inherent in the nature of neutrality' [4] he did no more than reflect the predominant view of his time. This was not, however, the only view, and Westlake, perhaps more justifiably from a historical viewpoint and certainly more prophetically, maintained that neutrality 'is not morally justifiable unless intervention in war is unlikely to promote justice', or could 'do so only at a ruinous cost to the neutral', for 'the general duty of every member of the society (of nations)[5] is to promote justice'.[6] Significantly, however, Westlake phrases

[1] Grotius, *op. cit.*, Bk. III, c. 17; Vattel, *op. cit.*, Bk. III, s. 135.

[2] *Neutrality*, I, The Origins (1935), pp. 8–10. Castren, *The Present Law of War and Neutrality* (1954), p. 51 *et seq.*

[3] For a collection of definitions see Hackworth, *Dig.*, Vol. VII, pp. 343–5.

[4] *International Law*, Vol. II, 6th ed., p. 515. As to its 'inherent' character there is clearly some doubt; Hall's view (*Int. Law*, 8th ed., p. 701) was that the duty of impartiality only became established after 1788. Politis, *Neutrality and Peace* (1935), p. 16, describes it as 'the last phase of the development' of the institution.

[5] Brackets mine.

[6] *International Law*, Vol. II, p. 90. See for a contrary view Jessup, *Neutrality*, Vol. IV, Today and Tomorrow (1938), pp. 77–82.

his view in terms of what is morally rather than legally justifiable, and in view of the state practice which had developed throughout the nineteenth century this qualification was inevitable. Indeed the emphasis throughout the Hague Conventions of 1907[1] is typically positivist in its insistence on impartiality.

However, with the gradual prohibition of war in positive international law it became possible in certain cases, as we have shown, to characterize a belligerency as illegal; this involved not only the recognition of a right of self-defence but also undermined the whole basis upon which the doctrine of impartiality had rested, namely the impossibility of distinguishing between delict and self-defence and the acceptance of an unlimited right to wage war. 'The historic foundation which underlay the modern formulation of the doctrine of absolute neutrality was the absolute right of the State to resort to war.' [2]

It is, therefore, essential to consider not only the development of a legal right of self-defence through the gradual prohibition of war and the use of force, but also the changes which ought logically to occur in the relationship between neutrals and belligerents as a result of that prohibition. That is not to say that these changes were ever accepted as part of international law, and we shall attempt to indicate where state practice has not developed consistently with logic but has remained impressed by the dictates of expediency or the inertia of positivist ideas. Furthermore, we are not here directly concerned with the problem of reconciling neutrality with participation in a system of collective security,[3] but rather with the immediate question of the effect on neutrality of a particular belligerency being classified as undertaken in self-defence.

Under the Covenant of the League[4] a signatory state resorting to war in disregard of the obligations contained in Arts. 12, 13 and 15 was clearly acting illegally. Faced with such illegality, once

[1] No. V, respecting the Rights and Duties of Neutral Powers and Persons in case of War on Land. No. XIII, concerning the Rights and Duties of Neutral Powers in Naval War.

[2] Oppenheim, *op. cit.*, 7th ed., p. 639.

[3] As to which see Lalive, 'International Organization and Neutrality', *BYBIL*, Vol. 24 (1947), p. 72. Whitton, 'La Neutralité et la Société des Nations', *R.C.*, 1927 (III), p. 453.

[4] See generally on this problem Whitton, *op. cit.*, ch. II, p. 474 *et seq.* *Collective Security*, ed. Bourquin, League of Nations International Studies Conference, Paris, 1936, especially Lauterpacht, p. 412 *et seq.*

a Member had determined that this state had resorted to war in breach of these obligations it could elect to treat the breach as an act of war against itself; in such a case the Member would lose neutral status. Again, in participating in military sanctions under Art. 16 a Member would similarly lose its neutral status, so that in both cases its position is not relevant to the problem under discussion, namely the extent to which the recognition of a right of self-defence has affected the law of neutrality.

On the other hand, however, in the absence of such an election each member was bound, under Art. 16(1), to discriminate against the state in breach of its obligations by means of the economic sanctions contained in the Article, and, under Art. 16(3), to afford support to other co-operating states in such financial and economic measures and also to afford passage through its territory to the forces of any of the Members co-operating to protect the covenants. These discriminatory measures were never deemed to involve the Member in belligerency, and it had been said that the Covenant-breaking belligerent must be deemed, in signing the Covenant, to have consented in advance to measures of discrimination being applied against him by those Members of the League who did not elect to declare war upon him.[1] To this extent, therefore, the Covenant afforded legal justification for a departure from the strict duty of impartiality normally incumbent on neutrals.

In general, however, the character of this discrimination is that of a sanction against the Covenant-breaking state, and *prima facie* it bears little relation to the position of any state which undertakes a war of self-defence in the defence of its rights. Not every illegal resort to war by one state would involve another in action in self-defence; indeed it was conceivable that there may be two opposing belligerents, both in breach of their obligations under the Covenant. However, it was probable that in most cases the resort to war would activate the right of self-defence in another Member, and the terms of the Covenant lend support to the view that in these circumstances the state acting in self-defence had a right to receive the support, by way of discrimination against the aggressor state, from other Members who chose to remain neutral. After all, Art. 10 did contain a guarantee by each Member of the territorial integrity and political independence of every other

[1] Oppenheim, *op. cit.*, Vol. II, 6th ed., p. 507.

Member, and the duty of discrimination under Art. 16(1) appears absolute in character. As Politis wrote in 1935, 'in principle, the duty of assistance already exists by virtue of Arts. 10 and 16 of the Covenant'.[1] In point of fact, however, this view was never taken although the possibility of such a view clearly did exist. The duty to discriminate under Art. 16(1) was never regarded as a specific duty owed to a Member acting in self-defence, and even as a duty to take sanctions against the aggressor owed to League Members generally it was evaded either by a refusal to characterize an aggression as a 'resort to war' [2] or else, eventually, by an interpretation of Art. 16(1) which denied its obligatory character.[3] It has been said, with considerable justification, that:

> La neutralité n'est pas exclusivement une notion juridique, c'est aussi une notion politique. Il est certain que la neutralité subsiste comme institution, et l'idée de neutralité continuera d'être à la base de la politique de plusieurs pays.[4]

The development of state practice in the inter-war years in this respect showed more concern with political convenience than with the juridical implications which the Covenant logically brought about. Certainly the practice of Members under the League affords no evidence that a state in the exercise of its legal right of self-defence could, as a matter of right, call upon neutral Members to discriminate against the aggressor.

The Pact of Paris necessarily posed the problem in more acute form, for there the prohibition of war as an instrument of national policy was unequivocal. On the other hand the Pact made no reference to the law of neutrality, nor did it contain any guarantee similar to Art. 10 of the Covenant or any obligatory sanctions similar to those in Art. 16, and the effect of the Pact on the duties

[1] *Op. cit.*, p. 87. For similar views see Whitton, 'Neutralité et la S.D.N.', *R.C.*, 1927 (II), p. 520; Redslob, *Traité*, p. 435; Rousseau, *Droit International Public* (1953), p. 673 *et seq.*: for a contrary view see Cohn, *Neo-Neutrality* (1939), pp. 78–9, whose premiss rejecting any distinction between defensive and offensive wars we should not accept.

[2] As in the cases of the Japanese invasion of Manchuria in 1931, of China in 1937.

[3] See the declaration by several European states in 1938, renouncing the obligatory character of sanctions under Art. 16(1)—*Acta Scandinavia* (ix), p. 128. Also the refusal in 1940 by Sweden and Norway to allow passage to British and French troops to be sent to Finland in pursuance of the Resolution of the League Assembly, Official Journal, 1939, p. 540.

[4] Boye, 'Règles de la Neutralité', *R.C.*, 1938 (II), p. 226.

of the neutral state was subject to considerable disagreement. Lauterpacht, as the editor of the sixth edition of Oppenheim, stated that the Pact 'has not directly affected the law of neutrality', but at the same time he was clearly aware of the juridical consequences which logic dictated although state practice might not support:

> There is no doubt that by destroying the basis of the traditional doctrine of neutrality as an attitude of absolute impartiality, namely, the unrestricted right of the sovereign states to go to war, the Treaty has provided the starting point for important changes in the law of neutrality.[1]

On the other hand other writers concluded that, since the Pact enabled action in violation of the Pact to be characterized as delictual, the neutral had a right,[2] and possibly even a duty,[3] to discriminate against the offending state and actually assist the state acting in self-defence. The celebrated Budapest Articles of Interpretation, adopted by the International Law Association at Budapest on September 10th, 1934,[4] drew similar conclusions by way of interpretation of the Pact and suggested, *inter alia*, that:

> In the event of a violation of the Pact by a resort to armed force or war by one signatory State against another, the other State may, without thereby committing a breach of the Pact or of any rule of international law, do all or any of the following things:
> (*a*) Refuse to admit the exercise by the State violating the Pact of belligerent rights, such as visit and search, or blockade etc.
> (*b*) Decline to observe towards the State violating the Pact the duties prescribed by international law, apart from the Pact, for a neutral in relation to a belligerent.
> (*c*) Supply the State attacked with financial or material assistance, including munitions of war.
> (*d*) Assist with armed forces the State attacked.

---

[1] *Op. cit.*, pp. 512–14. Also Cohn, *op. cit.*, p. 93: *contra*, Politis, *op. cit.*, p. 80.

[2] Boye, 'Shall a state which goes to war in violation of the Kellogg-Briand Pact have a Belligerent's rights in respect of Neutrals', *A.J.*, Vol. 24 (1930), p. 766.

[3] Quincey Wright, 'The Future of Neutrality', *Int. Concil.*, 1928, p. 362. Brierly, 'Some Implications of the Pact of Paris', *BYBIL*, Vol. 10 (1929), p. 211. Also Quincey Wright, 'The Meaning of the Pact of Paris', *A.J.*, Vol. 27 (1933), p. 39, at p. 59. He does, however, suggest that discrimination should not extend to the laws of war, a sound view later reflected in Art. 7 of the Budapest Articles of Interpretation.

[4] *I.L.A. Reports*, 38 (1935), 66, 67.

Although objections may be raised as to whether these Articles go beyond the task of interpretation,[1] and although it may rightly be said that to adduce rules as a matter of logic is not necessarily to state accepted rules of international law, the fact was that these Articles suggested the inevitable trend of legal development consistent with the maintenance of the principles of the Pact. Indeed it was to these rules that the United States authorities were later to refer in justifying their discrimination in favour of Great Britain in 1940,[2] and as Lauterpacht himself later admits:

> The historic foundation which underlay the modern formulation of the doctrine of absolute neutrality was the absolute right of the state to resort to war. That right was solemnly relinquished by practically all nations, including Germany, in the General Treaty for the Renunciation of War. Discrimination against the aggressor state and assistance to its adversary were in accordance with the purpose of the Treaty, whose indirect effect was to sap the foundations of the law of absolute neutrality.[3]

Moreover, though expressed as a view *de lege ferenda*, the Harvard Draft Convention on the Rights and Duties of States in Case of Aggression[4] drew somewhat similar conclusions in the case where, by reason of its violation of an obligation,[5] a state had resorted to armed force and thereby incurred international responsibility. In that event a state not itself the victim of any attack might assist the actual victim, the so-called 'Defending State', with armed force and thereby assume the role of a 'Co-Defending State'; or, in affording lesser assistance, assume the rôle of a 'Supporting State'.

These views were never, in their own time, an expression of international law as evidenced in the practice of states, for, though

[1] Lauterpacht, 'The Pact of Paris and the Budapest Articles of Interpretation', *Trans. Grotius Soc.*, Vol. XX (1935), p. 178. Also Hudson, M.O., The Budapest Resolution of 1934 on the Kellogg-Briand Pact of Paris, *A.J.*, Vol. 29 (1935), p. 92.

[2] U.S. Secretary of State Stimson before Senate Committee on Foreign Affairs, January 16th, 1941, in speaking of the Lease-Lend Bill; cited Hackworth, *Dig.*, Vol. VII, p. 680. Also U.S. Secretary Hull, January 15th, 1941, cited Hackworth, p. 689. U.S. Attorney-General Robert H. Jackson, Address to Inter-American Bar Association at Havana, March 27th, 1941, cited Hackworth, pp. 686–7.

[3] Oppenheim, Vol. II, 7th ed., p. 639.

[4] *A.J.*, Supp., Vol. 33 (1939), p. 823.

[5] Ibid., Art. 1(c) defines aggression.

they pointed to the conclusion which must necessarily follow if the full implications of the Covenant and the Paris Pact be realized, the fact remained that state practice throughout the inter-war years refused to accept these conclusions. It is necessary, therefore, to examine how in practice neutral states viewed their duties towards the state acting in self-defence, and secondly, how the defending state viewed its rights in relation to neutral states.

THE NEUTRAL STATE

An examination of state practice in the inter-war years reveals no evidence to support the thesis, tenable as a matter of logical interpretation of the Covenant and the Pact, that the 'neutral' state had a duty to assist the state acting in self-defence, and the latter a right to demand such discrimination. On the contrary, that practice reveals a determination to ignore the possibilities afforded by the characterization of a conflict as delictual on the part of one or both belligerents.

As early as 1921, at the Barcelona Conference on Freedom of Transit, convened under League auspices, a final statute contained in Art. 8 the following provision: 'This statute does not prescribe the rights and duties of belligerents and neutrals in time of war'.[1] In the following two years 'at least four important multi-partite conventions, signed by League members, contained similar recognition of the survival of neutrality'.[2] The Nine Power Treaty for the Protection of China, signed at the Washington Disarmament Conference on February 6th, 1922, by the U.S.A. and eight other states, members of the League, contained in Art. 6 an agreement to respect China's rights as a neutral. Numerous 'neutrality treaties' so-called were concluded, as for example the German-Soviet Treaty of 1926, the Austrian-Greek Treaty of 1921, the Serb-Italian Treaty of 1925, the Lithuanian-Soviet Treaty of 1926, the Italo-Soviet Pact of Friendship, Non-Aggression and Neutrality of 1933. Art. 2 of this last treaty illustrates the general tenor of these treaties, an obligation to remain neutral in the event of an attack upon either by a Third State:

[1] Hudson, *International Legislation*, Vol. I, pp. 625–35.

[2] Jessup, *Neutrality*, IV, p. 119. And see the lists cited by the same author; *Proceedings A.S.*, 1933, p. 134 *et seq.*

If either of the High Contracting Parties is attacked by one or more Powers, the other High Contracting Party undertakes to observe neutrality during the whole period of the conflict.[1]

Nothing could be further from an obligation to assist the victim of an aggression.

The Pact of Paris made no difference to this prevalent policy, for 1928 saw the adoption of a Convention on Maritime Neutrality by the Sixth International Conference of American States,[2] and, indeed, in the Chaco war neutrality was proclaimed by Argentina, Brazil, Chile and Peru.[3] Again, the Anti-War Treaty on Non-Aggression and Conciliation,[4] signed at Rio de Janeiro on October 10th, 1933, contained a condemnation of wars of aggression coupled with the adoption of a common attitude 'in their character as neutrals'. In the Italo-Abyssinian War the United States, together with most other states, maintained an attitude of strict impartiality[5] which one American writer has suggested 'carried with it an implied abandonment of the Pact of Paris'.[6] It has, of course, been suggested that this technical impartiality did in fact result in discrimination in favour of Abyssinia, since she would be supplied by the states Members of the League whereas Italy could turn neither to the League Members nor to neutrals for supplies.[7] In point of fact the practice of League Members was itself so predominantly neutral in the strict sense[8] that this view is unrealistic.

By 1938 several European states renounced the obligatory

[1] *League of Nations Treaty Series*, Vol. 146, p. 329. For an enumeration of some of these treaties see Barandon, *Le système juridique de la société des Nations pour le prevention de la guerre* (1933), pp. 346–7. Also Jessup, *op. cit.*, p. 119 *et seq.*

[2] Ratified by the U.S. in February, 1932. *U.S. Treaty Series*, No. 845, Washington, 1932.

[3] Wilson, 'War and Neutrality', *A.J.*, Vol. 27 (1933), p. 724.

[4] *A.J.*, Supp., Vol. 28 (1934), p. 79.

[5] See Resolution of U.S. Senate, August 31st, 1935: cited in Jessup, *Neutrality*, Vol. IV, p. 126; Whiteman, *Neutrality* (1941), pp. 21–2. For an impartial survey of U.S. policy see Cohn, *op. cit.*, p. 105 *et seq.*

[6] Fenwick, 'Neutrality and Responsibility', *A.J.*, Vol. 29 (1935), p. 664.

[7] Jessup, *op. cit.*, p. 132.

[8] The Co-ordination Committee set up by the League in 1935 to coordinate sanctions against Italy made several proposals (see *Off. Journal*, Spec. Supp., No. 150 (1936)), but on July 4th, 1936, such was the 'success' of these sanctions that the Assembly recommended to the Committee that it bring to an end the measures taken by members in accordance with these proposals, ibid., pp. 338–40.

character of sanctions under the Covenant and declared their neutrality,[1] and in 1940 Sweden and Norway were to refuse the request of the British and French governments to allow the passage of their troops in order to lend assistance to Finland in pursuance of the resolution of the League Assembly.[2] In part this consistent adherence to traditional neutrality rested on the argument that any discrimination by a third state would place upon that state the invidious burden of determining whether either state, and if so which, was acting in self-defence. The difficulties inherent in this decision are too obvious to be ignored, but at the same time this cannot provide either an explanation or a justification for this view, for in the cases of the Japanese invasion of Manchuria, of the Italian invasion of Abyssinia, and the Russian invasion of Finland the League made the necessary finding of aggression against one of the belligerents, and in two of those cases authorized sanctions.[3]

With the onset of the Second World War a decided change in state practice did occur, notably in the way in which the United States developed an ever-increasing policy of discrimination in favour of the Allies, until eventually she herself assumed belligerent status.[4] There are theoretically two possible constructions of such 'intervention'.

> Ils interviendront, en premier lieu, s'ils s'estiment personellement menacés par le politique de l'agresseur. Ils interviendront, en second lieu, s'ils ont le sens de l'intérêt général et le souci de maintenir l'ordre international.[5]

In other words it is possible to see this discrimination as a direct result of the necessity of self-defence of the United States herself, or it is possible to see it as a direct result of an obligation assumed, by reason of the qualification of the action of one belligerent as an aggression, to assist the victim of the aggression, the state waging war in self-defence. It is submitted that in the main the evidence supports only the first construction; it is clear throughout these measures of discrimination that the concept of self-defence was invoked as the legal justification for those departures from strict neutrality, but in all cases it was the defence

[1] *Acta Scandinavia* (ix), p. 128.

[2] Off. Journal, 1939, p. 540.

[3] See *ante*, pp. 137–8.

[4] For a survey of the change in the U.S. attitude see Komarnicki, R.*C*., 1952 (1), p. 456 *et seq.*

[5] Giraud, 'Théorie de la Légitime Défense', R.*C*., 1934 (111), p. 804.

of the United States herself.[1] There is little or no evidence that the United States ever deemed herself obliged to assist Great Britain by reason only of the fact that Great Britain waged a war of individual and collective self-defence against flagrant aggression.

The United States Neutrality Law of 1937[2] was framed in terms of complete impartiality, except in the case where a Latin-American state became engaged in war with a non-American state; this presupposed that the non-American state was the aggressor and, presumably, the Monroe Doctrine would afford the necessary basis upon which to discriminate or intervene in favour of the defending Latin-American state. That proviso apart, the United States was determined to remain indifferent to the question whether one belligerent exercised its right of self-defence against an aggression in breach of the Paris Pact. However, in 1939, by the Neutrality Act of November 4th of that year,[3] the lifting of the arms embargo contained in the 1937 Act enabled the transfer of arms to Britain and France via private entities;[4] at this stage the U.S. Government was not prepared to discriminate openly. It was not until 1940, with the transfer of destroyers to Great Britain,[5] that the United States revealed an open discrimination by an act which was *prima facie* contrary to international law; its justification, apparently, was that:

> . . . the obligation of abstinence must be deemed to depend upon the unwavering condition that non-participation is compatible with, and not subversive of, the requirements of self-defence.[6]

---

[1] There can be no question of the neutral's right to self-defence in respect of its own rights, for example when a belligerent invades its territory or otherwise violates its duties towards the neutral. See, as one example, the arming of merchant ships against illegal exercise of the right of visit and search or direct attack. *The Maria*, I, C. Rob, p. 340, *per* Sir William Scott, at p. 374. Rodick, *op. cit.*, pp. 103–4. For the U.S. attitude to this problem in 1917 see Hyde, *op. cit.*, Vol. III, p. 1994 *et seq.* Also Pearce-Higgins, *Defensively armed merchant ships* (1917), p. 25.

[2] May 1st, 1937; 50, Stat. 121. See Garner, 'The U.S. Neutrality Law of 1937', *BYBIL*, Vol. 17 (1938), pp. 44–6; Hyde, Vol. III, p. 2320.

[3] 154, Stat. 4.

[4] See Hyde, Vol. II, p. 2229.

[5] By executive agreement, September 2nd, 1940; see *A.J.*, Vol. 34 (1940), for numerous articles concerning this.

[6] Hyde, *op. cit.*, p. 2236. See also Sec. of State Hull before House Committee on Foreign Affairs, January 15th, 1941. Dept. of State Bulletin, January 18th, 1941, pp. 89–90.

Subsequently, in 1941, the discrimination developed via the 'Lease-Land Act',[1] an act which authorized the production and disposal of defence articles for the benefit of 'the government of any country whose defence the President deems vital to the defence of the United States'. Yet another form of discrimination was the freezing of foreign assets within the United States which were owned by the Axis powers or their nationals, or by states and their nationals which had come under the occupation of the Axis powers; the presidential authority for this action was found in the Trading with the Enemy Act of October 6th, 1917,[2] as amended, which demanded that such action was to be 'necessary in the interests of national defence and security'. Throughout these measures the insistence is on the self-defence of the United States, and assistance to a belligerent was to be afforded where the defence of that belligerent harmonized with the United States' own interests.

If confirmation of this be sought then the establishment of neutral protective zones 'as a measure of continental self-protection' by the American Republics in a statement known as the Declaration of Panama in October, 1939,[3] affords it. These claims to a protective jurisdiction on the high seas made no attempt to discriminate between belligerents, and, indeed, the British Admiralty protested against them.[4] It is not without significance that Mr. Stimson, Secretary of War, testified before the House Committee on Foreign Affairs on January 11th, 1941, in relation to the proposed lease-lend bill, and stated that, as a direct result of the breach of the Kellogg Pact by Germany the U.S. could:

> . . . decline to observe towards the State violating the pact the duties prescribed by international law. . . . Supply the State attacked with financial or material assistance, including munitions of war,[5]

[1] 55, Stat. 31. See citations in Hackworth, *Dig.*, Vol. VII, pp. 691–2.

[2] 40, Stat. 411. For amendments see Hyde, *op. cit.*, Vol. III, p. 2357, fn. 5; also Hackworth, *Dig.*, Vol. VII, p. 653 *et seq.*

[3] See Final Act of the Meeting of Foreign Ministers of the American Republics, Panama, September 23rd–October 3rd, 1939. Dept. of State Bull., October 7th, 1939, 321–2: cited in Hyde, *op. cit.*, Vol. III, p. 2348.

[4] Statement from British Admiralty, issued October 13th, 1939; *The Times*, January 16th, 1940.

[5] Cited Hackworth, *Dig.*, Vol. VII, p. 680. It is of interest to note that Stimson relies on the Budapest Articles in support of his contentions. For a more cautious attitude towards them see the Lord Chancellor in the House of Lords, February 20th, 1935; *Parl. Deb.* (H.L.), 5th Series, Vol. 95, cols. 1007, 1043.

thereby advocating a policy much more closely related to the pure fact of discrimination based on the Paris Pact, without reference to the necessity for the defence of the United States herself. The House Committee's own report[1] corrects this liberal view in soundly basing the United States policy on the assumption that the U.S. would throughout be acting in her own defence.

THE STATE ACTING IN SELF-DEFENCE

The complementary question arises whether, by virtue of the fact that a state wages war in self-defence, it becomes entitled to exceptional rights as a belligerent against neutrals, over and above what are normally conceived to be belligerent rights. This position is, as we have shown, perfectly feasible, and, indeed, one construction of Arts. 10 and 16 of the Covenant would support it; but in fact states have never regarded the distinction between delict and self-defence as warranting more than a right of the neutral to discriminate in favour of the state acting in self-defence, and have never recognized a duty to do so. If we interpret state practice correctly it is, in our submission, impossible to speak of a right to discrimination vested in the state acting in self-defence. On the contrary the traditional emphasis has been on the duty of any belligerent to respect neutral rights, and when Art. I of the Hague Convention of 1907[2] provided that 'the territory of neutral powers is inviolable' it did so without distinguishing between belligerents.

However, apart from this general question as to whether or not the state acting in self-defence has a right to discrimination in its favour by neutrals, there may arise specific situations in which a belligerent violates neutral rights and justifies the violation by relying on the right of self-defence. In certain cases the belligerent may temporarily occupy neutral territory and, as Oppenheim states:

> The question whether such occupation on the part of a belligerent would be excusable in case of extreme necessity, in self-defence, on

---

[1] H. Rept. 18, 77, Cong. First Session, pp. 5–6. Cited Hackworth, VII, p. 692.

[2] Conv. V, respecting the Rights and Duties of Neutral Powers and Persons in Case of War on Land, 1907.

account of the neutral's inability to prevent the other belligerent from making use of the neutral territory as a base for his military operations must, it is believed, be answered in the affirmative, since an extreme case of necessity in the interest of self-defence must be considered as an excuse.[1]

The infringement of neutral rights may also take other forms, such as the destruction of neutral military installations, fleets, or aircraft, or serious interference with neutral commerce upon the high seas. In all these cases, however, if the right of self-defence is to be relied on as a basis for such action against neutrals we must presuppose a breach of neutral duties by the neutral which violates or imperils the belligerent's rights so as to afford to the belligerent the right of self-defence. The position is correctly stated by Rodick in these terms:

> It is difficult to see how one can find a legal justification and excuse for a belligerent violation of neutral rights in a case where the neutral has not failed in any duty which it owes to the particular belligerent.[2]

In many cases the breach of duty will be found in the neutral's failure to use 'due diligence' to prevent its territory being used by one belligerent as a base for warlike operations against the other. Indeed, it is on this basis that the mining of the Norwegian leads in April, 1940, by the British fleet can be justified.[3]

To some extent the plea of self-defence becomes confused with that of reprisals, for a belligerent jeopardized by its enemy's violation of neutral rights may take reprisal action, aimed primarily at the opposing belligerent, which also adversely affects neutral rights, and the circumstances may be susceptible to argument based on both reprisals and self-defence. Yet the two grounds of justification are not coextensive, for whereas a belligerent may take proportionate reprisals against illegalities committed by its opponent, it is not every illegality which will also justify action in self-defence, for this last remedy is only available when the illegality results in a serious threat to the belligerent's existence or to those primary rights we have previously examined. For

[1] *Op. cit.*, Vol. II, 7th ed., p. 698.

[2] *Op. cit.*, p. 117. See also Art. 24, 'Harvard Draft Convention on Rights and Duties of Neutral States in Naval and Aerial War', *A.J.*, Vol. 33 (1939), Supp.

[3] See joint declaration by British and French governments; Hackworth, *Dig.*, Vol. VII, p. 148.

example, in the *Altmark* incident on February 16th, 1940,[1] when the British destroyer *Cossack* intercepted a German auxiliary vessel carrying British prisoners of war which had been voyaging inside Norwegian territorial waters for some 400 miles, the British government justified its violation of neutral territory on the ground that, since the Norwegian authorities had failed to remedy the illegality involved in the *Altmark's* passage, the U.K. herself became entitled to intervene. As Waldock says:

> . . . a duty was imposed on Norway to release the prisoners or at the very least to compel the Altmark to leave Norwegian waters,

and because of her failure to do so,

> . . . the U.K. thereby became entitled itself to intervene in Norwegian waters and remedy a breach of international law which, if consummated, would materially prejudice its interests.[2]

The principle justifying this intervention, in Waldock's view, appears to be that of self-preservation, for he says:

> Accordingly, where material prejudice to a belligerent's interests will result from its continuance (i.e. the breach of duty),[3] the principle of self-preservation would appear fully to justify intervention in neutral waters.[4]

Now if by self-preservation the legal concept of self-defence is intended, it may be doubted whether the interests of the U.K. affected by the Norwegian breach were sufficiently linked to her security as to prejudice that security. Derogation from neutral rights can only be justified by self-defence where the interests of the belligerent are vital enough to involve its security.[5]

Of a similar nature are the problems posed by the sort of impairment of neutral rights involved in the establishment of

[1] See Waldock, 'The Release of the Altmark's Prisoners', *BYBIL*, Vol. 24 (1947), p. 218, maintaining the legality of the British action. Also Bisschop, *Trans. Grotius Soc.*, Vol. 26 (1940), pp. 67–82. For doubts as to this see Hyde, *op. cit.*, Vol. III, p. 2339; Borchard, *A.J.*, Vol. 34 (1940), p. 289. For the Norwegian view see *Docs. on Int. Affairs*, 'Norway and the War', R.I.I.A. (1941), p. 35. For correspondence between G.B. and Norway see *Norway*, No. 1 (1950), Cmd. 8012.

[2] *Op. cit.*, p. 220.

[3] Brackets mine.

[4] Ibid., p. 236; he cites Hyde, Vol. II, 2nd ed., p. 2337, although Hyde disagrees on the relevance of that principle, 3rd ed., p. 2339.

[5] For disapproval of Waldock's argument see Stone, *Legal Controls of International Conflict*, p. 40; Borchard, *A.J.*, Vol. 34 (1940), pp. 289–94.

long-distance blockades and systems of control like the Navicert system. In the First World War Great Britain introduced measures of control which seriously infringed neutral rights to export and import goods not normally within the definition of contraband; these measures were authorized by the Retaliatory Orders in Council of March 11th, 1915, and January 10th, 1917.[1] In the Second World War they were repeated under the authorization of the Orders in Council of November 27th, 1939, and of July 31st, 1940.[2] These measures purported to be measures of reprisal against illegalities by Germany as opposing belligerent, although their justification has been stated in terms remarkably akin to those apt to phrase a claim of self-defence. Colombos regards their basis as:

> . . . the absolute necessity of resorting to retaliation as a protection against the serious menace to their rights and their very existence which the actions initiated by their adversary involved.[3]

In the *Stigstad*[4] Lord Sumner, delivering the judgment of the Privy Council, declared these Orders to be:

> . . . illustrations of the broad rule that belligerency and neutrality are states so related to one another that the latter must accept some abatement of the full benefits of peace in order that the former may not be thwarted in war in the assertion and defence of what is the most precious of all the rights of nations, the right to security and independence.[5]

However framed, whether as self-defence or as reprisals, it appears that a condition precedent to the application of these measures should be the commission of an international delinquency, a breach of duty, by the state against which the measures are directed.[6] The arbitration tribunal in *The Cysne*, an arbitration between Portugal and Germany in 1930, stated:

> . . . reprisals are not admissible against neutrals. There is no legal justification for reprisals except when they have been provoked by an act contrary to international law. This means that they are not admis-

[1] *London Gazette*, March 15th, 1915; *London Gazette*, January 12th, 1917. It seems no neutral during the First World War admitted the right to retaliation. Harvard Draft, *A.J.*, Supp., Vol. 33 (1939), pp. 407, 418–19.

[2] Statutory Rules and Orders 1939, No. 1709; ibid., 1940, No. 1436.

[3] *Law of Prize*, 1949, 3rd ed., p. 276.

[4] [1919] *A.C.* 279.

[5] Ibid., p. 288.

[6] See Hyde, *op. cit.*, p. 2346.

sible except against the State held guilty of the original violation of international law.[1]

Where, therefore, these measures are directed against neutrals, or by their terms are wide enough to include acts against neutrals which are more than merely incidental to reprisals against the other belligerent, it is essential to prove a breach of duty in the neutral in order to justify the measures. It is submitted that where the neutral fails to use due diligence in remedying belligerent illegalities, or permits those illegalities to continue to the serious detriment of another belligerent, this produces a state of *de facto* discrimination against the other belligerent which may amount to such a breach.[2] There can also be no question that the illegalities by Germany which gave rise to this British action were of a kind calculated to impair the very existence of Britain. Accordingly self-defence would seem an appropriate remedy even against neutrals, and, indeed, the plea of self-defence advanced at Nuremberg in respect of the invasion of Norway was rejected on the facts, not as a question of law.[3]

The more difficult position arises where there cannot be found any breach of duty in the neutral to justify infringement of his rights by a belligerent acting in self-defence. This may arise in two ways; firstly, when the neutral despite due diligence has been unable to prevent occupation of its territory or other violation of its rights by one belligerent which brings about a situation in which the opposing belligerent is constrained to act in self-defence.[4] Here, if one rests the right of intervention by this opposing belligerent on 'fault' in the neutral, the dilemma is clearly apparent, for the belligerent cannot, in self-defence, violate the rights of the 'innocent' neutral nor can he in reason be expected to tolerate the threat arising from his opponent's illegality.

[1] *A.D.*, 1929–30, case No. 287, p. 490. See also Harvard Draft Convention on Rights and Duties of Neutral States in Naval and Aerial War, *A.J.*, Vol. 33 (1939), Supp., Section 2, 179: 'A belligerent is not relieved of its duty to respect the rights of a neutral state as provided in this Convention, even when engaged in acts of reprisal or retaliation for illegal acts of its enemy.'

[2] See Hall, *International Law*, 8th ed., pp. 747–8.

[3] See *ante*, p. 142.

[4] Where the occupation brings neutral territory into the region of war, the opposing belligerent can clearly attack his enemy in that region. See the U.S. invasion of Luxembourg in November, 1918; Hyde, Vol. III, p. 2342. Also the Allied invasion of Greece in 1915 whilst Greece was still neutral. As to this see the view of the Graeco-German Mixed Arbitral Tribunal in the *Coenca Brothers Case* (1927), 7 T.A.M., p. 683, at pp. 686–7.

Secondly, the situation may arise where the belligerent must anticipate his opponent's violation of neutral rights in self-defence; where, for example, the belligerent occupies neutral territory,[1] or destroys neutral installations or fleets, in order to forestall their capture by the opposing belligerent. The classic example is, of course, the destruction of the Danish fleet at Copenhagen in 1807.[2] In such a case we are assuming neutral status and absence of consent to the belligerent action, and if neutral rights are to be protected the legal system must obviously contain some limitations on the right of the belligerent to take this kind of anticipatory action; as Hyde states:

> It is believed, however, that deference for the principle respecting the inviolability of neutral territory is of utmost importance to the family of nations, and that, accordingly, the mere fear entertained by a belligerent lest its enemy may wrongfully utilize neutral territory for a strategic end should rarely, if ever, be deemed to excuse an anticipatory invasion, designed to forestall a contemplated and hostile movement.[3]

---

[1] The British occupation of Iceland in May, 1940, seems an instance of this, though whether to forestall a German invasion or merely to provide bases for naval and air patrols of the northern sea routes seems open to question. See Churchill, *The Unrelenting Struggle* (1942), p. 182; *History of the Second World War*, 'The War at Sea', I, H.M.S.O., 1954, p. 345. Such was the German pretext on invading Belgium in 1914; British Docs. on the Origins of the War, XI, 1898–1914 (1926), p. 320. Allied occupation of the Faroes seems to have been by consent of the Governor; see statement by Mr. Butler, Under-Secretary for Foreign Affairs, H.C. Deb., 1939–40, Vol. 359, col. 799; also with Greenland, see Briggs, 'The Validity of the Greenland Agreement', *A.J.*, Vol. 35 (1941), p. 506; also with the Azores, see R.I.I.A. *Survey, 1939–46*, p. 281, and Churchill, *op. cit.*, III, p. 123.

[2] See Rodick, *Doctrine of Necessity*, p. 112; Stowell, *Intervention*, 1921, pp. 409–14. For a defence of the British action see Westlake, *International Law*, Vol. I, pp. 302–3; Hall, *International Law*, 4th ed., pp. 285–7. The destruction of the French fleet at Oran and Mers-el-Kebir in 1940 was a somewhat similar action, and Art. 8 of the French Armistice did provide for the passing under the control of the German authorities of the French fleet; the German undertaking not to use the fleet for their own purposes was regarded with scepticism by the British authorities. See Churchill, *Second World War*, II, p. 208 *et seq.* In this action, and again in the invasion of French North Africa, of Syria, and the attack on Dakar, the position was not quite parallel for there were two distinguishing factors; firstly the fact that France was not neutral but a former ally, forced to sign an armistice under duress, and secondly Great Britain recognized the Free French government in continuing the struggle from exile. We maintain these distinctions despite the fact that the Vichy government chose to equate its position after 1940 with that of neutrality. See Komarnicki, 'The Place of Neutrality in the Modern System of International Law', *R.C.*, 1952 (I), p. 453.

[3] *Op. cit.*, Vol. III, p. 2341. Cheng, *General Principles of Law*, p. 92, rejects the legality of such action in any circumstances.

At Nuremberg the German contention was that the invasion of Norway was motivated solely by a desire to forestall an Allied invasion, and, as we have seen,[1] the Tribunal rejected this argument on the facts; it is of interest to note that it did not reject, as a matter of law, the contention that a belligerent may invade neutral territory in order to forestall occupation by the opposing belligerent.

Perhaps the strict answer to this situation is that the belligerent can only act against the neutral by virtue of a right of necessity, and not by right of self-defence. The problem is not peculiar to international law and, indeed, exactly parallel situations arise in municipal law where A acts in self-defence against B but of necessity is forced in so doing to violate the rights of an innocent person C. In English law the better opinion appears to be that this is, so far as C is concerned, not self-defence; furthermore, there appears to be no duty to make compensation.[2] In the United States, the right of A against C, the innocent victim, appears to be more in the nature of a qualified and 'incomplete' privilege, so that where the infringement of C's rights is intentional (i.e. not such as to warrant the defence of inevitable accident) there is no liability save a duty to compensate C.[3] This result may appear contradictory, for one might question from whence the duty to compensate arises if there is no liability, but, as Bohlen has said,[4] the shift has been away from liability based on fault to a more practical if slightly illogical balancing of interests.

In international law it might be possible to argue for the limitation of the right of self-defence to cases where the violation of a state's rights is only justified as a reaction to a breach of duty

[1] See *ante*, p. 143. The view of the British prosecutor, Sir Hartley Shawcross, was that the right of self-defence would only become operative when force had been used against the neutral, see 3 I.M.T. (Nuremberg), p. 129.

[2] Winfield, *Torts*, 5th ed., p. 53 and pp. 58–9; Glanville Williams, *Criminal Law, The General Part*, pp. 573–4. Cases are few: in *Scott* v. *Shepherd* (1773), 2 W.Bl., de Grey, C.J., at p. 900, and Gould, J., at p. 898, thought neither Willis nor Ryal would have been liable as they acted 'under a compulsive necessity for their own safety and self-preservation'. *Greyvenstein* v. *Hattingh* [1911] A.C. 355 is unhelpful since there appears to have been consent by innocent third parties to trespass on their land (p. 358). English criminal law distinguishes self-defence from necessity—see R. v. *Dudley*, 14 Q.B.D., 273.

[3] Prosser, *Torts*, pp. 129–30, and also p. 137. U.S. Re-statement, *Torts*, ch. 45, s. 890, p. 476, suggests duty to compensate limited to trespass to land. The best treatment is by Bohlen, *Incomplete Privilege*, 39 H.L.R., 307–24.

[4] *Op. cit.*, at p. 316.

by that state. In that event action against a neutral such as we are now considering would, if we accept these analogies of private law, fall under the doctrine of necessity and one might hazard a duty to compensate. It is of interest to note that when Great Britain destroyed the Danish fleet at Copenhagen,[1] and the French fleet at Oran,[2] these actions were preceded by an offer to take into custody the neutral fleets and return *in specie* together with compensation for any deterioration. However, no compensation, so far as can be ascertained, was ever offered for the actual destruction of the fleets, nor does it appear possible to postulate, from the practice of states, a duty to compensate neutrals for such violations of their rights where the violation is not obviously illegal but made under a genuine plea of self-defence, or, more accurately, of necessity.

NEUTRALITY UNDER THE U.N. CHARTER AND THE RIGHT OF SELF-DEFENCE

Under the Charter the continued existence of a status of neutrality, or of something akin to neutrality, whether it be termed 'qualified neutrality' or 'non-belligerency', is beyond question;[3] indeed, the selection of an appropriate terminology has

[1] Rodick, *op. cit.*, p. 113; Hall, *op. cit.*, 4th ed., pp. 285–7.

[2] Churchill, *Second World War*, II, p. 208 *et seq.*

[3] The generally accepted view is that permanent neutrality is quite incompatible with membership. See discussion in the 1st Commission at San Francisco. UNCIO, Docs., Vol. VI, pp. 459–60. This must be so as far as Members are concerned and assuming the Charter operates as intended—see Kelsen, *Law of the United Nations*, p. 468. As far as non-members are concerned, our submission is that their position in relation to a state acting in self-defence is legally unaffected by the Charter. If they choose to discriminate in its favour they must be 'acting in accordance with the principles of the present Charter' (Art. 2(6)); but they can scarcely be under any duty to do so. The suggestion that Art. 2(6) would warrant the U.N. compelling discrimination runs contrary to the generally accepted principle '*pacta tertiis nec nocent nec prosunt*', although there may be justification for preventing discrimination in favour of the aggressor under this article. See Dehn, *The effect of the U.N. Charter on the Development of International Law*, with special reference to the Status of Neutrality and the Hague and Geneva Conventions, I.L.A. Report of the 41st Conference (Cambridge), 1946. Grieve, 'The Present Position of Neutral States', *Trans. Grotius Society*, Vol. 33 (1948), p. 114, disagrees with Dehn. On the general position of neutrality and preference for the term 'non-belligerency' see also Komarnicki, 'The Place of Neutrality in the Modern System of International Law', *R.C.*, 1952 (1), p. 399 *et seq.*, especially ch. IV; Kelsen, *Law of the U.N.*, p. 480; Beckett, *The North Atlantic Treaty*, p. 7; Lalive, 'International Organisation and Neutrality', *BYBIL*, Vol. 24 (1947),

little relevance save in so far as it indicates a variation from the rights and duties enjoined by the traditional law of neutrality. For our present purpose it is necessary to inquire whether, under the Charter, the characterization of a use or threat of force as delictual can be made, and whether, being made, it affects the rights and duties of non-belligerent states vis-à-vis a state which, as a result of the delict, is forced to take belligerent action in self-defence.

There is little doubt that, as a matter of law, this characterization can now be made. The basis of this characterization is Art. 2(4) which states:

> All Members shall refrain in their international relations from the threat or use of force against the territorial integrity or political independence of any state, or in any other manner inconsistent with the purposes of the United Nations.

However, the really significant change brought about by the Charter lies in the centralization of this task of characterization, or, to use more conventional terms, of determining the aggressor, and directing sanctions against it. This characterization is now primarily a matter for the competent organ or organs of the United Nations,[1] so that it will be convenient to treat the problem according to whether or not the characterization has been made by the United Nations.

Where the characterization has been made by a competent organ of the United Nations

The procedure envisaged by the Charter, and assuming the proper functioning of the organs of the United Nations, would be that the breach of Art. 2(4) by any state[2] would be determined

p. 72; Taubenfeld, 'International Actions and Neutrality', *A.J.*, Vol. 47 (1953), p. 384 *et seq.* And see also the discussions in the I.L.C. on the Pan-American Draft Declaration (U.N. General Assembly, Doc. A/285) in I.L.C. Summary Records A/CN.4/SR.9 at p. 15 and A/CN.4/SR.15, pp. 3–7.

[1] We say 'primarily' and not 'exclusively' for the reason that by Art. 24 the Members confer only 'primary' responsibility for the maintenance of international peace and security on the Security Council. A residual responsibility lies on the General Assembly under Arts. 10, 11 and 12 and also on the individual members by virtue of the Purposes and Principles of the Charter.

[2] The obligation under Art. 2(4) is certainly one of the Principles to which, under Art. 2(6), the Organization will ensure non-members conform. It would even apply to communities not strictly 'states', and has presumably been so applied in the Security Council resolution of June 25th, 1950, which determined that the 'authorities of North Korea' had committed a breach of the peace. U.N. Doc. S/1501.

by the Security Council and characterized as a 'threat to the peace, breach of the peace, or act of aggression' under Art. 39. Now the terms of these two articles are not synonomous; it may well be that a determination under Art. 39 could be made independently of any breach of Art. 2(4), but certainly it would seem such a breach ought, as a general rule, to be within the terms 'threat to the peace, breach of the peace, or act of aggression'. [1] Accordingly, the characterization of the use or threat of force as delictual, or as lawful in self-defence, ought, *prima facie*, to be made by the Security Council,[2] and assuming it is so made, the basis of neutrality as an attitude of complete impartiality is in theory destroyed.

However, it is not certain that a determination under Art. 39 is bound to take the form of a characterization of the use of force by one party as delictual, and by the other party as lawful self-defence.[3] It is more likely that the Security Council will not, at least in the initial stages, be concerned with allocating legal responsibility, but will take measures designed to restore international peace and security. Moreover, the fact that the Security Council has made a determination under Art. 39 does not involve any Member in a duty to discriminate.[4] The minimum obligation on Members is contained in Art. 2(5):

> All Members shall give the United Nations every assistance in any action it takes in accordance with the present Charter, and shall refrain from giving assistance to any State against which the United Nations is taking preventive or enforcement action.

This suggests that the obligation is to assist the United Nations in taking measures designed to restore international peace and security, rather than to assist the state acting in self-defence. Should the Security Council proceed to take action, then one or more members may well retain a non-belligerent status, either because the action takes only the form of a 'recommendation'

[1] See Kelsen, *op. cit.*, pp. 727, 737, for a criticism of the difference in terminology.

[2] We are, of course, excluding the possibility of the use or threat of force being either sanctions or action taken under Art. 107 or 53(1) against 'enemy states'.

[3] *Post*, pp. 251–6.

[4] Goodrich and Hambro, *Charter of the U.N.*, p. 262.

under Art. 39,[1] or because the action is pursuant to a decision under Art. 41 or under that part of Art. 42 permitting the pacific measures of 'demonstrations, blockade, and other operations . . .', or because states are exempt from belligerent action under Art. 48. In this condition of 'non-belligerency' such duties as arise from Art. 2(5) are not said to exist towards the states acting in self-defence, nor does the latter obtain any rights by virtue of that article. If illustration of this be sought, then one can point to the position of South Korea after members had taken action pursuant to the recommendation of the Security Council of June 27th, 1950;[2] it has nowhere been suggested that non-belligerents were under any 'duty' to discriminate in favour of South Korea, and, although South Korea was not a member state, it is not believed that the position would have been different had it been one.

It is also clear that, under the Uniting for Peace Resolution of November 3rd, 1950,[3] the so-called Acheson Plan, the General Assembly has also assumed the power to determine the existence of a 'breach of the peace or act of aggression'.[4] It is equally doubtful whether this determination is intended to be a characterization of the use of force as delictual or lawful self-defence. Its purpose will be to recommend the action necessary to restore international peace and security, rather than to allocate legal responsibility; and any action by Members is probably better construed as action to restore international peace and security than as action to assist the state acting in self-defence. Moreover, no legal obligation to take action exists here at all; not only are

[1] It is only a 'decision' which, under Art. 25, is legally binding on Members. See generally Kelsen, *op. cit.*, p. 444 *et seq.*; Jiménez de Arechaga, *Voting and the Handling of Disputes in the Security Council*, p. 179. And see S.C. Off. Rec., 5th Year, No. 17, pp. 13, 15.

[2] U.N. Docs., S/1511. A survey of the contributions of Members towards South Korea's struggle is given in an Appendix to Docs. Relating to the Korean Conflict, II, Special Release No. I/18. And see the Report of the Collective Measures Committee, G.A. Official Records, Sixth Session, Supp. No. 13 (A/1891), 1951.

[3] The resolution presupposes the failure of the S.C. to act by reason of the lack of unanimity of the permanent members. Its legality has been questioned; the problem is discussed in Kelsen, *Recent Trends in the Law of the United Nations*, ch. IV; Woolsey, 'The Uniting for Peace Resolution of the United Nations', *A.J.*, Vol. 45 (1951), p. 129.

[4] See the finding of the G.A. on February 1st, 1951, that the Central People's Govt. of China had engaged in aggression in Korea; Resolution of G.A. 327th Plenary Meeting (A/1771).

the recommendations of the General Assembly not binding,[1] but the minimum obligations contained in Art. 2(5) are limited by the phrase 'preventive or enforcement action', and it may be argued that this can only refer to action ordered or authorized by the Security Council under Chapter VII or Art. 53(1).[2] However, the obligation to assist the United Nations 'in any action it takes in accordance with the present Charter' remains, although it is impossible to construe from this anything more than an authorization to implement the recommendations of the Assembly by action which, apart from that authorization, might well be illegal.[3] Certainly it cannot be construed as a duty to discriminate in favour of the state acting in self-defence.

In both these cases, therefore, where either the Security Council or the General Assembly has determined the existence of a 'threat to the peace, breach of the peace, or act of aggression', the obligations on Members exist solely vis-à-vis the United Nations. There is no obligation to render assistance to the state acting in self-defence or to discriminate in its favour. It is not without significance that at San Francisco the New Zealand proposal to insert into the Charter a collective guarantee of the political independence and territorial integrity of members against aggression was rejected.[4] There may, however, be a residuary 'privilege' of discriminating in favour of the State acting in self-defence, but this should only be exercised in those cases where the determination by the United Nations organ leaves no doubt as to which state is acting in self-defence. Once this has been made abundantly clear, by an impartial organ of the world community, there can certainly be no duty of impartiality.

[1] This is something of a generalization, but certainly true in this connection. See Sloan, 'The Binding Force of a "Recommendation" of the General Assembly of the U.N.', *BYBIL*, Vol. 25 (1948), p. 1.

[2] See Beckett, *op. cit.*, p. 7. The Uniting for Peace resolution refers to 'collective measures' which, though authorized by Art. 1(1), are probably different from 'enforcement action' taken by the S.C. or under its direction.

[3] The Resolution of the General Assembly of February 1st, 1951 (A.1771), requested members 'to refrain from giving any assistance to the aggressor in Korea'; this implies the application of Art. 2(5) to action authorized under the Acheson Plan, although we cannot agree with this except to the extent indicated above. The subsequent authorization of discrimination by the imposition of an arms embargo on China (Resolution A/1805) is an illustration of an authorization of action which might otherwise be illegal as a departure from the duties of neutrality.

[4] U.N.C.I.O. Docs., Vol. VI, Commission I, General Provisions, p. 343.

Where the characterization has not been made by a competent organ of the United Nations

The possibility of a determination under Art. 39 not being made, despite the clearest evidence of a breach of Art. 2(4), is not unlikely. The voting procedure within the Security Council, demanding unanimity amongst the permanent members for this non-procedural vote, leaves the question open to all the hazards involved in the marked political disagreement existing amongst these permanent members. In such a case, where the Security Council's failure to make this characterization arises quite clearly from the lack of unanimity of the permanent members, it is arguable that by virtue of their residual power to determine a breach of Art. 2(4), the member states, acting individually or collectively, may themselves determine such a breach and discriminate in favour of any state which acts in self-defence. This discrimination can, from what has already been said of the Charter, only exist as a privilege, not a duty.[1]

It has been suggested that nothing in the Charter precludes the individual member from taking this course. Lauterpacht states:

> There is nothing in the Charter which obliges them (the Members)[2] to maintain an attitude of full neutrality in such cases. In the first instance, provided that there has been a case of armed attack, they may in the exercise of the right of collective self-defence under Art. 51 of the Charter take such action as they deem fit, including—apart from the right to go to war—the denial of the ordinary benefits of neutrality and measures of discrimination against the aggressor.[3]

It is also clear that the General Treaty for the Renunciation of War could provide for the parties to that treaty a basis for similar acts of discrimination.[4]

Whether the characterization, and consequent decision to discriminate, is made unilaterally, or collectively, or by an organ of some organization for collective self-defence acting on behalf of the members of that organization, does not, it is submitted, affect the legal quality of the decision, for it remains one not made by a competent organ of the United Nations. It may be that where discrimination by non-belligerents is practised as part of collective action by an organization in self-defence, the non-belligerent will choose to rely on the fiction that 'an attack against one is an

[1] Taubenfeld, *op. cit.*, p. 390. [2] Brackets mine.
[3] Oppenheim, *International Law*, II, 7th ed., p. 651. [4] Ibid.

attack against all'.[1] In this event the discrimination purports to be based on self-defence rather than on the duty to aid a state in self-defence. If, in fact, measures of discrimination are taken as a measure of self-defence, individual or collective, they are clearly permissible and no difficulty arises; the real difficulty occurs when states which have no right of self-defence, individual or collective, discriminate against one party to a conflict prior to any determination by a competent organ of the United Nations. The danger of states proceeding on their own initiative is that divergent characterizations may be made, either by single states, groups of states, or even different organizations for collective self-defence. For this reason Jessup concludes that:

> . . . it would be disastrous to agree that every state may decide for itself which of the two contestants is in the right and may govern its conduct according to its own decision, even if it were agreed that they would not actually support one or other side by force.[2]

Again, Dehn concludes that:

> Apparently the only safe course would thus be to adopt a status of strict non-intervention, withholding aid of every kind from each belligerent until the aggressor state had been identified, be it by a decision of the Security Council or by world opinion.[3]

He is here envisaging a 'temporary status', whereas the real problem arises when the deadlock within the Security Council will permanently prevent the making of the necessary characterization.

The dilemma lies between adopting a policy of neutrality and thus, in failing to assist the state in self-defence, countenancing the commission of a delict, or making an authoritative determination which may, in the outcome, prove to be wrong. It is believed that the only proper course for states which are not themselves placed in the necessity of self-defence, is for those states to abstain from intervention or discrimination until such time as a competent organ of the United Nations has determined what measures are necessary for the maintenance of international peace and security, and what part those states shall take in these

[1] See for example Art. 5, North Atlantic Treaty, concluded in Washington, April 4th, 1949. Text cited in *A.J.*, Vol. 43 (1949), Supp., p. 159.

[2] *Modern Law of Nations*, p. 205. He advocates a system of impartial blockade against both parties to the fighting pending an authoritative determination as to the respective merits of the parties.

[3] *Op. cit.*, p. 43.

measures. This view is elaborated at a later stage;[1] for the moment let it suffice to point out that the General Assembly, in its Resolution on the Duties of States in the Event of the Outbreak of Hostilities, on November 17th, 1950, recommended that states engaged in hostilities should 'take all steps practicable in the circumstances . . . to bring the armed conflict to an end at the earliest possible moment'.[2] It is difficult to see how intervention by states generally could prove consistent with this end.

The dilemma is not so real since the General Assembly's Resolution on Uniting for Peace, for the characterization by the General Assembly will not be made only in those cases where there are not two-thirds of the members willing that it should be made. Accordingly, for a state or group of states to continue to make such a characterization on their own initiative, and discriminate on that basis, would seem highly suspect when a two-thirds majority of world opinion cannot be secured in favour of such a course.[3] This new development impinges on the very basis of action by organizations for collective self-defence,[4] but for present purposes it would seem safe to assert that discrimination as a 'privilege' ought never, apart from the exercise of self-defence, to be exercised before both the Security Council and the General Assembly have had the opportunity of making the necessary characterization. In the absence of such characterization by both these organs, discrimination, if not forbidden by the Charter, is undertaken at a state's own risk and with full responsibility.

[1] *Post*, Chapter X.

[2] Resolution 378 (v); and see *post*, pp. 244–7.

[3] See the argument of U.S. Rep. during the consideration by the Security Council of the Greek question and following the Council's failure to adopt the recommendation of the Commission of investigation: 'the continued failure . . . of the Security Council to take effective action in the case because of the Soviet veto cannot . . . preclude individual or collective action by states willing to act, so long as they act in accordance with the general purposes and principles of the United Nations . . . This is particularly true where such individual or collective action is in support of a policy or course of action which has the clear approval of a clear preponderance of the permanent and non-permanent members of the Security Council'. U.N. Doc. S/PV, 180, pp. 56–65. This is substantially the same argument; lacking the clear approval of the preponderance of members of the U.N. the action would be equally questionable.

[4] See *post*, pp. 242–6.

CHAPTER IX

SELF-DEFENCE UNDER THE U.N. CHARTER

THE ORIGIN OF ART. 51

WE have seen that under the Covenant of the League and the Paris Pact the prohibitions against war were, by general consent, never taken to preclude the right of self-defence. It is, therefore, not surprising that the Dumbarton Oaks Proposals similarly contained no express reservation of a right of self-defence.[1] Indeed the terms of the prohibition of the 'threat or use of force in any manner inconsistent with the Purposes of the Organization' in Chapter II, Para. 4, are not apt to include legitimate action in self-defence. At San Francisco the view of Committee I in dealing with the effect of this prohibition[2] was that the 'use of arms in legitimate self-defence remains admitted and unimpaired',[3] apparently without the specific reservation which was introduced by Committee III/4 and which became Art. 51 of the Charter. The origin of Art. 51 is to be found in the discussions of this latter Committee and the report of its sub-committee III/4A, for in dealing with the problem of harmonizing existing regional arrangements with the proposed United Nations Organization these committees faced the problem of preserving a certain freedom of action in self-defence.[4] Chapter VIII (C) (1) of the Dumbarton Oaks Proposals stated that 'nothing in the Charter should preclude the existence of regional arrangements or agencies' but also stated

[1] The text of the Dumbarton Oaks Proposals is given in the British Commentary on the Charter of the United Nations, Cmd. 6666.

[2] Amended to the wording now used in Art. 2(4) of the Charter.

[3] *UNCIO*, Vol. VI, Report of Rapporteur of Committee I to Commission I, p. 459. This was also the Norwegian delegate's view, ibid., p. 334.

[4] For a history of the negotiations in Committee see Kunz, 'The Inter-American System and the U.N. Organisation', *A.J.*, Vol. 31 (1945), p. 758 *et seq.*; Canyes, 'The Inter-American System and the Conference of Chapultepec', *A.J.*, Vol. 39 (1945), p. 504 *et seq.*; Yuen-li-Liang, 'Regional Arrangements and International Security', *Trans. Grotius Society*, Vol. 31 (1946), p. 216, especially p. 226 *et seq.*; Krezdorn, *Les Nations Unies et les Accords Régionaux*, Thesis No. 100, published by University of Geneva, 1954, p. 117 *et seq.*; Nguyen Quoc Dinh, 'La Légitime Défense d'après la Charte des Nations Unies', *R.G.D.I.P.*, Vol. 52 (1948), p. 228.

under Chapter VIII (C) (2) that 'no enforcement action should be taken under regional arrangements or by regional agencies without the authorization of the Security Council'. Now in those proposals the vote by which the Security Council should give such authorization was not stated, but the statement of the Four Sponsoring Powers,[1] the so-called San Francisco Statement, concerning the operation of the voting procedure laid down in the new Art. 27, made it certain that this authorization would require the unanimity of the permanent members. The fear which presented itself to the minds of members of Committee III/4 was, therefore, that by the exercise of the veto a single permanent member might prevent the regional organization from taking any action. To those states which had signed the Act of Chapultepec on March 3rd, 1945,[2] at the Inter-American Conference, the problem had real significance, for they had there avowed their intention of resisting aggression by armed force if necessary. The connection between this Act and the introduction of Art. 51 was stated quite clearly by the Columbian delegate, Camargo, at the 4th Meeting on May 23rd, 1945:

> The Latin-American countries understood as Senator Vandenberg has said, that the origin of the term 'self-defence' is identified with the necessity of preserving regional systems like the Inter-American one . . . it may be deduced that the approval of this action implies that Chapultepec is not in contravention of the Charter.[3]

This concern was not limited to the members of the Inter-American system; the position of the Arab League,[4] of certain bilateral security arrangements in Europe to guard against renewed German aggression,[5] and even of the individual state's

[1] Text given in Goodrich & Hambro, *op. cit.*, pp. 216–18; *UNCIO* Doc. 852, III/1/37(1). The statement, made in response to a questionnaire submitted by a subcommittee of Committee III/1 (*UNCIO* Doc. 855, III/I/8/2(a)) did not deal specifically with this problem but the application of the non-procedural vote can be deduced from para. 1 of the Statement.

[2] Text in *A.J.*, Vol. 39 (1945), Supp., p. 108.

[3] *UNCIO*, Vol. 12, p. 680.

[4] Pact concluded March 22nd, 1945. For text see Dept. State Bulletin XVI, pp. 967–70; and see the view of the Egyptian delegate, *UNCIO*, Vol. 12, p. 682.

[5] See opinion of French delegate, *UNCIO*, Vol. 12, p. 681. Also Reid, 'Regionalism under the U.N. Charter', *Int. Concil.*, 1946, p. 120. For an example of these bilateral arrangements see Franco-Soviet Treaty of Alliance of December 10th, 1944, text in *A.J.*, Vol. 39 (1945), Supp., p. 83.

right to resort to self-defence needed clarification. As Evatt says:

> It was essential that there should be clear recognition of the right of a country to defend itself against aggression and to call its friends to its assistance under regional or other defensive arrangements.[1]

The draft of Art. 51 appears, after the rejection of an Australian proposal,[2] in the Report of Dr. V. K. Wellington Koo, as rapporteur of Committee III/4 to Commission III;[3] its author seems to have been Senator Vandenberg, though why the term 'armed attack' appears is not apparent.[4] Certainly the aggression defined in the third paragraph of the Act of Chapultepec is not limited to an 'armed attack', and though the reasons for the insertion of Art. 51 are tolerably clear, there is no explanation of this curious proviso 'if an armed attack occurs'. [5]

THE INTERPRETATION OF ART. 51

The correct interpretation of Art. 51 is, in our submission, only to be achieved by a full appreciation of its relation to Art. 2(4).[6] It is incontestable that prior to the Charter a right of self-defence was recognized by general international law, so that the question which must be posed is whether the Charter contains a prohibition of action which would normally be legitimate as the exercise of self-defence, a right admitted and recognized by the general law. We must presuppose that rights formerly belonging to member states continue except in so far as obligations incon-

[1] The United Nations (1948), p. 27.

[2] 2nd Meeting, May 9th; *UNCIO*, Vol. 12, p. 668. The proposal suggested an authorization of regional action should require only the votes of three permanent members and, in the event of failure to act or authorize such action, the signatories to a regional arrangement should be free to take action in accordance with that arrangement.

[3] *UNCIO*, Vol. 12, pp. 737–40; Doc. 904, III/4/13(1), p. 3.

[4] *The Private Papers of Senator Vandenberg* (1953), p. 186 *et seq*., confirm the view that Vandenberg was the chief instigator of the new article, but they contain no indication as to why the term 'armed attack' was included.

[5] The suggestion made by Waldock, 'The Regulation of the Use of Force by Individual States in International Law', *R.C.*, 1952 (II), 455, at p. 496, that the proviso results from the association of Art. 51 with Chapter VII does not appear convincing, for enforcement action under Chapter VII is conditioned by a determination of a 'threat to the peace, breach of the peace, or act of aggression', and there is no evidence to suggest these terms are limited to an 'armed attack'.

[6] This relation is discussed in detail by Pompe, *Aggressive War*, p. 102 *et seq.*

sistent with those existing rights are assumed under the Charter. As Goodhart has rightly said:

> The Members of the United Nations when exercising their inherent powers do so not by grant but by already existing right. The Charter limits the sovereign rights of the states; it is not a source of those rights.[1]

It is, therefore, fallacious to assume that members have only those rights which the Charter accords to them; on the contrary they have those rights which general international law accords to them except and in so far as they have surrendered them under the Charter. Kelsen, writing of the right of self-defence, says 'the right has no other content than the one determined by Art. 51'[2]; this is a fundamentally erroneous approach which produces a restricted interpretation of the article not warranted by the Charter.

Now the relevant obligation assumed by members is, *prima facie*, that contained in Art. 2(4):

> All Members shall refrain in their international relations from the threat or use of force against the territorial integrity or political independence of any state, or in any other manner inconsistent with the Purposes of the United Nations.

As we have seen, the view of Committee I at San Francisco was that this prohibition left the right of self-defence unimpaired; in the words of its rapporteur 'the use of arms in legitimate self-defence remains admitted and unimpaired'.[3] Indeed, it is difficult to see what other conclusion could be reached, for if we examine the substantive rights protected by self-defence the absence of any inconsistency with Art. 2(4) is apparent. Action undertaken for the purpose of, and limited to, the defence of a state's political independence, territorial integrity, the lives and property of its nationals[4] (and even to protect its economic independence) cannot

[1] 'The North Atlantic Treaty of 1949', *R.C.*, 1951 (11), p. 187, at p. 192.

[2] *Recent Trends in the Law of the United Nations*, p. 914. See also Nguyen Quoc Dinh, *op. cit.*, p. 244.

[3] *UNCIO*, Docs., Vol. VI, p. 459.

[4] See the replies of the Jewish Agency representative and of the representative of the Arab states to the questionnaire of the Security Council (S/753) adopted at its 295th Meeting in 1948. In answer to the question as to the basis upon which they justified the use of armed force outside their own territories they all invoked, *inter alia*, the protection of the lives and property of either the Arab or Jewish populations. See Off. Rec. S.C., 301st Meeting, May 22nd, 1948, pp. 7–10. All these states assumed this was not in breach of the Charter; for a contrary view see Pompe, *op. cit.*, p. 98.

by definition involve a threat or use of force 'against the territorial integrity or political independence' of any other state.[1] To the extent that action in self-defence would involve a breach of this obligation it would *ipso facto* cease to be within the requirements of self-defence as permitted by general international law. Nor can it be said that the protection of those same substantive rights by the exercise of self-defence is 'in any other manner inconsistent with the Purposes of the United Nations'; those purposes hinge primarily on the maintenance of international peace and security, and it would be a strange conclusion if a state's protection of its own legitimate interests were inconsistent with that end.[2] Indeed it is in the interests of its own security that the state exercises the right of self-defence and there can be no inconsistency between the security of a state's legitimate interests and the general security. A more substantial objection would be that the Purposes envisage 'collective measures' whereas action in self-defence is primarily a unilateral measure undertaken on the state's own responsibility; but this objection loses force when self-defence is conceived as an interim means of protection, available until those collective measures ensure the same protection of the individual state's rights, a protective right rather than a collective sanction.

For these reasons we would maintain that the obligation assumed under Art. 2(4) is in no way inconsistent with the right of self-defence recognized in international law. It remains to be seen whether Art. 51 itself contains any limitation on that right, and it is to an examination of the provisions of that article that we now turn.

[1] Goodhart, *op. cit.*, p. 202. Also Stone, *Legal Controls of International Conflict*, pp. 234–6, where he argues that the United Nations action in Korea could not violate Art. 2(4) since it involved no design or attempt against the territorial integrity or political independence of any state.

[2] It could be argued that the Security Council, in the execution of its primary responsibility for the maintenance of international peace and security, could take enforcement action under Chapter VII against a state exercising its right of self-defence, for the determination of a 'threat to the peace, breach of the peace, or act of aggression' under Art. 39 does not necessarily presuppose a delict. There might here be an inconsistency between self-defence and the Purposes of the Charter, but the position is difficult to envisage if the Security Council fulfils its own obligation of acting 'in conformity with the principles of justice and international law' (Art. 1(1)).

(a) *Nothing in the present Charter shall impair the inherent right of individual or collective self-defence*

This initial phrase is purely declaratory;[1] it takes the form of an assurance '*ex abundante cautela*', an assurance required by the representatives comprising Committee III/4 for reasons which we have already examined. Goodhart's opinion is that it 'need not have been included in the Charter at all if it is correct to say, as I believe it is, that the individual states are only deprived of the exercise of those powers which have been specifically forbidden to them. . . .' [2] The reference to an 'inherent' right suggests something of the philosophy of natural law, a tendency to regard the right as established by natural law rather than positive law, but this view is neither necessary nor helpful; it has been described as 'a theoretical opinion of the legislator which has no legal importance'.[3] Perhaps its only significance lies in its indication that the right is an existing right, independent of the Charter and not the subject of an express grant, so that it has a certain importance in refuting Kelsen's own view that the right has only such content as Art. 51 gives it. The term 'collective self-defence' has been regarded as an extension of the traditional right and a somewhat problematical term.[4] This is a question which will be dealt with in Chapter X in connection with the general concept of 'collective self-defence'.

(b) '*If an armed attack occurs*'

This proviso is open to two interpretations; on the one hand it is possible to construe this as a restriction on the traditional right of self-defence so that the right is now only available to Members who are the object of an actual armed attack. In this way Kelsen argues that:

> . . . this article applies only in case of an armed attack. The right of self-defence must not be exercised in case of any other violation of the legally protected interests of a Member.[5]

---

[1] Kelsen, *Recent Trends*, p. 913. [2] *Op. cit.*, p. 202.

[3] Kelsen, *Law of the United Nations*, p. 791.

[4] See Kelsen, 'Collective Security and Collective Self-Defence under the Charter', *A.J.*, Vol. 42 (1948), p. 792.

[5] *Law of the United Nations*, pp. 269, 797–8; also *A.J.*, Vol. 42 (1948), p. 792. There is considerable support for this view from other authors: Beckett, *op. cit.*, p. 13; Wehberg, 'L'Interdiction du Recours à la Force', *R.C.*,

The reasoning behind this view is that 'the Charter forbids any use of force on the part of the individual Members except for the exercise of the right of self-defence against an armed attack'. With respect, this statement is inaccurate and misleading, for the relevant prohibition is Art. 2(4) which contains no prohibition of the exercise of self-defence as permitted under the general law; moreover it is quite certain that under the general law the right was not limited to cases of an armed attack. This restrictive interpretation, if accepted, would involve two propositions; firstly that action in self-defence may not be 'anticipatory' but must await an armed attack, and secondly that self-defence is only legitimate where the measures used to violate the state's interests take the form of an 'armed attack'. The invalidity of this interpretation can be demonstrated both in the reasoning behind it and in the inaccuracy of the two propositions which arise from it.

The reasoning takes the form of an assertion that, because Art. 51 says nothing in the Charter forbids or prevents self-defence against an armed attack, it must therefore follow that self-defence is valid only against an armed attack—a complete *non sequitur*. It is tantamount to saying that therefore something in the Charter does prevent self-defence unless there is an armed attack; since the prohibition of Art. 2(4) leaves the traditional right unimpaired this is clearly untrue, for this declaratory clause of Art. 51 imports no additional obligation to that contained in Art. 2(4). The history of Art. 51 suggests nothing of an additional obligation; the *travaux préparatoires*, to which we may legitimately resort in the case of ambiguity,[1] suggest only that the article should safeguard the right of self-defence, not restrict it. The propositions which stem from this restrictive interpretation are equally doubtful; they represent a marked departure from the position under traditional international law, a restriction on the rights of sovereign states not lightly to be presumed, and they are also inconsistent with the practice of members since the Charter.

In the first place the right has, under traditional international law, always been 'anticipatory', that is to say its exercise was

1951 (1), at pp. 70, 81; Pompe, *op. cit.*, pp. 98, 100; Stone, *op. cit.*, p. 244, though he suggests (fn. 8) that anticipatory defence against troop concentrations on a state's border would be warranted; Tucker, 'The legal Interpretation of War', *I.L.Q.*, Vol. 3 (1950), at p. 29; Krezdorn, *op. cit.*, p. 122; Nguyen Quoc Dinh, *op. cit.*, pp. 240–4.

[1] See *ante*, p. 182.

valid against imminent as well as actual attacks or dangers. Indeed the *Caroline* is itself the classical illustration of this, and the practice of states subsequent to the Charter evidences no indication to accept a more restrictive interpretation of the right. In the discussions in the Security Council on the Kashmir dispute the representative of Pakistan justified the invasion of Kashmir by Pakistan forces as an essential (albeit anticipatory) measure to circumvent the imminent danger to Pakistan which would arise on the occupation of all Kashmir by India;[1] it was undisputed that no actual attack had occurred against Pakistan. The First Report of the United Nations Atomic Energy Commission in 1946 observed that:

> In consideration of the problem of violation of the terms of the treaty or convention, it should also be borne in mind that a violation might be of so grave a character as to give rise to the inherent right of self-defence recognized in Art. 51.[2]

It cannot be supposed that a treaty violation falls within the definition of an actual armed attack, so that the Commission clearly understood Art. 51 as permitting 'anticipatory' self-defence. Again, in the discussions of the General Assembly's Sixth Committee in 1952 in connection with the definition of aggression, the representatives of Belgium, Greece, the United Kingdom and the United States all considered that a state threatened with an impending attack might be justified in attacking first in self-defence.[3] A recent writer has also deduced from the judgment of the International Court of Justice in the *Corfu Channel Case* in 1949[4] the proposition that, so far as the right of self-defence is concerned,

> It is enough if there is a strong probability of armed attack—an imminent threat of armed attack[5]

---

[1] *Off. Rec. S.C.*, 5th Year, 464th Meeting, p. 7; S/PV. 464. The only objection to this construction of the Charter came from India, the other interested party, who pointed out that there had been no armed attack on Pakistan, ibid., 466th Meeting, p. 4 *et seq.* It is not possible to construe from the Pakistan argument any assertion that the imminent danger would come from India; the argument seems to be based, *inter alia*, on the broader ground that India's occupation of Kashmir would make the defence of Pakistan untenable.

[2] U.N. Doc. AEC/18/Rev. 1, p. 24. And see U.N. Repertory of Practice, 1955, Vol. II, p. 436.

[3] 278th–295th Meetings, January 5th–22nd, 1952.

[4] I.C.J. Reports, 1949, p. 5.

[5] Waldock, *op. cit.*, p. 500.

and considers that:

> At any rate, it is clear that the Court did not take a narrow view of the inherent right of self-defence reserved by Art. 51.[1]

The judgment is not free from ambiguity but, with respect to this writer, it is difficult to deduce from the judgment anything quite so definite. So far as the passage through the straits was concerned, the U.K. argument rested on the view that the passage was in the exercise of a right recognized by international law, and as a right of 'innocent' passage it did not cease to be innocent because of the precautions taken to meet the event of an attack by Albanian shore batteries. Neither the U.K. argument, nor the Court's judgment, expressly rested on the basis of self-defence.[2] The Court did state that the mission was designed to affirm a right which had been unjustly denied;[3] it also stated that:

> The intention must have been, not only to test Albania's attitude but at the same time to demonstrate such force that she would abstain from firing again on passing ships. Having regard, however, to all the circumstances of the case . . . the Court is unable to characterize these measures taken by the United Kingdom authorities as a violation of Albania's sovereignty.[4]

These findings relate more to the view that the U.K. action was not in breach of Art. 2(4) than to a direct finding with reference to the right of self-defence. They do, admittedly, bear on the right of self-defence, once it is conceded that the threat of force by an individual state can only be an exception to Art. 2(4) where it is self-defence; however, no statement to this effect was made and it is, therefore, impossible to draw firm conclusions from the judgment in relation to the right of self-defence. Had the Albanian shore batteries actually fired, then retaliation by the U.K. warships would clearly have been in the exercise of the right of self-defence; on the facts, however, the U.K. action seems to be based on the exercise of the right of innocent passage, a right not invalidated by the fact that it was accompanied by preparations for self-defence should the need arise.

[1] Waldock, *op. cit.*, p. 501.

[2] The reference to 'rights of self-defence and self-help' is made in the British argument relating to Operation Retail, the subsequent minesweeping of the Channel, and not to the passage through the Channel on October 22nd, 1946. See Statement of Sir E. Beckett, *Pleadings*, Vol. III, p. 296. Also reply of U.K., Vol. II, p. 284. As such it was rejected: I.C.J. Reports (1949), p. 35.

[3] I.C.J. Reports (1949), p. 30.

[4] Ibid., p. 31.

During the consideration of the complaint by Israel to the Security Council of the restrictions imposed by Egypt on the passage of ships through the Suez Canal, dated July 11th, 1951,[1] the plea of self-defence under Art. 51 was specifically raised by the Egyptian representative in order to justify these restrictions. Certain representatives argued the invalidity of this plea on the basis that no 'armed attack' had occurred against Egypt. The actual decision[2] of the Security Council was, however, that 'such practice (i.e. interference with passage)[3] is an abuse of the exercise of the right of visit, search and seizure', and found 'that that practice cannot in the prevailing circumstances be justified on the ground that it is necessary for self-defence'. The relevant prevailing circumstances, as recited in the resolution, appear to be not so much that at the time no armed attack was taking place against Egypt, but rather,

> That since the armistice régime, which has been in existence for nearly two and a half years, is of a permanent character, neither party can reasonably assert that it is actively a belligerent or requires to exercise the right of visit, search, and seizure for any legitimate purpose of self-defence.

It is not considered that this finding can constitute an assertion that the right of self-defence is limited to cases where an actual armed attack occurs; it is conceivable that had large-scale mobilization by Israel threatened an impending breach of the armistice, the prevailing circumstances might have justified this plea of self-defence.

It is not believed, therefore, that Art. 51 restricts the traditional right of self-defence so as to exclude action taken against an imminent danger but before 'an armed attack occurs'. In our view such a restriction is both unnecessary and inconsistent with Art. 2(4) which forbids not only force but the threat of force, and, furthermore, it is a restriction which bears no relation to the realities of a situation which may arise prior to an actual attack and call for self-defence immediately if it is to be of any avail at all. No state can be expected to await an initial attack which, in

[1] Off. Rec. S.C., 6th Year, Supp. for July, August, September, pp. 9 & 10, S/2241.

[2] Off. Rec. S.C., 6th Year, 558th Meeting, 1st September, 1951, para. 5, S/2298/Rev. 1.

[3] Brackets mine.

the present state of armaments, may well destroy the state's capacity for further resistance and so jeopardize its very existence.

The second proposition is equally unsupported, both by the traditional notion of self-defence and the present practice of states. It is well recognized that an armed attack is by no means the only form of aggression,[1] of imperilling a state's rights so that it may be compelled to resort to the exercise of a right of self-defence. The identification of aggression and an armed attack[2] is a gross over-simplification of a complex problem and one which has not been followed either in the definitions of aggression proposed in the International Law Commission[3] and the General Assembly,[4] or in the practice of states.[5] The proper interpretation of Art. 51 does not warrant this second proposition which, though it may, *prima facie*, simplify the problem of aggression, tempts writers into an unnecessary distortion of the term 'armed attack' so as to include the various forms of indirect aggression such as assistance to revolting minorities, bacteriological or gas warfare, or serious breaches of a Convention on Atomic Weapons. The preferable, and it is believed the correct, view is that expressed by Goodrich and Hambro:

> The provisions of Art. 51 do not necessarily exclude the right of self-defence in situations not covered by this Article. If the right of self-defence is inherent as has been claimed in the past, then each

---

[1] See generally *post*, ch. XI.

[2] For example Pompe, *op. cit.*, p. 98. This restricted notion of aggression is perhaps at the root of the assumption that self-defence lies only against an armed attack. Kelsen admits the narrowness of the view, *Law of U.N.*, p. 797.

[3] See Report on the work of the Third Session, Doc. A/CN.4/48, July 30th, 1951, p. 9, para. 49; the tentative formulation, not finally accepted, spoke of aggression as 'the threat or use of force . . . in any manner, whatever the weapons employed and whether openly or otherwise . . .'

[4] G. A. Res. 380 (v), adopted at 308th Plenary Meeting, 1950, and solemnly affirming that 'any aggression, whether committed openly or by fomenting civil strife in the interest of a foreign Power, or otherwise, is the gravest of all crimes against peace and security throughout the world'. Also G.A. Resolution, November 27th, 1948, at 167th Plenary Meeting; (193 (III)) endorsing UNSCOB findings.

[5] See the Yugoslavian complaint to the G.A. on November 9th, 1951 (A/1946). Chilean allegation that the political independence of Czechoslovakia had been violated by the threat of force by U.S.S.R., March 12th, 1948 (S/694). Complaint of Hyderabad by cable to S.G., August 21st, 1948, charging that India had exposed Hyderabad to violent intimidation, threats of invasion, frontier violations, and a crippling economic blockade 'intended to coerce it into a renunciation of its independence' (S/986).

Member retains the right subject only to such limitations as are contained in the Charter.[1]

It follows from this that the question of who decides when an armed attack occurs,[2] a question undetermined by the Charter, loses any special significance, for the right of self-defence is not confined to that eventuality. The question is in fact a broader one as to who decides, in the first place, whether the occasion has arisen which justifies the exercise of the right of self-defence. In the nature of things this must be a decision for the state invoking the right, but this does not imply that the state unilaterally determines the legality of such action as is taken, for this final decision ought properly to be made by an impartial body and not by the parties concerned.[3]

(*c*) '*Against a Member of the United Nations*'

The view has been expressed that the literal interpretation of this phrase would limit the members' right of self-defence to situations where the attack has been made on a member state.[4] On this interpretation members would have no right to assist non-members under the right of collective self-defence; the matter is of some importance since organizations in collective self-defence may, and do, contain non-members of the United Nations as, for example, with Italy's original membership of N.A.T.O.[5] Art. 51 cannot take away non-members' rights of self-defence,[6] so that if any restriction is intended it relates only to the freedom of members to associate themselves with non-members in their defence. Yet the conclusion that this restrictive effect is intended by Art. 51 depends on the same form of questionable reasoning which we have rejected in relation to the interpretation of the phrase 'if an armed attack occurs'. That is to say upon reasoning which suggests that, since Art. 51 acknowledges members' rights to associate in self-defence with members, this must by implication

[1] *Op. cit.*, p. 301.

[2] The question is posed by Kelsen, *Law of U.N.*, pp. 797–8.

[3] See *post*, p. 262.

[4] See Stone, *op. cit.*, p. 246, fn. 20.

[5] See also U.K.–Jordan Treaty of Alliance of March 2nd, 1946, which invokes Art. 51 although Jordan was not a U.N. member.

[6] Kelsen, *Law of U.N.*, p. 793, seems to suggest this is a corollary of the U.N.'s assumed right under Art. 2(6) to impose the obligations of Art. 2(4) on non-members. It would seem the preferable argument is quite simply that the Charter is *res inter alios acta* and does not, *prima facie*, purport to affect the rights of non-members.

mean there is no such right of association with non-members. Of this argument Goodhart has rightly said:

> Such a limitation on the rights of sovereign States would, however, have to be expressed in clear terms and cannot be supported by the doubtful rule of construction that *expressio unius est exclusio alterius.*[1]

The situation which arose in Korea when the Republic of South Korea, a non-member of the U.N., was attacked by forces from north of the 38th parallel on June 24th, 1950, was undoubtedly one in which South Korea was placed under the necessity of acting in self-defence; the resolution of the Security Council on June 25th[2] implied this in noting an 'armed attack' upon South Korea and in determining that the action of the North Korean authorities constituted a 'breach of the peace'. The reference to an 'armed attack' may be an indication that the Security Council considered Art. 51 applicable so as to warrant assistance to South Korea by virtue of members' rights of collective self-defence; indeed this is the only basis upon which the U.S. decision to authorize the intervention of U.S. air and sea forces on the side of South Korea, prior to the recommendation of the Security Council on June 27th[3] that members furnish assistance, can be justified. However, the practice on this occasion is inconclusive, for the U.S. authorities sought another justification[4] and

[1] *Op. cit.*, p. 202. The only possible exception to this is where a non-member is an 'enemy' state within the meaning of Arts. 107 and 53(i) and action is taken against a non-member pursuant to those articles. It is conceivable that here the right of collective self-defence would be denied to members, but this is inevitably so if action under these articles presupposes a renewal of aggression by such 'enemy' states as Art. 53(i) does; there can in any event be no right of association in collective self-defence with an aggressor. See Kelsen, *Law of U.N.*, p. 815; *Recent Trends*, pp. 917–18. Stone, *op. cit.*, p. 246, fn. 20, sees the conflict between collective self-defence with non-members and Arts. 107 and 53(i) as a conflict between 'liberties' not 'rights', resulting in an 'extra-legal conflict of naked power'. These views seem unnecessary for the reason stated above.

[2] Doc. S/1501. And see the further resolution of July 7th, 1950, welcoming the support by Members 'to assist the Republic of Korea in defending itself' (S/1588).

[3] Doc. S/1511.

[4] The U.S. representative at the 474th Meeting of the S.C. on June 27th seems to suggest that the Presidential Order to U.S. forces was in pursuance of the call of the S.C. to all Members to render assistance to the U.N., made under the resolution of June 25th (S/1501). S.C. Off. Rec., 5th Year, 474th Meeting, pp. 3–5. The French delegate took the same view, ibid., p. 9. It is extremely doubtful whether this initial resolution justifies such action, for the U.N. had at that stage taken no action which the United States could assist. See also on the U.S. intervention, Stone, *op. cit.*, p. 231, fn. 13.

subsequent action by other states was soundly based on the Security Council's recommendation of the 27th, so that it cannot be interpreted as action based on the right of collective self-defence with a non-member.

(*d*) '*Until the Security Council has taken the measures necessary to maintain international peace and security*'

This clause illustrates the essentially provisional nature[1] of action in self-defence under a centralized system; such a system presupposes that the right is inevitable as an interim measure of protection, but that it should cease when the machinery of the centralized system itself operates as an effective protection of the individual members' rights. Accordingly, under the Charter, such action by the individual state, or even by a number of states acting under the 'collective' right, is envisaged as a temporary measure and in no way a substitute for the collective action of the Organization.[2] This view is supported by the fact that all members have conferred primary responsibility for the maintenance of international peace and security on the Security Council. There would seem, therefore, to be a legal obligation to suspend individual or collective self-defence once the Security Council[3] has taken these measures. The paramount difficulty here lies in the question of competence to decide whether the Security Council has in fact taken 'the measures necessary to maintain international peace and security'. If this competence rests exclusively with the Security Council, then the decision of the Security Council that such measures had been taken, would of itself deny to the defending state its right to continue in its interim protection of its interests. Yet the decision of the Council without more cannot,

[1] Although this is true in principle, in practice the necessity of terminating action in self-defence by a non-procedural note involves the likelihood of an indefinite continuation of this 'provisional' action should there be a lack of unanimity amongst the permanent members.

[2] Kelsen, *Law of U.N.*, p. 800.

[3] The question may also arise where the General Assembly proceeds to take the necessary measures via recommendations to members under the Acheson Plan. Strictly speaking the obligation to suspend individual action relates only to the case where the S.C. has taken such measures, but in principle, if the Members have already agreed to the General Assembly assuming similar responsibilities for the maintenance of international peace and security, they can be said to have agreed to like limitations on their own powers.

one would suppose, terminate action in self-defence,[1] for the phrase 'measures necessary' implies positive action. Whether such positive action by the Council, or by member states pursuant to its decisions or recommendations, does in fact constitute the necessary measures must be decided on the facts of the individual situation. It may well be that in some circumstances an order to the attacking state which is obeyed so as to end the attack will be sufficient; in other circumstances nothing less than the use of armed force will suffice.

On the other hand, to allow the defending state to be the sole judge of whether the Council has taken the necessary measures, opens up the possibility of unilateral action ousting collective action in matters relating to international peace and security, and this would plainly contravene the very spirit of the Charter.[2] On balance, therefore, it is suggested that the preferable view, and one which is not excluded by the Charter, is that whether the necessary measures have been taken must be determined objectively, as a question of fact, and that both the S.C. and the defending state are able to reach their own decisions on this. Should these decisions conflict then the individual member admittedly runs the risk of its continued action being characterized as a 'threat to the peace, breach of the peace, or act of aggression' under Art. 39, but this is only a somewhat greater hazard that it runs in any event by resorting to self-defence and would probably be undertaken in preference to annihilation by the attacking state. This sort of dilemma arises from a paradoxical situation in which the collective organ can deny to a state its freedom of individual action in protection of its rights, without any guarantee that collective action will afford those rights an equal protection. The article refers to 'measures necessary to maintain international peace and security', not 'measures necessary to protect the legiti-

[1] *Contra*, it would seem, Waldock, *op. cit.*, p. 496. Stone, *op. cit.*, p. 244, regards the competence as exclusively within the S.C., apparently on the basis '*nemo iudex in sua causa*'. And see British Commentary on the Charter, Cmd. 6666, p. 9. 'It will be for the S.C. to decide whether these measures have been taken and whether they are adequate for the purpose.' For a contrary view see Goodrich and Hambro, *op. cit.*, p. 300, who suggest it is for each defending state to decide both when and for how long conditions exist which justify the exercise of the right.

[2] But see Krezdorn, *op. cit.*, p. 127: 'Nous inclinons cependant à penser que ce sont les Etats en exercice de légitime défense que décident quelles mesures doivent être considérées comme nécessaires pour rétablier la sécurité . . .'

mate interests of the state attacked', and though in principle one would say that the former phrase includes the sense of the latter, especially since the Council must act 'in conformity with the principle of justice and international law' (Art. 1(1)), there is no real assurance that the individual member's rights may not be sacrificed in the more general interest of the maintenance of international peace and security. In theory this should not be so, but in fact the risk of a 'political' decision by the Council is always present. Measures necessary to 'maintain international peace and security' are probably the measures referred to in Arts. 39, 41, and 42[1] and clearly exceed the limits of measures in self-defence.

Once these measures are taken, and assuming the individual state accepts their adequacy, any further action by the individual state, or by states associated with it in collective self-defence, ceases to be based on the right of individual or collective self-defence. The legal basis of continued action is to be found in the authorization[2] of the Security Council,[3] and 'l'action autonome de légitime défense se transformera ainsi en une action au nom des Nations Unies'.[4]

(e) *'Measures taken by Members in the exercise of the right of self-defence shall be immediately reported to the Security Council'*

This phrase imports a legal obligation to report immediately to the Security Council any measure actually taken by the Members in self-defence.[5] In contradistinction to Art. 54, which imposes on members of regional arrangements and regional agencies an obligation to report 'activities undertaken or in contemplation',

[1] Kelsen, *Law of U.N.*, p. 801.

[2] Authorization would include recommendations and, in the absence of agreements under Art. 43, provide the normal way of instigating collective measures.

[3] Kelsen, *Recent Trends*, p. 928, suggests that the S.C. action in its resolution of June 25th, 1950, terminated the South Korean right of self-defence; this seems a curious definition of 'action' and in any event that resolution could scarcely be considered the 'measures necessary to maintain international peace and security'. See Swedish delegate to 285th Plenary Meeting of the G.A.: 'Both the action of the U.S. and the decisions of other countries to assist South Korea are solidly based upon the provisions of Art. 51 of the Charter concerning collective self-defence', Off. Rec., Fifth Session, September 26th, 1950.

[4] Krezdorn, *op. cit.*, p. 127.

[5] See the Indian delegate's reply to the Pakistan plea of self-defence at the 466th Meeting of the Security Council. Off. Rec. S.C., 5th Year, No. 8, p. 4.

this Article does not involve any obligation to report preparatory measures.[1] The information which members supply under this article will afford a basis, though not the only basis, upon which any subsequent decision of the Council relating to the taking of provisional measures under Art. 40, or to a determination under Art. 39, or even enforcement action under Arts. 41 and 42, may be made. It will be noted that in the Resolution on Uniting for Peace[2] members are 'invited' to inform the Collective Measures Committee established thereunder, of measures taken to conform with the recommendation that the members maintain within national armed forces elements trained so as to be able to implement the General Assembly's recommendations. This, although not a legal obligation, is much nearer the obligation contained in Art. 54. There is no obligation or even invitation to report measures taken in self-defence to the General Assembly or any of its Committees. Indeed, since the statement of interested parties will always be suspect, the General Assembly appears to intend relying on the Peace Observation Committee[3] for fact-finding, and the Security Council itself will obviously need to supplement information supplied by interested parties by an independent investigation under Art. 34 or by a sub-committee under Art. 29.[4]

(*f*) *'And shall not in any way affect the authority and responsibility of the Security Council under the present Charter to take at any time such action as it deems necessary in order to maintain or restore international peace and security'*

This clause is perhaps superfluous and without legal effect.[5] It

[1] Goodrich and Hambro, *op. cit.*, p. 307. See *post*, p. 219, for a more detailed discussion of this distinction in relation to self-defence and regional arrangements.

[2] Doc. A/1481, para. 9. At the 367th Meeting of the General Assembly's First Committee on October 18th, 1950, the Soviet representative argued that this was a violation of Art. 51 which provides for a report to the Security Council. There are two arguments against this view; firstly the Resolution, para. 8, states that the obligation is 'without prejudice' to the use of elements under Art. 51, and this involves the obligation to report to the Security Council under Art. 51, and secondly the reports to be made to the Collective Measures Committee do not relate to measures taken in self-defence.

[3] Established in para. 3 of the Resolution.

[4] The distinction between these two procedures for fact-finding is not an easy one. See Jiménez de Arechaga, *Voting and the Handling of Disputes in the Security Council*, p. 75 *et seq.*

[5] Kelsen, *Law of United Nations*, p. 804.

reiterates the principle that the primary responsibility for the maintenance of international peace and security is vested in the Security Council,[1] and again illustrates the intended provisional nature of individual or collective action in self-defence.

[1] Principles already established in Arts. 24 and 39.

CHAPTER X

COLLECTIVE SELF-DEFENCE

THE use of the phrase 'collective self-defence' in Art. 51 has been the subject of criticism on the ground that it embodies a contradiction in terms. Kelsen argues that, since self-defence involves action which is by definition unilateral in character, to speak of a 'collective' unilateral right is to indulge in self-contradiction: for him the right of self-defence 'is the right of the attacked or threatened individual or State, and of no other individual or State'.[1] For similar reasons other authors have preferred to call the right 'not self-defence, but defence of another State'.[2] Now whatever are the merits of these criticisms, it is clear firstly that the provision was intended to cover the sort of collective action in self-defence which regional arrangements might wish to take and for which their constitutive treaties made provision,[3] and secondly that Art. 51 did not import any novel concept into international law and was declaratory of existing rights. The notion of a collective right of self-defence has long been accepted, although writers have differed in their views as to the basis of the right. It is of some importance to consider these views for, in the absence of a clear indication in the Charter as to what precise situation the right of 'collective self-defence' envisages, they may well indicate the nature of the action covered by this phrase, just as state practice may well indicate the nature of collective self-defence prior to the Charter.

THE THEORY OF THE COLLECTIVE RIGHT OF SELF-DEFENCE

So far as can be ascertained, there are three different theories as to the proper basis of the right. In the first place there is the view

[1] *Law of the United Nations* (1950), pp. 792, 797. See also Root, 'Observations on the Monroe Doctrine', *A.J.*, Vol. 17 (1923), p. 616.

[2] Kunz, 'Individual and Collective Self-Defence in Art. 51 of the Charter of the U.N.', *A.J.*, Vol. 41 (1947), p. 875. And see Stone, *Legal Controls of International Conflict*, p. 245; *contra*, Beckett, *The North Atlantic Treaty*, p. 13.

[3] *Post*, pp. 224–33.

that the right is based on the analogy with private law. Baty states:

> That self-defence, when legitimate, need not be limited to one's own defence, but may extend to the defence of states unjustly attacked, appears to follow from the analogy of private law.[1]

On similar reasoning Le Fur states:

> Le droit de légitime défense, entre Etats comme entre individus, ne vise pas seulement la défense personelle, mais aussi celle d'autrui.[2]

A survey of the provisions of some of the main systems of law on this point would seem to bear out the analogy which these writers seek to draw. The English Common Law clearly recognizes self-defence as going beyond the defence of one's own person or property, although the cases suggest there must be some relationship between the person attacked and the person who assists in his lawful defence.[3] The American Re-statement on the Law of Torts again both recognizes the right and limits it to the defence of those who are members of one's household, or those whom one is under a legally or socially recognized duty to protect.[4] Art. 328 of the French Criminal Code provides:

> Il n'y a crime, ni délit lorsque l'homicide, les blessures et les coups étaient commandés par le nécessité actuelle de la légitime défense de soi-même ou d'autrui.[5]

There would seem little question that, on the analogy of private law, the right is both individual and collective, and, since 'general principles of law' may be regarded as a legitimate source of public international law, the analogy serves to support the theory of the 'collective' right of self-defence. Of immediate interest, however, is the fact that the right is limited to those cases where there exists

[1] *Canons of International Law*, p. 99.

[2] 'Guerre juste et juste paix', *R.G.D.I.P.*, Vol. 24, p. 74. And see Fiore, *Diritto Internazionale*, ss. 241, 242, justifying collective intervention to protect the rights of strangers; Phillimore, 'Droits et Devoirs des Etats', *R.C.*, 1923 (I), p. 45. Descamps, 'Le Droit International Nouveau', *R.C.*, 1930 (I), pp. 399, 557 and 475, cites the Belgian Penal Code Art. 416 in support of this view.

[3] See *Russell on Crime*, 10th ed., Vol. I, p. 763. *Leward* v. *Basely* (1694), I Ld. Raym. 62, wife's defence of husband; *Tickel* v. *Read* (1772), Lofft. 215, master's defence of servant.

[4] S. 76.

[5] Recueil Sirey (1955): Garraud, *Précis de Droit Criminel*, 5th ed., pp. 329–340.

some sort of proximate relationship; the right extends to the defence of one's family, one's servants, and to those persons whom one is under a recognized duty to protect. These cases seem to presuppose an interest which the person has a right to defend, for example his interest in the integrity and well-being of his family or his servants; in Roman law the interest was confined to those cases where the 'protector' had rights of dominion over the persons he sought to protect in self-defence.[1] It is this element which distinguishes self-defence from action taken to defend some complete stranger in whose well-being the 'protector' has no special interest, for in the latter case, if the 'protector' intervenes to defend the stranger, it is generally by virtue of some duty imposed by the law to prevent a breach of the peace or grievous wounding;[2] it is not by virtue of a right of self-defence, either individual or collective. Even in the absence of a duty of positive action, assistance rendered to the stranger is legally distinct from self-defence, for its purpose is the maintenance of the public peace and not the protection of the intervener's substantive rights. For self-defence to apply there must be a violation of the intervener's own rights against which he may act in self-defence, but in those cases in which the law recognize a proximate relationship between the intervener or 'protector' and the actual victim such that the attack violates the 'protector's' legally recognized interests in the security of the victim the right of self-defence will be 'collective'. If this analysis is correct, then, when we carry the analogy into the international sphere it follows that the 'collective' right will exist where the state invoking the right can show some interest of its own which is violated by the attack launched upon another state. We must similarly presuppose a 'proximate relationship', though not necessarily in terms of geographical contiguity, which makes a direct violation of the rights of one state an indirect, but nevertheless real, violation of the rights of another state which comes to the former's aid by virtue of the latter's right of collective self-defence.

The second theory explaining the basis of the collective right

[1] Sohm, *Institutes of Roman Law*, 3rd ed., p. 224. Wrongs to persons or their property under the *potestas* of the paterfamilias were considered to be wrongs to the paterfamilias; Buckland, *Text-book of Roman Law* (1921), p. 104.

[2] As is the case in English law: 2 Hawkins' Pleas of the Crown, c. 12, s. 1. See Archbold, *Criminal Pleading, Evidence and Practice*, 33rd ed., p. 1074.

is one which is based upon the concept of a duty to maintain international peace and to redress a violation of the rules of international law.[1] As Redslob puts it:

> Le devoir de maintenir la paix, d'une part, et l'obligation de redresser la norme violée de l'autre, convergent et s'unissent dans le précepte de soutenir la légitime défense d'autrui.[2]

This theory meets with certain difficulties, for the existence of such duties in international law is highly questionable; Redslob himself frames this postulate under the general heading of 'Une Doctrine Marginale', and it appears to be a concept which goes beyond what the actual relationships of state would justify. Moreover, as Stowell has pointed out,[3] so long as the duty of vindicating the law depends on the sovereign decision of each state as to how and when this obligation shall be fulfilled, the content of such a 'duty' is problematical. The provisions of Art. 16 of the Covenant, and of the Kellogg-Briand Pact of 1928,[4] in which Redslob finds support for his thesis, can scarcely be held to have imposed a duty on signatories to vindicate a breach of the obligation

[1] The conclusion is almost inescapable that any postulation of a duty to maintain international peace, as a basis of the right of self-defence, is based upon the theory of the just war. Until any particular act of force by a state can be classed as either a delict or a sanction the postulate of such a duty seems an anomaly in the legal system. The existence of such a duty would make all treaties of assistance merely declaratory of existing international law; it cannot be supposed that, at least prior to the Charter, this was the case.

[2] *Traité de Droit des Gens*, p. 435. See also Grotius, *De Jure Belli ac Pacis*, Bk. I, cap. V, 2; Wolff, *Jus Gentium*, s. 656; Vattel, *Droit des Gens*, Bk. II, ch. I, s. 4.

[3] *Intervention in International Law*, p. 48. See the somewhat similar doubts of Wehberg, *The Outlawry of War* (1929), p. 99: 'But we ask what law gives a state the right to decide for itself whether the means of violence which it has used are justified by the higher interests of the international community. A state can represent these higher interests only as an organ of the international community.'

[4] See the statement of Stimson of December 30th, 1929: 'The Pact contains no covenant similar to that in the Covenant of the League of Nations providing for joint forceful action by the various signatories against an aggressor.' *A.J. Supp.*, Vol. 25 (1931), p. 90 note. This view would seem preferable, and it is difficult to see how the Pact supports Redslob's thesis. Tucker, 'The Legal Interpretation of War', *I.L.Q.*, Vol. 3 (1950), p. 20, regards the Paris Pact as, in effect, an extension of the right of self-defence by 'permitting other contracting parties the right to collectively assist the state acting in self-defence'. It is difficult to agree that the freedom of action which signatories reserved against a state breaking the Pact by depriving such state of benefits under the Pact has necessarily anything in common with the right of self-defence, either individual or collective.

contained in the Covenant and the Pact. Nor is it considered that the present development of the law justifies the assertion that each state has an interest in the general preservation of world peace, if by the term 'interest' we mean a legally recognized interest which a state may protect by the exercise of self-defence. Lauterpacht has said of the concept of collective self-defence:

> Such an extension of the notion of self-defence is a proper expression of the ultimate identity of interest of the international community in the preservation of peace.[1]

In fact, however, this interest is no more than the general interest (and we use the term without legal significance) which members of any community have in the preservation of peace within that community. If we return to the analogy of private law, it corresponds to the interest which individuals have in the preservation of order and which is expressed when the 'protector' assists the stranger in his defence; it is not such a legally recognized interest as the 'protector' has in his family or servants, and which he protects by the exercise of his right of self-defence. The danger inherent in admitting that, by virtue of an 'interest' in the maintenance of international peace and security, any state can assist another state deemed to be acting in self-defence, is that it opens up the possibility of unlimited action under a system of defensive alliances which would be quite contrary to the Charter system.[2]

It is, of course, possible for international law in the future, either by treaty or by developing a custom, to impose duties on states respecting the maintenance of international peace and security, and these would find their analogy in the duties which private citizens in English law have to prevent the commission of felonies or dangerous woundings.[3] To this extent the U.N. Charter contains the first real attempt to reconcile the imposition of duties to maintain international peace and security with the

[1] Oppenheim, *International Law*, Vol. II, 7th ed., p. 155. See Westlake, *International Law*, Vol. I, p. 320, for a justification of collective intervention in the support of justice or of the interests of third states so far as consonant with justice. Also Hall, *International Law*, 8th ed., p. 65. An even vaguer basis than the identity of interest in the preservation of peace is that of the identity of interest of mankind as such. See Descamps, 'Le Nouveau Droit International', *R.C.*, 1930 (I), at p. 475, where he states: 'Le peril crée, comme l' on a dit, un lien sacré de confraternité entre les hommes et peut leur imposer le devoir d'assister dans certains cas les victimes d'une injuste agression.'

[2] *Post*, pp. 244–7. [3] Kenny, *Outline of Criminal Law*, 16th ed., p. 473.

problem posed by the freedom which each sovereign state normally would have to decide when and how such a duty may be fulfilled. This decision is delegated to the Security Council which is invested with 'primary responsibility' for the maintenance of international peace and security, and whose decisions the member states are, under Art. 25, legally bound to accept. The duty to vindicate the law is conditional upon a decision of the Security Council which may, subject to certain provisos,[1] legally oblige a member to fulfil such a duty. Yet the action which any member may take in fulfilment of such a duty has little in common with the action it takes in collective self-defence under Art. 51. Similarly, although it has been suggested[2] that collective self-defence is the best means of fulfilling one of the primary purposes of the United Nations, namely 'to take effective collective measures for the prevention and removal of threats to the peace, and for the suppression of acts of aggression or other breaches of the peace' (Art. 1(1)), this function is equally clearly one quite distinct from self-defence; the identification of the two arises from a failure to distinguish the protective right of self-defence from collective sanctions. Stone has rightly said:

> So far is the inherent right of self-defence under Art. 51 from being a means of taking the 'collective measure for the prevention of threats to the peace and the suppression . . . of aggression' under Art. 1, paragraph 1, that large-scale resort to it would be rather the clear sign of the defeat of that principle. . . .[3]

The third theory explaining the basis of the collective right is founded on the principle that states may exercise collectively what is undoubtedly their individual right.[4] This, it is submitted,

[1] The legal obligation to participate in sanctions is conditional upon the state being bound by a special agreement under Art. 43, upon the conformity of the decision with the voting procedure of Art. 27, and possibly also with the Purposes and Principles of the Charter.

[2] Beckett, *The North Atlantic Treaty*, p. 35.

[3] *Legal Controls of International Conflict*, p. 264.

[4] This same principle justified the exercise of jurisdiction over the Major War Criminals of the European Axis by the four state signatories of the London Charter of August 8th, 1945. See Oppenheim, Vol. II, 7th ed., p. 581; Judgment of the Nuremberg Tribunal, Memorandum of the Secretary-General, A/CN.4/5, March 3rd, 1949, p. 79. The judgment is not unambiguous on this question of the legal basis of the Tribunal's jurisdiction, and it is particularly difficult to reconcile this view with the statement at page 216 (of text given in *A.J.*, Vol. 41 (1947)) although it goes on to state 'they have done together what any one might have done singly'.

provides by far the most satisfactory explanation of the collective right, for it demands that each participant in the collective action has an individual right of self-defence; the existence of its individual right, which is largely a question of fact in the circumstances, is the condition precedent to the state's participation in its collective enforcement. The analogy of private law supports rather than opposes this view, for the private law requirement of a legally recognized interest is comparable to the requirement that each participating state should possess a legally recognized interest which is violated, either by an attack upon itself or its neighbour. Beyond this point, when the participation involves not the protection of the state's own rights or interests, but the protection of the more general interest in the maintenance of international peace and the vindication of international law, such action ceases to fall within the concept of self-defence, either individual or collective.

The preference for this third theory and rejection of the second is based upon an examination of the possible factual situations which the right of self-defence might envisage, for it is believed that the proponents of the second theory confuse situations which are radically different. There are, in final analysis, three possible situations:

(1) State A violates the legally protected interests of State B. Here A is in breach of an established duty and B may exercise the right of individual self-defence.
(2) State A violates the legally protected interests of States B and C. Here A is in breach of an established duty vis-à-vis both B and C and both may exercise their rights of individual self-defence, in which case the position is as in (1) above, *or* may exercise these in concert; this is the position which is properly termed 'collective self-defence'. The essence of this position is that the participants base their action on a violation of their own legally protected rights or interests, and this remains true whether they are two or twenty-two in number.
(3) State A violates the legally protected interest of State B only; B exercises its right of self-defence and C joins in 'collective' action. Here the participant C cannot base its action on a breach of its own rights but falls back upon the

different concept of a 'duty' to maintain international peace and redress the violated norm, or an 'interest' in the maintenance of international peace and security.

Whatever be the merits or demerits of the term 'collective self-defence', it is submitted that the particular situation envisaged in (3) above is not one in which the participating state can claim to be acting in self-defence, individual or collective. The full relevance of this distinction between the right of self-defence, exercised collectively, and the administration of sanctions (or perhaps more correctly, so far as the Charter is concerned, the participation in collective measures for the maintenance of international peace and security)[1] is seen when we examine the present position under the Charter. For the moment, however, our contention is simply that a state resorting to force not in defence of its own rights, but in the defence of another state, must justify its action as being in the nature of a sanction and not as self-defence, individual or collective. The aim is to redress the violation of international law, not to protect its own rights. The requirements of the right of collective self-defence are two in number; firstly that each participating state has an individual right of self-defence, and secondly that there exists an agreement between the participating states to exercise their rights collectively. Before examining the developments which have taken place since the Charter on the basis of a right of collective self-defence, and the relevance of the distinction between self-defence and sanctions to these developments, it is fitting that we examine state practice prior to the Charter. For, even prior to the Charter, there had developed certain doctrines, of which the primary example is the Monroe Doctrine, from which the right of collective self-defence, recognized in the Charter, sprang.

STATE PRACTICE PRIOR TO THE CHARTER

The practice of certain states prior to the Charter affords evidence that they considered a 'proximate relationship' to exist between themselves and certain other states so that an attack upon those other states would constitute a threat to their own security. The classic example of this practice is, of course, the Monroe

[1] See *ante*, p. 19.

Doctrine, and it is proposed to deal with the Monroe Doctrine and certain similar doctrines advanced by Great Britain and Japan.

(*a*) *The Monroe Doctrine*

The reactionary policy of the Allied Powers in Europe after 1815, directed towards the suppression of any revolutionary régime, and in particular the circular from Troppau in 1823,[1] produced a special anxiety in the United States. It had been made known to the United States by Mr. Canning, the British Foreign Secretary, that the Powers of the Holy Alliance contemplated the extension of this policy of reaction to the Western Hemisphere, in particular to the Spanish colonies in South America.[2]

The attitude of the United States was publicly declared by President Monroe in his annual message of December 2nd, 1823,[3] the critical part of which stated:

> . . . We should consider any attempt on their part to extend their system to any portion of this hemisphere as dangerous to our peace and safety.[4]

In pursuance of this principle the United States protested against the European interventions in Mexico from 1825–60[5] and even more strongly, after the withdrawal of the English and Spanish naval forces from Vera Cruz in April, 1862, against the French occupation of Mexico under the Archduke Maximilian.[6] A later and important illustration of this attitude was seen in the interposition of the United States in the controversy between Great Britain and Venezuela over the boundary dispute of 1895, the United States maintaining not only that the dispute was a 'serious and direct menace to its own integrity, tranquillity,

[1] *Ante*, p. 44. There were in fact earlier indications of this same attitude towards the expansion of European possessions in the Americas. See Jefferson to Carmichael and Short, U.S. Mins. to Spain, March 23rd, 1793, cited Moore, *Dig.*, Vol. VI, p. 369. Also the attitude in 1811 in relation to Florida, ibid., p. 372, and to Cuba, ibid., p. 379. For detailed references to a vast literature on the subject of the Monroe Doctrine see Hyde, Vol. I, p. 281 fn.

[2] Mr. Canning to Mr. Rush, August 23rd, 1823, cited Moore, *Dig.*, Vol. VI, 392.

[3] For the full text of the message see Hyde, Vol. I, pp. 284–6.

[4] Ibid., p. 285.

[5] Moore, *Dig.*, Vol. VI, p. 477 *et seq.*

[6] An army of 50,000 men under General Sheridan was sent to the Rio Grande and General Scholefield was given authority to recruit a 'volunteer' army to assist the republican government of Mexico; it would not appear that this army ever actively opposed the French. See Moore, *op. cit.*, p. 498.

and welfare',[1] but that the refusal of Great Britain to arbitrate amounted to an appropriation of territory contrary to the principles of the Monroe Doctrine.[2]

Under this same principle the United States opposed even the indirect acquisition of control of American territory by non-American states through the medium of public agencies. In 1912 the Senate adopted a resolution that:

> When any harbour or other place in the American continents is so situated that the occupation thereof for naval or military purposes might threaten the communications or the safety of the United States, the government of the United States could not see without grave concern the possession of such harbour or other place by any corporation or association which has such a relation to another government, not American, as to give that government practical power of control for naval or military purposes.[3]

The fear on which this resolution was founded was that Japan might indirectly acquire a footing in territory adjacent to Magdalena Bay.

In June, 1940, Secretary of State Hull informed the Axis powers of Germany and Italy of the continuance of this policy.

> 'In accordance with its traditional policy relating to the Western Hemisphere, the United States could not recognize any transfer, and would not acquiesce in any attempt to transfer, any geographic region of the Western Hemisphere from one non-American power to another non-American power.' [4]

These examples suffice to show that from the point of view of the United States her security was so dependent on the security of the American Continent as a whole that any attack upon that continent would jeopardize her interests to such an extent as to afford to the United States the right of self-defence. There is

[1] Sec. of State Olney to Sir Julian Pauncefote, November 26th, 1895; Moore, *op. cit.*, p. 559.

[2] Moore, *op. cit.*, p. 575. Yet the U.S. did not, presumably, take the view that any dispute between an American and non-American state involved the interests of the U.S. In the dispute between Hayti and Germany in 1897, when Hayti was threatened by bombardment by German warships the U.S. chose not to interfere; see Mr. Sherman, Sec. of State to Mr. Powell, Min. to Hayti, December 22nd, 1897, cited Moore, *Dig.*, VI, p. 475. See also in relation to the German proposal to use force in order to coerce Venezuela to satisfy legitimate claims in 1901, Moore, VI, p. 586. In all these cases the United States was satisfied with the assurance that the action involved no possibility of occupation of American territory except for the specific purpose of enforcing claims.

[3] Hyde, Vol. I, p. 289.

[4] Ibid., p. 289.

ample evidence that for many years the United States maintained this view as a matter of unilateral policy and that its essential basis was the individual right of self-defence.[1] It was only gradually that the United States sought to secure the agreement of other American states in the essentials of the policy and their pledge of active co-operation so as to make the Monroe Doctrine not merely a policy of self-defence of the United States but of collective self-defence of the continent as a whole.[2] The culmination of this change, inevitable due to the growing independence of the other American states and their resentment of the professed right of intervention in their affairs by the United States, came at the Eighth International Conference of American States on December 24th, 1938, when there was approved, unanimously, a 'Declaration of the Principles of the Solidarity of America', more commonly known as the Declaration of Lima.[3] It was probably only at this stage that the Monroe Doctrine ceased to be a purely unilateral policy of the United States, and the true process of collectivization began. While the Declaration contained nothing more binding than an obligation of consultation at the initiative of any one of the signatory states,[4] the implication as to the char-

[1] Hughes, 'Observations on the Monroe Doctrine', *A.J.*, Vol. 17 (1923), p. 616; Clark, Memorandum on the Monroe Doctrine, Dept. State Publication No. 37, 1930; Fenwick, 'The Monroe Doctrine and the Declaration of Lima', *A.J.*, Vol. 33 (1939), p. 257; Root, 'The Real Monroe Doctrine', *A.J.*, Vol. 8 (1914), p. 432; Roosevelt, *L'Idéal Americain*, p. 113, cited in Planas-Suarez, 'L'Extension de la Doctrine de Monroe en Amerique du Sud', *R.C.*, 1924 (iv), p. 338; Rivier, *Principes du Droit des Gens* (1896), Vol. I, p. 406.

[2] For a summary of the negotiations by which the U.S. sought this, see Moore, *Dig.*, Vol. VI, pp. 417, 599–602. On the early reactions of the American states to this policy see Alvarez, *The Monroe Doctrine* (1924), pp. 10, 19; Trelles, 'La Doctrine de Monroe dans son développement historique', *R.C.*, 1930 (ii), p. 397; Planas-Suarez, *op. cit.*, p. 274; Moore, *Principles of American Diplomacy*, pp. 400–8. See Art. 8, Convention on Rights and Duties of States, December 26th, 1933; U.S. Treaty, Vol. IV, 4807, at p. 4809. Also Additional Protocol Relative to Non-Intervention, at Buenos Aires on December 23rd, 1936, Art. I; U.S. Treaty, Vol. IV, p. 4821. Also Art. 2 of the Convention for the Maintenance, Preservation and Re-Establishment of Peace, concluded on the same day, in which the parties agreed: 'that in the event of an international war outside America which might menace the peace of the American Republics, such consultation shall also take place to determine the proper time and manner in which the signatory states, if they so desire, may eventually co-operate in some action tending to preserve the peace of the American Continent', U.S. Treaty, Vol. IV, 4819.

[3] For the full text of the Declaration see Hyde, Vol. I, p. 303 fn.

[4] Ibid., para. 4.

acter of the Monroe Doctrine in the future was unmistakable.[1] At the First Meeting of the Foreign Ministers of the American Republics at Panama, on October 3rd, 1939, this shift from a unilateral to a collective right was further emphasized by a resolution providing for consultation should any region of America subject to the sovereignty of a non-American state be obliged to change its sovereignty and thereby produce a danger to the security of the American Continent.[2] A second meeting at Habana produced, on July 30th, 1940, a Final Act which included a resolution known as the 'Act of Habana concerning the Provisional Administration of European Colonies and Possessions in the Americas'. A supplementary Convention[3] took notice of the fact that, as a result of the European war, situations might arise in the American colonial possessions of the belligerent powers 'creating a state of danger to the peace of the continent', and accordingly declared, *inter alia*, that:

> Any transfer, or attempted transfer, of the sovereignty jurisdiction, possession or any interest in or control over any such region to another non-American State would be regarded by the American Republics as against American sentiments and principles and the rights of American states to maintain their security and political independence,

and that 'this community has . . . international juridical capacity' to act in the manner provided for in the Convention. The manner contemplated was the assertion of a provisional control over those European colonial possessions by this new juridical entity of American states.[4]

It is at this stage, then, that the Monroe Doctrine becomes a collective doctrine and not an assertion of unilateral policy by the United States. Although there were later cases of the United States acting unilaterally[5] in matters which, *prima facie*, affected

[1] See Fenwick, *op. cit.*, p. 257; 'The Monroe Doctrine has now taken on a multilateral character' (p. 266), and 'The Convention nevertheless affirmed the principle that the American Republics had a common interest in the protection of any one of their number against attack' (p. 261).

[2] Hyde, Vol. I, p. 304.

[3] The texts of these two instruments are set forth in the Dept. of State Bulletin, August 24th, 127 and 145 respectively.

[4] An Inter-American Commission for Territorial Administration was set up for this precise purpose (Art. XVI).

[5] E.g. the U.S. arrangement with the Danish government in exile in April, 1941, with reference to Greenland. Also the communication in June, 1940, of the policy of the U.S. to the Axis Powers; Dept. of State Bulletin, June 22nd, 1940, 681.

the security of the American continent as a whole, the change is, on the whole, a marked one. It is, of course, possible to see the Monroe Doctrine as a doctrine of state policy without any necessary relation to or basis upon the right of self-defence.[1] This ignores the fact that, since the policy involved a *prima facie* unlawful interposition in the relations of other states, the United States must find some legal justification for that interposition. To submit that a state may interpose in the affairs of other states, contrary to established legal principle, and justify this interposition without reference to legal principles is clearly wrong. The basis upon which the United States necessarily rested her policy was her right of self-defence; as Hyde states:

> The basis of the claim would be that the proper defence of the nation is rendered more difficult and its safety jeopardized by the transfer generally of American territory to non-American states . . . a moderate and reasonable enunciation of the principle of self-defence.[2]

(*b*) *The British and Japanese Doctrines*

It would be erroneous to assume that the United States has, alone of the world powers, maintained the principle that her security demanded a claim of special interests in parts of the world not within her territorial jurisdiction.

Great Britain has made similar claims in relation to Afghanistan, Persia and Egypt.[3] It was to enforce recognition of these claims that the British note of May 19th, 1928, was sent to the United States government in connection with the Treaty for the Renunciation of War or, as it is more commonly known, the Kellogg-Briand Pact of 1928. The British government therein stated:

> There are certain regions of the world the welfare and integrity of which constitute a special and vital interest for our peace and safety. . . . Their protection against attack is to the British Empire a measure of self-defence.[4]

---

[1] Hershey, *Essentials of International Public Law* (1912), pp. 152–3; Root, *op. cit.*, p. 427.

[2] *International Law*, Vol. I, p. 288; also Hughes, *op. cit.*, p. 615; Tower, 'The Origin and Meaning of the Monroe Doctrine', *A.J.*, Vol. 14 (1920), p. 24. See also the Report on the Pact of Paris submitted to the U.S. Senate by the Committee on Foreign Relations, cited Mandelstam, *L'Interpretation du Pacte Briand-Kellogg*, p. 33.

[3] Pearce-Higgins, 'The Monroe Doctrine', *BYBIL*, Vol. 5 (1924), p. 114.

[4] Cmd. 3109, p. 25; Cmd. 3153, p. 10; R.I.I.A. Documents, 1928, p. 5.

The reference to 'certain regions of the world' was not, on this occasion, further specified; to the extent that these regions included parts of the British Empire, subject to the sovereignty of Great Britain, the claim was perfectly legitimate. To the extent that these claims referred to regions under the sovereignty of other states the claim could not be justified as self-defence except upon proof that in fact an attack upon those regions would jeopardize Britain's security and violate her own rights.[1]

In April, 1934, Mr. Eijii Amau, as spokesman for the Japanese Foreign Office, stated his country's policy towards China in terms which were reminiscent of the more dictatorial pronouncements of the United States on the Monroe Doctrine. He said:

> We therefore oppose any attempt on the part of China to avail herself of the influence of any other country in order to resist Japan. We also oppose any action taken by China calculated to play one Power against another.[2]

This special position which Japan claimed on the basis of territorial propinquity is in some respects analogous to the special position claimed by the United States in the Western Hemisphere, although later developments indicated a marked difference in the intention of Japan as to the ultimate purpose of this claim to a special position. Although this claim was by no means novel,[3] it would not seem to have met with the agreement of other

[1] Wehberg, *The Outlawry of War* (1931), at p. 86, describes this as 'a very dubious reservation of a purely imperialistic nature which diminishes the significance of the Kellogg Pact to a considerable degree'. He accepts the reservation of the Monroe Doctrine and distinguishes the British claim on its lack of definition and limitation to a geographical region. For the opposition of the U.S.S.R., see Schwarzenberger, *Power Politics*, 2nd ed., pp. 506–7. Miller, *The Peace Pact of Paris* (1928), pp. 117–18, accepts this express reservation as being within the concept of self-defence previously stated by Mr. Kellogg, the U.S. Secretary of State, and as being outside the prohibitions of the treaty.

[2] Cited Hyde, 'Legal Aspects of Japanese Pronouncements in Relation to China', *A.J.*, Vol. 28 (1934), p. 431; also R.I.I.A. Documents, 1934, p. 472.

[3] An earlier illustration is the communication of January 18th, 1915, by the Japanese Minister at Peking to the President of the Chinese Republic, known as the 'Twenty-One Demands'. The fourth group of these demands, which insisted that China should not cede or lease any harbour, bay or island along the Chinese coast to any third Power, finds a parallel in the U.S. policy in 1912 towards Magdalena Bay; see *ante*, p. 209. See generally Keeton, *China, The Far East, and the Future* (1943), pp. 139–45.

states,[1] and, lacking the basis of consent, any action taken by Japan in furtherance of this policy which involved intervention or interposition in the affairs of China, or of other nations in their relations with China, would seem to require a plea of self-defence for its justification. In this event, the Japanese claims, measured by the requirements of the legal concept of self-defence, would not appear to have any legal basis except upon proof that her security was so dependent upon the security of China. It was not inconceivable that the situation in China might afford a real threat to the security of Japan, but the onus of proving this would lie on Japan.

In the statement of the British claims, quoted above, the connection between these claims of 'special interest' and the right of self-defence is clearly brought out, although it is unmentioned in the Japanese claims. Whether this connection is stated expressly or raised by implication, the right of self-defence cannot afford a legal basis to claims which fail to conform to the requirements which that concept clearly demands. The Japanese, British and Monroe doctrines are, in so far as they purport to be based on the legal concept of self-defence, subject to identical requirements. The proof of an immediate danger to the real interests of these states can conceivably be made in relation to a given situation. It would not seem possible to formulate a doctrine in advance, based upon hypothetical situations, and then justify all measures in pursuance of this doctrine as based upon the legal right of self-defence.

Moreover, at best the British and Japanese doctrines can only amount to an assertion which the United States made in the earlier stages of the Monroe doctrine, namely that their security is so essentially linked with that of certain other states as to make an attack on those other states a threat to their own security. This would, of course, always be a question of fact to be decided in the

[1] The partial recognition of this policy (contained in the 21 demands) by the United States in the exchange of notes of November 2nd, 1917, between Sec. Lansing and Viscount Ishii, the Japanese Ambassador to the U.S., was cancelled on April 14th, 1923, and was inoperative from that date. For text of exchange of notes see *A.J.*, Supp., Vol. 12 (1918), p. 1. For text of cancellation see *A.J.*, Supp., Vol. 17 (1923), p. 137. The lack of consent by China is evidenced by her fear that Art. 21 of the Covenant should in any way endorse this Japanese policy and afford a legal basis for it; see Miller, *Drafting of the Covenant*, Vol. I, p. 336.

circumstances and cannot be stated as a matter of principle. In any event it is an assertion of a right of individual self-defence and, in the absence of an agreement with the states directly attacked to exercise the individual rights of self-defence in concert, bears no real relation to the concept of collective self-defence.[1] The development of collective self-defence by these states needed not only the existence of the individual right of self-defence, but also an arrangement, whether formal or *ad hoc*, by the states affected directly or indirectly by an attack to exercise their rights of self-defence in concert. As we have seen, it is only since 1938 that the United States has really placed the Monroe Doctrine within the concept of collective self-defence properly so-called.

THE CHARTER AND 'COLLECTIVE SELF-DEFENCE'

Since the term 'collective self-defence' is not defined in the Charter, it is necessary to resort not only to general principles of law and the practice of states prior to the Charter, but also to the *travaux préparatoires* in order to clarify the meaning of the term under the Charter.

The connection between Art. 51 and the need to safeguard the freedom of action in self-defence contemplated by regional arrangements has already been stressed. The Act of Chapultepec of March 3rd, 1945, had stated:

> That any attempt on the part of a non-American State against the integrity or inviolability of the territory, the sovereignty or the political independence of an American State shall be considered as an act of aggression against all American States.[2]

In the fourth meeting of Committee III/4 at San Francisco on May 23rd, 1945, Camargo, speaking for Columbia, declared that:

> In the case of the American states, an aggression against one American state constitutes an aggression against all the other American states and all of them exercise their right of legitimate defence by giving support to the state attacked, in order to repel such aggression. This is what is meant by the right of collective self-defence.[3]

---

[1] See Théry, *Notion d'Agression*, p. 295 *et seq.*

[2] Section 5 (J). *A.J.*, Supp., Vol. 39 (1945), p. 109. This principle reproduced the 15th Declaration of the 2nd Meeting of the Ministers of Foreign Affairs, Havana, 1940.

[3] *UNCIO*, Docs., Vol. XII, p. 687.

With this view the Latin-American representatives agreed. The Egyptian representative stated[1] that Art. 51 would also cover action contemplated under the Pact of the Arab League, although the Pact simply states in Art. 6 that in case of aggression the attacked or threatened state may demand the convocation of the Council of the League which 'shall determine the measures necessary to repulse the aggression'.[2] Yet, whilst the Egyptian delegate declared himself to be against the inclusion of alliances and mutual assistance pacts, the French delegate was of the opinion that the formula adopted in Art. 51 'extends in general to cases of mutual assistance against aggression'.[3] It is difficult, therefore, to deduce from these discussions within the preparatory committees any clear indication of what the phrase 'collective self-defence' means.

The basis of the Act of Chapultepec was that 'an attack against one is an attack against all'; this may be intended as a statement of fact or as a legal fiction. Whether it would be true as a statement of fact would depend entirely upon the extent and gravity of the attack; whether, as a legal fiction, it is permissible under the Charter is open to serious question. In our submission the term 'collective self-defence', as used in the Charter, does no more than recognize that members may exercise collectively what is their individual right; it does not create new rights, nor, by permitting the use of a legal fiction, convert action unauthorized by a competent organ of the United Nations into action in the exercise of the right of collective self-defence. The situation which the Charter envisages by the term is that situation we have outlined at the beginning of the chapter as the second of three possible situations,[4] a situation in which each participating state bases its participation in collective action on its own right of self-defence. It does not, therefore, generally extend the right of self-defence to any state which desires to associate itself in the defence of a state acting in self-defence. The view that this is a possible construction of Art. 51[5] is, in our submission, based upon a misconception not only of the character of action in self-defence, but also of the whole system of the Charter in which Art. 51 finds its place. It is a view

[1] *UNCIO*, Docs., Vol. XII, p. 682. See Schwarzenberger, *Power Politics*, 2nd ed., pp. 511–12, on the origin of Art. 51.

[2] Pact of March 22nd, 1945. Text cited in *A.J.*, Vol. 39 (1945), Supp., p. 266.

[3] *Loc. cit.*, p. 681.

[4] See *ante*, p. 206.

[5] Tucker, 'The Legal Interpretation of War', *I.L.Q.*, Vol. 3 (1950), p. 29.

which derives from the assumption that, since states were formerly free to conclude any defensive treaty of alliance and to act on the obligation of assistance contained therein, that freedom or right is still preserved to member states under Art. 51. There are, however, several grounds for disagreeing radically with this view. Firstly the notion of freedom to conclude and act upon a defensive treaty of alliance developed in an age which knew no prohibition of the state's right to resort to war or to use force, or in which (as under the Covenant) the system of collective security was de-centralized. The system under the Charter is radically different, for the Charter contains not only a prohibition of the right to use force or the threat of force, but also a system of collective security in which primary responsibility for the maintenance of international peace and security is vested in the Security Council (Art. 24), and in which members agree to accept and carry out the decisions of the Security Council (Art. 25). This degree of centralization was never found under the League and it is, therefore, a false analogy which lies at the basis of an argument that because states were free to aid any other state in self-defence under the Covenant they are therefore free to do the same under the Charter. Moreover, to admit this freedom to lend assistance is to admit that states may, on their own initiative, assess the legality of another state's claim to exercise self-defence. This, it is believed, is entirely inconsistent with the whole plan of the Charter, which envisages the minimum of unauthorized action by individual states pending the intervention of the community on the authorization of a competent United Nations organ.

Secondly, this view is scarcely consistent with any analogy offered by private law; it has been shown that the concept of self-defence in private law presupposes an interest of a legal nature which the 'protector' has in the security of the actual victim. The right of intervention possessed by other persons is of an entirely different character, for it belongs to the realm of sanctions rather than to the concept of self-defence, individual or collective. Equally so in international law, the intervening state which has no 'legal' right in the security of the actual victim, which has not itself the right of self-defence, must justify its action as being in the nature of a sanction; it is not self-defence, individual or collective.

Thirdly, this view distorts the concept of 'self-defence' out of all recognition; on such a view 'collective self-defence' becomes assistance by one state, not itself possessing any right of self-defence, to another state which *may*[1] be exercising the right of self-defence. The range of individual state action, permissible without the prior authorization of a competent organ of the United Nations, becomes almost unlimited on this hypothesis. It cannot be a view consistent with the whole system of the Charter. The individual members cannot on the one hand delegate primary responsibility for the maintenance of international peace and security to the Security Council (Art. 24), and on the other claim this right of unilateral action to support any state which they consider to be acting in self-defence. This sort of freedom of alliance cannot stand together with a system of collective security as centralized as the United Nations Charter. The Charter clearly intends that the prohibition of Art. 2(4) will admit of only the minimum exception of self-defence, strictly construed, and subject to the overriding authority of the Security Council. The whole emphasis of the Charter is on collective action in the sense of action undertaken by the collectivity of states and authorized by the United Nations itself. It cannot be supposed that this extensive view of the scope of 'collective self-defence' would ever have been accepted at San Francisco; admittedly it may be a more convenient view at the present time in view of the frustration of the Security Council by the lack of unanimity amongst the permanent members. In fact one suspects that this extensive interpretation of the concept of 'collective self-defence' is due entirely to the political impasse within the Security Council which renders the effective operation of the machinery for collective action unlikely. However, the solutions to this problem are either the abandonment of the system of rights and duties contained in the Charter or the devising of substitute procedures for collective action *within* the United Nations. It is in fact the latter solution which has been adopted, as will presently be shown; for the moment let it suffice to say that the distortion of the concept of 'collective self-defence' is not a permissible solution.

The relative importance of Art. 51 in the general scheme of the

[1] Only a subsequent, impartial determination by an organ of the international community can really decide that it *is* exercising the right of self-defence. See the view of the International Military Tribunal, Judgment, October 1st, 1946; *A.J.*, Vol. 41 (1947), at p. 207.

Charter increased tremendously with the frustration of the centralized machinery for maintaining international peace and security. The lack of agreement between the permanent members of the Security Council, demonstrated in the application of the veto and the absence of any agreements under Art. 43 whereby members would place armed forces and facilities at the disposal of the Council, combined to bring about a measure of de-centralization quite unforeseen in an organization distinguished from the League by its increased centralization of enforcement machinery. The emphasis shifted, therefore, from Chapter VII of the Charter, and especially Arts. 39, 40, 41 and 42, to those other provisions of the Charter which provided for de-centralized but collective action. In the first place Art. 51, as we have seen, provided for 'collective self-defence', and a number of treaty arrangements based upon this right of collective self-defence have developed, arrangements of which the North Atlantic Treaty Organization is the prime example. On the other hand increased importance has also been placed on regional arrangements, whose continuance was ensured by Chapter VIII of the Charter, and, since the powers of such organizations vary according to whether they act pursuant to Art. 51 or Chapter VIII, it has been a matter of some controversy as to whether organizations avowedly based on Art. 51 are properly regional arrangements under Chapter VIII; the term regional arrangements, like the term collective self-defence, is left undefined by the Charter.[1] The essential difference is really twofold; firstly states organized for collective self-defence may exercise their rights without the prior authorization of the Security Council, whereas regional arrangements may take 'enforcement action' only with that authorization, and secondly under Art. 51 members are bound to report to the Security Council only 'measures taken . . . in the exercise of their right of self-defence', whereas

[1] A proposed definition was put forward by the Egyptian delegate at San Francisco but was rejected on the ground that it was not exhaustive, *UNCIO*, Docs., Vol. XII, pp. 854, 817. See also Saba, 'Les Accords Régionaux dans la Charte de l'O.N.U.', *R.C.*, 1952 (1), p. 635, at pp. 684–6; Yèpes, 'Les Accords Régionaux et le Droit International', *R.C.*, 1947 (11), at p. 252; Kelsen, *Law of United Nations*, p. 918 *et seq.*; Stone, *Legal Controls of International Conflict*, p. 247. The best definition, in our submission, is that by Van Kleffens in 'Regionalism and Political Pacts', *A.J.*, Vol. 42 (1949), p. 666, at p. 669; 'a voluntary association of sovereign states within a certain area or having common interests in that area for a joint purpose, which should not be of an offensive nature, in relation to that area'.

regional arrangements under Art. 54 must keep the Security Council 'fully informed of activities undertaken *or in contemplation*'.[1] These differences, measured against the background of the antagonism between the Eastern and Western powers, suffice to make the issue an important one, and we propose, therefore, to discuss the arguments in relation to N.A.T.O., although, it must be borne in mind, they are of general application and not necessarily limited to the nature of that particular organization.

(*a*) *Collective self-defence and regional arrangements*

The principal exposition[2] of the view that N.A.T.O. is an organization based on Art. 51 and not Chapter VIII of the Charter is to be found in the book entitled *The North Atlantic Treaty* by the former legal adviser to the British Foreign Office, Sir W. E. Beckett. In the main his argument is threefold.[3]

(i) Art. 53 envisages the use of regional arrangements for 'enforcement action' under the Security Council's authority, and this term, as evidenced by its use in Arts. 2(5) and 50,[4] refers to 'action ordered or authorized by the proper organ of the United Nations'.[5] Such action, he maintains, is essentially different from action in self-defence which under Art. 51 clearly does not require the prior authoriza-

[1] See in pursuance of this obligation the reports sent to the Security Council by the Chairman of the Organization of American States during December, 1948, when, after Costa Rica had telegrammed to the Security Council alleging an invasion by armed forces from Nicaragua on December 12th (S/116), the O.A.S. informed the Security Council that they were seized of the question (Letter of December 15th, 1948, S/1171).

[2] For other statements to the same effect see view of U.S. State Dept., The Atlantic Pact, Dept. of State Publication 3462 (March, 1949). And see the speech of Mr. Bevin, British Foreign Minister, in the House of Commons, H.C. Debates, Vol. 464, col. 2018.

[3] There are other subsidiary arguments which our own conclusions make it unnecessary to deal with; for example, Kelsen's argument that N.A.T.O. defines its own 'region' in Art. 6, Beckett's argument as to the illogicality of having members of the regional arrangement report measures 'in contemplation' and other members of the organization for collective self-defence but outside the region report only measures 'undertaken' (p. 17), and the superfluity of reporting treaties for collective self-defence in view of Art. 102, and the unreality of any greater obligation (p. 18).

[4] This article actually refers to 'enforcement measures' but Beckett submits there is no essential difference between the two, *op. cit.*, p. 7.

[5] Ibid., p. 7.

tion of the Security Council.[1] To this argument Kelsen has replied[2] that, though the phrase 'enforcement action' does, under Arts. 2(5), 2(7), and 50 have this meaning, it cannot bear such a meaning in the second section of Art. 53(1) which suggests that the obligation to secure prior authorization for enforcement action has an exception in 'measures against any enemy state'. If, therefore, the phrase 'enforcement action' would normally include such measures, the phrase cannot mean only measures ordered or authorized by the Security Council, for it has never been suggested that measures against enemy states require prior authorization. Kelsen's own conclusion, therefore, is that:

> 'The use of force in the exercise of the right of self-defence, too, is an enforcement action in this sense, that is to say, an enforcement action taken, not by the Security Council, but by members of the United Nations.' [3]

(ii) The matters with which regional arrangements are intended to deal are defined in Ch. VIII and do not include action in self-defence.[4] To this Kelsen replies that it would have been superfluous to specifically include this, since Art. 51 already states that 'nothing in the present Charter shall impair the inherent right . . .', and presumably this means nothing in Chapter VIII could do so; hence the superfluity of a specific mention of this 'matter'. In Kelsen's view the phrase 'such matters relating to the maintenance of international peace and security as are appropriate for regional action' is perfectly apt to include self-defence, for 'there can be no doubt that the organization of collective self-defence is a matter relating to the maintenance of international peace and security'.[5]

(iii) The hall-mark of a regional arrangement is that it contemplates measures in case of a conflict between members of that arrangement, whereas organizations in collective

[1] For the same conclusion see 'The North Atlantic Treaty in the U.S. Senate', *A.J.*, Vol. 43 (1949), p. 639.

[2] 'Is the North Atlantic Treaty a Regional Arrangement?', *A.J.*, Vol. 45 (1951), at p. 162, and by the same author in *Recent Trends in the Law of the U.N.*, p. 918 *et seq.* For similar reasoning by another author see Tucker, *op. cit.*, p. 30.

[3] *Loc. cit.*, p. 164.

[4] Beckett, *op. cit.*, pp. 17–18.

[5] *Loc. cit.*, p. 163.

self-defence contemplate only measures against threats from outside the organization. Whereas this might be the normal situation, on a strict interpretation of the Charter this is not necessarily so, and Kelsen rightly maintains that this particular argument 'has no basis in the Charter'.[1] Indeed, the U.S. Secretary of State, Dean Acheson, in a press conference on N.A.T.O. on March 18th, 1949, when questioned about the scope of Art. 4 of the treaty, expressed the opinion that members of N.A.T.O. would, under that article, act together against a threat to a member's political independence coming from within that member's own territory;[2] this is difficult to reconcile with the view that N.A.T.O. operates only against external aggressions.

It may well be that this controversy arises from an attempt to characterize organizations by form rather than by function, as being either organizations in collective self-defence or regional arrangements. If, as we suggest, we start from the premiss that members of an organization, whether a regional arrangement or not, can always exercise this right of self-defence, then the relevant question becomes not 'What sort of organization is this?' but rather 'What function is it exercising?' Once this latter question is answered it is then possible to define the obligations which are incumbent on members according to whether they are exercising their right of self-defence, or are purporting to take enforcement action—used in the only sense which harmonizes with the Charter as a whole, despite Kelsen's argument, namely, of action authorized by the Security Council. As Kelsen himself has said:

[1] *Loc. cit.*, p. 165. On this point Stone agrees with Kelsen (*op. cit.*, p. 248, fn. 29), but maintains this is not the decisive point. Stone's reasoning, in brief, is that the natural meaning of the phrase 'appropriate for regional action' in Art. 53(1) is action *within* the region; that otherwise the S.C. could invoke the aid of one regional arrangement against another; that settlement of disputes contemplated is clearly intra-regional and therefore it is natural to assume a similar limit on enforcement action; and that if an alliance for defence is a regional arrangement the obligation to report defence plans to a potential aggressor on the S.C. would be ludicrous. In our view the natural meaning is not the only meaning, and so far as the second argument is concerned this can scarcely be so if both regional arrangements are taking 'enforcement action'. The final argument is not really relevant once we distinguish the organization's functions as a regional arrangement from those it performs in collective self-defence.

[2] Cited in Salvin, 'The North Atlantic Treaty Organization', *Int. Concil.*, 1949, Appendix E, p. 431, at pp. 432–3.

> ... the wording of the Charter does not exclude organization of collective self-defence through regional arrangements as a substitute ... for collective security ... and the rule of Art. 53, that no enforcement action shall be taken without the authorization of the Security Council does not apply to the exercise of the right of collective self-defence organized in the regional arrangement because this rule is restricted by Art. 51.[1]

We might also add that it is perfectly possible for an organization primarily designed for collective self-defence to be used for enforcement action if the members agree[2] to carry out the recommendations or decisions of the Security Council so as to undertake action which is not action in self-defence.[3] Whether or not it could exercise other functions normally assigned to regional arrangements, as for example the pacific settlement of disputes, would depend upon whether it contained machinery appropriate to that task. Again, when preparatory measures are taken by the organization solely with a view to their use in self-defence, no obligation to report such measures arises; on the other hand when preparations are made for making forces available for use in enforcement action under the Security Council's authorization these would have to be reported as measures 'in contemplation' under Art. 54.

If, therefore, we can assume that organizations of states can exercise their rights of individual or collective self-defence regardless of whether they are formally designated organizations in collective self-defence or regional arrangements, the only relevant question is whether these organizations purport or claim to exercise a right of self-defence in any way inconsistent with the Charter. To answer this question will necessitate an inquiry into the basic provisions of the various organizations and a comparison of these provisions with the Charter.

[1] *Loc. cit.*, p. 164. For the same conclusion see Yuen Li Liang, 'Regional Arrangements and International Security', *Trans. Grotius Soc.*, Vol. 31 (1946), p. 216, at p. 228.

[2] That is assuming they have not concluded agreements under Art. 43.

[3] See *A.J.*, Vol. 43 (1949), p. 639: 'It can be utilized as a regional arrangement subject to the pertinent provisions of the Charter, if the members so desire.' And see also Ambassador Austin's assertion in the debate on the North Atlantic Treaty in the U.S. Senate that it was 'not necessary to define the organization of the North Atlantic community as exclusively a regional arrangement, or as exclusively a group for collective self-defence, since activities under both Art. 51 and Ch. VIII are comprehended in the Treaty'; Hearings, Pt. I, p. 22, cited in *A.J.*, Vol. 43 (1949), p. 638.

(*b*) *Treaty arrangements contemplating the use of force without the prior authorization of a competent organ of the* U.N.

In the main these arrangements claim expressly to be based upon Art. 51 of the Charter; Art. 5 of the North Atlantic Treaty refers to action which parties will take 'in the exercise of the right of individual or collective self-defence recognized by Art. 51 of the Charter of the United Nations . . .', and there are similar provisions in other treaties.[1]

To the extent that these treaties re-state obligations already existing under the Charter of the United Nations,[2] they are, for Members of the United Nations, primarily declaratory, and no question of inconsistency can arise. Indeed, many of these treaties attempt to avoid inconsistency by expressly asserting the paramountcy of their obligations under the Charter,[3] and Art. 103 of the Charter itself states the same principle.

In most of these treaties there is an obligation on Members to consult together in certain circumstances; Art. 4 of the North Atlantic Treaty may be taken as a typical example:

> The Parties will consult together whenever, in the opinion of any of them, the territorial integrity, political independence or security of any of the Parties is threatened.[4]

Consultation as such cannot involve the Parties in any breach of their obligations, for, since the primary and most fundamental

[1] For example, Art. 3, Rio Treaty; Art. IV, Brussels Treaty (Treaty of Economic, Social and Cultural Collaboration and Collective Self-Defence, Brussels, March 17th, 1948), *A.J.*, Vol. 43 (1949), Supp., p. 59. For a general survey of these treaties see Bebr, 'Regional Organizations', *A.J.*, Vol. 49 (1955), p. 166, at p. 175. Schwarzenberger, *Power Politics*, 2nd ed., pp. 525–6, examines the compatibility of N.A.T.O. membership with Britain's obligations under the Anglo-Soviet Alliance of May 28th, 1942.

[2] Such as the obligation 'to refrain in their international relations from the threat or use of force in any manner inconsistent with the purposes of the U.N.', found in Art. 1, N.A.T.; Art. 1, Rio Treaty; Art. 1, Manila Treaty (S.E.A.T.O.), signed at Manila, September 8th, 1954; text cited in *Manchester Guardian*, September 10th, 1954.

[3] For example, Art. 6, Manila Treaty; Art. 10, Rio Treaty; Art. V, Brussels; Art. 7, North Atlantic Treaty.

[4] See also Art. 7, Brussels; Art. 4(2), Manila Treaty; Arts. 6, 7, Rio Treaty; Art. 4, Soviet-Roumanian Treaty (February 4th, 1948), U.N. Treaty Series, Vol. 48, p. 189. Art. 4, Soviet-Chinese Treaty (February 14th, 1950), *A.J.*, Vol. 44 (1950), Supp., p. 84. Art. II, U.S.A.–Korean Treaty (October 1st, 1953), *A.J.*, Vol. 48 (1954), Supp., p. 147. Art. III, Tripartite Security Treaty between Australia, New Zealand and U.S.A. (September 1st, 1951), the so-called Anzus Pact, R.I.I.A. Documents, 1951, p. 677.

limitation on the freedom of the Parties to take collective action is contained in Art. 2(4) of the Charter, the question of inconsistency with the Charter really only arises when they contemplate action involving the 'threat or use of force'. Action of this nature must be in conformity with Art. 2(4) (which, it will be noted, brings in the general question of consistency with the Purposes of the United Nations), and Art. 51; the latter article, as we have seen, imposes certain positive obligations on Members in respect of their right of individual or collective self-defence. When action *prima facie* within the terms of the prohibition of Art. 2(4) is contemplated under these treaties certain questions arise; they are, namely, whether the circumstances in which such action is contemplated correspond with the circumstances in which that action is permitted by the Charter, whether in the execution of such action any inconsistency with obligations under the Charter is involved, and finally, whether such action is correctly and necessarily characterized as action in self-defence, individual or collective.

(i) *The definition of the Casus Foederis*

So far as this first question is concerned, it appears that the '*casus foederis*' is variously defined.[1] Art. 5 of the North Atlantic Treaty states that:

> The Parties agree that an armed attack against one or more of them in Europe or North America shall be considered an attack against them all and consequently they agree that, if such an armed attack occurs, each of them, in exercise of the right of individual or collective self-defence, recognized by Art. 51 of the Charter of the United Nations, will assist the Party or Parties so attacked by taking forthwith, individually and in concert with the other Parties, such action as it deems necessary, including the use of armed force, to restore and maintain the security of the North Atlantic area.

Consistency with Art. 51 is clearly intended by the use of the term 'armed attack'. Similarly Art. IV of the Manila Treaty refers to 'aggression by means of armed attack in the treaty area',[2]

[1] For an exhaustive compilation of terms used, both in treaties antedating the U.N. Charter and afterwards, see Secretary-General's Report on the Question of Defining Aggression, A/2211, October 3rd, 1952.

[2] There is appended to the text an 'Understanding of the U.S.A.' in these terms: 'The delegation of the U.S.A. in signing the present treaty does so with the understanding that its recognition of the effect of aggression and

Art. IV of the Anzus Pact refers to 'armed attack in the Pacific Area', and Art. VI of the Arab League Pact appears to equate a 'case of aggression or threat of aggression' with an 'attack'. The general tenor of the terms of these treaties suggests that it was intended to link them with the terms of Art. 51 of the Charter.

This is not the case, however, with the system of bilateral treaties which originally constituted the Soviet system of collective security.[1] In these treaties the *casus foederis* is defined more in terms of 'military aggression', 'aggression' and 'aggressive policy', than in terms of an armed attack. Moreover, so far as the treaties with states in Eastern Europe are concerned, they aim at security against renewed aggression by Germany or any state allying itself with Germany. The Soviet-Finnish Treaty of April 6th, 1948, is fairly typical; Art. 1(1) states:

> In the event of Finland or the Soviet Union, across the territory of Finland, becoming the object of military aggression on the part of Germany or any state allied to the latter, Finland, loyal to her duty as an independent state, will fight to repulse the aggression. In doing so, Finland will direct all the forces at her disposal to the defence of the inviolability of her territory on land, on sea, and in the air. . . .[2]

The Treaty of Friendship, Alliance, and Mutual Assistance between the U.S.S.R. and China is, not unnaturally, directed at Japan rather than Germany and is somewhat more widely phrased; Art. 1 states that the agreement is:

> . . . to take all the necessary measures at their disposal for the purpose of preventing a repetition of aggression and violation of peace on the part of Japan, or any other state which should unite with Japan, directly or indirectly, in acts of aggression. . . .[3]

---

armed attack and its agreement with reference thereto in Art. 4, para. one, apply only to Communist aggression, but affirms that in the event of other aggression or armed attack it will consult under the provisions of Art. 4.'

[1] See generally Kulski, 'The Soviet System of Collective Security Compared with the Western System', *A.J.*, Vol. 44 (1950), p. 453; also Bebr, *op. cit.*, p. 182.

[2] U.N. Treaty Series, Vol. 48, p. 149. The Brussels Treaty originally, in its Preamble, resolved 'to take such steps as may be held to be necessary in the event of a renewal by Germany of a policy of aggression'. But see Annex. I to the Final Act of the London Conference, October 3rd, 1954, deleting the phrase and substituting 'to promote the unity and to encourage the progressive integration of Europe', *N.A.T.O., 1949–54*, by Lord Ismay, p. 243. The Dunkirk Treaty between U.K. and France, March 4th, 1947, Treaty Series (67), 1946, Cmd. 7015, also deals explicitly with the renewal of German aggression.

[3] Signed at Moscow, February 14th, 1950, *A.J.*, Supp., Vol. 44 (1950), p. 84.

This type of phrasing, particularly in relating to states which ally themselves with either German or Japanese aggression 'directly or indirectly' or 'directly or in some other form',[1] is more comprehensive than the phrase 'armed attack', and it is for this reason that the Soviet collective security system has been criticized for its lack of uniformity with Art. 51.[2] It would appear that the legal basis of these treaties is, by implication from the use of terms like 'aggression' to define the *casus foederis*, supposed to be Art. 107 and not Art. 51. This view, though never expressly stated in the treaties, is supported by the fact that they all hinge upon aggression by an 'enemy' state within the definition of Art. 107. However, in so far as the treaties contemplate action against states other than Germany or Japan they clearly cannot fall within the terms of Art. 107; action of this nature will have to be justified under Art. 51. A marked change in the policy behind the Soviet security system has become evident in the Warsaw Pact of May 14th, 1955.[3] This treaty is clearly analogous to the Western multilateral treaties and sets up an organization to handle the procedures of consultation and of organizing a unified military command. The Warsaw Treaty Organization is clearly based on Art. 51; Art. 4 of the Treaty states:

En cas d'attaque armée en Europe contre un ou plusieurs Etats signataires du Traité par un Etat quelconque ou un groupe d'Etats, chaque Etat signataire du Traité, en exercise du droit de légitime defense individuelle ou collective, conformément à l'article 51 de la

---

[1] Art. 2, Polish-Bulgarian Treaty, May 29th, 1948; U.N. Treaty Series, Vol. 26, p. 213. And see Art. 2, Soviet-Yugoslav Treaty, April 11th, 1945: 'If one of the contracting parties should in the post-war period be drawn into military operations against Germany, which would have resumed her aggressive policy, or against any other state which would have joined Germany either directly or in some other form in a war of this nature, the other contracting party . . . etc.' This treaty was denounced by U.S.S.R. on September 28th, 1949, see R.I.I.A. Docs. 1949–50, p. 473. See also, for similar clauses, the treaties between U.S.S.R. and Hungary, February 18th, 1948; U.N. Treaty Series, Vol. 48, p. 163. U.S.S.R. and Poland, April 21st, 1945; U.N. Treaty Series, Vol. 12, p. 391. U.S.S.R. and Czechoslovakia, December 12th, 1943; *A.J.*, Supp., Vol. 39 (1945), p. 81.

[2] Kulski, *op. cit.*, pp. 460–1.

[3] Text given in Zbiór Dokumentów, No. 5, Warsaw, 1955. Extracts from Marshal Bulganin's speech at the opening of the Warsaw Conference on May 11th, 1955, are given in R.I.I.A. Calendar and Texts, May, 1955, Vol. 2, No. 5, at p. 138; these explain the Soviet views on the need for the new organization and explain its operation.

Charte des Nations Unies, prêtera à l'Etat ou aux Etats victimes d'une telle attaque une aide immédiate, individuellement, et en accord avec les autres Etats signataires du Traité, par tous les moyens qui lui sembleront nécessaires, y compris l'emploi de la force armée. . . .

We have previously indicated, however, that the right of self-defence is not limited to cases of an 'armed attack', so that the mere fact that the *casus foederis* is, in the bilateral treaties of the Soviet system, not limited to cases of an actual 'armed attack' is not, in our view, conclusive on the question of compatibility with the Charter. The real question, to which none of these treaties either of the Soviet or Western systems give a conclusive answer, is whether they contemplate the exercise of the remedial right of self-defence only in those cases where those substantive rights to which the remedial right of self-defence attaches are violated; what precise form the violation takes, whether it is an 'armed attack', 'aggression', or 'threat of aggression' is only relevant on the question of proof of violation. It is true that the North Atlantic Treaty (Art. 4), the Manila Treaty (Art. 4(2)), and the Rio Treaty (Art. 6) attempt some formulation of these substantive rights in the clauses dealing with the obligation to consult together. In the main, however, the clauses which govern the obligation to afford assistance[1] including the threat or use of force do not indicate that the 'armed attack' is necessarily action violating these substantive rights, no more than the Soviet bilateral treaties indicate the rights violated by the 'aggression' or 'aggressive policy' which is the chosen formula in those treaties.

The Rio Treaty is the most complex of all and merits detailed treatment. In distinguishing 'armed attack' from other aggressions, and aggressions within the Americas from those without, as well as differentiating between aggressors which are American from those which are not, the treaty envisages five different situations.

[1] And it makes no essential difference whether the obligation is to take immediate action to assist the victim of the armed attack or aggression, as in the Soviet treaties, the Rio Treaty and the North Atlantic Treaty, or whether the obligation is dependent on a decision of some organ set up by the Treaty, as in the Pact of the Arab League. The legal character of the action when taken is the same; there is, in the latter case, perhaps more assurance that assistance will be justified by reference to the conditions governing the right of individual or collective self-defence, but so long as the organ is not the Security Council or General Assembly, its decision does not affect the nature of the action.

1. An armed attack *within* the region defined in Art. 4, by either an American or a non-American state (Art. 3(3)).[1]
2. An armed attack *outside* the region of Art. 4 but within the territory of an American state (Art. 3(3)).[2]
3. An armed attack *outside* the region of Art. 4 and outside the territory of an American state (Arts. 3(3) and 3(6)).[3]
4. Aggression not taking the form of an armed attack, whether inside or outside the region of Art. 4 (Art. 6).
5. Threats of aggression, extra-continental or intra-continental conflicts, or any other fact or situation which might endanger the peace of America (Art. 6).

In situations one and two, this is 'considered as an attack against all the American states and, consequently, each one of the said Contracting Parties undertakes to assist in meeting the attack in the exercise of the inherent right of individual or collective self-defence, recognized by Art. 51 of the Charter of the United Nations'.[4] In the third situation this also constitutes an attack on all American states but, as distinct from the first two situations, no duty to afford immediate assistance to the victim state on its request arises. There is, however, a duty to consult and 'the Organ of Consultation shall meet immediately in order to agree on the measures which *must* be taken in case of aggression to assist the victim of aggression or, in any case, the measures which should be taken for the common defence and for the maintenance of the peace and security of the Continent'.[5] In the fourth situation

[1] For an example of this situation see the Costa Rican complaint against Nicaragua in a note of December 11th, 1948, to the Chairman of the Council of the O.A.S., discussed in *A.J.*, Vol. 43 (1949), p. 329, by Fenwick. See also Bebr, *op. cit.*, pp. 176–7. An account of the proceedings of the O.A.S. is given in the *Manchester Guardian* of January 18th, 1955.

[2] i.e. Hawaii.

[3] i.e. Canada or Greenland.

[4] Art. 3(1). Individual assistance can only be given at the request of the actual victim (Art. 3(2)). (But the request of any member state will summon the Organ of Consultation.) This obligation of automatic assistance is qualified by Art. 20 which provides that no state shall be required to use armed force without its consent. Fenwick, *A.J.*, Vol. 43 (1949), p. 313, regards this as a merely technical limitation on the obligation of Art. 3 'introduced so as to avoid the appearance of submitting to the decision of a two-thirds majority the constitutional right of the U.S. Congress to declare war'. When the attack is by another American state a special procedure applies. The Organ of Consultation may call upon both parties to suspend hostilities and restore the *status quo ante bellum*. The rejection of pacifying action will be considered in the determination of the aggressor (Art. 7).

[5] Art. 6.

this merely gives rise to the obligation to consult, but, as in the third situation, the Organ of Consultation must meet and take the measures indicated in Art. 6. In the fifth situation there is the same obligation to consult but the taking of measures by this Organ of Consultation appears to be optional due to the use of the word 'should' rather than 'must'.[1]

In Art. 9 the treaty gives a non-exhaustive definition of aggression which still leaves a discretion in the Organ of Consultation to characterize other acts as aggression:

> In addition to other acts which the Organ of Consultation may characterize as aggression, the following shall be considered as such:
> (*a*) Unprovoked[2] armed attack by a State against the territory, the people or the land, sea or air forces of another State.
> (*b*) Invasion, by the armed forces of a State, of the territory of an American State, through the trespassing of boundaries demarcated in accordance with a treaty, judicial decision, or arbitral award, or, in the absence of frontiers thus demarcated, invasion affecting a region which is under the effective jurisdiction of another State.

Since, however, the definition is not exhaustive, it remains possible for the Organ of Consultation to decide upon the measures enumerated in Art. 8, and including the 'use of armed force', to be taken 'if the inviolability or the integrity of the territory or the sovereignty or political independence of any American State should be affected (the word is weaker than threatened or violated)[3] by an aggression which is not an armed attack . . .' or if the peace of America is endangered 'by an extra-continental or intra-continental conflict, or by any other fact or situation'.[4] These causes, which may prompt the Organ of Consultation into taking a decision to use armed force, are by no means limited to an 'armed attack', nor do they bear any necessary relation to the breach of those substantive rights which, in our view, can alone justify the exercise of a right of self-defence. Admittedly the latter part of Art. 6 suggests a link with some notion of self-

[1] Kunz, 'The Inter-American Treaty of Reciprocal Assistance', *A.J.*, Vol. 42 (1948), p. 117.

[2] The notion of 'provocation' may be subject to different meanings: see S.G.'s Report on the Question of Defining Aggression, U.N. Doc. A/2211, October 3rd, 1952, at p. 49. Also the strictures of Alfaro in the I.L.C. (A/CN.4/L.8, pp. 10–11) where he regarded Art. 9 as 'introducing the vague, imprecise and uncertain element of provocation'.

[3] Brackets mine.

[4] Art. 6, Rio Treaty.

defence in referring to 'measures . . . to assist the victim of aggression . . . for the common defence and for the maintenance of the peace and security of the Continent'. Yet the link is vague and imprecise, and the phrasing has the sound of a political document or manifesto rather than a definition of legal rights.

There is in all these treaties too much concern with the *casus foederis* and its definition, and too little concern with the content of the rights which, if the treaties really are based upon the right of self-defence, they purport to protect. They run the danger of any definition which is formal and bears no stated relationship to the substantive rights involved. The rights of 'territorial integrity, political independence, or security' are referred to in Art. IV of the North Atlantic Treaty, but the reference relates to the obligation to consult, not the obligation to render assistance involving armed force; also, in Art. 9 of the Rio Treaty, the reference to a right of territorial integrity is made by implication when the treaty deals with the forms of hostile action which the Organ of Consultation may characterize as aggression. It is fairly clear that none of these treaties, of either the Soviet or the Western systems, really attempt a definite statement of the rights which they claim to protect by the series of mutual obligations contained in the treaties. It may be, of course, that in stating that the parties to the treaty will take action 'in the exercise of the inherent right of individual or collective self-defence recognized by Art. 51 of the Charter of the United Nations',[1] or by the use of terms like 'armed attack' or 'aggression', it is necessarily implied that the obligations under the treaty are all to be read subject to the limitations and conditions imposed upon the exercise of the right of self-defence by general international law and the Charter. To this extent the treaties would merely provide additional obligations not inconsistent with the general law, or else provide a degree of organization for the exercise of rights sanctioned by the general law. The danger lies, however, in the possibility of states acting on the literal interpretation of these treaties, without reference to the limitations and conditions imposed upon this exercise of the right of self-defence by the general law. For example, it is not every 'armed attack' which can be automatically characterized as illegal; we have previously indicated that a state may, in the exercise of the right of self-defence, take 'anticipatory'

[1] Art. 3(1) North Atlantic Treaty.

action against an imminent threat to its security which leaves no other course of action open to the state apart from completely jeopardizing its existence. Situations such as that occurring when a state is faced with large-scale mobilization by an avowedly belligerent neighbour on its frontiers, or that envisaged by the U.N. Atomic Energy Commission[1] as resulting from a serious breach of a treaty prohibiting the manufacture of nuclear weapons, are examples of the kind of situations which, in our view, would justify anticipatory action involving armed force and, possibly, a transgression of the territory of the threatening state. Action of this nature would, *prima facie*, fall within the definition of an armed attack adopted by the North Atlantic Treaty or the Rio Treaty,[2] for example; the literal application of the treaty provisions, without regard for the general law, would involve the parties in action against a state itself acting in self-defence. Moreover, the literal application of these treaties would treat isolated attacks upon the ships or aircraft of one of the members as a *casus foederis*,[3] and set into motion the whole series of obligations of assistance, again without regard to the requirement of proportionality which is an essential condition of the exercise of the right of self-defence under the general law.

The conclusion seems inescapable that, to avoid a conflict with the conditions imposed on the exercise of the right of self-defence by general international law, the application of the terms of these treaties (both Soviet and Western) demands the use of discretion in the light of those conditions of general international law. The individual state may have the opportunity to exercise such discretion in view of the type of qualifying clause which describes the manner in which the obligation of immediate assistance is to be performed—as is seen in Art. 5 of the North Atlantic Treaty

[1] U.N. Doc. AEC/18/Rev. 1, p. 24.

[2] At least in so far as the obligation of immediate assistance arises under Art. 3. The definition of aggression under Art. 9 refers to 'Unprovoked armed attack' and, for the purposes of a decision of the Organ of Consultation, avoids this difficulty.

[3] This results from the definition of an 'armed attack' in Art. 6 of the North Atlantic Treaty (as amended), Art. 9, Rio Treaty. It must probably be assumed that the attacks are 'acts of State' and not unauthorized acts of individual members of the armed forces. This seems to be implied from the phrase 'armed attacks by any State' in Art. 3, Rio Treaty; the North Atlantic Treaty does not use the phrase 'by any State' but presumably this would be the normal interpretation.

which contains the phrase 'by taking forthwith . . . such action as it deems necessary'.[1] Where the decision to use armed force rests with an organ set up by the treaty, the states collectively, acting through this organ, may exercise a similar discretion, although Art. 9 of the Rio Treaty states that the Organ of Consultation 'shall' consider the acts enumerated there as aggression, and to this extent appears to curtail the discretion of the Organ. Unless, however, discretion is exercised by the parties to these treaties, acting individually or collectively through an organ, there is no absolute assurance that the automatic and literal application of their provisions will necessarily be limited to the exercise of the right of self-defence, whether individual or collective, sanctioned by general international law.

(ii) *The question of consistency with the special obligations imposed under Art. 51*

There are, apart from the limitations and conditions imposed by general international law, certain special obligations imposed by Art. 51 relating to the exercise of the right of self-defence by members of the United Nations. These are the obligation to report immediately to the Security Council measures taken in the exercise of the right, and also the obligation to cease action in self-defence when the Security Council 'has taken the measures necessary to maintain international peace and security'.[2] Certain of the treaties faithfully repeat these obligations in express terms: Art. 5 of the North Atlantic Treaty states:

> Any such armed attack and all measures taken as a result thereof shall immediately be reported to the Security Council. Such measures shall be terminated when the Security Council has taken the measures necessary to restore and maintain international peace and security.[3]

Art. 4 of the Warsaw Pact contains a restatement of these obligations, but the bilateral security treaties concluded by the U.S.S.R.

[1] Fenwick, 'The Atlantic Pact', *A.J.*, Vol. 43 (1949), p. 314, regards this formula as due to the constitutional problems of the U.S.A. touching the Presidential power to commit forces and the Congressional right to declare war; it presumably was not intended to bring in a discretion for the purpose of deciding the validity of the action under international law. Almost identical phrasing is found in Art. 4 of the Warsaw Treaty.

[2] See *ante*, p. 195.

[3] See also Art. 4, Manila Treaty; Art. 5, Brussels Treaty; and Arts. 3 and 5 of Rio Treaty.

do not contain similar provisions, and it has been suggested that for this reason these treaties are to that extent illegal.[1] There is, in our submission, no basis for this view; the obligations to report measures undertaken, and to cease such measures once the Security Council has taken the measures necessary to restore and maintain international peace and security, arise from the Charter and a re-statement of them is unnecessary. It would, of course, be illegal to stipulate in these treaties conduct inconsistent with these obligations, but the mere omission to re-state the duties imposed by the Charter is not in itself illegal.

(iii) *The legal character of the action contemplated under the treaties*

The final, and perhaps most substantial, question is whether the action contemplated under these treaties, whether of the simple bilateral type or of the more complex form, is correctly characterized as action in self-defence, individual or collective. If, as we suggest, the right of self-defence is available only to a state which defends its own substantive rights, and the difference between the individual and the collective right lies in whether states exercise their right of self-defence individually or in concert, then the question arises whether the action contemplated by these treaties is necessarily of that character.

These treaties are based upon the principle that an attack against any one party is an attack against the other party or parties to the treaty; the principle is the same whether the operative phrase, the *casus foederis*, is 'armed attack', 'aggression' or 'aggressive policy'. As an abstract statement this must be a legal fiction; in the concrete situations envisaged by these treaties it may also be a statement of actual fact. It is not difficult to envisage a direct attack against a state in Western Europe which, in view of the magnitude of the attack and the evidence of a wider aggressive intention which it affords, in fact threatens the security of all the states in the northern part of the Western Hemisphere. The interdependence of the securities of a number of states may, in this

[1] Kulski, *op. cit.*, p. 462. The Manila Treaty also contains no re-statement of these obligations. See also the Balkan Pact of August, 1954, between Greece, Turkey and Yugoslavia; text cited in *A.J.*, Vol. 48 (1954), Supp., p. 47. This Pact makes the termination of the parties' defensive measures dependent on the Security Council's 'effectively applied measures mentioned in Art. 51' (Art. 7(1))

age, be stated without real fear of contradiction; it would result in an attack against one constituting in fact, and not merely as a legal fiction, a violation of the right to independence and security of other states. On the other hand it would be ludicrous to suppose that merely by the conclusion of a treaty any two states could bring mutual assistance within the concept of self-defence—at least if this is to be a juridical concept and not a term of diplomacy. To state, for example, that an attack upon Chile, say by one of its South American neighbours, is an attack upon the United Kingdom or Turkey would be a possible statement, but it would belong to the realm of fiction rather than fact. Consequently, should either the United Kingdom or Turkey afford military assistance to Chile in those circumstances, their action would only by a travesty of terminology be called collective self-defence. It is not believed that the juridical concept of a right of self-defence can be stretched to an extent which is so far removed from fact by using this fiction of 'an attack against one is an attack against all'.

It is for this reason, it is believed, that these treaties are concluded between states in some geographical proximity to each other; many of them are restricted in their application to defined regions. Whether it be the 'North Atlantic area' defined in Art. 6 of the North Atlantic Treaty,[1] the European area of the Brussels Treaty[2] or the Warsaw Treaty, the region defined in Art. 4 of the Rio Treaty, or the 'Pacific area' defined in Art. 8 of the Manila

[1] For the current definition of the region, amending Art. 6 on the accession of Greece and Turkey, see Art. II of the Protocol to the North Atlantic Treaty, London, October 17th, 1951. Text given in Western Co-operation, Central Office of Information, London, September, 1953, p. 71.

'For the purpose of Art. 5, an armed attack on one or more of the Parties is deemed to include an armed attack

(i) on the territory of any of the Parties in Europe or N. America, on the Algerian Departments of France, on the territory of Turkey or on the islands under the jurisdiction of any of the Parties in the North Atlantic area north of the Tropic of Cancer;

(ii) on the forces, vessels or aircraft of any of the Parties when in or over these territories or any other area in Europe in which occupation forces of any of the Parties were stationed on the date when the Treaty entered into force or the Mediterranean Sea or the North Atlantic area north of the Tropic of Cancer.'

[2] Art. IV, now Art. V of the revised Treaty. See Annex 1 to the Final Act of the London Conference. Text in *N.A.T.O. 1949–54*, by Lord Ismay, p. 242.

Treaty,[1] the regional nature of these treaties suggests an interdependence in fact of the security of the member states. It approximates to the 'proximate relationship' of kinship which in private law justifies assistance by one person to another within the concept of self-defence. Within the defined area the statement that an attack against one state is an attack against all must be taken to be a statement of the belief of the parties that the security of each is so dependent on the security of every other party, that a violation of the rights of one party would in fact also constitute a violation of the rights of all other parties. The treaties therefore establish a means by which these states, each having the right of individual self-defence, may exercise their rights collectively. It is significant that in the Declaration by the governments of the United States, the United Kingdom and France, recorded at the London Conference in October, 1954, these governments stated that:

> They will regard as a threat *to their own peace and safety* any recourse to force which in violation of the principles of the United Nations Charter threatens the integrity and unity of the Atlantic Alliance or its defensive purposes.[2]

and in these circumstances they considered Art. 4 of the North Atlantic Treaty would be applicable. This declaration, with its insistence on a threat 'to their own peace and safety' implies that each one of the three states would deem itself to be in a state of individual self-defence—and the North Atlantic Treaty would provide the means of exercising these individual rights collectively. Similarly, Art. IV of the Anzus Pact states:

> Each Party recognizes that an 'armed attack' in the Pacific Area on any of the Parties would be dangerous *to its own peace and security*.[3]

---

[1] Art. IV (i) of the Manila Treaty refers to 'armed attack in the treaty area against any of the parties or against any State or territory which the parties by unanimous agreement may hereafter designate would endanger its own peace and safety . . .' A Protocol has designated the States of Cambodia and Laos and the free territory under the jurisdiction of the State of Vietnam as being within these terms.

[2] *N.A.T.O.*, Lord Ismay, p. 242. Compare also the U.S. President's decision to defend Formosa and the Pescadores as being within the American 'defensive perimeter'; the basis for this view seems to be that invasion of these islands by hostile forces would involve a threat to the security of the Philippines and ultimately to the U.S.A. itself. See report of Congress Proceedings in *Manchester Guardian*, January 26th, 1955. The full text of the Presidential message is given in the same newspaper of the previous day.

[3] Italics mine. See also Art. 4(1) of the Manila Treaty.

Yet, even with the restriction implicit in the limiting of membership to states within a defined region, it is not necessarily true that every armed attack would, even within the region, in fact constitute an attack on each party so as to allow to each party the right of self-defence; and yet without this individual right they can scarcely claim to participate in a collective exercise of the right of self-defence. It is possible to imagine an armed invasion of Greece, for example, arising out of difficulties on her northern frontiers and taking the form of a limited invasion into Greek territory by forces of a neighbouring state (which state alleges the action is by way of reprisals) which, though technically within the terms of Art. 4 of the North Atlantic Treaty, could not possibly be said to constitute in fact an armed attack on every N.A.T.O. member. In such a case intervention by states like the U.S.A., Canada or Norway could not really be justified on the basis of the right of self-defence, individual or collective, if that right is to retain a juridical connotation and not dissolve into a description of political affiliations. It is not suggested that it is only geographical proximity which can constitute that interdependence between states which is essential before an attack upon one is also an attack upon the other. Though the *nexus* between states which have such an interdependence is normally of a geographical kind, it is not permissible to assume that only this kind of link is sufficient to afford an adequate basis for the exercise of the right of collective self-defence.[1] Interdependence can be of a political character: for example, the link between members of the British Commonwealth is political rather than geographical, and it may be perfectly proper to treat an attack upon any one member of the Commonwealth on any considerable scale as an attack upon the Commonwealth as a whole. There may also be ties of an economic or strategic character which make the security of one state dependent upon the security of another; indeed the British interests in the Middle East may be of this character, and reference has already been made to the British reservation in signing the Pact of Paris in 1928.[2] It is perhaps more the reality of the interdependence

[1] See Nguyen Quoc Dinh, 'La Légitime Défense d'après la Charte des Nations Unies', *R.G.D.I.P.*, Vol. 52 (1948), p. 223, at p. 245, who concludes that 'la légitime défense collective devrait, à notre avis, s'appeler légitime défense régionale'; this has, admittedly, some basis in the discussion in Committee III/4 at San Francisco but nothing in that discussion excludes a wider view.

[2] *Ante*, p. 212.

than the kind of interdependence which is vital here, and the important question is always, in final analysis, whether an attack upon one state in fact threatens the security of the other. The existence of geographical proximity, political, economic, or even cultural ties relates really to the question of proof of interdependence. The difficulty is, of course, to distinguish real interdependence which can alone afford a legal basis for the right of collective self-defence from a mere claim to 'spheres of interest' which ranks as a political rather than a legal doctrine. It is a distinction which must, however, be drawn if collective self-defence is to retain a juridical connotation.

Each member of a collective security arrangement, whether regional in character or not, would, therefore, in each case have to decide whether in the light of the conditions imposed on the exercise of the right of self-defence by general international law the state had the right of self-defence to exercise according to the treaty arrangements for the collective exercise of such a right. Reliance on the treaty is not enough, for the obligations contained in the treaty are subject to the over-riding obligations contained in the Charter, and Art. 2(4) is categorical. Unless the states using force or the threat of force in pursuance of their obligations under a collective security treaty can show that their action was authorized by a competent organ of the United Nations, they must show their action is justified as being in the exercise of the right of individual or collective self-defence,[1] and this right is governed by general international law, not by these collective security treaties, whether bilateral or multilateral. Moreover, the requirement of proportionality would exclude a general right of intervention by all parties to the treaty, if the effect of that general intervention would be to meet the *casus foederis* with a disproportionately large amount of force. The view put forward in the De Brouckère Report in 1926, that not every act of violence justifies its victim in resorting to self-defence in our submission is still sound, for 'legitimate defence implies the adoption of measures proportionate to the seriousness of the attack and justified by the imminence of the danger'.[2] This applies with equal force to third

[1] Assuming the action is not directed against an 'enemy' state under Art. 107 or Art. 53(1).

[2] Report of December 1st, 1926; see League of Nations Doc. C.740.M.279. 1926.IX, Docs., Series III, p. 101.

states claiming the right to intervene by virtue of the concept of 'collective self-defence'.

The only other possible explanation of the nature of the action contemplated under these treaties is that, where the conditions governing the exercise of the right of self-defence are not satisfied, participation in collective action by members not satisfying those conditions is still justified as action taken for the purpose of maintaining international peace and security within a particular region. This is not the avowed nature of the action; the Western treaties and the Warsaw Treaty at least avowedly claim their juridical basis in the right of self-defence, but as a purpose of the organization it is sometimes stated that the organization will take 'such action as it deems necessary, including the use of armed force, to restore or maintain the security of the North Atlantic area',[1] or whatever the appropriate area is. Art. 5 of the Rio Treaty suggests this alternative basis for action taken by providing for the reporting of action taken or in contemplation to the Security Council 'in the exercise of the right of self-defence or for the purpose of maintaining inter-American peace and security'. However, it is possible the latter alternative refers to the action which the Organization of American States would take as a regional arrangement pursuant to an authorization of the Security Council; the North Atlantic Treaty does not expressly contemplate the Organization being used as a regional arrangement, although there is nothing to prevent its members taking action to maintain or restore international peace and security pursuant to a request of the Security Council. To the extent that the automatic or literal application of these treaties could warrant action not strictly within the concept of self-defence, at least for some of the members of the organization, this other basis would seem to be the only one available. The action taken would be in the nature of collective security action rather than action in collective self-defence. It would be, within the region, a substitute for the kind of collective security which, under the Charter, the Security

[1] Art. 5, N.A.T.O. See also the Preamble to the Brussels Treaty: 'To afford assistance to each other, in accordance with the Charter of the U.N., in maintaining international peace and security and in resisting any policy of aggression.' See also the Warsaw Treaty which refers to consultation 'dans l'intérêt de l'organization de la défense commune et du maintien de la paix et de la sécurité' (Art. 3) and measures necessary 'de rétablir et de maintenir la paix et la sécurité internationales' (Art. 4).

Council was designed to take. The phrase 'to restore or maintain the security of the North Atlantic area' is, literally, a regional definition of the functions relating to the maintenance of international peace and security for which, on a global basis, the Security Council has been given primary responsibility. The Warsaw Treaty, in Art. 4, is even wider in phrasing for it refers to 'les mesures communes qu'il sera nécessaire d'entreprendre afin de rétablir et de maintenir la paix et la sécurité internationales' without any limitation as to region. These phrases bear close analogy to the phrasing used with reference to the Security Council's powers in Arts. 24, 39, 42, and 43 of the Charter. To regard the action of these treaty organizations as a regional substitute for the action which, under the Charter, it was contemplated that the Security Council would take is consistent with the fact that in the main they developed after 1946 and after the Security Council had begun to demonstrate the lack of real unanimity amongst the permanent members and, as a result, the unlikelihood of its fulfilling this function. It is also consistent with the attitude of the United Kingdom, France, and the U.S.A. in relation to the situation in the Middle East; the Tripartite Declaration of May 25th, 1950[1] states that these powers have 'deep interest in . . . the establishment and maintenance of international peace and security in the area . . . (and) should they find that any of these States (the Middle East States)[2] was preparing to violate frontiers or armistice lines, would, consistently with their obligations as members of the United Nations, *immediately* take action, both *within and outside*[3] the United Nations, to prevent such violation'. Kunz, writing of the N.A.T.O., says:

> But the Treaty certainly had in view the fact that the Security Council is paralysed by the veto; here as in the United Nations as a whole Art. 51 is being used more and more as a substitute, as Ersatz for the non-existing general collective security and sanctions. But self-defence under Art. 51 gains, under such conditions, a very different meaning and becomes a technique pretty near to the old-fashioned

---

[1] *The Times*, May 26th, 1950. See also the debate in the Commons on February 13th, 1950, in which the U.K. Prime Minister seems to suggest 'action' involves the use of force; reported in *Manchester Guardian*, February 14th, 1956; but see the report in *Manchester Guardian*, February 15th, 1956, of the statement by a Foreign Office spokesman that forces would not be used without the consent of the countries to which they would be sent.

[2] Brackets mine.

[3] Italics mine.

right to resort to war, especially as there is no juridical control over the exercise of self-defence.[1]

With that analysis of the reasons for the development of N.A.T.O. we would agree; we would not, however, agree that either the political conditions of post-war, or these treaties, can alter the concept of self-defence. To distort that concept to cover collective action by states, some of which may have no right of self-defence, may produce a politically desirable result; it does not produce a legal basis for such action recognized by international law. If the juridical concept of self-defence is to have any meaning it must, in our view, be distinguished from collective action for the purpose of maintaining international peace and security within a defined region. The latter we would characterize as collective security action.[2]

This is not to suggest that such collective security action is necessarily illegal; but, not being self-defence, its legality depends on considerations different to those governing the legality of action in collective self-defence. The other considerations are, firstly, that until the Charter is amended or abandoned it is the Security Council which is vested with primary responsibility for collective security,[3] whether regional or global. It follows that normally the prior authorization of the Security Council is a condition precedent to the right of members to take collective security action; this is borne out by Art. 52 which prevents regional arrangements from taking such action except with prior authorization from the Security Council. Secondly, since the responsibility of the Security Council is primary and not exclusive, and since the Security Council may well be prevented from fulfilling its responsibilities due to a lack of unanimity amongst the permanent members, there is a secondary responsibility on the totality of the U.N. members. Yet this responsibility lies on the totality of members acting collectively; the reference to 'collective measures' in Art. 1(1) of the Charter must mean measures taken on the authorization of the totality of the members as represented by the General Assembly, and not to groups of members as

[1] *Op. cit.*, p. 120. And see Fenwick, *A.J.*, Vol. 43 (1949), p. 315; also Surrey, 'The Emerging Structure of Collective Security Arrangements. The North Atlantic Treaty', Proceedings A.S. (1950), p. 9.

[2] For the difference between the two concepts see Kelsen, *Collective Security and Collective Self-Defence under the Charter of the* U.N., Vol. 42 (1948), p. 783.

[3] Art. 24, Charter of United Nations.

represented by a regional arrangement or collective security organization. There is, since the General Assembly Resolution on Uniting for Peace of November 3rd, 1950,[1] a specific procedure set up whereby the General Assembly may recommend or authorize members to take action of this kind when the Security Council fails to fulfil its primary responsibility due to the lack of unanimity of the permanent members. It is submitted, therefore, that before individual members or groups of members can take collective security action (as opposed to action in collective self-defence) it must clearly be shown that both the Security Council and the General Assembly have failed to take the necessary action. Only then can it be said that members have a residual responsibility in the matter. Moreover, whereas the Security Council's failure may be explicable by reason of the power of veto, this cannot be said of the General Assembly; the 'failure' of the General Assembly can only be attributed to a refusal of the necessary two-thirds majority of Members to take or authorize collective measures in the circumstances. In identical circumstances the action of a number of states, parties to a collective security arrangement, in arrogating to themselves the right to take collec-

[1] Off. Rec. G.A., Fifth Session, Plen. Meeting, pp. 341–7. The legal character of action taken pursuant to a recommendation of the General Assembly under this resolution is, in our view, that of 'collective measures' for the purpose of maintaining international peace and security (Art. 1(1)). This seems to follow from the resolution itself which refers to recommendations 'with a view to making appropriate recommendations to Members for collective measures . . . to maintain or restore international peace and security'. For a similar construction see Kelsen, *Recent Trends*, p. 975. Also McDougall & Gardner, 'The Veto and the Charter: an Interpretation for Survival', *Yale L.J.*, Vol. 60 (1951), p. 258, at pp. 288–91. Also Woolsey, 'The Uniting for Peace Resolution of the U.N.', *A.J.*, Vol. 45 (1951), p. 129, at p. 137. The view has been taken that this Resolution is itself based upon the right of collective self-defence preserved under Art. 51. See Stone, *Legal Controls of International Conflict*, at p. 275: 'The Uniting for Peace Resolution A is thus seen to fit into the anarchic self-defence derogation from the Charter far more naturally than it can be forced (if it can be forced at all) into its collective peace enforcement provisions'. Various delegates have, in the debates on the Resolution, also attempted to argue its validity on the basis of Art. 51. See Off. Rec. G.A., Fifth Session, 360th, 361st, 364th Meetings of First Committee. This view is, in our opinion, mistaken; the Resolution contemplated action for collective security, not collective self-defence. See Waldock, 'The Regulation of the Use of Force by Individual States in International Law', *R.C.*, 1952 (11), at p. 505, for a rejection of the view that the Acheson Plan is based on self-defence rather than on the G.A.'s secondary responsibility for the maintenance of international peace and security.

tive action when the General Assembly itself is not prepared to recommend such action would be extremely suspect.[1]

It is for the foregoing reasons that, rejecting the plea that the intervention of British and French forces in Egyptian territory in October, 1956, was justified in self-defence,[2] it is submitted that the alternative plea that the action was aimed at the separation of the Israeli and Egyptian forces and the maintenance of international peace and security in the Middle East must also be rejected. This latter construction of the intervention was stated in the Prime Minister's speech in the Commons on October 31st,[3] in his broadcast to the nation on November 4th,[4] and again in the House of Commons on November 1st;[5] it also figured repeatedly in government statements subsequent to those dates.

It may be doubted whether, on the facts, the action taken was wholly consistent with this aim,[6] for, even accepting the argument that a landing was only militarily feasible in the Canal area, this does not explain the absence of any kind of forceful measures to compel the withdrawal of Israeli forces from Egyptian territory. The mere fact that Israel had, and Egypt had not, accepted the ultimatum issued jointly by Britain and France on October 30th it not a sufficient explanation, for that begs the question of the right of those states to issue such an ultimatum involving, as it did, the threat of force. However, the crucial issue is not so much one of the consistency of this construction with the facts, but of the legality of state action involving the use or threat of force, other than self-defence, unauthorized by the United Nations.

[1] Bebr, *op. cit.*, p. 166, at p. 175, concedes that 'It is conceivable that such a recommendation might be used in an attempt to curb the independence of regional organizations and initiate some United Nations control over them.'

[2] *Ante*, p. 104, for a rejection of the view that the intervention was justified in self-defence in order to protect the lives and property of nationals. The other plea of self-defence of the installations in the Canal itself (see Lord Chancellor, November 1st, in House of Lords; text in *Manchester Guardian*, November 2nd) was inapplicable in the absence of any real evidence of a danger to those installations or to shipping in the Canal. The ultimate damage to the Canal, by the illegal blocking of the Canal by Egypt, came as a reaction to the allied landings.

[3] Parl. Debates (H.C.), Vol. 558, col. 1452.

[4] Text in *Manchester Guardian*, November 5th, 1956.

[5] Parl. Debates (H.C.), Vol. 558, col. 1653.

[6] Indeed the aim itself is suspect; see the unguarded statement of the Minister of Defence in the House of Commons on November 8th: 'The whole point of this is that the Canal cannot and must not be solely the concern of the Egyptian government,' *Manchester Guardian*, November 9th, 1956.

There can be no question but that this action was not authorized by the Security Council or the General Assembly. The resolution introduced by the United States in the Security Council on October 30th, calling on *all* states not to use force or the threat of force was vetoed by the United Kingdom and France against an otherwise majority vote of seven members.[1] This was not a case of action desired by the Council but which the Council itself was unable to recommend because of a single veto. The General Assembly's resolution of November 2nd also, by a majority of 64 votes to 5, with 6 abstentions, urged an immediate cease-fire and a halt to the movement of military forces into the area;[2] despite this the first actual landings by British and French troops took place three days later.

The danger of conceding to individual states or even groups of states the right to take collective security action, unauthorized by the competent organs of the United Nations, lies in the possibility that antagonistic groups may each reach a decision that action is necessary 'to maintain or restore international peace and security' and under a claim of right plunge the world into war.[3] It was for this reason that the Royal Institute of International Affairs Study Group in 1938 considered that, in order to prevent regional pacts degenerating into alliances of the pre-war pattern, an essential condition of their right to take action for the maintenance of international peace and security was that they should act only with the prior authority of the Council of the League or the P.C.I.J.[4] It was, in our belief, a realization of this danger which at San Francisco led to the rejection of the Australian proposal that in the event of the Security Council failing to act each member state retained the right to take such action as it deemed

[1] *Manchester Guardian*, October 31st, 1956.

[2] *The Times*, November 3rd, 1956. The Assembly reiterated its call to France, the U.K., and Israel on November 8th and November 24th: see U.N. News, London Release Nos. SCS/17, SCS/36.

[3] This danger was also realized when, in the Locarno Pact, Art. 4 distinguished between aggression which gave parties generally a right to intervene only on the permission of the Council of the League and 'flagrant' aggression which gave a right to intervene immediately. Treaty of Mutual Guarantee, Locarno, October 16th, 1925: text in *A.J.*, Supp., Vol. 20 (1926), p. 22. The definition of a 'flagrant' aggression in Art. 2 still leaves room for a subjective judgment, just as the definition of aggression does; the same problem remains. Scharzenberger, *op. cit.*, p. 529, points out the danger of self-defence pacts degenerating into the old pattern of defensive alliances.

[4] *International Sanctions* (1938), p. 135.

necessary in the interest of international peace and security.[1] For similar reasons writers have urged neutrality rather than intervention in a conflict in which the aggressor has not been determined by a competent organ of the United Nations.[2] The General Assembly resolution on the Duties of States in the Event of the Outbreak of Hostilities[3] provides that a state engaged in hostilities should 'take all steps practicable in the circumstances and compatible with the right of self-defence to bring the armed conflict to an end at the earliest possible moment'; a general right of intervention conceded to the allies of the immediate participants could scarcely be regarded as consistent with the aim of this resolution. For the concession of a right to decide upon action in the interest of international peace and security (and against which state or states) to every state brings about a potentially anarchical situation. It is, therefore, an additional reason for restricting the concept of collective self-defence; in stating that this concept requires each participating state to be exercising an individual right of self-defence, based on a violation of its own substantive rights, we believe this is the maximum concession which can be made if the prohibition of Art. 2(4) is to retain any meaning.

It is readily admitted that once we assume the impotency of the competent organs of the United Nations this view has serious disadvantages. To oppose all collective action (other than that which is strictly self-defence) not sanctioned by a competent United Nations organ, would (on that assumption) open the way for piecemeal aggression; each victim would fall in turn with no hope of assistance from friendly nations. There are, however, weighty reasons against accepting these serious disadvantages of the view as conclusive arguments against it. Firstly, these practical disadvantages stem from the system of rights and duties with which members surrounded themselves on signing the Charter; the

[1] In Committee III/4 at the 2nd Meeting on May 9th, *UNCIO*, Docs., Vol. 12, p. 668. And see the New Zealand proposal to include a collective guarantee of every member against aggression, also rejected. 1st Commission, General Provisions, June 6th, 1945; *UNCIO*, Docs., Vol. 6, pp. 343–4.

[2] Jessup, *Modern Law of Nations*, p. 205.

[3] Resolution 378(v), November 17th, 1950. The original Yugoslav proposal contained terms advocating a withdrawal of troops within 24 hours, Doc. A/1399, September 27th, 1950. The Resolution omitted any specific time limit.

restrictions contained in the Charter on the freedom of unilateral action, of action involving force unsanctioned by the competent U.N. organ, were really feasible only on the assumption that the Security Council would fulfil the responsibilities assigned to it. In fact it has not done so, but the consequences of this, however disadvantageous, are reasons for questioning the political wisdom of the Charter scheme; they are not reasons for extending and distorting the legal concept of self-defence. The content of that legal right is not subject to change due to an admittedly inconvenient political position. Secondly, of course, this dilemma has been mitigated by the assertion of the right to recommend action to members by the General Assembly; since the Acheson Plan it is not possible to make the assumption that there is no competent organ of the United Nations really capable of authorizing collective action in the interests of international peace and security. This new development seems to take the force from the argument, of a political rather than legal character, for extending the concept of collective self-defence to cover intervention by any state to assist the victim of an aggression.

There does, however, remain the final problem inherent in any system of collective security of the legality of action to assist a state pending the decision of the competent organ. Even under the Acheson Plan, although an emergency meeting of the Assembly may be called within twenty-four hours, the necessary investigation of the facts or even the formal procedure for taking a decision may take time. As Kelsen has said:

> Between the moment the illegal attack starts and the moment the centralized machinery of collective security is put into action, there is, even in case of its perfectly prompt functioning, a space of time, an interval, which may be disastrous to the victim.[1]

During the interim period, pending a decision of the competent organ of the United Nations, the victim state is not devoid of assistance, for those of its neighbours who are themselves placed under the necessity of self-defence by the illegal attack, whose own right of self-defence is activated by the attack, may exercise this right of self-defence in concert with the original victim. If prior provision has been made for this action in collective self-defence by treaty so much the better. Moreover the greater the

[1] *A.J.*, Vol. 42 (1948), p. 785.

scale of the attack the wider the range of neighbouring states imperilled by the attack and able to invoke their right of self-defence. This right would not, in our opinion, justify a general right of intervention at this stage; states not individually in a state of self-defence would have no right to take action or join in collective action. To allow them to do so would, at this stage, completely nullify the whole system of collective security and signal a return to the very anarchy which the system of collection security is designed to prevent. The right of states which are not acting in self-defence to intervene must await the authorization of the competent organ of the centralized machinery, and this obligation cannot be avoided by a perversion of the concept of collective self-defence.

If it should still be contended that in an age of nuclear warfare the destructive power of an initial attack could completely destroy a state entitled only to assistance from other states placed under the necessity of exercising their right of self-defence, then it is only possible in reply to suggest that the technological advances of modern warfare may well have made any system of collective security *simpliciter* archaic and outmoded. The only real solution to this problem lies either in combining the system of collective security with some means for depriving all the individual states of the kind of armaments which, by their immediate destructive power, make the system unworkable; or in moving towards a system of world federation in which component states would be completely disarmed. It is not our intention to ignore these difficulties, but only to state the conviction that they are not solved by distorting the concept of self-defence, individual or collective, out of all legal recognition.

It is conceded that these views are based upon the assumption that the system of rights and duties imposed by the Charter is still binding upon members. The position might arise in which, due to the frustration of the machinery envisaged in Chapter VII for the maintenance of international peace and security and in particular the failure to implement Art. 43, members take the view that the Charter no longer represents the fundamental law of international society or even a literally binding treaty.[1] This view, impliedly invoking the doctrine *clausula rebus sic stantibus*, would

[1] See Wortley, 'The Veto and the Security Provisions of the Charter', *BYBIL*, Vol. 23 (1946), at p. 109.

perhaps enable the members to assume a greater freedom of action based upon a right to take such action as is necessary to maintain or restore international peace and security. It is not believed that states have yet taken that view, a view which involves substantial repudiation of the Charter, and the inauguration of the Acheson Plan may well have forestalled the necessity for taking such a view. If, in the future, the necessity for taking that view should arise, then members would fall back upon the system of rights and duties imposed by general international law, apart from the Charter, and the legality of their actions would have to be determined exclusively by that law.

CHAPTER XI

SELF-DEFENCE AND AGGRESSION

IN the attempt to define aggression considerable emphasis has generally been placed upon the inter-relation of that concept and the concept of self-defence. The view has often been expressed that self-defence and aggression are correlative terms, that aggression gives rise to the right of self-defence and that, since they are counterparts of the same concept viewed from different sides, to define one is to define the other. For example, in the note of June 23rd, 1928, addressed by the United States government to those governments invited to sign the Pact of Paris it was said, by way of objection to the French proposal to include a specific recognition of the right of self-defence in the proposed Pact,[1]

> Express recognition by the treaty of this inalienable right, however, gives rise to the same difficulty encountered in any effort to define aggression. It is the identical question approached from the other side.[2]

The same view is implicit in the attempts to categorize the individual use of force into either self-defence or aggression[3] and, as Fitzmaurice, the United Kingdom delegate to the Sixth Committee of the General Assembly on January 9th, 1952, said:

[1] U.S. Dept. State, the General Pact for the Renunciation of War, 1928, pp. 36–7; convenient text in Shotwell, *op. cit.*, App. VI; see *ante*, pp. 132–4. For the same view see Eagleton, 'The attempt to define Aggression', *Int. Concil.*, 1930, p. 609; Report by the Secretary-General on the Question of Defining Aggression (A/2211), p. 60; in the discussion of the General Assembly's Sixth Committee in January, 1952, see the views of Petrzelka (Czechoslovakia) at the 286th and 333rd Meetings. Also Vignol, *Definition de l'Agresseur*, p. 127: 'la théorie de la guerre juste et cette de la légitime défense sont les deux faces d'un même problème.'

[2] Proposal of April 20th, 1928, text in Shotwell, *War as an Instrument of National Policy*, App. IV.

[3] See definition by Alfaro submitted to the International Law Commission in its Third Session (A/1858, paras. 46 and 49): 'the only two purposes for which states can legitimately use force are: first, to exercise the inherent right of individual and collective self-defence; and second, to stop aggression and restore international peace and security'. Also that submitted by Amado (A/1858, para. 40): 'Any war not waged in exercise of the right of self-defence or in application of the provisions of Art. 42 of the Charter of the United Nations is an aggressive war.'

The whole problem resides precisely in knowing when the war is being waged as a matter of self-defence and when it is being waged as a matter of aggression. . . . If there is no definition of self-defence there is no definition of aggression.[1]

This identification of the problems of defining these two concepts of self-defence and aggression is, in our view, open to serious criticism. This criticism is twofold. In the first case the context within which a definition of aggression has been sought has been either that of military aggression, conceived as the simple act of taking the initiative in military action, or that in which the state first committing any one of a series of defined acts is automatically deemed to be the aggressor. This, in fact, was the basis of the Litvinoff definition proposed to the Disarmament Conference in 1933,[2] of the proposed Act relating to the Definition of the Aggressor, prepared by the Committee on Security Questions of that conference,[3] and of the recent Soviet proposal submitted to the Sixth Session of the General Assembly on January 5th, 1952.[4] As Politis, in his report to the Committee in 1933, explained:

It is clearly specified that the State which will be recognized as the aggressor is the first state which commits one of the acts of aggression. . . . The chronological order of the facts is decisive here.[5]

Within this context, when aggression is treated as a pure question of fact, there can be no correlation between aggression and self-defence, for the problem of self-defence is essentially a problem of legal responsibility. Moreover, the context of military aggression is too limited in an age which is marked by the development of the technique of 'ideological', 'economic', and 'indirect' aggression for there to be any real correlation between a definition of

[1] Cited in Fitzmaurice, 'The Definition of Aggression', *Int. & Comp. L.Q.*, 1952 (1), p. 137. See also Fitzmaurice's views in the 292nd Meeting; Off. Rec. General Assembly's Sixth Committee, Sixth Session.

[2] League of Nations, Records of the Conference for the Reduction and Limitation of Armaments, Series D, Vol. 5, p. 237.

[3] Ibid., Conference Docs., Vol. II, pp. 683–4.

[4] A/C.6/L.208.

[5] Conference Docs., Vol. II, p. 680. See for the same view Vignol, *Définition de l'Agresseur*, 1933, p. 32: 'L'agresseur est l'Etat qui prend l'initiative d'une guerre injuste.' For a rejection of this view see Redslob, *Histoire des Grands Principes du Droit des Gens*, 1923, p. 282: 'L'agresseur n'est point celui qui accomplit le premier fait d'armes ou qui franchit le premier la frontière ennemie. L'agresseur est l'état qui commit un impiètement tel sur la souveraineté d'autrui que l'adversaire est reduit à la lutte armée comme à un dernier moyen de salut.'

aggression within that context and a definition of self-defence based upon the need to protect the security of a state against the various forms of illegal conduct other than military attack. As Pompe has said:

> As soon as acts and situations not consisting in the immediate use of military force against another state are taken into consideration, the narrow concept of aggression is given up and aggression and defence are no longer clear-cut concepts complementing each other. Such action can consist in a general mobilization, in military intimidation, in a policy of economic boycott, in warlike propaganda in the press, and also in a fear of aggression on the part of the military attacker.[1]

It has been shown[2] that the Charter does not confine the right of self-defence to this narrow context of military force.

In the second case, a more telling criticism is that any identification of the problems of defining aggression and self-defence necessarily assumes that the two concepts are required for identical purposes. The problem of definition, treated without regard to the purpose for which the definition is required, is bound to produce widely divergent views; it is, therefore, to the question of the purpose of a definition that we now turn.

THE PURPOSE OF THE DEFINITION OF THE CONCEPTS OF AGGRESSION AND SELF-DEFENCE

The concept of aggression

The definition of this concept is, at the present time, essentially a problem connected with the development of a system of collective security.[3] The need for a definition is the need for knowing the circumstances in which the machinery of the collective security system will operate and the conditions upon which intervention in the collective interest in the maintenance of international peace and security will be warranted.

Under the United Nations Charter the condition precedent for the application of the enforcement procedures under Chapter VII is a determination that there exists a 'threat to the peace, breach of the peace, or act of aggression' (Art. 39). Similarly, a recommendation by the General Assembly under the Resolution on Uniting for Peace[4] presupposes a finding that there exists a

[1] *Op. cit.*, p. 56. [2] *Ante*, pp. 187–93.

[3] Secretary-General's Report, *op. cit.*, p. 6.

[4] Off. Rec. G.A., Fifth Session, 302nd Plen. Meeting, pp. 341–7; see *ante*, p. 177.

'breach of the peace or act of aggression'. What is required, therefore, more than a definition of aggression, is a definition of the broader phrase 'threat to the peace, breach of the peace, or act of aggression',[1] for upon any one of these three conditions the Security Council (and, upon one of the last two conditions, the General Assembly) can call into operation the collective machinery for the purpose of maintaining international peace and security.

It is abundantly clear that the purpose of collective action under the Charter is the restoration of international peace and security; this is the criterion by which the justification of the action is measured. That this criterion predominates is clearly shown by the Charter. The purposes of the United Nations are, *inter alia*,

> To maintain international peace and security, and to that end, to take effective collective measures for the prevention and removal of threats to the peace, and for the suppression of acts of aggression or other breaches of peace. . . . (Art. 1(1)).

In this context it is clear that 'the peace' means 'international peace'; this is borne out by the fact that the obligation to settle international disputes by peaceful means is demanded so 'that international peace and security, and justice, are not endangered' (Art. 2(3)). The executive organ of the United Nations, the Security Council, is delegated with 'primary responsibility for the maintenance of international peace and security' (Art. 24), and enforcement action is designed 'to maintain or restore international peace and security' (Art. 39). Even in the Uniting for Peace Resolution by which the General Assembly assumes the power to recommend to members that they take collective measures when the Security Council has 'because of lack of unanimity of the permanent members' failed to exercise its primary responsibility, the express purpose of the recommended collective measures is 'to maintain or restore international peace and security'.[2]

[1] Maktos (U.S.A.) criticized the U.S.S.R. proposal to define only aggression and not also 'threats to the peace, breaches of the peace', saying that, thus limited, the question was 'purely academic'; Off. Rec. G.A., Sixth Committee, Sixth Session, 282nd Meeting; see also Peruvian delegate, ibid., 289th Meeting. For similar criticisms by writers see Komarnicki, *op. cit.*, p. 85; Kelsen, *op. cit.*, p. 727.

[2] Ibid., Resolution A (1). And see Komarnicki, 'La definition de l'Agresseur', *R.C.*, 1949 (11), p. 85; 'Le critère principal d'après la Charte, c'est l'infraction à l'ordre international, c'est-à-dire au maintien de la paix et de la sécurité international.'

If this, then, is the purpose for which intervention is required, this suggests that what these organs are concerned with is first and foremost a situation of *fact*, a situation which contains the element of a threat to international peace and security. These organs are not, at this stage, concerned with the problem of legal responsibility and the respective rights of the states immediately involved in the situation. They are concerned with, above all else, a question of fact: 'c'est là, avant tout, la contestation d'un fait'.[1] As Pompe has said:

> . . . international practice has followed the tendency to consider war or armed conflict as a situation to which the collective security organ should try to put an end by mediation and conciliation, leaving aside the question of responsibility for its origin.[2]

This, it will be recalled, was the view put forward in the Rutgers Memorandum of 1928[3] which, in advocating a shift in emphasis from Art. XVI of the Covenant to Art. XI, suggested the postponement of questions of responsibility to the primary problem of stopping the conflict. The same approach is evident in the League's treatment of the Chaco dispute between Bolivia and Paraguay; the conclusion of the League's Commission was:

> No inquiry into the question of responsibility for the war as long as there is any possibility of peaceful settlement. An inquiry would only be in place if all such possibilities had vanished.[4]

Recently the General Assembly's Resolution on the Duties of States in the Event of the Outbreak of Hostilities,[5] passed on November 17th, 1950, provides for the case in which 'a State *becomes engaged in armed conflict* with another State or States . . .', and imposes on the state a duty to proclaim its readiness, on a

[1] Cavaré, 'Les Sanctions dans le Pacte de la S.D.N. et dans la Charte des Nations Unies', *R.G.D.I.P.*, 1950, at p. 659. For similar views in the Sixth Committee of the General Assembly see Off. Rec. G.A., Sixth Session, Sixth Committee, 292nd Meeting, Fitzmaurice (U.K.); Seventh Session, 330th Meeting, Mme Bastid (France), 332nd Meeting, Armado (Brazil). For contrary view see Théry, *op. cit.*, pp. 63–4; also *International Sanctions*, R.I.I.A., 1938, p. 13.

[2] *Op. cit.*, p. 41. See also Unden, 'La guerre d'agression comme problème de Droit International', *Int. Concil.*, 1930, p. 12; Wright, *A.J.*, Vol. 29 (1935), p. 379.

[3] League of Nations, Minutes of the Second Session of the Committee on Arbitration and Security, Doc. C.A.S. 10, 1928, IX, 3, p. 24 *et seq.*

[4] Text of Commission's Report cited in *A.J.*, Vol. 28 (1934), Supp., p. 198. Off. Journal, Spec. Supp. No. 132, p. 48 (see Conclusion No. 1 of Chapter IV).

[5] Resolution 378A(v), para. 1(*a*) and (*b*).

condition of reciprocity, to cease fire and withdraw its military forces: the obvious intent of this resolution is to concentrate on ending the conflict and to postpone the question of legal responsibility.

The reason for postponing the question of responsibility is not only that a decision on this might prejudice the chances of a peaceful settlement, but also that in the initial stages the question of actual responsibility may not admit of a clear answer. It may, in fact, need thorough investigation of all the facts, present and antecedent, before this issue of responsibility can be settled; in the nature of things, since the efficacy of any international action is dependent on the speed with which it is taken, the task of investigation and assessment of responsibility must be postponed. If an analogy is sought from private law it is this: the policeman who is called to a street brawl does not and cannot inquire first who attacked whom; he stops the fight by acting on both parties and postpones the question of responsibility to the last.[1]

If, then, we can assume that the purpose of a definition at this stage is to determine whether, as a question of fact, the situation constitutes a threat to international peace and security, it is clear that a definition which attempts to answer the question of legal responsibility is entirely out of place. For this reason the concepts of self-defence and aggression cease to bear any necessary correlation, for self-defence is essentially a legal concept and one entirely dependent on legal responsibility. It has been too rarely observed that the function of a definition of aggression for the purpose of an organ empowered to intervene in the interests of international peace and security is quite different from the function of a definition of aggression or self-defence for the purpose of allocating legal responsibility. There have been exceptions: in the Report of the Royal Institute of International Affairs on International Sanctions in 1937, Gaythorne-Hardy expressed a dissenting view that:

> ... rules for the determination of the aggressor ... involve a confusion of thought, and are based upon a misconception of the function and purpose of the League sanctions. The League, in applying

---

[1] Unden, *op. cit.*, p. 33, described the appropriate function of the Council of the League in saying that its repressive measures 'n'entrent pas dans la catégorie des peines: ce sont plutôt des mesures de police destinées à empêcher les hostilités et à rétablir la paix'.

sanctions, is not concerned with the merits of the dispute; its object is to stamp out the spark of war before it can spread to a general conflagration.[1]

The same difference in the function of a definition of aggression obtains under the Charter. Waldock has said:

Aggression as a legal concept now has significance in two related but distinct contexts:

(1) When the Security Council makes a 'determination' of an 'act of aggression' under Art. 39 of the Charter in order to bring into being its powers to take enforcement action. Alternatively, when the General Assembly makes a finding of an 'act of aggression' under the Uniting for Peace Resolution in order to make recommendations for collective measures to maintain or restore peace.

(2) When a State or an individual in a State is charged before a tribunal with having committed the criminal offence of 'aggression' under international law.[2]

A similar acuteness and awareness of this difference has also been shown in the Sixth Committee of the General Assembly in 1952 but, unfortunately, it was shown too rarely and expressed with too little force.[3]

It follows from the foregoing that the lack of correlation between the concepts of aggression and self-defence may, in theory, lead to collective action for the purpose of maintaining international peace and security being taken under the authorization of the Security Council or the General Assembly *against* a state

[1] *International Sanctions*, 1938, p. 187, fn. 1. See also *Collective Security*, p. 336, statement of Mantoux: 'The important thing is to remember that the question of the ending of hostilities is distinct from the question of the settlement of a conflict. The first wrong which must be determined is the wrong done by the party resorting to force; whether that party had valid reason for resorting to force is a question which it is time enough to consider when hostilities have been ended.'

[2] 'The Regulation of the Use of Force by Individual States in International Law', *R.C.*, 1952 (11), p. 455, at p. 506.

[3] Off. Rec. G.A., Sixth Committee, Sixth Session, 285th Meeting, Cortina (Argentine); Seventh Session, 330th Meeting, Mme Bastid (France); 334th Meeting, Roling (Netherlands): 'The Netherlands delegation considered that a distinction should be made between the two objects the General Assembly had had in mind in calling, under Resolution 599 (vi), for a definition of aggression. The Assembly's object had been, first, to contribute to the maintenance of international peace and security by formulating a definition for the guidance of the competent organs of the United Nations, and secondly, to promote the development of international law by providing directives for the judges called upon to try persons guilty of international crimes. Quite clearly, a guide intended for politicians differed fundamentally from one intended for jurists.'

exercising a right of self-defence. Certainly the Charter does not presuppose that enforcement action can only be undertaken against delictual conduct.[1] However, the possibility of conflict between a state taking measures of self-defence and the enforcement action or collective measures of the general organization is limited by the proviso to Art. 51 that the right of self-defence exists only 'until the Security Council has taken the measures necessary to maintain international peace and security';[2] this proviso would also apply by analogy to collective measures under the Acheson Plan. The solution in practice in the vast majority of cases will be found in the identification of measures of self-defence with the object of the international organ in maintaining international peace and security and the integration of the individual with the collective use of force.

The concept of self-defence

The purpose of this concept is not, as with aggression, to define the circumstances in which the competent organs of the collective security will take action to maintain international peace and security, but rather to define the situations in which the state, acting without the authorization of those competent organs, may use force to protect those essential rights on which its security depends. The essence of this concept is that it is concerned with legal responsibility; the right of self-defence presupposes the delictual character of the conduct of states against which action is taken, and questions of convenience, desirability, or political wisdom are irrelevant to it. Moreover, the criterion of self-defence, namely the imminent or actual danger to the state's security, has no necessary coincidence with the criterion of collective action for the restoration or maintenance of international peace and security. Not every situation which justifies a state in exercising its right of self-defence will constitute a threat to international peace and security so as to warrant the intervention of the collectivity of states. Conversely, a situation constituting a threat to international peace and security may arise in which neither of the parties can claim to be acting in self-defence: the case of two states engaging in conflict, each with aggressive intent and determined to conquer the other, is not unfeasible.

[1] Oppenheim, *International Law*, Vol. II, 7th ed., p. 160, and see p. 163; also Kelsen, *Law of United Nations*, pp. 724 ff. [2] *Ante*, p. 195.

Once this identification between the concepts of aggression and self-defence is rejected, certain consequences follow. For example, it is no longer sound to assume that, because certain kinds of conduct are excluded from a definition of aggression, there is no right of self-defence against such conduct. Certain kinds of conduct were excluded from the definition of aggression embodied in the Act relating to the Definition of the Aggressor drawn up by the Committee on Security Questions in 1933, and the definition proposed by the U.S.S.R. to the General Assembly in 1952. 'Frontier Incidents' were as such excluded from the list of acts constituting aggression and were, in fact, expressly stated not to constitute sufficient justification for attack.[1] This has not only given rise to speculation as to what constitutes a 'frontier incident' as opposed to invasion,[2] but it has also been assumed that the right of self-defence is therefore excluded in the case of 'frontier incidents'; as Fitzmaurice said in the Sixth Committee at the 281st Meeting in 1952,

> . . . a potential aggressor would be able to provoke even the most serious frontier incidents with impunity, because any military reaction on the part of the other state would automatically constitute aggression.[3]

This is by no means a necessary conclusion, at least if the determination of aggression is not automatic but results from the application of the definition in the light of facts other than the bare fact of the provoked state crossing the frontier.[4] It is, in our

[1] Protocol annexed to Art. 2 of the Act.

[2] The de Brouckère report to the Preparatory Commission of the Disarmament Conference, dated December 1st, 1926, contains a description rather than a definition: League of Nations Doc. C.740.M.279, 1926, IX, p. 93. See also the statements of Spiropolous (Greece) in the Sixth Committee, Off. Rec. G.A., Sixth Session, Sixth Committee, 279th Meeting, para. 13; Ogrodzinski (Poland), ibid., 283rd Meeting, para. 9.

[3] Off. Rec. G.A., Sixth Session, Sixth Committee, 281st Meeting, para. 10.

[4] Whether the definition proposed by the U.S.S.R., which Fitzmaurice is criticizing, necessarily means that the commission of any one of the defined acts is *ipso facto* aggression is not entirely clear; apparently it does, and on this assumption can be criticized, but see the statement of the Soviet delegate Vishinsky at the 331st Meeting to the effect that the Soviet definition 'in no way implied that earlier events should be disregarded in determining which party had committed aggression'. Similarly Politis stated in relation to the 1933 definition: 'the strictness of the definition of the aggressor does not necessarily lead to the automatic application of sanctions' (Conf. Docs., Vol. II, p. 679), although *semble* it would lead automatically to characterization as aggression.

opinion, perfectly consistent to define aggression so as to exclude frontier incidents and at the same time recognize that the provoked state has a right of self-defence. Provided the frontier incident is on a scale such that it does not contain a danger to international peace and security (and therefore warrant collective intervention authorized by the competent organ of the international community), there is no reason to suppose that the proportionate reaction of the provoked state should constitute a threat to international peace and security. After all, for the defensive measures to be within the right of self-defence they must be proportionate and confined to the necessity of the case. Any other conclusion would bring about the ludicrous result that frontier detachments would be unable to take any defensive measures other than those confined entirely to their own state's territory.[1] It is, moreover, a result which contrasts oddly with the statement that attacks upon the vessels or aircraft of another state constitute aggression.[2] The distinction between these two situations is difficult to discover; in either case whether the situation involves a threat to international peace and security depends entirely on the scale and gravity of the situation, and that alone should determine whether 'aggression' has occurred; and in either case it is equally ludicrous to suppose that proportionate measures of self-defence cannot be taken. One cannot deny to the frontier detach-

[1] This, in fact, was the view taken by Politis, Conference Docs., Vol. II, p. 680. Such a view would even prevent counter-bombardment for 'bombarding the territory of another state' is defined as aggression in the Litvinoff definition and included in the second criterion of the Politis definition (see Conference Docs., Vol. II, p. 681). The fact that the Commission of Enquiry into the frontier incidents between Bulgaria and Greece in 1925 determined that Greece, in occupying a part of Bulgarian territory, had acted contrary to the Covenant does not support Politis' view; that finding is explicable entirely on the ground that the Greek measures were on the facts disproportionate (League of Nations Doc. C.727.M.270, 1925, VII) and see *ante*, p. 129.

[2] Art. 1(c) of the Litvinoff definition refers to 'attacking the naval or air forces of another state' as aggression; the Act referred to 'attack . . . on . . . the vessels or aircraft of another state' and Politis justified the wider definition in saying 'no distinction has been made according to whether these vessels or aircraft belong to the armed forces of the state or are of a non-military character belonging either to the state or its nationals' (Conference Docs., Vol. II, p. 681). But see for a contrary view Alfaro in his memorandum to the I.L.C. (A/CN.4/L.8, p. 11); the U.S.S.R. proposal of 1952 refers simply to 'the carrying out of a deliberate attack on the ships or aircraft of the latter' (A/C.6/L.208). The view that attacks upon the ships or aircraft of a state constitutes aggression has also been taken in various regional defence treaties: Art. 6, N.A.T.O.; Art. 9, Rio Treaty (see *ante*, ch. X).

ments or to the ships or aircraft immediately attacked the right to take proportionate measures of self-defence; nor can one deny that in so doing they act as state agencies, exercising the state's right of self-defence, and that for their action the state bears full responsibility.

Other omissions from the Soviet definition of aggression which have met with criticism in the Sixth Committee are the cases of destruction of the population of a state by technical methods such as bacteriological warfare,[1] the participation in a war of nationals of a neutral country,[2] or the undertaking or encouragement of terrorist activities.[3] Without entering into the merits of a dispute as to whether these forms of state conduct or these situations should be considered as a sufficient threat to international peace and security to warrant the intervention of the collectivity of states—that is entirely a question of policy—it is clear that, whether or not these situations involve a threat to international peace and security, if they involve a threat to the security of a particular state then, assuming the conditions governing self-defence are satisfied, a right of self-defence arises.

It is also provided in the Litvinoff definition that justification for an attack cannot be based upon the internal situation of a state, of which one instance is given as 'possible danger to life or property of foreign residents'.[4] Again, as with frontier incidents which are similarly excluded as sufficient 'provocation', this produces confusion when applied indiscriminately to the two concepts of self-defence and aggression. It may be a perfectly proper policy to decide that threats to the life or property of foreign residents shall not be deemed of sufficient gravity as to involve a threat to international peace and, therefore, warrant the application of enforcement measures by the organized community of states. It is not, however, either a necessary or a proper conclusion from that to determine that therefore the state whose nationals are affected has no right of self-defence—for there

[1] Ammoun (Lebanon), Off. Rec. G.A., Sixth Session, Sixth Committee, 286th Meeting, para. 27; Spiropoulos (Greece), ibid., 292nd Meeting, para. 3.

[2] Van Glabbeke (Belgium), ibid., 287th Meeting, para. 38, citing the illustration of Chinese intervention in Korea through 'volunteers'; also Fitzmaurice (U.K.), ibid., 292nd Meeting, para. 40.

[3] Secretary-General's Report (A/2211), p. 49; see *ante*, p. 45.

[4] League of Nations Records of the Conference for the Reduction and Limitation of Armaments, Series D, Vol. 5, p. 237; clause 2A(c) of the definition; see also the Protocol to the proposed Act, ibid., Vol. 2, pp. 683–4.

may well be involved a threat to that state's essential rights.[1] The policy behind the proposed Act of 1933 was explained by Politis in these terms:

> Provocation is either one of the acts of aggression defined in Art. 1—in such case the State which has been the victim of such an act can obviously retaliate by acts of a similar nature and no difficulty arises—or provocation consists in a breach of international law or in the unfriendly attitude of Governments or public opinion without the commission of an act of aggression.[2]

Now this strict dichotomy advocated by Politis confuses the requirements of a definition of aggression for the purposes of an agency entrusted with collective enforcement of international peace and security with the requirements of a definition of self-defence for the purposes of a state taking unilateral action. In the latter context it is, in our view,[3] improper and inconsistent with established principle to deny to the state the right of self-defence. Provided the measures taken in the protection of the lives and property of nationals conform to the requirements of the right of self-defence, that is to say are proportionate and limited to the necessity of the case, there is no reason to suppose that either the threat to those nationals or the taking of measures of protection will constitute a threat to international peace and security. In so far as measures of protection exceed what is proportionate and necessary then, no doubt, international peace and security will be endangered and those measures may properly be determined as aggression. However, the criterion applicable to that question would be whether a threat to international peace and security exists; the criterion applicable to the question whether self-defence is justifiable will be whether a threat to the protecting state's rights exists.

A further divergence between the functions of a definition of self-defence and aggression is seen when we consider those forms of conduct which are termed 'indirect aggression'. *Prima facie*, since this conduct does not involve the use of force, it is less likely that its effect will be to endanger international peace and

[1] *Ante*, p. 94; and see views of Fitzmaurice (U.K.), Off. Rec. G.A., Sixth Session, Sixth Committee, 292nd Meeting.

[2] League of Nations Conference for the Reduction and Limitation of Armaments, Docs., Vol. II, p. 682; see also Secretary-General's Report, *op. cit.*, p. 49.

[3] *Ante*, ch. V.

security; there is, therefore, some reason for excluding it from a definition of aggression for the purposes of an international security organ. Yet, again, this is purely a question of fact and of policy; as we have previously indicated,[1] there is no inherent reason why the economic policies of a state, or methods of ideological warfare and hostile propaganda, should not be considered aggression if in fact they endanger international peace and security. The whole question resolves itself into one as to the stage at which the community generally feels that the adverse effect of a state's conduct justifies the intervention of the community.

The fact that these forms of 'indirect aggression' are not accepted within the definition of aggression for the purpose of an international security organ bears no relation to the question whether, against these forms of injurious conduct, the individual state whose own security is endangered has the right to resort to self-defence. It has been suggested previously that against delictual conduct not involving the use or threat of force the right of self-defence will rarely justify measures involving force;[2] this results not from an arbitrary restriction of self-defence to measures involving force but from the essential requirement of proportionality. The criterion by which the legality of the measures used in self-defence will be judged is that of proportionality, and international law has never recognized a hard-and-fast rule confining self-defence to delictual conduct involving force. In many cases, however, the appropriate and proportionate reaction to 'indirect aggression' will take the form of legislative measures, of an assertion of an exceptional jurisdiction not normally sanctioned by international law, or of the refusal to accept obligations normally owed to the delinquent state. These measures are, in their very nature, unlikely to affect international peace and security, and remain solely within the context of self-defence.

For these reasons, therefore, it is submitted that in considering whether a situation affords a state the right of self-defence the only relevant concept is that of self-defence; the concept of aggression, as it has been elaborated during the course of the last forty years,

[1] *Ante*, pp. 42, 113. For a survey of criticisms directed to the lack of inclusion of these forms of indirect aggression in the Soviet definition of 1952, see Secretary-General's Report, *op. cit.*, pp. 55–9.

[2] *Ante*, p. 24.

has an entirely different purpose and can afford no guide to the question whether a right of self-defence exists.

It is, finally, obvious that, though in the nature of things the decision to resort to self-defence rests initially with the individual state whose rights are violated,[1] since that decision rests on a unilateral judgment on the respective legal rights of the states concerned, it cannot be final or conclusive. The decision to exercise self-defence is a preliminary decision for which the state bears full responsibility, and it cannot be maintained that its own judgment is conclusive on the question of the respective rights of the parties concerned. No one state can arrogate to itself the final right to determine unilaterally the question whether another state is in breach of established duties. That question must ultimately be determined by an impartial international organ, whether judicial or executive in character. When the United States government in its note of June 23rd, 1928, stated:

> Every nation is free at all times and regardless of treaty provisions to defend its territory from attack or invasion and it alone is competent to decide whether circumstances require recourse to war in self-defence,[2]

it is only to be implied that, in the first instance, the individual state alone assumes responsibility to make that decision. It is not a necessary or justifiable conclusion from this that this decision is conclusive or final on the ultimate question of the legality of its action: *nemo judex in sua causa*. The view of the Japanese government that its action in Manchuria in 1931[3] could not be questioned was, therefore, completely unfounded and in fact rejected by the Lytton Commission and the League.[4] As has been shown,[5] this view was rejected by the British prosecutor at

[1] Giraud, 'La Théorie de la Légitime Défense', *R.C.*, 1934 (111), at p. 809. Wright, *A.J.*, Vol. 27 (1933), at p. 46.

[2] U.S. Dept. State, the General Pact for the Renunciation of War, 1928, pp. 36–7.

[3] Statement of Japanese delegate to Council of League, November 21st, 1933, cited in *A.J.*, Vol. 27 (1933), p. 100.

[4] See adoption of Lytton Report by the Assembly of the League on February 24th, 1933; convenient text in *A.J.*, Vol. 27 (1933), Supp., p. 119; and see *ante*, p. 33. For the same view see Wright, 'The Meaning of the Pact of Paris', *A.J.*, Vol. 27 (1933), pp. 46–7; Brierly, 'Some Implications of the Pact of Paris', *BYBIL*, Vol. X (1929), p. 209; Giraud, *op. cit.*, p. 810.

[5] *Ante*, p. 140.

Nuremberg,[1] by the United States prosecutor,[2] and by the International Military Tribunal itself which stated:

> But whether action taken under the claim of self-defence was in fact aggressive or defensive must ultimately be subject to investigation and adjudication if international law is ever to be enforced.[3]

The question of responsibility

If the notion that a state can unilaterally and finally determine the legality of its own action in self-defence is rejected, it follows that provision ought to be made for the impartial determination of this question. Only in this way can the prohibition of recourse to force achieve a truly normative character and thus give to the concept of self-defence a full, juridical value. The issue of legal responsibility will invariably have to be postponed until after international peace and security has been restored and, on this final issue, both the concept of aggression and that of self-defence may be relevant; moreover, at this final stage they bear a far closer correlation than they can possibly bear at the stage where an organ of the collective security system is deciding whether to intervene. This is a consequence of the difference which exists between an executive decision to intervene to maintain international peace and security, and a judicial or quasi-judicial decision allocating legal responsibility. The correlation may not, however, be exact, and this becomes evident when we examine and distinguish the questions of state and individual responsibility.[4]

(i) *Responsibility of states.* It is advisable to distinguish what we should term 'provisional' responsibility, that is to say the responsibility which the international organ, entrusted with the maintenance of international peace and security, will impose during the continuation of the hostilities or situation for conduct which has

[1] Trial of Major War Criminals, Vol. XIX, pp. 481–2, speech of Shawcross.
[2] Ibid., p. 421, speech of Mr. Justice Jackson.
[3] *A.J.*, Vol. 41 (1947), p. 207.
[4] Wright, 'Proposal for an International Criminal Court', *A.J.*, Vol. 46 (1952), p. 60, at p. 66, criticizes the failure of the Committee on International Criminal Jurisdiction (Geneva, 1951) to distinguish the two in its Draft Statute for an International Criminal Court: for text see Report to General Assembly, A/AC.48/4.

the effect of hindering the organ's measures to restore international peace and security, from the 'final' responsibility which must be determined by an international organ and which is concerned with the merits of the case in its entirety. It is clear that, as a matter of expediency and without pre-judging the respective merits of the parties, the Security Council or General Assembly may indicate certain provisional measures to prevent an aggravation of the situation.[1] These measures may take the form of cease-fire orders, orders to withdraw troops behind their own frontiers or behind demarcated truce-lines, or calling upon the parties to resort to arbitration or peaceful means to settle the dispute.[2] Disobedience to these orders may properly be characterized as conduct involving responsibility,[3] but it is clearly not the same responsibility as that involved in the dispute as a whole. It is, for example, conceivable that a state genuinely taking up arms in self-defence will, during the course of hostilities, incur responsibility of this 'provisional' character by its failure to conform to measures ordered by the Council; for example, by refusing to withdraw its forces or cease fire. This is always a possibility in view of the scope for difference of opinion as to whether the Council has 'taken the measures necessary to maintain international peace and security' (Art. 51).

It may, therefore, be possible to characterize conduct in defiance of these provisional measures as 'aggression' for the purpose of determining the future course of the executive organ's measures for the maintenance of international peace and secur-

[1] Art. 40, U.N. Charter: presumably the General Assembly can, by analogy, indicate similar provisional measures under the Resolution on Uniting for Peace.

[2] For the practice of the Security Council in relation to this article see U.N. Repertory of Practice of U.N. Organs., Vol. II, New York, 1955, pp. 357–80. The refusal to arbitrate had, under the proposed Geneva Protocol of 1924, been suggested as conclusive as to the party guilty of aggression (see *ante*, p. 126); this test can, in our view, only be one applicable to the ascertainment of 'provisional' responsibility.

[3] This idea was paramount in the Report approved by the Committee of the Council of the League on March 15th, 1927 (Off. Journal, 1927, pp. 832–3): that report stated 'If in spite of all steps here recommended, a "resort to war" takes place, it is probable that events will have made it possible to say which state is the aggressor and in consequence it will be possible to enforce more rapidly and effectively the provisions of Art. XVI.' This same idea is seen in the Rutgers Memorandum, League of Nations, Disarmament, 1928 (IX), 6, p. 142, para. 117(e); also the Politis Memorandum on Security, ibid., p. 132, para. 79.

ity;[1] it is obvious, however, that aggression in this sense has no necessary correlation with either the concept of self-defence or the more fundamental issue of final responsibility.

The question of final responsibility calls for an inquiry of a judicial or quasi-judicial nature rather than a political decision, and if the concept of aggression is used to indicate final legal responsibility then there is no need to rely on presumptions from facts such as the refusal to arbitrate or the taking of the initiative in hostilities, for the factors affecting the issue of final responsibility are unlimited. As Wright has said:

> The test . . . to be applied by a juridical body in the calm after the hostilities are over . . . should embody that justice which requires that due weight be given to all the facts of the situation as it appeared or reasonably should have appeared to the litigants at the time.[2]

It is at this stage that all the antecedent facts such as mobilization, degree of re-armament, political policy, propaganda, espionage, and the attitude of a state's press[3] may be brought in evidence. The inquiry, by whatever international organ it is undertaken, is directed to the question of which party or parties violated the legal rights of other states, and thus, in this final stage, the concept of aggression, if used to characterize the delictual conduct of a state, will bear a close correlation to that of self-defence. The correlation need not be exact, for it is possible for neither party to be successful with a plea of self-defence, since not every reaction to a delict is self-defence. In the main, however, that correlation will exist and it is for the international organ, acting in a

[1] That this would be the purpose of the Security Council seems to be implied in its Resolution of July 15th, 1948, on the Palestine situation; it declared 'that failure by any of the Governments or authorities concerned to comply with the preceding paragraph of this resolution would demonstrate the existence of a breach of the peace within the meaning of Art. 39 of the Charter requiring immediate consideration by the Security Council *with a view to such further action under Ch. VII of the Charter as may be decided upon by the Council.*'

[2] 'The Concept of Aggression in International Law', *A.J.*, Vol. 29 (1935), at p. 386.

[3] These facts are in isolation inconclusive and become useful indications of responsibility only when placed in the entire context of a given situation. See view of Alfaro in the I.L.C., A/CN.4/L.8, pp. 19–20; also view of Permanent Advisory Committee of League of Nations, Records of IVth Assembly, Minutes of Third Committee (Off. Journal, Spec. Supp. No. 16, p. 117). Also Wright, *op. cit.*, p. 378, for an analysis of the various kinds of facts which might be relevant at this stage of the inquiry.

judicial or quasi-judicial capacity, to determine the issue of final responsibility on the basis of the legal rights of the parties.

At the present stage of development of international institutions it is likely that the inquiry may have to be conducted by a political organ, albeit acting quasi-judicially; either by the Security Council or the General Assembly, or a subsidiary organ appointed for the purpose. Ideally it is a question which should be referred to the International Court of Justice, but, until such time as that tribunal has compulsory jurisdiction, it is not possible to exclude settlement by organs of a political character.

(ii) *Responsibility of individuals*. Reference has previously been made to the concept of individual responsibility for a war of aggression accepted by the International Military Tribunals at Nuremberg and Tokyo.[1] It was in relation to 'aggression' as a Crime against Peace that the defence of self-defence became relevant and, as we have seen,[2] the criminal responsibility of the individuals charged with this crime at Nuremberg was linked with the delictual character of the war waged by their state, so that the plea of self-defence was available to the individuals only when the act of war undertaken by the state could be said to have been in self-defence.

The development of a notion of individual responsibility need not, however, proceed on this close identification of state and individual responsibility. In the first case, if 'aggression' in relation to individuals is to be used as a penal concept it may call for clearer definition than that used in relation to states, for, as Waldock has said, 'too wide a power of judicial legislation vested in a criminal court is scarcely consistent with the maxim *nullum poenum sine lege*'.[3] Secondly, the notion of individual responsibility may be extended to cover crimes other than acts of aggression: and thirdly, the individuals responsible may not be responsible as

[1] See *ante*, pp. 138–45.

[2] *Ante*, p. 139.

[3] *Op. cit.*, p. 507. Perhaps the most difficult problem here is to define the stage at which authorities of a state become 'responsible', particularly in relation to the separate crimes of conspiracy and complicity (Art. 2(12), Draft Code). The Report of the I.L.C. (Doc. A/1858) states: 'There can be no question of punishing as accomplices in such an offence all the members of the armed forces of a state or the workers in war industries.' See also Pompe, *op. cit.*, p. 351, for an analysis of the burden of proof in relation to this particular offence.

authorities of a state but as individuals, so that no identification between their responsibility and the state's responsibility can be assumed.

This development can best be illustrated by the Draft Code of Offences Against the Peace and Security of Mankind, adopted by the International Law Commission in its Third Session in 1951.[1] Individual responsibility is envisaged for a number of offences, one of which is Art. 2(1):

> Any act of aggression, including the employment by the authorities of a State of armed force against another State for any purpose other than national or collective self-defence or in pursuance of a decision or recommendation by a competent organ of the United Nations.

The crime of 'aggression' is here defined with rather more precision than in Art. 6 of the London Charter in that it excludes armed force in self-defence or in pursuance of a decision or recommendation by a competent organ of the United Nations. A more precise definition would, at that stage, have prejudiced the work of the Sixth Committee and the International Law Commission in defining aggression. In our submission, however, the concept of 'aggression' used in relation to acts by the authorities of a state has no necessary connection with the concept of 'aggression' for the purposes of enforcement action taken by the United Nations: aggression in relation to individuals must be based solely upon questions of legal responsibility.

The relevance of self-defence to other acts characterized as crimes under international law by the Code depends entirely upon the character of the offence. Self-defence can only justify measures which are appropriate to the protection to those legal rights or interests of the state which we have outlined in Part I of this work; it follows, therefore, that certain offences can never meet with the defence of self-defence. For example, specified as criminal under Art. 2(8) are

> Acts by the authorization of a State resulting in the annexation, contrary to international law, of territory belonging to another State or territory under an international régime.

[1] Report of the I.L.C. Third Session, Off. Rec. G.A., Sixth Session, Supp. No. 9, Doc. A/1858: convenient text in *A.J.*, Vol. 45 (1951), Supp., p. 126. For critical analysis of the Draft Code see Pompe, *op. cit.*, p. 338 *et seq.*; Parry, 'Some Considerations upon the Content of a Draft Code', *I.L.Q.*, Vol. 3 (1950), p. 208; Johnson, 'Code of Offences against Peace and Security', *Int. & Comp. L.Q.*, Vol. 4 (1955), p. 445 and see *ante*, p. 46.

Clearly annexation can never be a means of protecting those legal rights for which self-defence is a permissible remedy, so that self-defence cannot be a defence to this crime.[1]

It is also apparent that the Code envisages criminal responsibility of individuals who are not acting as 'authorities of a State', so that, whether these criminal acts are termed 'aggression' or 'offences against the peace and security of mankind', the responsibility of these individuals may have no necessary link with state responsibility. Furthermore, even supposing self-defence is an appropriate plea in defence, a concept of 'self-defence' for this purpose cannot be the same concept as that used in connection with state responsibility. If the plea is admissible at all its substance will be determined by analogy with private law[2] and not with reference to the protection of the legal rights of the state.

The final question which arises in relation to individual responsibility is that of jurisdiction.[3] As yet there is no real agreement on the advisability of establishing an international criminal court. The Draft Statute for an International Criminal Court[4] is unlikely to receive acceptance in the foreseeable future and, indeed, in any event envisages the possibility of states setting up independent tribunals to try offenders over whom they have jurisdiction 'according to the general rules of international law'.[5]

[1] Nor, presumably, to the offences under Art. 2(5), (6), (9(iv)(v)), (10), (11).

[2] Art. 2 of the Draft Statute for an International Criminal Court (see below fn. 4) states: 'The Court shall apply international law, including international criminal law, and, where appropriate, national law.' This would enable the Court to apply self-defence as a private law concept to offences by individuals not acting as authorities of a state, or even to individuals accused of war crimes, etc., where self-defence under international law is irrelevant.

[3] This question was put aside in the Draft Code of Offences; the Report of the I.L.C. suggested merely that 'a transitional measure might be adopted providing for the application of the code by national courts'.

[4] Drafted by the Committee on International Criminal Jurisdiction (Geneva, 1951); for text see *A.J.*, Vol. 46 (1952), Supp., p. 1. See G.A. Resolution of December 19th, 1948 (260(iii)6), requesting the I.L.C. to consider the desirability of establishing an international judicial organ with criminal jurisdiction; also Secretary-General's Memorandum on Historical Survey of the Question of International Criminal Jurisdiction (A/CN.4/7). For discussion on the Draft Statute in the Sixth Committee see Off. Rec. G.A., Seventh Session, Sixth Committee, 321st Meeting, 1952. See also Wright, 'Proposal for an International Criminal Court', *A.J.*, Vol. 46 (1952), p. 60; Yuen-li-Liang, 'Notes on the Establishment of an International Criminal Jurisdiction', *A.J.*, Vol. 46 (1952), p. 73, *A.J.*, Vol. 47 (1953), p. 638; Finch, 'Editorial Comment', *A.J.*, Vol. 47 (1953), p. 89.

[5] Art. 55.

CHAPTER XII

CONCLUSIONS

THE right of self-defence in international law is one form of self-help; it can be distinguished by its purpose and character from other forms of self-help and from collective action by the international community for the preservation of international peace and security. As a means of protecting certain essential rights of a state, the exercise of the right of self-defence inevitably finds a place in a system of international law which affords no guarantee of the protection of those essential rights by the organized community of states. The characteristics of the right of self-defence can be ascertained from the writings of jurists, from state practice, and from decisions of both municipal and international tribunals, and these sources evidence a fair measure of agreement. These characteristics are the following:

(1) The right of self-defence lies against conduct by states which is delictual as being in breach of a duty established by international law.

(2) The exercise of the right of self-defence presupposes the absence of any alternative means of protection for certain essential rights of the state which are endangered.

(3) The danger to those rights must be serious, and must be actual or imminent.

(4) The measures of self-defence taken must be reasonable, limited to the necessity of protection, and proportionate to the danger.

The right of self-defence is, however, not a right *stricto sensu* but a 'privilege' which legalizes action otherwise illegal taken in the protection of certain essential rights *stricto sensu* upon which the security of the state depends. The nature of the measures taken under the privilege of self-defence vary according to the form which the danger takes, and the criterion of the legality of the measures taken in self-defence is proportionality. The measures taken must be in proportion to the danger and must never be excessive or go beyond what is strictly required for the protection of the substantive rights which are endangered. This view, which it is submitted conforms to the view adopted by states, rejects any artificial distinction between measures involving the use of force and those not involving the use of force. Whilst it is conceded that the right of self-defence generally applies within the context of force, it is neither a necessary nor an accurate conclusion that the right of self-defence applies only to measures involving the use of force. The function of the right of self-defence is to justify action, otherwise illegal, which is necessary to protect certain essential rights of the state against violation by other states.

The substantive rights to which self-defence pertains, and for which it serves as a means of protection are:

(*a*) The Right of Territorial Integrity.
(*b*) The Right of Political Independence.
(*c*) The Right of Protection over Nationals.
(*d*) Certain Economic Rights.

These rights cannot, however, be stated in absolute terms: they exist within a legal system which has as its purpose the protection of similar rights in other states and the maintenance of peace and security generally. It is, therefore, impossible for the state to assert these rights in a way which is inconsistent with either a recognition of equal rights in other states or the general interest in the preservation of international peace and security. For this reason, to take one example, the state cannot assert its right to territorial integrity and claim the right of self-defence in circumstances which deny to another state the right of self-defence against a danger to its security arising within the former's territory. Nor, to take another example, can the state assert its right to defend its territory against action by the international community, duly authorized, and taken for the purpose of maintaining international peace and security. These substantive rights are always relative to the rights of other individual states, and to the rights of the community as a whole; the principle of the 'relativity of rights' prevents an assertion of 'absolute' rights which is inconsistent with the basic aims of the legal system upon which they depend.

The dynamic character of international society precludes the assumption that these rights are necessarily of an enduring character. At the present time the absence of a guarantee that states generally will afford to aliens within their territory the protection of life and property, which is the proper aim of any civilized legal system, affords sufficient justification for the inclusion of a right of protection over nationals abroad within the right of self-defence. The time may come when states generally can give and maintain such a guarantee; in that event the protection of nationals abroad may well cease to form part of the right of self-defence. The same dynamic element in international society may, in contrast, promote an increasing interdependence between states in the economic field. This will involve not only the necessity for a more comprehensive regulation of state economic activity by international law, but also the wider recognition of the right of self-defence against activities which are economically injurious and in breach of duties established by that law.

The development of international society also brings with it means of injuring a state's security which are not subject to regulation by the international legal system. The new techniques of subversive activities and ideological propaganda, for example, call for a specific regulation; the right of self-defence in relation to these new techniques will only have a juridical connotation when their use can be characterized as delictual. Similarly, these new techniques afford to individuals an unprecedented power of endangering a state's security. Yet the legacy of the dualist doctrine is seen in the tardy development of the notion of individual responsibility. At the present time the state can only protect these essential 'rights' against individuals by assuming a power to legislate under its own law in order to penalize the conduct of individuals which injures its security. There is, however, no obligation on other states to recognize this jurisdiction, and there is no duty to give effect to it by surrendering to the injured state those individuals who are within their territory.

The traditional duty of non-intervention, and the prohibition of the use or threat of force against a state's territorial integrity or political independence, are not, today, really adequate to ensure that all forms of conduct by states or individuals which are genuinely detrimental to the security of other states, can be characterized as delictual. It is impossible to accept the consistency between a legal system founded on respect for the independence of states and the continued legality of certain injurious forms of conduct. Moreover, until these forms of conduct can be characterized as delictual, there is no place for the 'right' of self-defence in regulating the power of states to take counter-measures for the protection of their security and independence. These protective counter-measures, and the injurious conduct they are designed to meet, take place in an area of inter-state relationships in which a legal distinction between the two is impossible.

By far the greatest difficulty in postulating a right of self-defence in international law as it existed in the nineteenth and early twentieth centuries was, however, the existence of the state's unlimited 'right' to go to war. Whilst, within the domain of the law of peace, the right of self-defence (or more accurately those substantive rights it served to protect) found some correlation in the duties imposed on states by international law, within the domain of the law of war these duties disappeared. They could not exist side by side with the unlimited 'right' to go to war, for this 'right' involved a complete negation of the rights of political independence and territorial integrity which in peace were assured to other states. This difficulty could not be avoided by ignoring the consistent trend of state practice and by deducing the rights and duties of states from rational principles. The conduct of states had ceased to be guided by or to conform to rational principles, and a theory of international law which bore no relation to the behaviour of the subjects of that law was unacceptable as a statement of legal principles. The difficulty was eventually overcome in the only way possible, by a prohibition of the unlimited right to war in a rule accepted as law by the majority of states.

The trend towards a prohibition of the state's unlimited right to resort to war has been described; the Covenant of the League, followed by the Pact of Paris, brought about a situation in which self-defence became legally meaningful. The Nuremberg Judgment endorsed this trend by declaring a war waged in pursuance of this unlimited right to be not only delictual, but also criminal. This trend has been continued by the United Nations Charter which, whilst extending the prohibition to the use or threat of force, expressly reserved to Members the right of self-defence. It is now possible, with certain exceptions, to characterize the use or threat of force as a delict, or as a sanction (that is to say action authorized by a competent organ of the United Nations), or as self-defence.

This development does not, however, solve certain related problems; the existence of a rule by which the characterization, as a matter of substantive law, may be made, does not of itself provide the means by which the characterization may be made. Yet, excluding the case in which force is used on the express authority of a competent organ of the United Nations (when, therefore, its character is clear), the use or threat of force by individual states will have to be characterized as delictual or as action in self-defence. Initially, as we have indicated, this characterization will have to be made by the state or states immediately affected; these states can only resort to self-defence against a use or threat of force which is delictual. It is, however, a decision for which the individual state or states assume full responsibility; it is not a decision which is final or conclusive on the question of legal responsibility, but one which is subject to the overriding authority of the Security Council, and probably the General Assembly, and also to eventual review by an impartial organ entrusted with the task of allocating legal responsibility between the states involved.

Whether or not the Security Council or the General Assembly were ever intended to undertake the task of allocating legal responsibility is extremely doubtful. Our own conclusion is that it is rather their function to intervene or to authorize intervention by Members when, as a question of fact, there is a situation which calls for action to maintain or restore international peace and security; these organs are not, certainly at the initial stage, concerned with questions of legal responsibility. This raises the question of whether states not themselves placed in the necessity of self-defence, can decide for themselves the issue of legal responsibility and discriminate or intervene in favour of the state which, according to *their* decision, is acting in self-defence. Our own view is that states cannot do this consistently with their obligations under the Charter. Whilst it is admitted that the possibility of distinguishing between a delictual use of force and action in self-defence destroys the fundamental assumption upon which the idea of impartial neutrality rests, it is submitted that the duty of Members is to abstain from intervention until authorized to act by a competent organ of the United Nations. To concede a general right of intervention, without the authorization of a competent organ, would, in our view, be entirely inconsistent with the system of collective security envisaged by the Charter and, in particular, the delegation of primary responsibility for the maintenance of international peace and security to the Security Council.

This limitation on the freedom of action of Members cannot be overcome by relying on an extended interpretation of the right of 'collective self-defence'. That right permits collective action by states which each have the individual right of self-defence, and which they choose to exercise in concert. The tendency to distort this concept of 'collective self-defence', whilst it may meet a politically inconvenient situation which arises from the frustration of the Security Council, can only destroy the right of collective self-defence as a legal concept.

The arguments against this restrictive view of the freedom of individual action under the Charter are based, in final analysis, upon the impotency of the Security Council and the decided advantage to the potential aggressor which this restriction on individual action would give. These arguments are valid enough for the purpose of a possible revision of the Charter; they may be valid enough for a complete abandonment of the Charter. They are not, in our view, valid as reasons for distorting the meaning of the obligations contained in the Charter so long as those obligations are accepted as subsisting. The solution to the difficulty posed by the frustration of the very organ to which primary responsibility for the maintenance of international peace and security was delegated, and on which the whole system of collective security depends, must be sought either in the abandonment of the Charter system, or in the devising of substitute procedures within the United Nations. The General Assembly's Resolution on Uniting for Peace points to the adoption of the latter alternative.

Finally, it may be observed that the emphasis placed upon the maintenance of international peace and security in the Charter has overshadowed the problem of allocating legal responsibility for a conflict. In the nature of things, the determination of the question of legal responsibility must be postponed to the primary task of restoring international peace and security; yet, if international law is to be respected, and if the concept of self-defence is to achieve recognition as a legal concept, the question of legal responsibility must eventually be answered. It is doubtful whether the Security Council or the General Assembly are really competent to answer this question, for they are both political organs, and the question of legal responsibility is eminently justiciable. There is no real difficulty over the existence of rules by which the issue can be settled; the criteria are now present in international law, and the real difficulty appears to be one of providing a tribunal with compulsory jurisdiction over states and, since individual responsibility may be involved, over individuals. The right of self-defence can only achieve full recognition in a legal system which embodies the compulsory settlement of the question of legal responsibility on which the whole concept of self-defence depends.

BIBLIOGRAPHY

BOOKS

ALEXANDROWICZ, *International Economic Organisations*, London, 1952.
ALVAREZ, *The Monroe Doctrine*, New York, 1924.
ARCHBOLD, *Criminal Pleading, Evidence and Practice*, 33rd ed.
AYALA, *De Jure et Officiis Bellici*, trans. in Classics of International Law, Publications of Carnegie Endowment, ed. J. B. Scott.

BAKER, *The Geneva Protocol*, London, 1925.
BARANDON, *Le Système juridique de la Société des Nations pour le prévention de la guerre*, trans. from German, Paris, 1933.
BARROWS, *William M. Evarts*, Univ. of N. Carolina Press, 1941.
BATY, *Canons of International Law*, London, 1930.
BECKETT, *The North Atlantic Treaty*, London, 1950.
BELLI, *De Re Militari et Bello*, trans. in Classics of International Law, Publications of Carnegie Endowment, ed. J. B. Scott.
BLUNTSCHLI, *Theory of the State*, Oxford, 1898.
——, *Le Droit International Codifié*, 3rd ed., trans. from German, Paris, 1881.
BORCHARD, *Diplomatic Protection of Citizens Abroad*, New York, 1916.
BORQUIN, ed. of *Collective Security*, League of Nations International Studies Conference, Paris, 1936.
BRIÈRE DE LA, *Le Droit de Guerre Juste*, Paris, 1938.
BRIERLY, *Law of Nations*, 3rd, 4th and 5th ed.
BRIGGS, *Law of Nations, Cases, Documents, and Notes*, 2nd ed.
BUCKLAND, *Textbook of Roman Law*, 1921.

CALVO, *Le Droit International*, 5th ed., 1896.
CASTREN, *The Present Law of War and Neutrality*, Helsinki, 1954.
CHENG, *The General Principles of Law*, London, 1953.
CHOATE, *The Two Hague Conferences*, Princeton, 1913.
CHURCHILL, *The Second World War*, Vols. I and II, London, 1948–9.
CLARKE, *Right to Protect Citizens in Foreign Countries by landing Forces*, Dept. of State, Washington, 1912, re-ed. 1929.
COBBAH, *National Self-Determination*, Oxford, 1945.
COHN, *Neo-Neutrality*, Columbia, 1939.
COLOMBOS, *International Law of the Sea*, 3rd ed., London, 1954.
——, *Law of Prize*, 3rd ed., London, 1949.

DÉAK and JESSUP, *A Collection of Neutrality Laws*, 2 vols., Washington, 1939.
—— ——, *Neutrality*, 4 vols., Columbia, 1935.
DICKINSON, *Equality of States*, Harvard, 1920.
DUGUIT, *Etudes de Droit Public*, Paris, 1901.
DUNN, *Protection of Nationals*, Baltimore, 1932.
DUPUIS, *Le Principe d'équilibre et le Concert Européen*, Paris, 1909.

EAGLETON, *Responsibility of States*, New York University Press, 1928.
EVATT, *The United Nations*, Oxford, 1948.

FAUCHILLE, *Traité de Droit International*, 2 vols., Paris, 1922.
FENWICK, *International Law*, New York, 1924.
FIORE, *Diritto Internazionale Codificato*, 5th ed., New York, 1918 (trans. Borchard).
FORD, *The Anglo-Iranian Oil Dispute* 1951–2, Univ. of California Press, 1954.
FREEMAN, *The International Responsibility for Denial of Justice*, London, 1938.
FRIEDMANN, *Expropriation in International Law*, London, 1953.

GAYTHORNE-HARDY, *A Short History of International Affairs*, 1920–38, Oxford, 1939.
GARNER, *International Law and the World War*, 2 vols., 1920.
GENTILI, *De Jure Belli*, trans. in Classics of International Law, Publications of Carnegie Endowment, ed. J. B. Scott.
GIERKE, *Political Theories of the Middle Ages*, trans. Maitland, Cambridge, 1900.
GOODRICH and HAMBRO, *Charter of the United Nations*, 2nd ed., 1949.
GREGORY, *Tariffs, A Study in Method*, London, 1921.
GROTIUS, *De Jure Belli ac Pacis*, trans. in Classics of International Law, Publications of Carnegie Endowment, ed. J. B. Scott.

HABERLER, *Theory of International Trade*, London, 1936.
HACKWORTH, *Digest of International Law*, 7 vols., Government Printing Office, Washington, 1940.
HALL, W. E., *International Law*, 8th ed. by Pearce-Higgins, 1924.
HALL, *Readings in Jurisprudence*, 1938.
HANKEY, *Politics, Trials, and Errors*, Oxford, 1950.
HART, *The Monroe Doctrine*, Boston, 1916.
HERSHEY, *Essentials of Public International Law*, New York, 1912.
HILL, *Claims to Territory in International Law and Relations*, Oxford, 1945.
HINDMARSH, *Force in Peace*, 1933.
HOGAN, *Pacific Blockade*, Oxford, 1908.
HOHFELD, *Fundamental Legal Conceptions*, Yale University Press, 1923.
HUDSON, *International Legislation*, 9 vols., 1919–45.
HYDE, *International Law*, 3 vols., 1945.

ISMAY, LORD, *N.A.T.O., The First Five Years*, 1949–54, Printed in Netherlands.

JESSUP, *The Law of Territorial Waters and Maritime Jurisdiction*, 1927.
—— *Modern Law of Nations*, New York, 1948.
JIMÉNEZ DE ARECHAGA, *Voting and the Handling of Disputes in the Security Council*, New York, 1950.

KEETON, *China, The Far East and the Future*, London, 1943.
KELSEN, *Principles of International Law*, New York, 1952.

KELSEN, *Law of the United Nations*, London, 1950.
—— *Recent Trends in the Law of the United Nations*, London, 1951.
KENNY, *Outline of Criminal Law*, 1952, ed. J. W. C. Turner.
KOCOUREK, *An Introduction to the Science of Law*, Boston, 1920.
—— *Jural Relations*, 12th ed., 1928.
KOMARNICKI, *La Question de l'Integrité territorial dans le Pacte de la S.D.N.*, Paris, 1923.
KREZDÔRN, *Les Nations Unies et les Accords Régionaux*, Geneva, 1954.

LANGER, *Seizure of Territory*, Princeton, 1947.
LAPRADE, *England and the French Revolution*, 1909.
LAUTERPACHT, *Private Law Sources and Analogies of International Law*, 1927.
—— *The Function of Law in the International Community*, Oxford, 1933.
—— *International Law and Human Rights*, 1950.
LAWRENCE, *International Law*, 3rd ed., revised, 1905.
LE FUR, *Guerre Juste et Juste Paix*, Paris, 1920.
LEVAL, *De la Protection Diplomatique des Nationaux à l'Etranger*, Brussels, 1907.
LISSITZYN, *The International Court of Justice*, New York, 1951.

MANN, *The Legal Aspect of Money*, 2nd ed., Oxford, 1953.
MANNING, *Peaceful Change*, London, 1937.
MASTERSON, *Jurisdiction in Marginal Seas*, New York, 1929.
MCNAIR, *Law of Treaties*, Oxford, 1938.
MILLER, *The Geneva Protocol*, New York, 1925.
—— *The Peace Pact of Paris*, London, 1928.
—— *The Drafting of the Covenant*, 2 vols., New York, 1928.
MOORE, *Digest of International Law*, 8 vols., Washington, 1906.
—— *International Arbitration*, 6 vols., Washington, 1898.
—— *Principles of American Diplomacy*, 1905.
—— *Collected Papers*, 7 vols., Yale University Press, 1944.
MORRISON, *The Outlawry of War*, Chicago, 1927.
MUNCH, *Les Origines et l'Oevre de la S.D.N.*, 2 vols., Copenhagen, 1923–4.
MYERS, *The Origin and Conclusion of the Paris Pact*, Boston, 1929.

NEILSON, *The Tragedy of Europe*, 5 vols., Appleton Wisc., 1940–6.
NUSSBAUM, *Money in the Law*, Chicago, 1939.

OFFUTT, MILTON, *Protection of Citizens Abroad by the Armed Forces of the United States*, John Hopkins Univ. Studies in Historical and Political Science (1928).
OPPENHEIM, *International Law*, 2 vols., editions cited.

PHILLIMORE, *Commentaries on the Law of Nations*, 1854.
PIGGOTT, *Nationality*, 2 vols.
PITTARD, *Protection des Nationaux*, Geneva, 1896.
PITT-COBBETT, *Leading Cases in International Law*, 3rd ed., London, 1913.
POLITIS, *Neutrality and Peace*, 1935.

POMPE, *Aggressive War an International Crime*, 1953.
PRADIER-FODÉRÉ, *Traité de Droit International*, 6 vols., 1885–94.
PUFENDORF, *De Jure Naturae*, trans. in Classics of International Law, Publication of the Carnegie Endowment, ed. J. B. Scott.

RAY, *Commentaire du Pacte*, Paris, 1930.
REDSLOB, *Traité de Droit des Gens*, Paris, 1950.
—— *Histoire des Grands Principes du Droit des Gens*, 1923.
RIVIER, *Principes du Droit des Gens*, 2 vols., 1896.
RODICK, *The Doctrine of Necessity in International Law*, 1928.
ROLIN, *Le droit moderne de la guerre*, 3 vols., Brussels, 1920–1.
ROUSSEAU, *Droit International Public*, Paris, 1953.
RUSSELL, *On Crime*, 10th ed., J. W. C. Turner.

SALMOND, *Jurisprudence*, 3rd ed., 1910.
SCHWARZENBERGER, *Manual of International Law*, 3rd ed.
—— *Power Politics*, 1951.
SCOTT, *The Hague Conventions and Declarations of* 1899 *and* 1907, 1915.
—— *The Hague Peace Conferences of* 1899 *and* 1907, 2 vols., Baltimore, 1909.
—— *Hague Court Reports*, New York, 1916.
SHOTWELL, *War as an Instrument of National Policy*, London, 1929.
SMITH, *Law and Custom of the Sea*, London, 1948.
SOHM, *Institutes of Roman Law*, 3rd ed.
SOLAGES DE, *La Théologie de la Guerre Juste*, Toulouse, 1946.
STONE, *Legal Controls of International Conflict*, London, 1954.
STOWELL, *Intervention in International Law*, 1921.
—— *International Law*, London, 1931.
STRAUS-HUPÉ and POSSONY, *International Relations*, 2nd ed., New York, 1954.
STURZO, *The International Community and the Right of War*, London, 1929.
STUYT, *The General Principles of Law*, The Hague, 1946.
SUAREZ, *Selections from Three Works*, trans. in Classics of International Law, Publications of Carnegie Endowment, ed. J. B. Scott.

THÉRY, *Notion d'Agression*, Paris, 1937.
TOBIN, *The Termination of Multilateral Treaties*, Columbia, 1933.
TOWLE, *International Trade and Commercial Policy*, New York, 1947.
TOYNBEE, *Survey of International Affairs*, 1920–3, London, 1925.

VANDERPOL, *La Doctrine Scolastique du Droit de Guerre*, Paris, 1919.
VATTELL, *Le Droit des Gens*, trans. in Classics of International Law, Publications of Carnegie Endowment, ed. J. B. Scott.
VICTORIA, *De Indis et de Jure Belli*, trans. in Classics of International Law, Publications of Carnegie Endowment, ed. J. B. Scott.
VIGNOL, *Definition de l'Agresseur*, 1933.
VINER, *Dumping, A Problem in International Trade*, 1923.

WEHBERG, *The Outlawry of War*, Washington, 1931.
WESTLAKE, *International Law*, Cambridge, 1904.

Wheaton, *International Law*, 6th ed. by A. Berridale Keith, 2 vols., London, 1929.

Whiteman, *Neutrality*, Yale University Press, 1941.

Whiteman, M., *Damages in International Law*, 3 vols., Washington, 1937.

Williams Fischer, *Some Aspects of the Covenant*, 1934.

—— *Chapters on Current International Law and the League of Nations*, London, 1929.

Williams, B., *State Security and the League of Nations*, Baltimore, 1927.

Wilson, *The International Law Standard in Treaties of the United States*, Harvard, 1953.

Wolff, *Jus Gentium*, trans. in Classics of International Law, Publications of Carnegie Endowment, ed. J. B. Scott.

Wright, *The Enforcement of International Law through Municipal Law in the United States*, 1915.

Zimmern, *The League of Nations and the Rule of Law*, London, 1936.

ARTICLES

Barratt, The Real Monroe Doctrine, *Trans. Grotius Soc.*, Vol. 14, 1929.

Bebr, Regional Organisation: A United Nations Problem, *A.J.*, Vol. 49, 1955.

Beckett, The Exercise of Criminal Jurisdiction over Foreigners, *BYBIL*, Vol. 6, 1925.

—— Diplomatic Claims in respect of Injuries to Companies, *Trans. Grotius Soc.*, Vol. 17, 1931.

Borchard, The A.G.'s Opinion on the Exchange of Destroyers, *A.J.*, Vol. 34, 1940.

Bourquin, Crimes et Délits contre la sureté des Etats Etrangers, *R.C.*, 1927 (I).

Boye, Règles de la Neutralité, *R.C.*, 1938 (II).

—— Shall a State which goes to war in violation of the Kellogg-Briand Pact have a Belligerent's rights in respect of Neutrals, *A.J.*, Vol. 24, 1930.

Brierly, Règles du Droit de la Paix, *R.C.*, 1936 (IV).

—— Some Implications of the Pact of Paris, *BYBIL*, Vol. 10, 1929.

Briggs, Neglected Aspects of the Destroyer Deal, *A.J.*, Vol. 34, 1940.

—— The Validity of the Greenland Agreement, *A.J.*, Vol. 35, 1941.

Brown, The Armed Occupation of Santo Domingo, *A.J.*, Vol. 11, 1917.

—— International Responsibility in Haiti and Santo Domingo, *A.J.*, Vol. 16, 1922.

Canyes, The Inter-American System and the Conference of Chapultepec, *A.J.*, Vol. 39, 1945.

Cavaré, Les Sanctions dans le Pacte de la S.D.N. et dans la Charte des Nations Unies, *R.G.D.I.P.*, Vol. 21, 1950.

Cheng, The Anglo-Iranian Oil Dispute, *World Affairs*, 1951.

Chester, Diplomacy of the Quarter-Deck, *A.J.*, Vol. 8, 1914.

COLOMBOS, The Paris Pact, otherwise called the Kellogg Pact, *Trans. Grotius Soc.*, Vol. 14, 1928.
COMYNS-CARR, The Judgment of the I.M.T. for the Far East, *Trans. Grotius Soc.*, Vol. 34, 1948.
CURTIS, The Law of Hostile Military Expeditions as Applied by the United States, *A.J.*, Vol. 8, 1914.

DELBEZ, La notion juridique de guerre, *R.G.D.I.P.*, Vol. 24, 1953.
DESCAMPS, Le Droit International Nouveau, R.*C*., 1930 (I).
DICKINSON, The Analogy between natural persons and international persons in the Law of Nations, *Yale L.J.*, Vol. 6, 1918.
DYKE VAN, The Responsibility of States for International Propaganda, *A.J.*, Vol. 34, 1940.

EAGLETON, Attempt to Define Aggression, *Int. Concil.*, 1930.
—— Excesses of Self-Determination, *Foreign Affairs*, 1953.
—— The Individual in International Law, Proceedings A.S., 1946.
ELBE VAN, The Evolution of the Concept of the Just War in International Law, *A.J.*, Vol. 33, 1939.

FACHIRI, Expropriation and International Law, *BYBIL*, Vol. 6, 1925.
—— International Law and the Property of Aliens, *BYBIL*, Vol. 10, 1929.
FENWICK, Neutrality and Responsibility, *A.J.*, Vol. 29, 1935.
—— Neutrality on the Defensive, *A.J.*, Vol. 34, 1940.
—— Draft Code of Offences against the Peace and Security of Mankind, *A.J.*, Vol. 46, 1952.
—— Intervention, Individual and Collective, *A.J.*, Vol. 39, 1945.
—— The Monroe Doctrine and the Declaration of Lima, *A.J.*, Vol. 33, 1939.
—— The Atlantic Pact, *A.J.*, Vol. 43, 1949.
FINCH, The Treaty between the United States and Haiti, *A.J.*, Vol. 10, 1916.
—— The Nuremberg Trial and International Law, *A.J.*, Vol. 41, 1947.
FITZMAURICE, The Law and Procedure of the I.C.J., *BYBIL*, Vol. 27, 1950.
—— The Definition of Aggression, *Int. & Comp. L.Q.*, Vol. 1, 1952.
FRANKEL, The Anglo-Iranian Dispute, 1952, *Yearbook of World Affairs*, Vol. 6.

GARNER, The U.S. Neutrality Law of 1937, *BYBIL*, Vol. 19, 1938.
GIDEL, La Mer Territoriale et le Zone Contigue, R.*C*., 1934 (II).
GIRAUD, La Théorie de la Légitime Défense, R.*C*., 1934 (III).
GOODHART, The North Atlantic Treaty of 1949, R.*C*., 1951 (II).
GREEN, Recent Practice in the Law of Extradition, *Current Legal Problems*, 1953.
GRIEVE, The Present Position of Neutral States, *Trans. Grotius Soc.*, Vol. 33, 1947.

HERSHEY, Incursions into Mexico and the Doctrine of Hot Pursuit, *A.J.*, Vol. 13, 1919.
HINDMARSH, Self-Help in Time of Peace, *A.J.*, Vol. 26, 1932.
HOLLAND, War Sub-Modo, *L.Q.*R., Vol. 19, 1903.

HORWITZ, The Tokyo Trial, *Int. Concil.*, 1950.

HUDSON, The Budapest Resolution of 1934 on the Kellogg-Briand Pact of Paris, *A. J.*, Vol. 29, 1935.

HUGHES, Observations on the Monroe Doctrine, *A.J.*, Vol. 17, 1923.

HURST, Nationality of Claims, *BYBIL*, Vol. 7, 1926.

HYDE, Legal Aspects of the Japanese Pronouncements in Relation to China, *A.J.*, Vol. 28, 1934.

JENNINGS, The Caroline and McLeod Cases, *A.J.*, Vol. 32, 1938.

JOHNSON, Code of Offences against Peace and Security, *Int. and Comp. L.Q.*, Vol. 4, 1955.

KELSEN, Collective Security and Collective Self-Defence under the Charter of the U.N., *A.J.*, Vol. 42, 1948.

—— The Rights and Duties of States, *A.J.*, Vol. 44, 1950.

—— Is the North Atlantic Treaty a Regional Arrangement?, *A.J.*, Vol. 45, 1951.

KOMARNICKI, La Definition de l'Agresseur, R.*C.*, 1949 (II).

—— The Place of Neutrality in the Modern System of International Law, R.*C.*, 1952 (I).

KULSKI, The Soviet System of Collective Security Compared with the Western System, *A.J.*, Vol. 44, 1950.

KUNZ, Individual and Collective Self-Defence in Art. 51 of the Charter of the U.N., *A.J.*, Vol. 41, 1947.

—— The Inter-American Treaty of Reciprocal Assistance, *A.J.*, Vol. 42, 1948.

LALIVE, International Organisation and Neutrality, *BYBIL*, Vol. 24, 1947.

LAUTERPACHT, Revolutionary Propaganda by Governments, *Trans. Grotius Soc.*, Vol. 13, 1927.

—— Revolutionary Activities by Private Persons against Foreign States, *A.J.*, Vol. 22, 1928.

—— Boycott in International Relations, *BYBIL*, Vol. 14, 1933.

—— The Pact of Paris and the Budapest Articles of Interpretation, *Trans. Grotius Soc.*, Vol. 20, 1934.

—— Allegiance, Diplomatic Protection and Criminal Jurisdiction over Aliens, *Cambridge L.J.*, Vol. 9, 1947.

MANDELSTAM, L'Interpretation du Pacte Briand-Kellogg, R.*G.D.I.P.*, 1933.

MANNER, The Object Theory of the Individual in International Law, *A.J.*, Vol. 46, 1952.

MANNING, The Proposed Amendments to the Covenant of the League of Nations, *BYBIL*, Vol. 11, 1930.

McDOUGALL and GARDNER, The Veto and the Charter: An Interpretation for Survival, *Yale L.J.*, Vol. 60, 1951.

McNAIR, Extradition and Exterritorial Asylum, *BYBIL*, Vol. 28, 1951.

—— The Legal Meaning of War, *Trans. Grotius Soc.*, Vol. 11, 1926.

MILHAUD, L'Organisation économique de la Paix, R.*C.*, 1926 (V).

NGUYEN QUOC DINH, La Légitime défense d'après la Charte des Nations Unies, *R.G.D.I.P.*, Vol. 52, 1948.
NICOLOFF, An 'Act for the Protection of Peace' in Bulgaria, *A.J.*, Vol. 45, 1951.

PANDELFORD, American Rights in the Panama Canal, *A.J.*, Vol. 34, 1940.
PARRY, Plural Nationality and Citizenship with Special Reference to the Commonwealth, *BYBIL*, Vol. 30, 1953.
—— Some Considerations upon the Content of a Draft Code, *I.L.Q.*, Vol. 3, 1950.
PATTERSON, Les Bases économiques de la Paix, R.*C.*, 1931 (III).
PEARCE-HIGGINS, The Monroe Doctrine, *BYBIL*, Vol. 5, 1924.
PELLA, Towards an International Criminal Court, *A.J.*, Vol. 44, 1950.
PHILLIMORE, Droits et Devoirs Fondamentaux des Etats, R.*C.*, 1923 (I).
PLANAS-SUAREZ, L'Extension de la Doctrine de Monroe en Amerique du Sud, R.*C.*, 1924 (IV).
POTTER, L'Intervention en droit international moderne, R.*C.*, 1930 (II).
PREUSS, International Responsibility for Hostile Propaganda, *A.J.*, Vol. 28, 1934.

RAUCHBERG, Les Obligations juridiques des Membres de la Société des Nations pour le Maintien de la Paix, R.*C.*, 1931 (III).
REID, Regionalism under the U.N. Charter, *Int. Concil.*, 1946.
ROLIN, Du Droit à la Neutralité ou du droit de reste neutre, et Grotius et Vattel, *Bull. de la Classe des Lettres de l'Academie Royale*, 1920.
ROOT, The Real Monroe Doctrine, *A.J.*, Vol. 8, 1914.
ROSENNE, L'Execution et la mise en vigeur des décisions de la Cour Internationale de Justice, R.*G.D.I.P.*, Vol. 24, 1953.
RUTGERS, La Mise en Harmonie du Pacte de la S.D.N. avec le Pacte de Paris, R.*C.*, 1931 (IV).

SALVIN, The North Atlantic Pact, *Int. Concil.*, 1949.
SCHWARZENBERGER, The Protection of British Property Abroad, *Current Legal Problems*, 1952.
—— The Province and Standards of International Economic Law, *I.L.Q.*, Vol. 2, 1948.
—— The Most Favoured Nation Standard in British State Practice, *BYBIL*, Vol. 22, 1945.
—— Jus Pacis ac Belli? *A.J.*, Vol. 37, 1943.
—— The 'Aid Britain' Bill and the Rights and Duties of the U.S.A. as a Neutral Power, *Trans. Grotius Soc.*, Vol. 27, 1941.
—— The Fundamental Principles of International Law, R.*C.*, 1955 (I).
SCHWELB, Crimes Against Humanity, *BYBIL*, Vol. 23, 1946.
SLOAN, The Binding Force of a 'Recommendation' of the General Assembly of the U.N., *BYBIL*, Vol. 25, 1948.
SPENCER, The Monroe Doctrine and the League Covenant, *A.J.*, Vol. 30, 1936.

SURREY, The Emerging Structure of Collective Security Arrangements, The North Atlantic Treaty, Proceedings A.S., 1950.

TAUBENFELD, International Actions and Neutrality, *A.J.*, Vol. 47, 1953.
TAYLOR, The Nuremberg War Crimes Trials, *Int. Concil.*, 1949.
TRELLES, La Doctrine de Monroe dans son développement historique, R.C., 1930 (II).
TUCKER, The Legal Interpretation of War, *I.L.Q.*, Vol. 3, 1950.

UNDEN, La Guerre d'agression comme problème de Droit International, *Int. Concil.*, 1930.

VERDROSS, Idées Directrices de l'O.N.U., R.C., 1953 (II).
VULCAN, L., L'Execution des Décisions de la Cour Internationale de Justice d'aprés la Charte des Nations Unies, *R.G.D.I.P.*, Vol. 51, 1947.

WALDOCK, The Control of the Use of Force by Individual States in International Law, R.C., 1952 (II).
—— The Release of the *Altmark's* Prisoners, *BYBIL*, Vol. 24, 1947.
WEHBERG, Le Protocol de Genève, R.C., 1925 (II).
—— 'L'Interdiction du Recours à la Force, R.C., 1951 (I).
WHITTON, Efforts to Curb Dangerous Propaganda, *A.J.*, Vol. 41, 1947.
—— Cold War Propaganda, *A.J.*, Vol. 45, 1951.
—— La Neutralité et la Société des Nations, R.C., 1927 (II).
WILLIAMS GLANVILLE, The Juridical Basis of the Right of Hot Pursuit, *BYBIL*, Vol. 20, 1939.
WILSON, War and Neutrality, *A.J.*, Vol. 27, 1933.
WOOLSEY, The Settlement of the Chaco Dispute, *A.J.*, Vol. 33, 1939.
—— The Unilateral Termination of Treaties, *A.J.*, Vol. 20, 1926.
—— The Uniting for Peace Resolution of the U.N., *A.J.*, Vol. 45, 1951.
WORTLEY, The Veto and the Security Provisions of the Charter, *BYBIL*, Vol. 23, 1946.
WRIGHT, The Test of Aggression in the Italo-Ethiopian War, *A.J.*, Vol. 30, 1936.
—— The Concept of Aggression in International Law, *A.J.*, Vol. 29, 1935.
—— Proposals for an International Criminal Court, *A.J.*, Vol. 46, 1952.
—— The Bombardment of Damascus, *A.J.*, Vol. 20, 1926.
—— Changes in the Conception of War, *A.J.*, Vol. 18, 1924.
—— The Outlawry of War, *A.J.*, Vol. 19, 1925.
—— The Law of the Nuremberg Trial, *A.J.*, Vol. 41, 1947.
—— The Meaning of the Pact of Paris, *A.J.*, Vol. 27, 1933.
—— The Transfer of Destroyers to Great Britain, *A.J.*, Vol. 34, 1940.

YÈPES, Les Accords Régionaux et le Droit International, R.C., 1947 (II).
YUEN-LI-LIANG, Regional Arrangements and International Security, *Trans. Grotius Soc.*, Vol. 31, 1946.

DOCUMENTS

American State Papers, Foreign Relations of the United States, 1870– .

British Commentary on the Charter of the U.N., London, H.M.S.O., Cmd. 6666, 1945.

British and Foreign State Papers, 1812– .

Bulletin Officiel du VII Congrès Universelle de la Paix, Berne, 1856.

General Pact for the Renunciation of War, Washington, 1928.

Hansard, Parliamentary Debates, House of Commons, Official Report.

Hansard, Parliamentary Debates, House of Lords, Official Report.

Harvard Research Draft Code on Territorial Waters, *A.J.*, 1929, Supp.

" " " Convention on State Responsibility, *A.J.*, 1929, Supp.

" " " Convention on Jurisdiction with respect to Crime, *A.J.*, 1935, Supp.

" " " Law of Treaties, *A.J.*, 1935, Supp.

" " " Convention on Extradition, *A.J.*, 1935, Supp.

" " " Convention on Rights and Duties of States in Case of Aggression, *A.J.*, 1939, Supp.

" " " Convention on Rights and Duties of Neutral States in Naval and Aerial War, *A.J.*, 1939, Supp.

Hudson's World Court Reports, Vols. I–III, Washington, 1934–8.

H.M.S.O., History of the United Nations War Crimes Commission and the Development of the Laws of War, London, 1948; The War at Sea, I, ed. S. W. Roskill, 1954.

International Law Association, Report of Conferences, 38 (1935), 41 (1946).

International Court of Justice, Reports and Pleadings, 1947– .

League of Nations:

- Official Journal, I–XXI, February, 1920–March, 1940.
- Records of the Assembly.
- Treaty Series, Vol. I, No. 1 (September, 1920)—Vol. 205.
- First Report of the Committee on Amendments to the Covenant, June 17th, 1921, C.110.M.62, 1921, V.
- Report of the Commission on the Graeco-Bulgarian Dispute, C.727.M.270, 1925, VII.
- Documents of the Preparatory Commission for the Disarmament Conference (De Brouckère Report), December 1st, 1926, C.740.M.279, 1926, IX.
- Rutgers Memorandum on Arts. 10, 11 and 16 of the Covenant submitted to the Committee on Arbitration and Security, C.165.M.50, 1928, IX.
- Report of the Commission of Enquiry (Lytton Commission) on Sino-Japanese Dispute 1931–3, C.663.M.320, 1932, VII.
- Report of the Commission on the Chaco Dispute, May 11th, 1934, C.154.M.64, 1934, VII.
- Records of the Conference for the Reduction and Limitation of Armaments, Series B (Minutes of the General Commission), Vol. II, Series D, Vol. V.

Report of the Committee on Security Questions (Politis Report), May 24th, 1933, Conference Docs., Vol. II (1935, IX, 4).

Malloy's Treaties; Treaties, Conventions, International Acts, Protocols, and Agreements between the U.S.A. and other Powers (1776–1909), Washington, 1910, 2 vols.

Martens, Nouveau Receuil Générale des Traités, etc., 2nd Series (1876–1908), 35 vols.

Permanent Court of International Justice, Publications:
Series A, Judgments;
Series B, Advisory Opinions;
Series A/B, Cumulative Collection of Judgments and Advisory Opinions given since 1931;
Series C, Acts and Documents relating to Judgments and Advisory Opinions.

Proceedings of the Hague Peace Conference, Vols. I–III, New York, 1921.

Ralston and Doyle, Venezuelan Arbitrations of 1903, etc., Washington, 1904.

Receuil des Décisions des Tribunaux arbitraux mixtes institués par les Traités de Paix, 9 vols. and 1 fasc., Paris, 1922–30.

Receuil Sirey, Code d'Instruction Criminelle, Paris, 1955.

Royal Institute of International Affairs:
Survey of International Affairs, 1929, 1939–46.
Documents on International Affairs, 1929.
Calendar and Texts, 1955.
International Sanctions, Oxford, 1938.
Norway and the War, 1941.

Statutory Rules and Orders, published by authority, H.M.S.O.

Treaty Series, U.S. Dept. of State, publications of treaties of the United States according to number.

Trial of the Major War Criminals before the International Military Tribunal, December 14th, 1945–October 1st, 1946, 42 vols., Nuremberg, 1947.

Trial of the Japanese War Criminals, Dept. of State Publications, No. 2613, Far Eastern Series 12, Washington, 1946.

United Kingdom Treaty Series. Treaties presented by the Secretary of State for Foreign Affairs to Parliament, Vol. I (1892) and a volume each year.

United Nations:
Treaty Series . . . Treaties and International Agreements Registered or filed and recorded with the Secretariat of the U.N., 1946– .
Documents of the Conference on International Organization, San Francisco, 1945, 16 vols.
Yearbook, Dept. of Public Information, 1947– .
Official Records, General Assembly, 1946– .
Official Records, Security Council, 1946– .
Documents relating to the Korean Conflict, No. 1/18, Parts I–III, September, 1950–April, 1951.
Legislative Series: Laws and Regulations on the Régime of the High Seas, 2 vols., 1951–2.
Report of U.N. Atomic Energy Commission, Doc. AEC/18/Rev.1.

Report to General Assembly of Committee on International Criminal Jurisdiction, Geneva, 1951, Doc.A/AC.48/4.
Repertory of Practice of the U.N. Organs., Vols. I–V, New York, 1955.
Secretary-General's Memorandum on a Draft Declaration on Rights and Duties of States, December 15th, 1948, Doc. A/CN.4/2.
Memorandum on a Historical Survey of the Question of International Criminal Jurisdiction, 1949, Doc. A/CN.4/7.
Memorandum on the Charter and Judgment of the Nurnberg Tribunal: History and Analysis, March 3rd, 1949, Doc. A/CN.4/5.
Report on the Question of Defining Aggression, October 3rd, 1952, Doc. A/2211.
Reports of the International Law Commission, covering Second Session, June 5th–July 29th, 1950, Doc. A/1316; Third Session, May 16th–July 27th, 1951, Doc. A/1858.
Western Co-operation, Central Office of Information, London, 1953.
Zbiór Dokumentów, No. 5, Warsaw, 1955.

INDEX

www.ingramcontent.com/pod-product-compliance
Ingram Content Group UK Ltd.
Pitfield, Milton Keynes, MK11 3LW, UK
UKHW041450071026
15587UKWH00010B/732

9 781584 778554